TEACH YOURSELF BOOKS

CHINESE

Dedication

In joyous memory of my sister, Janet Anderson, whose life continues to bless.

CHINESE

Elizabeth Scurfield

TEACH YOURSELF BOOKS

Long-renowned as the authoritative source for self-guided learning – with more than 30 million copies sold worldwide – the *Teach Yourself* series includes over 200 titles in the fields of languages, crafts, hobbies, sports, and other leisure activities.

British Library Cataloguing in Publication Data
Scurfield, Elizabeth
 Chinese.
 1. Chinese language
 I. Title
 495.1

Library of Congress Catalog Card Number: 92-80862

First published in UK 1991 by Hodder Headline Plc, 338 Euston Road, London NW1 3BH

First published in US 1992 by NTC Publishing Group, 4255 West Touhy Avenue, Lincolnwood (Chicago), Illinois 60646 – 1975 U.S.A.

Typeset by Graphicraft Typesetters Ltd, Hong Kong.
Printed in England by Cox & Wyman Ltd, Reading, Berkshire.

Impression number 17   16   15   14   13   12   11   10
Year   1999   1998   1997   1996

Contents

Acknowledgements

My grateful thanks to all those who with their encouragement, criticism and help in all forms (from typing to welcome cups of tea) have made this publication possible.

In particular I wish to thank friends and colleagues from the Beijing Yuyan Xueyuan (Beijing Languages Institute), Xiong Wenhua and Li Dejin; Professor Kang Hongjin from the Chinese People's University; Vita Revelli for her loving support, and the publishers for their patience. My special thanks to Paula Jervis who willingly gave hours of her expertise on the text and tape and without whose hard work the Vocabularies would never have appeared.

Introduction

The first question you may ask is Why learn Chinese? The answers could vary enormously based on your particular interests but I offer a few tentative suggestions here. The Chinese are the largest single ethnic grouping in the world, so a *form* of Chinese is spoken by more people than any other language. Chinese is also the world's oldest language, its written records stretching back about 3500 years. Surely a good reason for more people to learn it? Most people imagine Chinese must be a very difficult language to learn. However, after shedding some of the possible preconceptions about language that you may have, you may well find that spoken Chinese is not as difficult as you had thought – you may even find it comparatively easy! The written language is a different kettle of fish entirely, being made up of individual characters which do have to be memorised but hopefully Chapter 13 will whet your appetite and make you eager for more.

China's cultural and philosophical heritage is enormous, a rich storehouse of knowledge and wisdom waiting to be tapped and although it would be foolish to pretend that by working through this book you will have access to very much of it in the original, it will, at the very least, have given you the possibility of seeing a little into that inscrutable Oriental mind and of making interesting and valuable comparisons with your own culture and way of thinking. I have found these reasons stimulating enough to go on studying Chinese for over 20 years and propose to go on doing so for at least another 20 or so! The Chinese have a saying:

Xue dao lao, huo dao lao, hai you sanfen xue bu dao.
Study reach old, live reach old, still have three-tenths study not reach.

This is certainly true as far as Chinese is concerned, but the rewards are great. It will take time, but if you can keep your mind open you will be surprised at the results.

Zhu ni xuexi yukuai!
Wish you study happy!

The Chinese language

Some of you will have heard of the term 'Mandarin' or 'Mandarin Chinese' which was how the West referred to the language spoken by the officials or 'mandarins' at the Imperial Court. It was then broadened to refer to the northern dialect, a version of which is spoken by over 70% of the Chinese or Han people and has become the *lingua franca* for the whole of China. This national language is known in China as *putonghua* 'common speech' which is now sometimes referred to in the West as Modern Standard Chinese although the term Mandarin still lingers on. Beijing (Peking) pronunciation is taken as the standard but there are many regional variations, some not easy to cope with. Try and find someone who claims to have a fairly standard accent to practise with in the first instance and listen hard to the cassette which is available with this book. *Putonghua* is taught in schools and used in universities and colleges all over China. The majority of TV and radio programmes as well as films for the cinema are also made in *putonghua*. This means that hopefully you will be understood all over China although you will sometimes have difficulty in understanding non-standard accents. Chinese have this problem too!

Putonghua is known as *huayu* in overseas Chinese communities and as *guoyu* 'national language' in Taiwan, but it is all the same language. There are many different dialects in Chinese, some of which are as different from one another as say English is from French, although they all have the same written language. The Cantonese dialect *guangdonghua* is spoken in Canton, Hong Kong and the New Territories and by many of the Chinese you will find in Britain. Many more Hong Kong Chinese are now learning *putonghua* so this is the one to go for!

Romanisation

The written language does not have a phonetic alphabet but various systems have been devised for transcribing Chinese sounds into the Latin script. The standard form in use today is known as *pinyin* (literally 'spell sound') which was adopted as the official system of the People's Republic of China in 1958. It has now been almost universally adopted in the West for transliterating Chinese personal and place names, replacing the Wade–Giles system which had been used previously. A few examples using the two different systems are given below.

Pinyin	*Wade–Giles* (and earlier)
Deng Xiaoping	Teng Hsiao-p'ing
Mao Zedong	Mao Tse-tung
Beijing	Peking
Guangzhou	Kwangchow (Canton)
Tianjin	Tientsin

Pinyin is used as a tool to teach children starting elementary school the correct pronunciation of the Chinese language and to enable them to write little essays in Chinese before they have mastered enough characters. It is taught for a relatively short time in the north where *putonghua* is widely spoken as a first language but for a longer period in the south where many children speak a different dialect at home. Difficult characters in children's books often have the *pinyin* in brackets next to them as an aid to learning. Many street signs in big cities are written in *pinyin* as well as characters, which can be quite useful when you are trying to find your way around!

Mao Zedong once expressed the aim of eventually turning the Chinese written language into an alphabetic system of writing but this idea seems to have been quietly dropped. Aesthetically and visually pleasing, Chinese characters are too much part of the

Chinese national heritage to disappear without a very long struggle, if ever.

The Chinese language is essentially still based on the character, which is *per se* monosyllabic (one character representing one idea) so the single-syllable morpheme is the basic unit in Chinese. As a result, there is still discussion in China as to what units of speech should be written together in *pinyin*. In general I have tried to keep to the system adopted by the Beijing Languages Institute for its textbooks, using the *Xiandai Hanyu Cidian* (Modern Chinese Dictionary) produced by the Chinese Academy of Social Sciences as a definitive reference. Thus 'syllables' are written separately except where they are seen as being one idea. I have, however, kept verb-objects separate for clarity.

Sounds and tones: general introduction

There are just over 400 basic monosyllables in Chinese which seems an incredibly small number and must be the result of sound-simplification over a few thousand years. It is not surprising therefore that the language has so many homophones, but the difficulty is alleviated somewhat by the fact that Chinese is a tonal language. Tones are obviously one way of coping with this phonetic poverty. There are four tones in *putonghua*, so by multiplying 400 by four we get a total of approximately 1600 separate items, although not all basic sounds exist in all four tones. The other way is by combining two syllables with a similar meaning into one 'word'. For example, *ài* and *qíng* mean 'love' and 'feelings' respectively and could be confused with other 'words' if used separately, but together they can only mean 'love' *àiqíng*. This makes communication considerably easier all round.

What we mean by 'syllable' in Chinese is usually composed of an initial and a final. The initial, if there is one, is a consonant at the beginning of the syllable and the final is the rest of the syllable, e.g. *hang* in which *h* is the initial and *ang* is the final.

Initials

Modern Chinese has 21 initials, 23 if you count 'w' and 'y' which some people regard as semi-vowels. There is also a sound 'ng' which only occurs at the end of a syllable as in English. These include six pairs (i.e. twelve initials of which six are aspirated and six are not). These twelve are all voiceless. (Aspirated means that the air is puffed out strongly when you make these sounds.) If you hold a piece of paper in front of your mouth it should move when you make an aspirated sound, but not when you make an unaspirated one. Voiceless means that the vocal chords do not vibrate. The six pairs are:

Unaspirated	*Aspirated*	*Description (all voiceless)*
'b' like **b** in *b*ore	'p' like **p** in *p*oor	labial plosive
'd' like **d** in *d*oor	't' like **t** in *t*ore	alveolar plosive
'g' like **g** in *g*uard	'k' like **c** in *c*ard	velar plosive
'z' like **ds** in a*ds*	'c' like **ts** in i*ts*	blade-alveolar affricate
'zh' like **j** in *j*elly	'ch' like **ch** in *ch*illy	blade-palatal (or retroflex) affricate *The tongue must be curled back*
'j' like **g** in *g*enius	'q' like **ch** in *ch*ew	front-palatal affricate *Tongue flat, corners of lips drawn back as far as possible*

Other small groups could be:

'm' like **m** in *m*e	voiced, labial, nasal
'n' like **n** in *n*eed	voiced, alveolar, nasal
'ng' like **ng** in si*ng*	voiced, velar, nasal
'sh' like **sh** in *sh*y	voiceless blade-alveolar fricative *The tongue must be curled back*
'r' like **r** in *r*ay	voiced, blade-palatal fricative *The tongue must be curled back with only slight friction*
's' like **s** in *s*ay	voiceless blade-alveolar fricative *Tongue flat, corners of lips drawn back*
'x' like **sh** in *sh*eet	voiceless, palatal fricative *Tongue flat, corners of lips drawn back as far as possible*
'f' like **f** in *f*an	voiceless labio-dental fricative
'h' like **ch** in lo*ch*	voiceless velar fricative *Arch the back of the tongue towards the roof of the mouth*
'l' like **l** in *l*ie	voiced alveolar lateral
'w' like **w** in *w*ay	voiced labial-velar approximant
'y' like **y** in *y*ell	voiced palatal approximant

Points to notice:

(i) 'c', 'q' and 'x' bear little resemblance to Western alphabetic values so take particular care with them.
(ii) Pay attention to the retroflexes 'zh', 'ch', 'sh' and 'r' which are made with the tongue curled back. Southern Chinese have difficulty with them too!

It should be stressed that the examples given above can only be approximate equivalents so the purchase of the tape which accompanies the book is strongly recommended.

Finals

There are 36 finals in Chinese. A final is a simple or compound vowel or a vowel plus a nasal consonant. A few 'syllables' may have no initial consonant but every one has to have a vowel. The following tables should be of some assistance in guiding you, although the tape is essential if you are to attempt more than an approximate pronunciation of the sounds.

'a' like **a** in f**a**ther

'ai' like **i** in b**i**te

'ao' like **ow** in c**ow**

'an' like **an** in m**an**

'ang' like **ang** in b**ang**

'e' like **ur** in f**ur**

'ci' like **ay** in pl**ay**

'en' like **un** in **un**der

'eng' like **ung** in d**ung**

'i' (after z, c, s,
   zh, ch, sh and r *only*)
   like **er** in wond**er**

'i' like **ea** in t**ea**

'ia' like **ja** in German *ja*

'iao' like **eow** in m**eow**

'ie' like **ie** in French Pi**e**rre

'iu' like **yo** in *yo*-yo

'ian' like **yen** in *yen*

'in' like **in** in b**in**

'iang' like **yang** in *yang*

'ing' like **ing** in r**ing**

'iong' like **Jung** in *Jung*
   (the psycho-analyst)

('y' replaces 'i' at the beginning of syllables if there is no initial consonant)

'o' like **ore** in m**ore**

'ou' like **o** in g**o**

'ong' like **ung** in J**ung**

'u' like **oo** in m**oo**

'ua' like **ua** in s**ua**ve

'uo' like **war** in *war*

'uai' like **wi** in s**wi**pe

'ui' like **weigh** in *weigh*

'uan' like **wan** in *wan*gle

'un' like **won** in *won*drous

'uang' like **w–ong** in *wrong*
   without the 'r' (very
   approximate)

('w' replaces 'u' at the beginning of syllables if there is no initial consonant)

'ü' like **eu** in pn**eu**monia

'üe' like **eu** of pn**eu**matic
   plus *air* said quickly

'üan' like **eu** of pn**eu**matic
   plus *end* said quickly

'ün' like **eu** of pn**eu**matic
   plus p**un** said quickly

(Written as *yu, yue, yuan* and *yun* as complete syllables)

er as in *err* making the 'r' retroflex

Please note the following:

(i)   The **'-i'** in *zi, ci, si, zhi, chi, shi* and *ri* is quite different from the '-i' with all the other consonants which is a long '-i' This 'i' is more or less only there for cosmetic reasons because no syllable can occur without a vowel. Say the consonant and 'sit on it' and you have the sound.

(ii) 'e' is made by dropping the jaw straight down. If you have difficulty, get hold of your jaw, pull it down and make the sound!

(iii) 'a', 'i', 'o', 'u' and 'ü' – the degree to which the mouth is opened gets narrower and narrower as the lips get rounder and rounder. (Look in a mirror!)

(iv) 'ang', 'eng', 'ong' are nasalised vowels. Again, the mouth aperture gets narrower, the lips rounder. Hold your nose as you practise these sounds. You should be able to feel the vibration!

(v) '-ian' is pronounced as '-ien'.

(vi) 'ü' occurs only with the consonants 'n', 'l', 'j', 'q' and 'x'. As 'j', 'q' and 'x' cannot occur as j+u, q+u or x+u, the Chinese in their wisdom have seen fit to omit the umlaut (¨) over the 'u' in *ju*, *qu* and *xu*! N and l, however, occur as both *nu* and *nü*, *lu* and *lü* so the umlaut has been retained.

(vii) The '-r' suffix may be added to some words e.g. *bian* → *bianr*, *wan* → *wanr*, *hai* → *hair*, *tian* → *tianr* and is used extensively in the Beijing dialect. Normal 'spelling' practice is to add the '-r' but you can choose whether or not to say it. I have sometimes used it so that you can become familiar with it.

Tones

The tone is the variation of pitch whether it be rising, falling or continuing. In speech we move smoothly from one tone to another, not in leaps and bounds. Every syllable in Chinese has its own definite tone and so tones are as important as vowels and consonants in forming syllables. *Putonghua* has four distinct tones so almost every basic monosyllable can be rendered in four different ways. These four tones all fall within your natural voice range, so some people speak Chinese at a higher or lower pitch than others because their voices are naturally higher or lower. You don't have to have a particular type of voice to speak Chinese. Now to the four tones themselves.

The first tone is a high, level tone and is represented as ' ¯ '. The tonemark is placed over the vowel (if there is only one vowel) e.g. *zhōng* 'middle' or on the main vowel of a syllable where there are two or three vowels, e.g. *gāo* 'tall', but *tiē* 'to stick'.

The second tone is a high, rising tone and is represented by the tonemark ´, e.g. *guó* 'country'.

The third tone is a falling and rising tone. It descends from below the middle of the voice range to nearly the bottom and then rises to a point somewhere near the top. It is represented by the tonemark ˇ, e.g. *jiǎn* 'to cut'.

The fourth tone is a falling tone. It falls from high to low and is represented by the tonemark ˋ, e.g. *zhù* to 'live'.

Figure 1 may help to make this clearer:

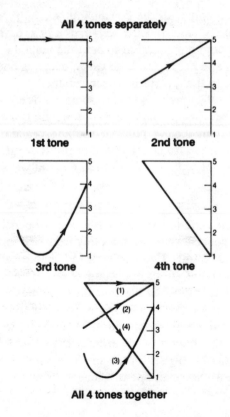

All 4 tones separately

1st tone   **2nd tone**

3rd tone   **4th tone**

All 4 tones together

The common problems that occur are:

(a) pitching the first tone too high,

(b) getting the second and fourth tones confused,

(c) getting down on the third tone but not being able to get up again.

Below are the solutions and how to practise the tones (you may need a mirror):

First tone: Pitch it where *you* feel comfortable. Say 'oo' as in 'zoo' and keep going for as long as you can. You should be able to keep it up for maybe half a minute. When you have got used to that, change to another vowel sound and practise that in the same way and so on.

Second tone: Raise your eyebrows every time you attempt a second tone until you get used to it. This is infallible!

Third tone: Drop your chin onto your neck and raise it again. Then practise the sound doing the movement at the same time.

Fourth tone: Stamp your foot gently and then accompany this action with the relevant sound.

Try saying two third tones together. Difficult isn't it? When this happens, the first one is said as a second tone but it is still marked as a third in the text, otherwise you may think that the syllable in question is always a second tone, which it is not: *Nǐ hǎo* is said as *Ní hǎo* 'How are you?' If *three* third tones occur together, the first two are said as second tones: *Wǒ yě hǎo* is said as *Wó yé hǎo* 'I'm OK too'.

Bù (不) is *fourth* tone but it becomes second before another fourth tone. As this is a straightforward rule I have marked *bu* as second tone when it occurs before a fourth in the text.

Yī (一) is first tone as an ordinary number: *yī* 'one', *shíyī* 'eleven', *yīyuè* 'January' but when it precedes other syllables it is fourth tone before first, second or third tones and becomes second tone before another fourth tone: *Yìxiē* 'some', *yìqǐ* 'together' *yílù* 'all the way'. It has been so indicated in the text. (Many dictionaries list *bu* and *yi* always as fourth tone and first tone respectively.)

Note that in the phrase *yí ge rén* 'one measure word person' the *ge* is said without a tone, although it is actually fourth, but it still carries enough weight to change the *yi* into a second tone.

Neutral tone: some syllables in Chinese are toneless or occur in the neutral tone.

(i)   Particles are always in the neutral tone.
(ii) The second half of a reduplicated word is often in the neutral tone: *gēge* 'elder brother', *māma* 'mum', *bàba* 'dad', *mèimei* 'younger sister'.
(iii) Syllables such as *zi* that only have a 'fill-in' function (i.e. to make the word disyllabic) are toneless: *bēizi* 'cup', *bèizi* 'duvet', *zhuōzi* 'table', *yǐzi* 'chair'.
(iv) The second syllable in compound words is sometimes toneless and is so indicated in the text. In another context it may have a full tone. Some people may pronounce certain words with a tone, some without, as in the word *dōngbiān* 'east side' which may also be pronounced as *dōngbian* particularly when 'r' is added: *dōngbian(r)*.

In actual speech, tones are rarely given their full value but they have to be learnt as if they were. Stress and intonation are also very important but this is best learnt by imitating the speakers on the tape as closely as possible without thinking too much about individual tones, and by listening to any Chinese native speaker. Intonation does not *remove* tones, it only modifies them. Learn the tone which goes with a word and as you listen and speak more you will hopefully find that you increasingly pick up the correct tones and intonation.

Just as a final word on tones, it's amazing how much most Chinese understand even if your tones are largely wrong so don't give up just because you think you haven't got the right ear! The Chinese love punning so I expect they enjoy lots of jokes at our expense, but does it really matter? Tones come with practice, listening and imitating – don't try too hard with them.

The following ten sounds, each written in the four different tones and therefore represented by four different characters, should serve to illustrate some of the points I have been making.

四声 (4 tones)

1 一
yī (one)

姨
yí (aunt)

椅
yǐ (chair)

亿
yì (hundred million)

2 屋
wū (house)

无
wú (none)

五
wǔ (five)

雾
wù (fog)

3 烟
yān (cigarette)

盐
yán (salt)

眼
yǎn (eye)

燕
yàn (swallow)

4 妈
mā (mother)

蔴
má (hemp)

马
mǎ (horse)

骂
mà (scold)

5 八
bā (eight)

拔
bá (to pull up)

把
bǎ (to hold)

爸
bà (father)

6 靴
xuē (boot)

学
xué (study)

雪
xuě (snow)

血
xuè (blood)

7 汤
tāng (soup)

糖
táng (sugar)

躺
tǎng (to lie down)

烫
tàng (scalding hot)

8 腰
yāo (waist)

摇
yáo (shake)

咬
yǎo (to bite)

药
yào (medicines)

9 枪
qiāng (gun)

墙
qiáng (wall)

抢
qiǎng (to rob)

呛
qiàng (irritate the throat)

10 书
shū (book)

熟
shú (ripe)

鼠
shǔ (a rat)

树
shù (tree)

Working through the book

A few sentences introduce the text of each chapter. By Chapter 20 this introduction is also written in Chinese. Almost all the texts are dialogues which allow scope for good, colloquial Chinese to be used, but the continuous passages used in Chapters 7–10 mean that a great deal of useful vocabulary can be introduced in a fairly natural way.

Chapters 1–5 are in *pinyin* romanisation with a literal translation directly underneath to enable you to see how the 'nuts and bolts' of the language work. There is an idiomatic translation on the right.

Chapter 6 shows many of the objects to be found in a house and lists the vocabulary for them. This can be used for reference at a later stage.

Chapters 7–10 are in *pinyin* with an English translation directly underneath. The beginning and end of each sentence in Chinese and English is indicated with a '/' to enable you to mentally 'line up' the two more easily.

Chapter 11 has the dialogue in *pinyin* with an English translation following. This will give you a real chance to see how much you have learnt without referring to the English as soon as you hit a problem!

Chapter 12 is a small reference grammar, expanding on a few of the points referred to in the chapters themselves. Some of them are presented in tabular form for ease of reference.

Chapter 13 gives an introduction to Chinese characters, their background and how to write them, with many useful examples.

Chapters 14–18 are in characters with the *pinyin* romanisation underneath. The vocabularies show all the new characters used in that chapter even if they have appeared in *pinyin* in previous chapters. In addition the vocabularies of 14 and 15 show the radicals or significs of all the characters introduced in that particular chapter. 14–18 also contain tables showing the stroke order of Chinese characters.

Chapters 19–22 have the character text in a block followed by the *pinyin* also in a block. You can decide to work in *pinyin* or characters or both.

Some of you may not want to get too involved in the learning and writing of characters, so I have made it possible to work through the entire book almost solely in *pinyin*, but do still read the introductory chapter on characters (Chapter 13) to understand how they work, as this is essential background knowledge as well as good fun. Conversely, those who are particularly interested in characters can go back to Chapters 1–11 and write out the texts in Chinese characters for extra practice. You will find the character texts for Chapters 1–5 and 7–11 at the back of the book, pp 344–54.

Within each chapter, the text appears first followed by the vocabulary in the order in which it appears. In the vocabularies I have sometimes split up a word by means of a dash to show how the different parts fit together but have kept to the orthodox system in the text, grammar points and exercises. The grammar section deals with the new grammar points, also in the order in which they appear in the text. Any exercise relating to a particular grammar point follows on directly after that grammar point. Each chapter also contains at least one item of interest about the Chinese way of life. These have been put in boxes to make them more accessible.

At the end of each chapter are exercises of a more general kind. Both these and the information passages often contain useful supplementary vocabulary. The new words in the exercises which do not appear in the vocabulary proper of a subsequent chapter *are* included in the Vocabularies at the back of the book, but without a chapter number. This is to avoid confusion with the new words which occur in the texts. (It was impossible to include *all* supplementary vocabulary for reasons of space.)

A Key to the Exercises precedes the *pinyin*-characters–English Vocabulary and the English–Chinese (*pinyin*) Vocabulary which give all the vocabulary items (*pinyin* and English) which have occurred in the texts in alphabetical order. Note that in the English–Chinese (*pinyin*) Vocabulary, entries beginning with 'be' have been listed under the second item for ease of reference so that 'be willing' for instance will be found under 'willing', 'to be engaged' under 'engaged' and so on. This also applies to similar entries such as 'feel jealous' which are glossed under 'jealous'. Do remember that variations are possible in some of the answers to the exercises so don't assume you're always wrong. Bear in mind too that the exercises are there to help you to learn as well as to practise what you have learnt, so not all the answers will be immediately obvious.

A final note regarding Chinese grammar. Over 20 years of experience have taught me that I should never be too categorical as far as Chinese grammar is concerned and always to preface remarks with 'nearly' 'always', 'almost invariably', etc. If I have forgotten to do so at any point in this book please regard it as said. *Putonghua* is still developing as a language so that even Chinese linguistics experts may, for example, hold a three-day meeting to discuss '*le*'. It is as exciting to be in on this as it is to be learning a language with its roots 3500 years in the past – with Chinese you have both!

List of abbreviations

adj.	adjective	n	noun
adv.	adverb	N	proper name
aux. v.	auxiliary verb	**num.**	numeral
CDE	compound directional ending	o	object
		pp	pronoun plural
coll.	colloquial	ps	pronoun singular
conj.	conjunction	**PW**	place-word
DE	directional ending	**prep.**	preposition
dem. adj.	demonstrative adjective	**QW**	question word
		RV	resultative verb
dem. p.	demonstrative pronoun	**RVE**	resultative verb ending
interj.	interjection	s	subject
MW	measure word	**TW**	time word
neg.	negative	v	verb
		v-o	verb-object

Note: I have chosen what I felt to be the most helpful grammatical descriptions. Other people may well use another term for auxiliary verb, resultative verb and so on.

1

Making Friends (*i*)

Mr King (*Wáng xiānsheng*) has come to China to teach English at Beijing University. Mr Li (*Lǐ xiānsheng*) is a friend and colleague of Mr King's Chinese teacher in Britain. The meeting takes place in Mr Li's office.

Lǐ	*Wáng xiānsheng, nǐ hǎo!* King/first-born/you/good/	How do you do, Mr King.
Wáng	*Lǐ xiānsheng, nǐ hǎo!* Li/first-born/you/good/	How do you do, Mr Li.
Lǐ	*Qǐng zuò.* Invite/sit/	Please, sit down.
Wáng	*Xièxie.* Thank/	Thank you.
Lǐ	*Qǐng hē kāfēi.* Invite/drink/coffee/	Have some coffee.
Wáng	*Xièxie, wǒ bù hē kāfēi.* Thank/I/not/drink/coffee/	No thanks, I don't drink coffee.
Lǐ	*Nàme, Zhōngguó chá* So/middle country/tea/ *xíng bu xíng?* be OK/not/be OK/	Would you like some China tea then?
Wáng	*Xíng, xièxie nǐ! Wǒ hěn* Be OK/thank/you/I/very/ *xǐhuan hē Zhōngguó* like/drink//middle country/ *chá.* tea/	Yes, thank you, I'm very fond of China tea.

xiānsheng (n)	*Mr, gentleman*	**wǒ** (ps)	*I, me*
nǐ (ps)	*you*	**bù** (neg.)	*not*
hǎo (adj.)	*good*	**nàme**	*in that case, so*
qǐng (v)	*to invite*	**Zhōngguó** (N)	*China*
zuò (v)	*to sit*	**chá** (n)	*tea*
hē (v)	*to drink*	**xíng** (v)	*to be all right*
kāfēi (n)	*coffee*	**hěn** (adv.)	*very*
xièxie (v)	*to thank*	**xǐhuan** (v)	*to like*

Grammar

1 NAMES

In Chinese, names always appears in the following order: surname, given name (Christian name), title (when used), e.g. *Máo Zédōng tóngzhì*, where *Máo* is the surname, *Zédōng* the given name and *tóngzhì* 'comrade'.

2 NǏ HǍO

Some Chinese adjectives can also function as verbs so *hǎo* means 'to be good' as well as 'good'. (Some people call such adjectives stative verbs.) Thus no separate verb for 'to be' is used. Note word order in '*Wáng xiānsheng, nǐ hǎo*'. Mr King comes first in Chinese.

3 USE OF *QǏNG*

Qǐng means 'to invite or to request somebody to do something'. Do not think of it as 'please' as this will create problems with word order later on. Note also that Chinese verbs are invariable, the same form is used throughout.

4 NEGATION WITH *BÙ*

With one exception (the verb 'to have' *yǒu*), all verbs are negated by putting *bù* in front of them.

5 QUESTIONS *XÍNG BU XÍNG*

One common way of asking a question in Chinese is to put the positive and negative forms of the verb together in that order: *Xíng bu xíng?* 'Is it all right (or not)?' The answer is not 'yes' or 'no' but either the positive form of the verb, in this case *xíng* or the negative form, i.e. *bù xíng*. (This construction is often referred to as the choice-type question form.) Note that the second half of the question, i.e. *bù* plus the verb, is sometimes written without tones·as it is normally said unstressed in everyday speech. I have followed this convention at times to familiarise you with it.

6 POSITION OF ADVERBS

Most adverbs in Chinese precede the verb, e.g. 'I like you very much' is *Wǒ hěn xǐhuan nǐ.*

7 TONE OF *BÙ*

Bù is normally fourth tone (ˋ) but changes to second tone (´) when followed by another fourth tone, e.g. *bú zuò* not bù zuò. Also note that in *Xíng bu xíng?*, *bu* is toneless.

EXERCISE 1.1

Make the following sentences negative:
Wǒ hē kāfēi → Wǒ bù hē kāfēi. (Check the tone-mark on *bu* is correct).

1 *Wǒ zuò.*
2 *Nǐ hǎo.*
3 *Wǒ hē chá.*
4 *Nǐ xǐhuan Zhōngguó.*
5 *Lǐ xiānsheng xièxie wǒ.*
6 *Wáng xiānsheng qǐng nǐ hē Zhōngguó chá.*

EXERCISE 1.2

Make the following statements into questions and then answer them first in the positive and then in the negative:
Nǐ hē chá. → Nǐ hē bu hē chá? → Wǒ hē chá.
Wǒ bù hē chá.

1 *Wǒ xǐhuan hē kāfēi.*
2 *Nǐ xièxie wǒ.*
3 *Wáng xiānsheng qǐng wǒ zuò.*
4 *Lǐ xiānsheng xǐhuan hē shuǐ* (water).

EXERCISE 1.3

Translate into colloquial English:
1 *Wáng xiānsheng qǐng wǒ hē Zhōngguó chá.*
2 *Lǐ xiānsheng hěn bù xǐhuan Wáng xiānsheng.*

3   *Wáng xiānsheng yě* (also) *bù hěn xǐhuan Lǐ xiānsheng.*
4   *Nǐ bú xièxie wǒ, nàme wǒ yě bú xièxie nǐ.*

EXERCISE 1.4

Translate into Chinese:
1   How do you do, Mr King. Please sit down.
2   I don't drink tea.
3   In that case, will coffee do?
4   Thank you, coffee would be marvellous.
5   I like you very much.
6   Please have [some]* China tea.
7   He (*tā*) doesn't like me either. (Use *yě*.)

* English words in square brackets should *not* be translated into Chinese.

On Meeting People

On meeting somebody for the first time on a formal occasion, the Chinese will usually shake hands and incline the head a little at the same time in greeting. This will probably be accompanied by such questions as *Nín guìxìng?* 'What is your surname?' (*Lit.* you [polite form] expensive surname) or *Qǐng wèn dàmíng?* 'May I ask your (famous) name?' or *Jiǔyǎng, jiǔyǎng.* 'I'm very pleased to meet you (*Lit.* long time raise head looking for you to come).'

In less formal situations, an older person may pat a younger one on the shoulder, close friends of the same sex may hug each other and pat each other on the back a few times and say for instance, *Nǐ hái huózhe?* 'You're still alive!' or *Shénme fēng bǎ nǐ chuī lái?* 'What wind blew you here?'. Secondary school students still stand up when the teacher comes in and chorus out *Lǎoshī hǎo!* 'How do you do teacher' (*Lit.* teacher good!) and the teacher will normally answer *Tóngxuémen hǎo!* 'How do you do students' (*Lit.* 'fellow students good').

Hopefully this will give you a few guidelines which you can then supplement from your own observations.

2

Making Friends (*ii*)

Mr King has invited Mr and Mrs Li (*Lǐ tàitai*) to his room for a drink.

Lǐ	*Wáng xiānsheng, wǒ gěi nǐ* King/first-born/I/give/you/ *jièshào yíxià, zhè shì wǒ* introduce/ /*this/be/I/ *àiren, Zhōu Déjīn.* love person/Zhou/Dejin/	Mr King, may I introduce my wife, Zhou Dejin?
Wáng	*Lǐ tàitai, nín hǎo!* Li/Mrs/you/good/	How do you do, Mrs Li.
Lǐ (t.)	*Wáng xiānsheng, nín hǎo!* King/first-born/you/good/ *Rènshi nín, wǒ zhēn gāoxìng.* Know/you/I/really/happy/	How do you do, Mr King. I'm really pleased to meet you.
Wáng	*Qǐng zuò, qǐng zuò. Hē* Invite/sit/invite/sit/Drink/ *yì bēi jiǔ ba.* one/cup/alcohol/ /	Please sit down. How about a drink?
Lǐ	*Xièxie, wǒ hē yì bēi.* Thank/I/drink/one/cup/	Thanks, I'll have one.
Wáng	*Lǐ tàitai ne?* Li/Mrs/ /	What about you, Mrs Li?
Lǐ (t.)	*Xièxie, wǒ bú huì* Thank/I/not/know how to/ *hē jiǔ.* drink/alcohol/	No thanks. I don't drink.

Wáng	*Nàme, júzizhī hǎo ma?*	What about an orange juice
	So/orange juice/good//	then?
Lǐ (t.)	*Hǎo, xièxie nín.*	Fine, thank you.
	Good/thank/you/	

* Extra obliques (/) signify the existence of a Chinese word which has no simple English equivalent.

gěi (prep.; v)	*for; give*	**gāoxìng** (adj.)	*happy*
jièshào (v)	*to introduce*	**yī** (num.)	*one*
yíxià	*see Exercise 2.2*	**bēi** (MW)	*cup(ful)*
		jiǔ (n)	*alcohol*
zhè (dem. p./adj.)	*this*	**ba**	*particle indicating suggestion*
shì (v)	*to be*		
àiren (n)	*husband, wife*	**ne**	*question particle*
tàitai (n)	*Mrs, wife*		
nín (ps)	*you (polite form)*	**huì** (aux. v.)	*to know how to; can; will*
rènshi (v)	*to know, recognize*	**júzi-zhī** (n)	*orange juice*
zhēn (adv.; adj.)	*really; true, real*	**ma**	*question particle*

Grammar

1 USE OF *GĚI*

Gěi may be used in several ways. Its basic meaning is as a verb meaning 'to give': *Wǒ gěi nǐ júzizhī* 'I'll give you orange juice' or it can stand with a personal noun or pronoun *before* the verb with the meaning of doing the action of the verb *for* that person: *Wǒ gěi nǐ hē* 'I'll drink (it) for you'. 'To introduce A to B' is *gěi B jièshào A* in Chinese.

2 *YÍXIÀ*

The subtlety of the Chinese language lies in the way it conveys nuances of meaning. In this context *yíxià* softens the abruptness of

Wǒ gěi nǐ jièshào without having any specific meaning, although in other contexts it can mean 'on one occasion' or 'have a little go at doing the action of the verb'.

3 USE OF *SHÌ*

The verb 'to be' is used much less in Chinese than in English. It is mostly to be found in A=B sentences: *Lǐ tàitai shi nǐ àiren* 'Mrs Li is your wife'. The test of whether *shi* has been used correctly is to turn the sentence round and if it still makes sense (albeit clumsily) then the *shi* is correct: *Nǐ àiren shi Lǐ tàitai* 'Your wife is Mrs Li'. Note that *shi* is unstressed unless the speaker wishes to emphasise it: *Tā* (she) *shì nǐ àiren* 'She is your wife'. (Doubt having been cast as to whether or not she was.)

4 *NÍN*

Nín is the polite form of *nǐ* but it is not used frequently. It is used to indicate respect, e.g. when addressing one's 'elders and betters'. It is *not* used in the plural. The table below lists the other personal pronouns.

Personal pronouns			
wǒ	*I, me*	**wǒmen**	*we, us*
nǐ	*you* (sing.)	**nǐmen**	*you* (pl.)
nín	*you* (sing. polite)		
tā	*he, she, it*	**tāmen**	*they, them*

5 TOPIC CONSTRUCTION

The Chinese are very fond of this construction and use it frequently. It consists of stating what you are going to talk about *first*, often in the very broadest sense, and *then* going on to state your view or reaction to it.

Rènshi nín, wǒ zhēn gāoxìng.

topic   reaction

6 MEASURE WORDS

In Chinese something called a measure word has to be used between a number and its noun. Different measure words are used with different categories of nouns. For example *běn* is used for books and magazines whereas *zhāng* is used for rectangular, flat objects such as tables, beds, maps, but is not a true measure as to length or anything else. Some measure words like *bēi* are actual indicators of quantity. The noun accompanying the number and measure word is often omitted when it is clear from the context what this is. For example, Mr Li says in answer to Mr King's question that he will *hē yì bēi* (*jiǔ* 'understood'). For a more comprehensive table of measure words see Chapter 12, pages 114–115.

7 BA

Ba is placed after a verb or phrase to denote a suggestion or to ask for confirmation of a supposition: *Hǎo ba* 'Is that all right then?'.

8 NE

When the same question is put to two or more people consecutively *ne* is usually used to replace the question which has been put to the first person. For example, Mr King suggests to Mr Li that he might like a drink and then turns to Mrs Li and asks: *Lǐ tàitai ne*?

9 HUÌ

One of several auxiliary verbs expressing 'to be able to, can'. *Huì* conveys the idea of 'knowing how to, having learnt it'. It is used to express knowledge of a foreign language: *Wǒ huì Yīngwén* 'I know English' and ability to smoke or drink, etc. 'I don't drink (alcohol)' becomes *Wǒ bú huì hē jiǔ* ('I **don't know how to** drink alcohol') in Chinese. Its other meaning is to express the possibility that something 'will happen in the future': *Tā huì lái* 'He will come'. Both meanings are used in the exercises.

10 QUESTION PARTICLE

The addition of *ma* at the end of any statement makes it into a question. For example: *Júzizhī hǎo* becomes *Júzizhī hǎo ma*?

Numbers 0–99					
0	líng	8	bā	16	shíliù
1	yī	9	jiǔ	17	shíqī
2	èr	10	shí	18	shíbā
3	sān	11	shíyī (10 + 1)	19	shíjiǔ
4	sì	12	shí'èr (10 + 2)	20	èrshí (2 × 10)
5	wǔ	13	shísān	30	sānshí
6	liù	14	shísì	65	liùshíwǔ
7	qī	15	shíwǔ	99	jiǔshíjiǔ

An apostrophe (') is used to show where the break comes between two syllables if there is any possible ambiguity in pronunciation so it is *shí'èr* and not *shíèr*.

Female equality

In the People's Republic of China (PRC) *àiren* means 'husband' or 'wife', but in overseas Chinese communities such as Singapore and Hong Kong it can still mean 'lover', so be careful how you use it! A Chinese woman, married to a Mr Zhang is seldom, if ever, addressed as Mrs Zhang (*Zhāng tàitai*), unless she is an overseas Chinese or is being addressed by a foreigner. She keeps her maiden name and when being introduced, this will be given together with her 'Christian name', e.g. *Zhōu Déjīn*. A foreigner married to a Mr King may be variously addressed as *Wáng tàitai* or *Wáng fūrén*.

EXERCISE 2.1

True or false?
1 *Lǐ xiānsheng bù hē jiǔ.*
2 *Lǐ tàitai hē júzizhī.*

3 *Lǐ xiānsheng gěi Wáng xiānsheng jièshào tā àiren.*
4 *Lǐ tàitai rènshi Wáng xiānsheng bù gāoxìng.*
5 *Zhōu Déjīn huì hē jiǔ.*

EXERCISE 2.2

Re-arrange the words given to produce the meaning in brackets:
   Yì bēi hē huì wǒ jiǔ. [I (can) drink a little alcohol.]
→ *Wǒ huì hē yì bēi jiǔ.*

1 *Gāoxìng Lǐ tàitai nín rènshi zhēn wǒ.* [I'm really happy to meet you, Mrs Li.]
2 *Ba júzizhī nàme hǎo.* [How about an orange juice, then.]
3 *Hē wǒ xǐhuan hěn jiǔ.* [I adore drinking.]
4 *Bù hē sì huì bēi pútáojiǔ* (grape alcohol) *nín.* [You won't drink four glasses of wine.]
5 *Gěi wǒ àiren Lǐ xiānsheng wǒ jièshào.* [I introduce my wife to Mr Li.]

EXERCISE 2.3

Translate into colloquial English:
Wáng xiānsheng qǐng Lǐ xiānsheng hē jiǔ. Lǐ xiānsheng hěn gāoxìng. Tā hěn huì hē jiǔ. Tā àiren Zhōu Déjīn ne? Tā àiren bú huì hē jiǔ. Tā hē júzizhī. Tā yě hěn bù xǐhuan Lǐ xiānsheng hē jiǔ.

EXERCISE 2.4

Translate into Chinese:
1 Do you drink?
2 I'm a teetotaller. What about you? (Use *nín*.)
3 Mr Zhou, may I introduce you to my wife?
4 Does she know him?
5 [When]* my husband smokes (*xī yān* v-o), I'm very cross.
6 How about [some]* coffee? (Use *ba*.)
7 Mr Zhang (Zhāng) doesn't know English (Yīngyǔ).
8 You won't drink seven glasses of wine.

  * NB The English words in square brackets should not be translated into Chinese.

3

Making Friends (*iii*)

Mr King continues his conversation with Mr and Mrs Li.

Wáng	*Lǐ xiānsheng, nǐmen yǒu* Li/first-born/you (pl)/have/ *xiǎoháir ma?* children/ /	Do you have any children, Mr Li?
Lǐ	*Yǒu, wǒmen yǒu liǎng ge –* Have/we/have/2/MW/ *yí ge nánháir, yí ge* 1/MW/male child/1/MW/ *nǚháir.* female child/	Yes, we have two; a boy and a girl.
Wáng	*Nánháir jǐ suì?* Male child/how many/years/ *Nǚháir jǐ suì?* Female child/how many/ years/	How old are they?
Lǐ	*Nánháir shísì suì, nǚháir* Male child/14/years/female *jiǔ suì.* child/9/years/	The boy is 14, the girl is 9.
Lǐ (t.)	*Wáng xiānsheng,* King/first-born/ *jié hūn le ma?* tie marriage/ / /	Are you married, Mr King?

Wáng	*Méi yǒu.*	No, I'm not.
	Not/have/	
Lǐ (t.)	*Yǒu duìxiàng ma?*	Do you have a steady
	Have/facing image/ /	girlfriend?
Wáng	*'Duìxiàng' shì shénme*	What does the word
	Facing image/be/what/	*duìxiàng* mean?
	yìsi?	
	meaning/	
Lǐ	*'Duìxiàng' shì nǚ*	*Duìxiàng* means girlfriend.
	Facing image/be/female/	Do you have a girlfriend?
	péngyou de yìsi. Nǐ yǒu	
	friend/ /meaning/You/have/	
	nǚ péngyou ma?	
	female/friend/ /	
Wáng	*Yǒu.*	Yes, I do.
	Have/	
Lǐ (t.)	*Tā zài nǎr? Tā yě*	Where is she? Is she in
	She/be at/where/She/also/	China too?
	zài Zhōngguó ma?	
	be at/middle country/ /	
Wáng	*Duì, tā yě zài Zhōngguó.*	Yes, she is.
	Correct/she/also/be at/	
	middle country/	
Lǐ	*Wǒ xiǎng qǐng nǐmen*	I'd like to invite you both
	I/feel like/invite/you (pl)/	over to our home. What do
	qù wǒmen jiā wánr, hǎo ma?	you say?
	go/our/home/play/good/ /	
Wáng	*Nà tài hǎo le.*	That would be great.
	That/too/good/ /	
Lǐ (t.)	*Nǐmen míngtiān*	Are you free tomorrow
	You (pl)/tomorrow/	evening?
	wǎnshang yǒu kòng ma?	
	evening/have/space/ /	
Wáng	*Yǒu kòng.*	Yes, we are.
	Have/space/	
Lǐ	*Nàme, qǐng nǐmen liǎ*	Then how about you both
	So/invite/you (pl)/two/	coming over for a meal

	míngtiān wǎnshang qù	tomorrow evening?
	tomorrow/evening/go/	
	wǒmen jiā chī fàn ba.	
	our/home/eat/cooked rice/ /	
Wáng	*Nà tài xièxie nǐmen le!*	Thank you very much
	That/too/thank/you (pl.)/ /	indeed. What time shall we
	Jǐ diǎn zhōng qù ne?	come?
	How many/point/clock/go/ /	
Lǐ (t.)	*Liù diǎn zěnmeyàng?*	How would 6 o'clock suit
	6/point/how about it/	you?
Wáng	*Xíng, jiù liù diǎn ba.*	Fine, 6 o'clock then.
	Be all right/then/6/point/ /	

yǒu (v)	*to have*	**yě** (adv.)	*also, too*
xiǎoháir (n)	*child (small)*	**duì** (adj.)	*correct*
liǎng (num.)	*two*	**xiǎng** (aux. v.; v)	*to feel like*
gè (MW)	*see 3.1* *		*doing some*
nán (adj.)	*male*		*thing; to think*
nǚ (adj.)	*female*	**qù** (v)	*to go*
jǐ (QW)	*how many*	**jiā** (n)	*home; family*
	(less than 10)	**wán(r)** (v)	*to have fun*
suì (n)	*year (of age)*	**nà** (dem. p./adj.)	*that*
jié hūn (v-o)	*to marry, to get*	**tài** (adv.)	*too*
	married	**míngtiān** (TW)	*tomorrow*
le	*modal particle*	**wǎnshang** (TW)	*evening*
méi (neg.)	*not (only used*	**yǒu kòng** (v-o)	*to have free*
	with yǒu)		*time*
duìxiàng (n)	*steady boy- or*	**liǎ** (num + MW)	*two*
	girlfriend	**chī fàn** (v-o)	*to eat (meal)*
shénme (QW)	*what*	**diǎn zhōng**	*o'clock*
yìsi (n)	*meaning*	(MW + n)	
péngyou (n)	*friend*	**zěnmeyàng**	*what about*
de	*marker*	(QW)	*(it)?, how?*
zài (v; prep.)	*to be at; at*	**jiù** (adv.)	*then; just, only,*
nǎr (QW)	*where*		*merely*

* i.e. Chapter 3, grammar point 1.

Grammar

1 MORE ON MEASURE WORD *GE*

Gè is by far the most common measure word in Chinese and is used with a whole range of nouns which do not have their own specific measure word. When in doubt as to which measure word to use, use *gè* – not all Chinese get their measure words right every time either! When said in normal speech, *gè* is usually toneless (see pages xvii- xviii).

2 MORE ON NUMBERS *ÈR* AND *LIǍNG*

Liǎng (two of a kind) is used with measure words instead of *èr*, so 'two children' is *liǎng ge xiǎoháir* not *èr ge xiǎoháir*. Some people find it helpful to think of *liǎng* as the bound form 'two of a kind'. *Liǎ* (an abbreviated form for *liǎng ge*) is often used with personal pronouns we, you (plural), they, instead of *liǎng ge*, thus 'the two of us' may either be *wǒmen liǎ* or *wǒmen liǎng ge*.

3 QUESTION WORDS AND THEIR POSITION

In Chinese, question words such as *jǐ* 'how many' (generally expecting an answer less than ten) and always used with a measure word, *duōshao* 'how many' (indicating any number), *shénme* 'what', *shénme shíhou* 'when' (*Lit.* what time), *shéi* 'who' (also pronounced *shuí*), *nǎr* 'where', *jǐ diǎn (zhōng)* 'what time' (*Lit.* what o'clock), *zěnmeyàng* 'what about it, how', appear in the sentence in the **same** position as the word which replaces them in the answer: *Tāmen jǐ suì?* 'How old are they?' *Nánháir shísì suì, nǚháir jiǔ suì.* (Note that no verb is necessary when stating age in terms of years.) *Tā zài nǎr? Tā yě zài Zhōngguó.*

The particle *ne* is often to be found at the end of the sentence containing a question word and has a softening effect. It also helps to make the sentence feel more balanced. Try saying such sentences with and without *ne* and hear the difference:

Jǐ diǎn zhōng qù?   *Jǐ diǎn zhōng qù **ne**?*

Tā zài nǎr?   *Tā zài nǎr **ne**?*

Note that sentences containing question words do **not** take *ma*.

EXERCISE 3.1

Replace the **bold** words with an appropriate question word:

*Nánháir **wǔ** suì → Nánháir jǐ suì?*

1 *Wǒmen hē júzizhī.*
2 *Lǐ xiānsheng hé* (and) *Lǐ tàitai yǒu liǎng ge xiǎoháir.*
3 *Pútáojiǔ hěn hǎo.*
4 *Wáng xiānsheng de nǚ péngyou zài Běijīng.*
5 *Tāmen míngtiān wǎnshang qī diǎn zhōng qù chī fàn.*
6 *Wáng xiānsheng qǐng tāmen chī fàn.*

4 VERBAL SUFFIX *-LE*

Le is the delight of all Chinese grammarians, but only its more straightforward aspects will be dealt with in this book. Here it is put *after* the verb to indicate that the action of the verb has been completed:

Wáng xiānsheng jié hūn le ma? If he had been married the answer would have been: *Jié hūn le.* The negative form of this construction is *méi yǒu* + *verb* where the *yǒu* may be omitted. The *verb* may be omitted when answering a question with *-le* in the negative but *yǒu* then has to be retained, so Mr King could equally well have replied: *Méi yǒu jié hūn* or *Méi jié hūn* instead of *Méi yǒu*. There is no completed action indicated in the negative so there is no *-le*. Note that the negative form of *yǒu* is *méi yǒu* not bù yǒu. This is the one exception to the rule that all verbs are negated by *bù*. (See 1.4.)

The question form is made by adding *ma* to the statement or *méi yǒu* after it:

Wáng xiānsheng jié hūn le ma? or *Wáng xiānsheng jié hūn le méi yǒu?* This is identical to the choice-type question form found in 1.5 except that the verb is **not** repeated. (*Yǒu* is never omitted in this type of question form.) Another alternative question form is: *Wáng xiānsheng jié hūn méi jié hūn?*, the answers, whether positive or negative, being as before.

5 MARKER *DE*

Two nouns may be linked by *de*, the first being subordinate to the second. Whatever comes **after** *de* is the main idea, i.e. what is being talked about, and what precedes *de* gives additional information about that main idea. Thus the sentence: *Duìxiàng shi nǚ péngyou de yìsi* tells us that the *yìsi* 'meaning' of *duìxiàng* is *nǚ péngyou*. In *péngyou de xiǎoháir* we are told that the *xiǎoháir* is 'a friend's' (*xiǎoháir*).

De is also used with pronouns in the same way: *Nǐ de jiā* 'your home'; *wǒ de bēizi* 'my cup'. For obvious reasons some students tend to regard this *de* as being possessive, but as can be seen from the first example this may be misleading. One way out of this difficulty might be to regard *wǒ de, nǐ de*, etc. simply as possessive adjectives meaning 'my', 'your' and not as *wǒ + de*, etc.

In close personal relationships: *tā māma* 'his mum', *nǐ àiren* 'your husband/wife', *wǒ péngyou* 'my friend' the *de* may be omitted. A Chinese newspaper article or official spokesman will also refer to China and to the Chinese government as *Wǒ guó* ('my country' – 'China') and *Wǒ zhèngfǔ* ('my government' – 'the Chinese government').

6 ANSWERING QUESTIONS

Although questions in Chinese are not answered with 'yes' or 'no' (see 1.5) the answer is sometimes prefaced with a *duì* 'correct' or a *bú duì* (which is often reduced to a simple *bù*). The text provides a good example of this: Mr Li asks if Mr Wang's girlfriend is in China too and he replies: *Duì, tā yě zài Zhōngguó*. If the answer had been negative, he might well have replied: *Bù, tā bú zài Zhōngguó* or *Bù, tā zài Yīngguó* (Britain).

7 *TÀI* VERB *LE*

As *le* is Chinese grammar's *bête noire*, any hints on its usage are indispensable. For example, it is almost invariably to be found together with the adverb *tài* 'too' as in *tài hǎo le* 'great', *tài xièxie nǐmen le* 'thank you very much indeed'. Don't ask me why!

8 ADVERBIAL PHRASES OF TIME (TIME WHEN)

As is stated in 1.6, most adverbs in Chinese **precede** the verb. Adverbs of 'time when' are no exception to this rule (for adverbs of 'time how long' see 10.12), so that in *Qǐng nǐmen míngtiān lái* 'Please come tomorrow' *míngtiān* precedes *lái*. This is the reverse of normal English usage. Such adverbs can also precede the subject or topic for emphasis. For example *Wǒ jīntiān lái, míngtiān wǒ bù lái* 'I'll come today, (but) I am **not** coming tomorrow'.

9 VERB-OBJECT CONSTRUCTIONS

This construction is a feature of the Chinese language so that whereas an English speaker is quite happy with simply stating that

'He likes eating' or that 'She is going to eat', a Chinese will normally say that he likes 'eating cooked rice' or that she is 'going to eat cooked rice' (*chī fàn*), where *chī* is the verb 'to eat' and *fàn* the object 'cooked rice'. There are numerous examples of this construction, some of the most common are given in the following table.

chī fàn	*to eat*	**shuì jiào**	*to sleep*
cooked rice		sleep sleep	
dú shū	*to study*	**shuō huà**	*to speak,*
read books		speak speech	*talk*
huà huàr	*to draw,*	**tán huà**	*to chat*
draw drawings	*paint*	chat speech	
paint paintings		**xī yān**	*to smoke*
jiāo shū	*to teach*	smoke tobacco/	
teach books		cigarettes	
kāi chē	*to drive*	**zǒu lù**	*to walk*
drive vehicle		walk road	
kàn shū	*to read*	**zuò chē**	*to go*
read books		sit vehicle	*(by some*
lù yīn	*to record*		*form of*
record sound			*transport)*
qǐng kè	*to invite*		
invite guest	*somebody*		
	for a meal		

Even *jié hūn* (tie marriage) is strictly speaking a verb-object construction and not a compound verb. The test is whether *le* can be inserted between the two parts or not. If it can, (and only finding or hearing examples can sometimes tell you this) then it is a verb-object construction, so we can say *chī le fàn* but we cannot say *xiè le xie* (*xièxie*) or *xǐ le huan* (*xǐhuan*). Classical Chinese is monosyllabic (one-syllabled), whereas modern Chinese has become increasingly disyllabic (two-syllabled) so the verb-object construction can be seen as conforming to this trend. Of course if the verb in question already has an object, then these 'fill-in' objects are not used.

NB There is great confusion as to whether these verb-objects should be written as one or two words in *pinyin*. I have kept them separate in the interests of clarity.

10   TELLING THE TIME

Question: *Xiànzài* (now) *jǐ diǎn (zhōng)?* (*lit.* Now/how many/ points/clock)

Answer: *Xiànzài yì diǎn zhōng.* (*lit.* Now/one/point/clock)

Zhōng is normally omitted except when asking the time or on the hour, where it is optional.

liǎng diǎn (zhōng)

sān diǎn (líng) wǔ fēn (minute)
líng 'zero' is optional

sì diǎn shíwǔ fēn or
sì diǎn yí kè
(one quarter)

wǔ diǎn sānshí fēn
or
wǔ diǎn bàn (half)

liù diǎn sìshíwǔ fēn
or *liù diǎn sān kè*
(three quarters) or
chà yí kè qī diǎn
(lack/one/quarter/7/
point)

qī diǎn wǔshí fēn or
chà shí fēn bā diǎn
(lack/10/unit/8/point)

For more information on time in general see Chapter 12, p. 116.

EXERCISE 3.2

What time is it on each of the clocks below?

1

5

2

6

3

7

4

8

11 THE ADVERB *JIÙ*

Jiù is used in many different ways, some of which you will meet in this book. Here it is used to link two clauses together and at the same time show acceptance: *Xíng, jiù liù diǎn ba.* As an adverb, *jiù* can never precede a noun or pronoun. Note that *ba* also expresses agreement or approval here (cf. 2.7).

Chinese straight talking

The Chinese love to know everybody else's business and do not feel at all inhibited about enquiring how much you paid for your house, your car, your record-player, your television, your clothes or anything else. They are always particularly interested in your age, marital status and whether you have children and if not why not! Although customs are changing gradually, it is still extremely unusual for a Chinese adult in his or her 30s to be unmarried or childless. Conversely it is quite in order for you to ask the same sort of questions. Being of a 'curious' disposition myself I have always felt very much at home in China. Of course, as contact with the outside world increases, many more Chinese are learning that some foreigners regard such questions as impolite and therefore may, on occasions, restrain their natural curiosity (and genuine openness) on such matters.

EXERCISE 3.3

The following sentences are incorrect, they contain common errors (the Chinese call such sentences *bìngjù* 'sick sentences'). Give the correct version. *Tā jié hūn míngtiān → Tā míngtiān jié hūn*

1 *Wǒ yǒu èr ge xiǎoháir.*
2 *Tā bù yǒu nǚháir.*
3 *Nǐmen yǒu liù péngyou.*
4 *Zhōngguó shi nǎr?*
5 *Jǐ suì tāmen?*
6 *Wǒmen qù shí diǎn zhōng.*

7 *Zěnmeyàng hē lǜ* (green) *chá?*
8 *Zhōu Déjūn méi yǒu jié hūn le.*
9 *Wáng tàitai bù chī fàn wǎnshang.*
10 *Zhāng xiānsheng xiǎng qǐng wǒmen, jiù wǒmen bù qǐng tā.*

EXERCISE 3.4
Translate the following passage into colloquial English:

Wǒmen yǒu sì ge xiǎoháir, sān ge nǚháir, yí ge nánháir. Wǒ de péngyou hěn duō (many). *Wǒ qǐng liǎng ge péngyou míngtiān wǎnshang lái* (come) *wǒmen jiā chī fàn. Wǒ àiren hěn bù gāoxìng yīnwèi* (because) *tā bú rènshi tāmen.*

EXERCISE 3.5
Translate into Chinese:
1 The girl is three years old, the boy is two.
2 Is he married? No, he isn't.
3 Are you (plural) going to his home for a meal tomorrow evening?
4 Where is she now (*xiànzài* TW)? She is in London (*Lúndūn*).
5 Do you (singular) have a steady boyfriend? No I don't. I am only (use *cái*) 15!
6 The two of us are really fond of coffee.
7 What time will you be at home?/How about 7 o'clock?/Fine, 7 it is then. (Use *jiù*.)
8 My wife is smashing, but (*dànshi*) she doesn't like talking much (*shuō huà*).
9 Where is your friend? I'd like to invite him for a meal.

At the Lis' (*i*)

Mr King and his girlfriend Miss Shaw *(Shǐ xiǎojie)* have arrived at the Lis' for dinner.

Wáng	*Wǒ gěi nǐmen jièshào yíxià,* I/give/you/introduce/ / *zhè wèi shì wǒ de nǚ* this/MW/be/my/female/ *péngyou, Shǐ Àilǐ. Zhè wèi* friend/Shi Aili/This/MW/ *shì Lǐ xiānsheng, zhè wèi* be/Li/first-born/this/MW/ *shì Lǐ tàitai.* be/Li/Mrs/	May I introduce you to my girlfriend, Shi Aili? This gentleman is Mr Li and this is Mrs Li.
Lǐ ⎱ **Lǐ (t.)** ⎰	*Shǐ xiǎojie, nín hǎo!* Shi/Miss/you/good/	How do you do, Miss Shaw.
Shǐ	*Lǐ xiānsheng ﹅ Lǐ tàitai,* Li/first-born/Li/Mrs/ *nǐmen hǎo!* you/good/	How do you do, Mr and Mrs Li.
Lǐ	*Qǐng suíbiàn zuò ba.* Invite/follow convenience/ sit/ /	Please make yourselves comfortable.
Lǐ (t.)	*Shǐ xiǎojie, nín yě shì cóng* Shi/Miss/you/also/be/from/ *Yīngguó lái de ma?* hero country/come/ / /	Are you from Britain too, Miss Shaw?

Shĭ	*Shì, wǒ yě shì cóng* Be/I/also/be/from/ *Yīngguó lái de.* hero country/come/ /	Yes, I am.
Lĭ	*À, nǐmen liǎ dōu shì* Ah/you/two/both/be/ *Yīngguórén.* hero country people/	Ah, you are both British.
Lĭ (t.)	*Shĭ xiǎojie, nín zài zhèr zuò* Shi/Miss/you/at/here/do/ *shénme?* what/	What are you doing here Miss Shaw?
Shĭ	*Wǒ zài zhèr xuéxí Hànyǔ.* I/at/here/study/Chinese language/	I'm studying Chinese language here.
Lĭ	*Nín zài nǎ ge xuéxiào* You/at/which/MW/school/ *xuéxí Hànyǔ?* study/Chinese language/	Which school are you (studying Chinese language) at?
Shĭ	*Wǒ zài Běijīng Dàxué xuéxí* I/at/Beijing/big study/study/ *Hànyǔ.* Chinese/	I am studying (Chinese language) at Beijing University.
Lĭ	*Xuéxiào lǐ shēnghuó* School inside/life/ *zěnmeyàng?* how/	What's it like there?
Shĭ	*Hěn búcuò!* Very/not wrong!	It's great!
Lĭ (t.)	*Nǐmen yídìng hěn è le.* You/definitely/very/hungry// *Wǒmen chī fàn ba. Jīntiān* We/eat/meal/ /Today/ *wǎnshang chī Zhōngguó cài* evening/eat/China/dish(es)/ *xíng ma?* be OK/ /	You must be ravenous. Let's eat. We are going to eat Chinese tonight, if that's all right with you?

Wáng	*Hǎo jíle!*	Marvellous!
	Good/extremely/	
Lǐ	*Bié kèqi, zìjǐ lái ba.*	Make yourselves at home.
	Don't/be polite/self/come//	Do help yourselves. Can
	Nǐmen huì yòng kuàizi ma?	you use chopsticks?
	You/know/use/chopsticks//	
Wáng	*Huì yòng, dànshi yòng de bù*	Yes, but not very well.
	Know/use/but/use/not/	
	hǎo.	
	good/	
Lǐ	*Méi guānxi...Ǹg, nǐmen*	It doesn't matter...Hm,
	Not/concern/Hm/you/	you are both pretty good.
	dōu yòng de búcuò a!	
	both/use/not bad//	
Lǐ (t.)	*Wǒ zuò cài, zuò de bù*	Sorry, I'm not much of a
	I/make/dish/make/not/	cook.
	hǎo, qǐng yuánliàng.	
	good/invite/forgive/	
Shǐ	*Nín zuò cài, zuò de hěn*	You cook very well.
	You/make/dish/make/very/	
	hǎo.	
	good/	
Lǐ (t.)	*Shǐ xiǎojie huì zuò cài ma?*	Can you cook, Miss
	Shi/Miss/know/make/dish//	Shaw?
Shǐ	*Huì yìdiǎnr, dànshi*	A little, but I am a very
	Can/one drop/but/	plain cook.
	jìshù bù gāo!	
	technique/not/tall/	
Wáng	*Tā Yīngguó cài*	She cooks wonderful
	She/hero country/dish/	English food.
	zuò de fēicháng hǎo.	
	make/extremely/good/	
Lǐ	*Zhōngguó cài zuò de*	What about Chinese food?
	Middle country/dish/make/	
	zěnmeyàng?	
	how/	
Shǐ	*Wǒ Zhōngguó cài*	I'm not much good at
	I/middle country/dish/	making Chinese food.

zuò de bù zěnmeyàng.
make/not/how/

Lǐ (t.) *Nǐmen zuìhǎo shǎo shuō* You'd better talk less and
You/most good/less/speak/ concentrate more on your
huà, duō chī fàn ba, food, otherwise it'll all get
speech/more/eat/meal/ / cold!
yàobùrán cài dōu liáng le!
/otherwise/dish/all/cool/ /

wèi (MW)	*for persons (polite)*	**jīntiān** (TW)	*today*
xiǎojie (n)	*Miss, young lady*	**cài** (n)	*dish; vegetable*
		(adj. +) jíle	*extremely (+ adj.)*
suíbiàn	*do as one pleases*	**bié** (adv.)	*don't*
shi...de	*see 4.4*	**kèqi** (adj.)	*polite (lit. guest air)*
cóng (prep.)	*from*	**zìjǐ** (p)	*oneself*
Yīngguó (N)	*Britain, England*	**yòng** (v)	*to use*
lái (v)	*to come*	**kuàizi** (n)	*chopsticks*
à (interj)	*ah, oh*	**dànshi** (conj.)	*but*
dōu (adv.)	*both, all*	**-de**	*see 4.8*
Yīngguórén (n)	*British (person)*	**méi (yǒu)**	
zhèr (PW)	*here*	**guānxi**	*it doesn't matter*
zuò (v)	*to do, to make*	**ńg** (interj.)	*hm*
xué(xí) (v)	*to study*	**yuánliàng** (v)	*to forgive*
Hànyǔ (n)	*Chinese language*	**yìdiǎn(r)** (n)	*a little*
		jìshù (n)	*technique*
nǎ (QW)	*which?*	**gāo** (adj.)	*tall, high*
xuéxiào (n)	*school*	**fēicháng** (adv.)	*extremely*
Běijīng Dàxué (N)	*Beijing University*	**bù zěnmeyàng**	*not up to much*
		zuì (adv.)	*most*
(n +) lǐ	*inside (+ n)*	**zuìhǎo** (adv., adj.)	*had better; best*
shēnghuó (n, v)	*life; to live*	**shǎo** (adv., adj.)	*less; few*
búcuò	*pretty good*	**shuō huà** (v-o)	*to speak, talk*
yídìng (adv.)	*certainly, definitely*	**duō** (adj., adv.)	*more; many*
		yàobù(rán) (conj.)	*otherwise*
è (adj.)	*hungry*		
le	*new situation le*	**liáng** (adj.)	*cool*

Grammar

1 MORE ON MEASURE WORDS

When *zhè* 'this' and *nà* 'that' occur with a noun in the singular or as pronouns (with a singular noun understood) or with a number, then the appropriate measure word must be inserted:

zhè wèi xiǎojie 'this MW (unmarried) young lady'

nà wèi xiānsheng 'that MW gentleman'

zhè wèi 'this MW one (person understood)'

nà liǎng ge rén 'those two MW people'

This rule applies equally well to such question words as *jǐ* 'how many' and *nǎ* 'which': (both of which must be followed by measure words):

Q. *Tā gěi nǐ jǐ bēi jiǔ?* 'How many glasses of alcohol did he give you?'

A. *Tā gěi wǒ sān bēi jiǔ.* 'He gave me three.'

Q. *Nǐ zài nǎ ge xuéxiào xuéxí Hànyǔ?* 'Where do you study Chinese?'

A. *Wǒ zài Běijīng Dàxué xuéxí Hànyǔ.* 'I study Chinese at Beijing University.'

Note that *wèi* is normally used with more formal nouns such as *xiānsheng, xiǎojie,* etc. but not with nouns such as *rén.* The *xiǎo* in *xiǎojie* is pronounced second tone in practice, as *jiě,* though neutral here, still carries enough weight to turn *xiǎo* into a second. Convention has us write it as third tone however.

EXERCISE 4.1

Insert the missing measure words in the following sentences:

Nà xuéxiào búcuò. → *Nà ge xuéxiào búcuò.*

1 *Zhè xiǎojie zài Běijīng Dàxué xuéxí Hànyǔ.*

2 *Nǎ xiānsheng shì nǐ àiren?*

3 *Wáng tàitai yǒu jǐ xiǎoháir?*

4 *Nà wǔ rén dōu shì nǐ péngyou ma?*

5 *Tāmen jǐ zhōng lái wǒmen jiā chī fàn?*

2 FOREIGN NAMES (I)

Certain very common and/or very well-known foreign surnames and Christian names have set equivalents in Chinese, e.g. Smith: *Shǐmìsī (Shǐ mì sī),* John: *Yuēhàn (Yuē hàn).* Thus John Smith

would be written *Yuēhàn•Shǐmìsī*, the '•' between the two indicating that the name is foreign. Since the majority of Chinese
names consist of three characters or 'syllables', most foreigners
who regularly come into contact with Chinese people often adopt a
three syllable name. Sometimes all three syllables are an approximate transliteration of the foreign surname, otherwise the Chinese
practice of generally having one syllable for the surname and two
for the given or Christian name is adopted. Thus Miss Shaw has
adopted the Chinese surname *Shǐ* 'history' and the given name *Àilǐ*
(ài lǐ) 'loves principle'. Almost all Chinese given names have a
meaning, hence the origin of such names as 'Beautiful Jade' and
'Flowering Plum Blossom' which appear in some English transla-
tions of Chinese literature and a good transcription of a foreign
name should follow this practice.

3 ADVERBIAL PHRASES OF PLACE

Adverbial phrases of place usually consist of a preposition and a
place-word and are generally put before the verb as in:

Wǒ zài zhèr xuéxí Hànyǔ. 'I study Chinese here.'

Other prepositions such as *cóng* 'from' and *dào* 'to' also function
in this way:

Tā cóng Zhōngguó lái. (*Lit.* He/from/China/comes) 'He comes from
                China.'

Wǒmen dào Měiguó qù. (*Lit.* We/to/beautiful country/go) 'We go to
                America.'

When an adverbial phrase of 'time when' (see 3.8) and an
adverbial phrase of place both occur before the verb, the rule is
time **before** place:

Nǐmen jīntiān zài wǒ jiā chī fàn. 'You are eating at my home today.'
(*Lit.* You/today/at/my/home/eat/cooked rice/.)

Note that words such as -*lǐ* 'inside', 'on', 'under', etc. occur **after**
the noun to which they refer. These will be dealt with in more
detail in a later chapter.

4 SHÌ...DE

An adverbial phrase of time, manner or place is emphasised by
putting *shì* in front of it and *de* after it. This construction can only
be used where the action of the verb has been completed, it cannot
be used for present or future actions:

Q.   Shǐ xiǎojie, nín yě shì cóng Yīngguó lái de ma?

A.   Shì, wǒ yě shì cóng Yīngguó lái de.

A negative answer might have been:

Bù, wǒ shì cóng Déguó (Germany) *lái de.*

The stress does not always show in the English translation but the following examples may illustrate the point more clearly:

Q.   Nǐ shì bā diǎn zhōng lái de ma? 'Did you come at 8?' (Was it at 8 that you came?)

A.   Bù, wǒ shì qī diǎn bàn lái de. 'No, at 7.30' (It was at 7.30 that I came.)

Q.   Nǐ shì zuò chē (sit vehicle) *lái de ma?* 'Did you come by bus/car?' (Was it by bus/car that you came?)

A.   Bù, wo shì zǒu lù lái de. 'No I came on foot.' (It was on foot that I came.)

5   ABBREVIATIONS

You might be forgiven for thinking that given the nature of the Chinese language, abbreviations would be out of the question, but you would be wrong. The Chinese love abbreviations, the pithiness of which has echoes of their classical past. Hence *Běijīng Dàxué* 'Beijing University' becomes *Běidà, Nánjīng Dàxué* 'Nanjing University' becomes *Nándà* and so on. As you can see the first syllable from each word has been picked out to form the abbreviation. The most likely targets for abbreviations are institutions and political movements.

6   THE PARTICLE *LE*

When *le* occurs at the end of a sentence it is often referred to as the 'modal particle *le*'. In this text it is used to indicate that a new state of affairs or situation has appeared:

Nǐmen yídìng hěn è le 'You must be starving' (whereas previously you weren't);

Cài dōu liáng le 'All the food is getting/will get cold' (whereas previously it was piping hot!)

You might find it helpful to think of this as the 'new situation' *le* or the 'change of state' *le*. This has to be accepted in its very broadest sense as the Chinese almost always use it with such questions as:

Xiǎoháir jǐ suì le? 'How old is the child?' (*Lit.* Child/how many/
    years/become)

Xiànzài jǐ diǎn le? 'What time is it?' (*Lit.* Now/how many/o'clock/
    become)

where the concept of a change of state has been stretched to its
limits.

7 DON'T! *BIÉ*

The negative imperative is formed by putting *bié* in front of the
verb or adjective acting as a verb:

Bié kèqi! 'Don't stand on ceremony!' *Bié shuō huà!* 'Don't speak!'

If *le* is added after the verb or adjective acting as a verb, the com-
mand is softened and sounds much less like an order:

Bié hē jiǔ le! 'Now, now, no drinking!'.

8 *DE* WITH THE COMPLEMENT OF DEGREE

The Chinese character for this *de* is quite different from the *de* in
Chapter 3, but they are identical in *pinyin* because they are the
same sound and are both toneless. The function of this *de* is to indicate what the Chinese call the complement of degree, i.e. it is used
with a word indicating manner or degree as in the following
pattern:

    Yòng de hěn hǎo 'to use something (very) well'.

The table below shows the essential workings of the complement
of degree.

(a)	Positive form:	S V *de* CD *Tā yòng de hěn hǎo.*	He uses it (very) well.
(b)	Negative form:	S V *de bu* CD *Tā yòng de bù hǎo.*	He doesn't use it well.
(c)	Question form with *ma*:	S V *de* CD *ma?* *Tā yòng de hǎo ma?*	Does he use it well?
(d)	Question form without *ma*:	S V *de* CD *bu* CD *Tā yòng de hǎo bu hǎo?*	

(e)	Question form using *zěnmeyàng*:	*S V de zěnmeyàng?* *Tā yòng de zěnmeyàng?*	How does he use it?
(f)	With an object:	*S V₁ O V₁ de CD* *Tā yòng kuàizi yòng de hěn hǎo.*	He uses chopsticks well.
(g)	With an object omitting the first verb:	*S O V de CD* *Tā kuàizi yòng de hěn hǎo.*	
(h)	With object as topic:	*O S V de CD* *Kuàizi tā yòng de hěn hǎo.*	(i) As for chopsticks he uses them (very) well. (ii) He uses chopsticks (very) well.

Note that:

1 It is the complement of degree and **not** the verb which has things done to it when we use this construction in the negative or question form [see table above *(a)–(e)*].

2 The complement of degree marker *de* must always directly follow its verb. If there is an object then the construction is as in *(f)* or *(g)* above.

3 If we wish to emphasise the **object** this may be put before the subject and the first verb is omitted as in *(h)*. This has the effect of making the object into a kind of topic which the speaker then goes on to talk about [see 2.5].

4 When adjectives such as *hǎo* act as verbs and are standing alone, they are normally preceded in the affirmative by the adverb *hěn* 'very'. Although in these cases *hěn* does not have the full force of the English word 'very' its function is to indicate that the statement is absolute. Without *hěn* some kind of contrast or comparison is implied:

> *Tā hǎo.* 'He is nice' (implying that someone else isn't)
> *Tā hěn hǎo.* 'He is (very) nice' is complete in itself and has no such overtones..

The same rule applies when these adjectives are used as complements of degree in the positive form [see *(a)*, *(f)*, *(g)* and *(h)* above]; but not in the negative or question forms [see *(b)*, *(c)*, *(d)* and *(e)*].

EXERCISE 4.2

Make the following statements into sentences using the complement of degree given in brackets. Give more than one form where appropriate:

> *Tā chī fàn (hěn duō)* → *Tā chī fàn, chī de hěn duō.*
> → *Tā fàn chī de hěn duō.*
> → *Fàn tā chī de hěn duō.*

1 *Wǒmen xuéxí (hěn shǎo)*
2 *Nǐmen shuō Hànyǔ (búcuò)*
3 *Tā shēnghuó (bù zěnmeyàng)*
4 *Nà ge rén zuò Zhōngguó cài (hěn hǎo)*
5 *Zhè ge péngyou shuō huà (bù duō).*

EXERCISE 4.3

Turn the following statements into questions (three forms) and then answer them in the negative:

> *Nà ge xiǎoháir zuò de hěn hǎo.* → *Nà ge xiǎoháir zuò de hǎo ma?*
> → *Nà ge xiǎoháir zuò de hǎo bu hǎo?*
> → *Nà ge xiǎoháir zuò de zěnmeyàng?*
>
> Negative → *Nà ge xiǎoháir zuò de bù hǎo.*

1 *Tā shuō Hànyǔ shuō de hěn hǎo.*
2 *Wǒ yí ge péngyou* (my one MW friend = one of my friends) *hē jiǔ hē de hěn duō.*
3 *Shǐ xiǎojie xuéxí de hěn màn* (slow).
4 *Gōngrén* (worker) *jīntiān lái de hěn shǎo.*
5 *Yīngguórén zuò Yīngguó cài, zuò de hěn hǎo.*

9 *DUŌ/SHǍO* + VERB

Duō or *shǎo* before the verb conveys the idea of doing more or less of the verb: *shǎo shuō huà* 'speak less', *duō chī fàn* 'eat more'. This construction can only be used with full verbs and not with adjectives used as verbs. (*Shǎo gāo* does not mean 'to be less tall'. This phrase would be meaningless.)

Interrogation – Chinese style?

Mr and Mrs Li have not previously met Miss Shaw so they are anxious to find out who she is and what she does where. This is very typical of a first meeting – somewhere, you are being fitted into an imaginary filing system!

Modesty

When talking to a second party, the Chinese have a long cultural tradition of denigrating themselves and their achievements but of praising the other party. They will do this both spontaneously and in response to compliments paid. As food is a major topic of conversation for the Chinese, this cultural tendency is often very pronounced when the quality and quantity of a meal are under discussion. Remarks by the host and the hostess that it is only 'a very simple meal' *yí dùn biàn fàn* (*Lit.* one/MW/simple/cooked rice) and 'there are no dishes worth speaking of' *méi shénme cài*, are almost *de rigueur* even though guests know they have gone to enormous trouble and expense to prepare the meal. Good examples of this modesty are Mrs Li's *Wǒ zuò cài, zuò de bù hǎo, qǐng yuánliàng* and Miss Shaw's very Chinese answer to the question as to her own cooking ability: *Huì yìdiǎnr, dànshi jìshù bù gāo*. Of course it is common practice for the listener to follow up such remarks with a compliment to the speaker as occurs here. Mrs Li's cooking is delicious *Nǐ zuò cài, zuò de hěn hǎo*, and Miss Shaw cooks wonderful English food *Tā Yīngguó cài zuò de fēicháng hǎo*!

EXERCISE 4.4

Answer the following questions on the text:

1 *Wáng xiānsheng de nǚ péngyou shì shéi* (who)?
2 *Shǐ xiǎojie shì bu shi Yīngguórén?*
3 *Shǐ xiǎojie zài Zhōngguó zuò shénme?*
4 *Zài Běijīng Dàxué shēnghuó hǎo ma?*
5 *Tāmen jīntiān wǎnshang chī shénme cài?*

6 *Wáng xiānsheng hé* (and) *Shǐ xiǎojie kuàizi yòng de hǎo bu hǎo?*
7 *Lǐ tàitai zuò cài zuò de zěnmeyàng?*
8 *Shǐ xiǎojie huì bu hui zuò Yīngguó cài?*

EXERCISE 4.5

Translate the following passages into colloquial English:

1 *Wǒ huì zuò cài dànshi zuò de bù hǎo. Wǒ de nǚ péngyou shuō wǒ de jìshù bù gāo. Wǒmen yǒu hěn duō Zhōngguó péngyou, tāmen zuò Zhōngguó cài zuò de búcuò. Tāmen yòng kuàizi yě yòng de hěn hǎo. Nǐ ne?*

2 *Wǒ yí ge péngyou qù Fǎguó* (France) *gōngzuò* (to work). *Fǎguó cài hěn hǎo chī—tā chī de hěn duō. Xiànzài tā hěn pàng* (fat) *le. Tā àiren shuō: 'Nǐ shǎo chī fàn, duō gōngzuò zěnmeyàng?'. Wǒ péngyou shuō: 'Shǎo chī fàn hǎo dànshi duō gōngzuò bù hǎo!'*

EXERCISE 4.6

Translate into Chinese:

1 I myself (*zìjǐ*) can't cook but my husband cooks marvellously.
2 Are you French? We are both French too.
3 Did that gentleman come at 2.30? No, he came at 3. (Use *shì... de*)
4 Where are you studying Chinese? How are you getting on?
5 He came from America. He is working here.
6 What's the time? You must be starving!
7 I've got no free time today but I'm not working tomorrow. Would 10 o'clock suit you? (Use *xíng.*)
8 She's not very good at using chopsticks but she cooks really good Chinese food.

5

At the Lis' (*ii*)

Mr King and Miss Shaw are just finishing their meal at the Lis'.

Lǐ	*Bié kèqi, zài duō*	Don't stand on ceremony,
	Don't/polite/again/more/	go on, eat a bit more.
	chī yìdiǎn(r).	
	eat/a little/	
Wáng	*Chī bǎo le, cài dōu hěn*	I've had enough, it was
	Eat/full//dishes/all/very/	delicious.
	hǎo chī.	
	good/eat/	
Lǐ (t.)	*Nǐmen yuànyì hē kāfēi háishi*	Would you like tea or
	You/want/drink/coffee/or/	coffee?
	hē chá?	
	drink/tea/	
Wáng	*Wǒ suíbiàn.*	I'm easy.
	I/follow convenience/	
Shǐ	*Hē chá ba.*	Let's have tea.
	Drink/tea/ /	
	(Hē wán le chá)	(After having tea)
	Drink finish/ /tea/	
Lǐ (t.)	*Shǐ xiǎojie, kànyikàn wǒmen*	Would you like to have a
	History/Miss/look look/we/	look round our little house,
	de xiǎo fángzi ba?	Miss Shaw?
	/little/house/ /	

Shǐ *Hǎo, xièxie nín.*
Good/thank/you/
Yǒngshòu, nǐ
Eternal longevity/you/
péi Lǐ xiānsheng tán huà
accompany/Li/Mr/chat/
ba...
speech/ /

Yes, please. Yongshou, you chat to Mr Li.

Lǐ (t.) *Zhè shì chúfáng, dìfang hěn*
This/be/kitchen/place/very/
xiǎo, suǒyǐ bīngxiāng 、
small/therefore/ice box/
xǐyījī dōu
wash clothes machine/both/
fàng zài wàimiàn tīng lǐ.
put/in/outside/hall inside/
Wǒmen zhǐ yǒu sān ge
We/only/have/3/MW/
fángjiān, érzi yì jiān, nǚ'ér yì
room/son/1/MW/daughter/
jiān...
1/MW/

This is the kitchen, it's very small so we have put the fridge and the washing machine in the hall outside. We only have three rooms, one for our son, one for our daughter...

Shǐ *Háizimen yǒu zìjǐ de fángjiān*
Children/have/own/ /room/
kěyǐ ānānjìngjìng de dú shū.
can/quiet/ /read/book(s)/

Children can study in peace if they have their own room.

Lǐ (t.) *Wǒ hé lǎo Lǐ de fángjiān zhǐ*
I/and/old/Li/ /room/only/
hǎo yòu dāng
good/again/serve as/
wòshì yòu dāng
bedroom/again/serve as/
kètīng.
sitting-room/ .

Old Li's and my room has to serve both as bedroom and sitting-room.

Shǐ *Nǐmen de kètīng bùzhì de*
You//sitting-room/decorate/
hěn piàoliang. Diànshì
very/beautiful/Television/

Your sitting room is beautifully furnished. Is it a colour TV or black and white?

shì cǎisè de háishi
be/colour/ /or/
hēi-bái de?
black and white/ /

Lǐ (t.)   *Shì cǎisè de. Yào bu yao*
Be/colour/ /Want/not/want/
kàn yíxià?
look/ /

It's colour. Would you like
to watch something?

Shǐ   *Bú yòng le. Shíjiān bù zǎo le,*
Not/use/ /Time/not/early/ /
wǒmen (yīng)gāi huí qu le.
we/ought to/return/go/ /

No, thanks. It's getting late,
we ought to be getting back.

Wáng   *Shíjiān guò de zhēn kuài. Lǐ*
Time/pass/really/fast/Li/
xiānsheng、Lǐ taitai, wǒmen
Mr/Li/Mrs/we/
děi zǒu le, xièxie nǐmen de
must/leave/ /thank/you/ /
rèqíng zhāodài.
warm-hearted/hospitality/
Wǒmen wánr de fēicháng
We/have fun/extremely/
gāoxìng, gěi nǐmen tiān le bù
happy/for/you/add/ /not/
shǎo máfan.
few/trouble(s)/

The time's flown. Mr and
Mrs Li, we must be on our
way, thank you for your
marvellous hospitality.
We've had a wonderful
time and caused you no end
of trouble.

Lǐ   *Méi shénme, huānyíng*
Not have/what/welcome/
nǐmen zài lái wánr.
you/again/come/have fun/

Not at all, feel free to come
again.

Wáng/   *Yídìng lái. Xièxie nǐmen.*
Shǐ   Certainly/come/Thank/you/
Zàijiàn.
Again see/

Thank you, we certainly
will. Goodbye.

Lǐ   *Màn zǒu, màn zǒu.*
Slow/go/slow/go/

Mind how you go.

From Chapter 5 onwards, the appropriate measure word (MW) is placed in square brackets after its noun unless it is *ge*, in which case it is omitted. Some nouns have two measure words, *ge* and a more formal one. Where this is so, both have been indicated.

zài (adv.)	*again*	**lǎo** (adj.)	*old*
chī-bǎo (RV)	*to eat one's fill*	**zhǐ hǎo** (adv.)	*have to*
hǎo chī (adj.)	*tasty, delicious*	**yòu…yòu**	*both…and…*
yuànyì (aux. v)	*to be willing; to want*	**dāng** (v)	*to serve as; be*
		wòshì (n)	*bedroom*
háishi	*or (used in questions)*	**kètīng** (n)	*living-room, lounge*
-wán (RVE)	*to finish verb + -ing*	**bùzhì** (v)	*to decorate*
		piàoliang (adj.)	*beautiful*
kàn (v)	*to look; to see; to watch; to read*	**diànshì** (jī) (n) [**tái**]	*television*
xiǎo (adj.)	*small*	**cǎisè** (n)	*colour, multicoloured*
fángzi (n) [**suǒ, ge**]	*house*	**hēi-bái** (adj.)	*black and white*
		yào (aux. v, v)	*want to, must, to want*
péi (v)	*to accompany*		
tán huà (v-o, n)	*to chat; conversation*	**bù…le**	*not…any more*
		shíjiān (n)	*time*
chúfáng (n) [**jiān, ge**]	*kitchen*	**zǎo** (adj.)	*early*
		(yīng)gāi (aux. v)	*ought, should*
dìfang (n)	*place*		
suǒyǐ (conj.)	*therefore*	**huí** (v)	*to return*
bīngxiāng (n)	*refrigerator*	**guò** (v)	*to pass, to cross*
xǐyījī (n) [**tái**]	*washing machine*	**kuài** (adj.)	*quick, fast*
		děi (aux. v)	*must, need*
fàng (zài) (v)	*to put (in)*	**zǒu** (v)	*to leave, to walk, to go*
wàimiàn (PW)	*outside*		
tīng (n)	*hall*	**rèqíng** (adj.)	*warm-hearted, enthusiastic*
zhǐ (adv.)	*only*		
fángjiān (n)	*room*	**zhāodài** (n, v)	*hospitality, to entertain*
érzi (n)	*son*		
jiān (MW)	*for room*	**tiān** (v)	*to add, increase*
nǚ'ér (n)	*daughter*	**máfan** (n/v, adj.)	*trouble, troublesome*
háizi (n)	*child*		
kěyǐ (aux. v)	*can, may*	**méi (yǒu)**	
ānjìng (adj.)	*quiet*	**shénme**	*it's nothing*
…de	*see 5.6*	**huānyíng** (v)	*to welcome*
dú shū (v-o)	*to study*	**zàijiàn**	*goodbye*
hé (conj.)	*and*	**màn** (adj.)	*slow*

Grammar

1   RESULTATIVE VERBS (I)

Not all compound (two syllable) verbs are resultative, e.g. *rènshi*, *jièshào* and *xuéxí* are not. At this stage the easiest way to recognise resultative verbs is by their endings. We have three examples of common resultative verb endings (or complements of result) in this chapter viz. -*bǎo*, -*wán* and -*qù*. *Chī bǎo* means to 'eat one's fill' where *chī* is the verb and *bǎo* is the resultative verb ending expressing satisfaction of appetite. *Bǎo* can only be used with *chī* in this way but it can stand on its own, meaning 'to be full'.

Wǒ bǎo le 'I'm full' (change of state *le*). *Hē wán* means 'to finish drinking' where *hē* is the verb and *wán* is the resultative verb ending expressing completion. Unlike -*bǎo*, -*wán* may be found with many different verbs, e.g. *kàn, zuò, shuō, chī*.

RESULTATIVE VERBS (II): SIMPLE DIRECTIONAL ENDINGS

...-*qù* is a directional ending indicating direction **away** from the speaker or point of reference and is used with verbs of motion and transference of something or somebody from one place to another. Thus *huí qu* means to go back:

Wǒmen gāi huí qu le 'We ought to be going back' (change of state *le*), i.e. previously we didn't have to go back, now we do...-*lái* is used in exactly the same way but to indicate direction **towards** the speaker or point of reference. *Huí lai* would mean 'to come back', the point of reference being where the speaker is when using it. For other common resultative verb endings of both types see the relevant sections in Chapter 12, pp. 118–119.   NB *Lái* and *qù* are normally toneless when used as simple directional endings.

EXERCISE 5.1

Insert *lái* or *qù* in the following sentences depending on the position of 'the speaker' which is given in brackets:

Zhào xiānsheng huí dàxué _____ *le.* (We all stayed in town) → *Zhào xiānsheng huí dàxué qu le.*

1 *Dèng xiǎojie yào huí Zhōngguó* _____. (Point of reference is where she is now, i.e. *Yīngguó*)
2 *Érzi jìn* (enter) *kètīng* _____ *le.* (Everybody is in the lounge)
3 *Tā jìn wòshì* _____ *le.* (Everybody is in the lounge)

4 *Nǐmen yīnggāi huí jiā* ____. (Parents to children on the phone)
5 *Wǒ xiǎng huí Yīngguó* ____. (Speaker is in China).

2 *HÁISHI* IN QUESTIONS

Háishi 'or' is placed between two statements thereby making them alternatives from which the listener must choose **one**:

*Nǐmen yuànyì hē kāfēi **háishi** hē chá?* 'Would you like tea or coffee?'
If the subject or object in both halves is the same it need not be repeated (this holds true for any two clauses, not just ones using *háishi*, and is a feature of Chinese), but there must be a **verb** in both halves even if it is the same verb:

Nǐ mǎi (buy) *bīngxiāng **háishi** tā mǎi?* 'Are you buying the fridge or is he?'

Note in another example from the text:

*Diànshì shì cǎisè de **háishi** hēi-bái de?* the *shì* in *háishi* is allowed to stand for the verb *shì* in the second half – this is the only exception to the rule. Try saying *háishi shì* and you'll understand why.

EXERCISE 5.2

Make the two statements into one question using *háishi*:

Nǐmen kàn diànshì.
Nǐmen kàn shū (v-o read). } → *Nǐmen kàn diànshì **háishi** kàn shū?*

1 *Tāmen xǐhuan chī fàn.*
  Tāmen xǐhuan shuō huà.
2 *Dèng tàitai yào mǎi* (buy) *bīngxiāng.*
  Dèng tàitai yào mǎi xǐyījī.
3 *Zhōu xiānsheng qù Fǎguó.*
  Zhāng xiānsheng qù Fǎguó.
4 *Shíjiān guò de kuài.*
  Shíjiān guò de màn.
5 *Wǒ péngyou de fángzi méi yǒu chúfáng.*
  Wǒ péngyou de fángzi méi yǒu yùshì (bathroom).
6 *Nǐ xuéxí Hànyǔ.*
  Nǐ xuéxí dìlǐ (geography).

3 REDUPLICATION OF VERBS

In much the same way as *yíxià* in 2.2, repeating the verb has the effect of softening the suggestion, question or statement. Monosyllabic verbs often have *yi* inserted between the two parts when they are repeated e.g. *kànyikàn*. Disyllabic verbs cannot be treated in this way so *jièshàoyijièshào* would be incorrect. Again, like *yíxià*, repeating the verb can also convey the meaning of 'having a little go' at doing the action of the verb in both the sense of a trial and in doing something fairly quickly. It can also indicate repetition of the action with verbs such as *fùxí* 'to revise'.

4 FÀNG + ZÀI

Zài + Place-Word is used after certain verbs such as *fàng* 'to place', *xiě* 'to write', *jì* 'to record', *zhù* 'to live', *shuì* 'to sleep', *zuò* 'to sit' and *zhàn* 'to stand'. As we have seen in 4.3, adverbial phrases of place generally occur before the verb so these are exceptions to that rule. Some people say that *zài* is acting as a resultative verb ending in such cases, i.e. that something or somebody comes into existence at some place as a result of the action of the verb. (It may just be simpler to memorise these verbs separately when they are used in this way.)

5 PLURALISER SUFFIX -*MEN*

We have already met -*men* used after pronouns in the singular to make them plural, *wǒ* becomes *wǒmen*, etc. Where it is deemed necessary to avoid ambiguity it can also be used after nouns indicating people to show that these are plural, although it is used quite sparingly and often only under certain conditions. The suffix -*men* is commonly used when addressing people in a speech.

Péngyoumen! 'Friends', *Tóngzhìmen!* 'Comrades' (This could be thought of as the Friends, Romans and Countrymen use of -*men!*) or when making a statement about people in general as in the text:

Háizimen yǒu zìjǐ de fángjiān…

but is not used when the people are specified in any way:

Chúfáng lǐ de háizi 'The children in the kitchen' (and not *Chúfang lǐ de háizimen*). It is probably best avoided unless you are sure of your ground.

6 ADVERBS + *DE*

Certain adjectives can be used both **before** verbs as adverbs (adverbial adjuncts) and **after** verbs as complements of degree.

Such adverbs indicate the manner or state of an action and are used with the particle *de* before the verb:

Tā hěn gāoxìng de qù tāmen jiā wánr 'He went off very happily to their home (to enjoy himself)'.

The Chinese character for this *de* is again quite different from the *de* we met in Chapters 3 and 4 but it is identical in *pinyin*. *De* may be omitted if the adverb is not itself modified, i.e. if there is no *hěn*, *fēicháng*, etc. in front of it:

Tā nŭlì xuéxí Hànyŭ 'She studies Chinese hard'.

7 ADJECTIVES

Monosyllabic adjectives generally occur directly before the noun they refer to but as soon as they are modified by *hěn, fēicháng*, etc., the marker *de* (see 3.5) must be inserted between the adjective and its noun:

Hăo rén 'Good person/people' but *Hěn hăo de rén* 'Very good person/people'.

8 REDUPLICATION OF ADJECTIVES

Some adjectives can also be repeated to indicate some degree of intensification:

hóng liăn '(a) red face' but *hónghóng de liăn* 'a *really* red face'.

With disyllabic adjectives the first syllable is repeated and then the second:

gāogāoxìngxìng (not *gāoxìnggāoxìng*) with the fourth syllable being stressed. Adjectives are often reduplicated when used as adverbs as in 5.6, with reduplicated disyllabic adjectives generally taking *de* before the verb. The *de* is optional with reduplicated monosyllabic adjectives:

Háizimēn gāogāoxìngxìng de qù xuéxiào 'The children go happily to school'.

Nǐmen gāi hǎohāor (de) xuéxí 'You ought to study hard'.

Note that in spoken Chinese, the second syllable of a reduplicated monosyllabic adjective is often pronounced in the first tone and takes an 'r' on the end. Not all adjectives can be reduplicated or used as adverbs in this way so it is advisable to learn them as you go along. In addition to *hǎo*, monosyllabic adjectives such as *kuài, màn* and *zǎo* frequently occur in this capacity.

9 HÉ

Hé 'and' cannot be used nearly so frequently as 'and' in English. It can only be used to join two noun constructions or pronouns, but **not** to join two verbs or two verbal clauses:

Wǒ hé Lǐ xiānsheng 'Mr Li and I' (in Chinese *wǒ* normally comes first).

Zhōngguórén hé Fǎguórén dōu xǐhuan chī fàn. 'The Chinese and the French both enjoy eating'.

Now, however, some intellectuals who have been exposed to European languages may use *hé* to join two verbs or two verbal clauses.

10 *LǍO* AND *XIǍO*

Instead of using the Chinese equivalent of Christian names when addressing colleagues or people in your peer group on an informal basis, *lǎo* or *xiǎo* is often put before the surname depending on whether the person in question is older or younger than you. Thus an older colleague with the surname *Zhāng* would become **lǎo** *Zhāng*, whereas a younger colleague called *Dīng* would be **xiǎo** *Dīng*. There is no hard and fast rule about this, however, and some people in the same peer group who become **xiǎo** or **lǎo** will still be **xiǎo** or **lǎo** even in their fifties, sixties and beyond **within** that peer group. The choice of which one to use largely depends on your own judgement, but normal practice is to follow the form of address used by your colleagues who have been there longer. It also conveys a feeling of intimacy, note that *Lǐ tàitai* refers to her husband as **lǎo** *Lǐ*. It is not generally used when addressing foreigners.

11 *YÒU...YÒU...*

Yòu...yòu... is used with two verbs or with two adjectives acting as verbs to express the meaning 'both...and...'

Tā yòu gāo yòu hǎokàn. 'He's both tall and good-looking' (good look/see).

Wǒ hé lǎo Lǐ de fángjiān zhǐ hǎo yòu dāng wòshì yòu dāng kètīng.
'Lao Li's and my room has to serve both as bedroom and sitting-room.'

12 THE NOMINALISER *DE*

(a)   Following on from 3.5 we see that *de* placed after a pronoun or adjective makes it into a noun:

Diànshì shì cǎisè de háishi hēi-bái de? 'Is it a colour TV or (a) black and white (one)?'

Nán de sì suì. 'The boy (*Lit.* the male one) is 4.'

Xiǎoháir shi tā de. 'The child is his/hers.'

Thus *wǒ de* on its own means 'mine', *nǐ de* 'yours', etc.

(b)   Where an adjective and a noun form one idea, *de* is omitted:

Rèqíng zhāodài 'kind hospitality'.

Fǎwén zázhì 'French magazines'.

13 *BÙ* VERB *LE*

The negated form of the change of state *le* (see 4.6) is *bù* verb...*le* which conveys the meaning that the subject (if there is one) no longer does the action of the verb or that the situation as stated by the verb is no longer the case:

Shíjiān bù zǎo le (*Lit.* time not early any more) 'It's getting late'.

Wǒ bù hē jiǔ le (*Lit.* I not drink wine any more) 'I've given up drinking'.

This is the only case in which *bù* can occur with *le*. Note that if the verb is *yǒu* then *méi* has to be used instead of *bù*:

Wǒ méi yǒu diànshì le 'I no longer have a TV'.

14 AUXILIARY VERBS

There are several examples of auxiliary verbs in the text, viz. *yuànyì, kěyǐ, yào, gāi* and *děi*. (We have already met *xǐhuan* and *xiǎng* in previous chapters.) These occur **before** action verbs or verbal expressions and cannot take verbal endings or verbal suffixes. Compare the seven examples below:

Wǒ yuànyì hē kāfēi 'I'm for coffee' (as opposed to anything else).

Wǒ xiǎng hē kāfēi 'I'd like some coffee' (now or in the near future).

Wǒ xǐhuan hē kāfēi 'I like (drinking) coffee' (permanent state of mind).

Wǒ yào hē kāfēi 'I want some coffee' (now or in the near future, expressing a stronger desire than *xiǎng*).

Wǒ (yīng)gāi hē kāfēi 'I ought to drink coffee' (it is less fattening, etc.).

Wǒ děi hē kāfēi 'I must drink coffee' (necessity).

Wǒ kěyǐ hē kāfēi 'I can drink coffee' (capability or permission).

For further information on auxiliary verbs see Chapter 12, pp.120–22.

15   *DUŌ* AND *SHǍO* + NOUN

Duō and *shǎo* are exceptions to the rule that monosyllabic adjectives directly precede their nouns or that when modified they must take *de*. They cannot stand on their own before the noun but occur with *hěn* and without *de*:

Hěn duō rén 'many people'.

Shǎo is more likely to occur with *bù* with the meaning of 'quite a lot of' or 'quite a few':

Bù shǎo máfan 'quite a lot of trouble'.

It is important to note, however, that Chinese usage differs from the English in that a sentence such as 'many people go/went' is much more likely to be expressed as *qù de rén hěn duō* rather than *hěn duō rén qù*, although both are grammatically correct.

16   PUNCTUATION

In a list, even if it only consists of two items, e.g. *bīngxiāng、diyī*, the Chinese use a form of pause-mark or *dùnhào* (、) between the items and not a comma. A comma is reserved for longer pauses.

Polite talk

The Chinese have a whole series of expressions for almost every social occasion ranging from *Chī bǎo le ma?* 'Have you eaten your fill?' or *Chī fàn le ma?* 'Have you eaten?' to *Huí lai le ma?* 'Have you come back?'. You might only have gone out to pump up your bicycle tyres but are still asked if you are back when you return five minutes later! Such expressions serve as a means of phatic communion between individuals, giving a feeling of community at very little cost to the individuals themselves. Mr King's little speech as he and Miss

Shaw are about to leave contains several typical examples
of this 'polite talk' which we would consider as clichés but
which appear very natural to the Chinese. *Gěi nǐmen tiān le
bù shǎo máfan* is a wonderful example of this. *Màn* 'slow'
features quite widely in polite talk with such exhortations as
Nǐmen mànmānr chī 'Take your time (over eating)' if somebody has finished eating and he or the host does not wish the
others to feel they have to follow suit. *Nǐmen mànmānr zuò ba*
'Sit slowly' you are told when the person you have come to
see is nowhere to be seen and you are in for a long wait!
When taking leave of somebody, the standard parting remark
is 'go slowly' (usually repeated) *Màn zǒu, màn zǒu.* (If you are
on your bicycle [or horse] it becomes *Màn qí, màn qí* 'Ride
(astride) slowly'!).

EXERCISE 5.3

Correct the word order in the following sentences:

Nǐ kàn diànshì zài zhèr → Nǐ zài zhèr kàn diànshì.

1 *Dìfang xiǎo, bīngxiāng、xǐyījī dōu zài zhèr fàng.*
2 *Xiǎoháir hē niúnǎi* (milk) *zài chúfáng xiànzài.*
3 *Tā yuànyì qù zǎozāor.*
4 *Wǒ tiān le hěn duō máfan gěi nǐmen.*
5 *Lǐ lǎoshī* (teacher) *huí gāogāoxìngxìng de dàxué qu le.*
6 *Rén de wàimiàn dōu shì nánde.*

EXERCISE 5.4

Translate into colloquial English:

Jīntiān wǎnshang xiǎoháir qù wǒ māma nàr (my mum's place).
*Dìfang hěn dà, bīngxiāng、xǐyījī tā dōu yǒu. Háizi xǐhuan wánr, wǒ
māma yě xǐhuan dài* (to take) *tāmen qù kàn diànyǐng* (film) *dànshi tā
yòu méi yǒu qián* (money) *yòu méi yǒu shíjiān; zhǐ hǎo ràng* (let)
tāmen zài dà huāyuán (garden) *lǐ wánr. Wánr wán le tāmen kěyǐ zuò
zài chúfáng lǐ tán huà、chī fàn. Chī wán fàn tāmen kěyǐ kàn* (cǎisè)
diànshì.

EXERCISE 5.5

Translate into Chinese:

1   My friend and I (5.9) would like to go to America (*Měiguó*).
2   Where is he watching TV? In the bedroom or in the sitting-room? (Leave out *lǐ*.)
3   Father (*Fùqīn*) says he doesn't recognise you any more.
4   (When) he got old, (he) (*jiù*) gave up drinking. (Use *jiù* in the second clause and change of state *le* in both clauses.)
5   She likes teaching and studying. (Use *yòu...yòu* plus v-o constructions.)
6   He's no alternative but to stand (*zhàn*) there. (Use *zhǐ hǎo*.)
7   I'll finish decorating the living-room and then (*jiù*) quietly read a book.
8   Thank you for your wonderful hospitality. I'll certainly come again.

6

In the House

A HOUSE, *FÁNGZI* [*SUŎ, GE*]

1	roof	*wūdǐng*		7	tree	*shù* [*kē*]
2	window	*chuānghu*		8	vegetables	*shūcài*
3	door	*mén*		9	curtain	*chuānglián*
4	garage	*chēkù*			ground floor	*yìlóu*
5	flowers	*huā* [*duǒ*]			first floor	*èrlóu*
6	garden	*huāyuán*				

LIVING ROOM, *KÈTĪNG*; DINING ROOM, *FÀNTĪNG*

1	sofa	*shāfā*	18	radio	*shōuyīnjī*
2	chair	*yǐzi [bǎ]*			*[tái, ge]*
3	window	*chuānghu*	19	tape	*lùyīnjī*
4	curtain	*chuānglián*		recorder	*[tái]*
5	carpet	*dìtǎn*	20	video	*lùxiàngjī*
		[kuài]		recorder	*[tái]*
6	electric fan	*diànshàn*	21	coffee	*chájī*
7	picture	*huàr*		table	*[zhāng, ge]*
		[zhāng]	22	table	*zhuōzi*
8	bookcase	*shūjià*			*[zhāng]*
9	vase	*huāpíng*	23	knife	*dāozi [bǎ]*
10	dictionary	*zìdiǎn [běn]*	24	fork	*chāzi [bǎ]*
11	novel	*xiǎoshuō*	25	spoon	*sháozi*
		[běn]	26	salt	*yán*
12	book	*shū [běn]*	27	pepper	*hújiāo*
13	telephone	*diànhuà(jī)*	28	mustard	*jièmo*
		[tái]	29	glass	*bōlibēi*
14	television	*diànshì(jī)*	30	vinegar	*cù*
		[tái]	31	soya sauce	*jiàngyóu*
15	table lamp	*táidēng*	32	cup	*bēizi*
16	electric light	*diàndēng*	33	radiator	*nuǎnqìpiàn*
17	ashtray	*yānhuīgāng*		(central heating	*nuǎnqì)*

KITCHEN, *CHÚFÁNG* [*JIĀN, GE*]

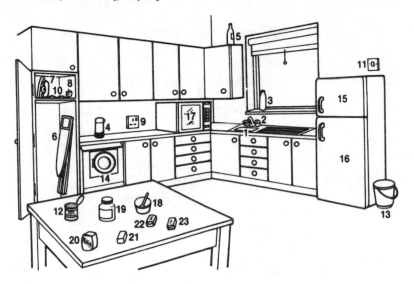

1	sink	*xǐwǎnchí, chízi*	12	tin/can	*guàntóu*
			13	pail, bucket	*shuǐtǒng*
2	tap	*lóngtou*	14	washing	*xǐyījī*
3	bottle	*píngzi*		machine	[*tái*]
4	Thermos	*rèshuǐpíng*	15	freezer	*bīngguì*
	flask		16	refrigerator	*bīngxiāng*
5	wine bottle	*jiǔpíng*	17	microwave	*wēibōlú*
6	ironing board	*tàngyījià*		oven	
7	iron	*yùndǒu*	18	sugar	*táng*
8	plug	*chātóu*	19	coffee	*kāfēi*
9	socket	*chāzuò*	20	flour	*miànfěn*
10	electric	*diànxiàn*	21	Indian tea	*hóngchá*
	cable	[*gēn*]	22	Chinese tea	*lùchá*
11	switch	*kāiguān*	23	Jasmine tea	*huāchá*

BEDROOM, *WÒSHÌ [JIĀN]*

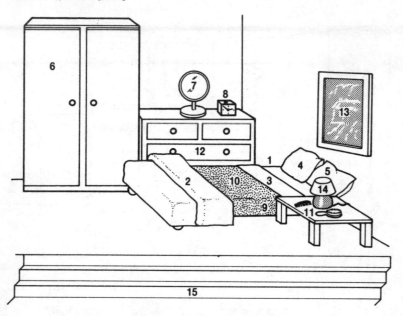

1	double bed	*shuāngrén-chuáng [zhāng]*	7	mirror	*jìngzi [kuài]*
	(single bed, | *dānrén-chuáng)*	8	alarm clock	*nàozhōng*
			9	mattress	*chuángdiàn*
2	duvet, quilt	*bèizi [chuáng]*	10	blanket	*tǎnzi [zhāng]*
3	sheet	*chuángdān*	11	brush or comb	*shūzi [bǎ]*
4	pillow	*zhěntou*	12	chest of drawers	*wǔdǒuchú, wǔdǒuguì*
5	pillow case	*zhěntào*	13	picture	*huàr [zhāng]*
6	wardrobe	*yīguì*	14	table lamp	*táidēng*
			15	stairs, staircase	*lóutī*

BATHROOM, *XĬZĂOJIĀN* OR *YÙSHÌ*

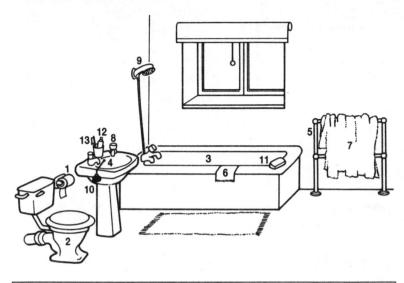

1	toilet paper	*wèishēngzhǐ* [*juǎn*]	7	bath towel	*yùjīn, dà máojīn* [*kuài*]
2	toilet	*cèsuǒ*	8	tap	*lóngtou*
3	bath	*xǐzǎopén, yùpén*	9	shower	(*línyù*) *pēntóu*
4	washbasin	*xǐliǎnpén*	10	plug	*sāizi*
5	towel rail	*máojīnjià*	11	toilet soap	*xiāngzào* [*kuài*]
6	face flannel	*miànjīn, máojīn* [*kuài*]	12	toothpaste	*yágāo* [*tǒng*]
			13	toothbrush	*yáshuā* [*bǎ*]

Although an increasing number of Chinese possess some modern appliances, some of the washing machines, showers, toilets and such like that you will see in less affluent homes, hotels or work units definitely belong to another era.

7

My Family

Zhang Zhanyi is an attendant at the Beijing Hotel. In this lesson he introduces himself and his family:

Wǒ jiào Zhāng Zhànyī. / Wǒ jiā zài Běijīng. / Wǒ jiā yǒu wǔ kǒu rén / –

My name is Zhang Zhanyi. / My home is in Beijing. / There are 5 people in my family / –

bàba、māma、gēge、jiějie hé wǒ. / Wǒ méi yǒu dìdi, yě méi yǒu mèimei. /

Mum, Dad, an elder brother, an elder sister and me. / I haven't got any younger brothers or sisters. /

Wǒ jiějie sānshí suì, hái méi yǒu zhǎo dào duìxiàng ne (= hái méi yǒu jié hūn ne!),

My elder sister is 30 and still hasn't got a steady boyfriend (i.e. is still unmarried),

zhè zhǒng qíngkuàng zài Zhōngguó hěn shǎo. / Gēge bǐ jiějie xiǎo liǎng suì,

this is very unusual in China. / My brother is 2 years younger than my sister,

bǐ wǒ dà yí suì bàn. /

but 1½ years older than me. /

Bàba、māma niánjì bǐjiào dà le. / Bàba jīnnián liùshíyī suì, shì (yí) ge lǎo jiàoyuán,

Mum and Dad are getting on a bit. / Dad is 61 this year, he has been a teacher for many years,

zài Běijīng Yǔyán Xuéyuàn jiāo wàiguó liúxuéshēng Hànyǔ. /
and teaches foreign students Chinese at the Beijing Languages Institute. /
   Māma bǐ bàba xiǎo sān suì, yǐqián shì ge gōngrén,
Mum is 3 years younger than Dad, she used to be a (factory) worker
xiànzài yǐjīng tuìxiū le. / Tāmen liǎ shēntǐ fēicháng hǎo. /
but she's (already) retired now. / They are both in excellent health. /
   Jiějie zài yīyuàn dāng yīshēng, gēge zài bùduì dāng bīng,
My sister is a doctor in a hospital, my elder brother is in the army,
suǒyǐ tāmen bù cháng(cháng) zài jiā. /
so they are not at home very much. /
   Wǒ zài Běijīng Fàndiàn dāng fúwùyuán, gōngzuò yǒu yìdiǎn(r) dāndiào
I am an attendant at the Beijing Hotel, my work is a bit monotonous
dànshi wǒ hé tóngshìmen de guānxi hěn hǎo, suǒyǐ hái guò de qù. /
but my work mates and I all get along very well so it's not too bad. /
   Wǒmen yì jiā rén gǎnqíng yě dōu hěn hǎo, rìzi guò de hái búcuò! /
We're a very close family too, so life is pretty good on the whole! /

jiào (v)	*to be called, to call*	**bǐjiào** (adv.)	*relatively*
kǒu (MW)	*for family members*	**jīnnián** (TW)	*this year*
bàba (n)	*daddy, dad*	**jiàoyuán** (n)	*teacher (as a profession, not a title)*
māma (n)	*mummy, mum*	**Běijīng Yǔyán**	*Beijing*
gēge (n)	*elder brother*	**Xuéyuàn** (N)	*Languages*
jiějie (n)	*elder sister*		*Institute*
dìdi (n)	*younger brother*	**jiāo** (v)	*to teach*
mèimei (n)	*younger sister*	**wàiguó** (adj., n)	*foreign (country)*
zhǎo (v)	*to look for*		
-dào (RVE)	*to manage to do the action of the verb, up to*	**liúxuéshēng** (n)	*student studying abroad*
		yǐqián (adv., conj.)	*previously, before*
zhǒng (MW)	*sort, kind*		
qíngkuàng (n)	*situation*	**gōngrén** (n)	*worker*
bǐ (prep.)	*compared with*	**xiànzài** (TW)	*now, at present*
dà (adj.)	*big, grown up*	**yǐjīng** (adv.)	*already*
bàn (num)	*half*	**tuìxiū** (v)	*to retire*
niánjì (n)	*age*	**shēntǐ** (n)	*health, body*

yīyuàn (n)	*hospital*	gōngzuò (n, v)	*work, to work*
yīshēng (n)	*doctor* (as a profession, not a title)	dāndiào (adj.)	*monotonous, dull*
		tóngshì (n)	*colleague, fellow worker*
bùduì (n)	*army*		
bīng (n)	*soldier*	guānxi (n)	*relation(ship)*
cháng (cháng) (adv.)	*often*	hái (adv.)	*still, in addition*
		gǎnqíng (n)	*feeling, emotion*
Běijīng		rìzi (n)	*day, date*
Fàndiàn (N)	*Beijing Hotel*		
fúwùyuán (n)	*attendant*		

Grammar

1 MORE ON NAMES

A Chinese wishing to know your name can either ask for your surname *Nǐ xìng shénme?* (*Lit.* You surnamed what?) 'What is your
surname?', to which the reply is *Wǒ xìng Zhāng/Lǐ/Wáng*, etc. or for
your given name, which in the reply is almost invariably prefaced by
the surname. Thus *Nǐ jiào shénme míngzi?* (*Lit.* You called what
given name) 'What is your name?' normally elicits the response *Wǒ
jiào* or *Wǒ (de) míngzi jiào* Surname (one character) + given name
(normally two characters though single ones do exist)

2 'MUM AND DAD' OR 'DAD AND MUM'?

Note the word order of the following: *bàba* precedes *māma, gēge*
precedes *jiějie* and *dìdi* precedes *mèimei*.

3 USE OF *YĚ*

Yě joins two verbal clauses here and although its basic meaning
remains unchanged it may be translated as 'either' or 'and' when
used in this way. The example from the text: *Wǒ méi yǒu dìdi yě méi
yǒu mèimei* could also have read *Wǒ méi yǒu dìdi hé mèimei*. (NB *hé*
can only join two noun constructions or pronouns). To an English
speaker the latter appears neater but the Chinese seem to like the
construction with *yě* and use it frequently:

Wǒ jiāo Yīngyǔ, yě jiāo Fǎyǔ 'I teach English and French'.

although *Wǒ jiāo Yīngyǔ hé Fǎyǔ* would be equally correct.
Note that when *dōu* and *yě* occur together *yě* always precedes *dōu*.
(See the example in the text.)

4 *HÁI MÉI YǑU...NE*

Méi yǒu (*Lit.* not have) precedes the verb to indicate that the action of the verb has **not** taken place. *Yǒu* may be omitted:

Tā méi (yǒu) jié hūn 'He/she isn't/hasn't married'.

The addition of *hái* before *méi* and *ne* at the end of the clause convey the idea that the situation is ongoing, thus in:

Wǒ jiějie...hái méi yǒu zhǎo dào duìxiàng ne

the expectation appears to be that she will or that at least she's still in with a chance!

5 THE COMPARATIVE WITH *BǏ*

The simplest form of comparative is *A bǐ* B + appropriate adjective:

Gēge bǐ jiějie xiǎo (*Lit.* Elder brother/compared with/elder sister/ small)

        'Elder brother is younger than elder sister.'

Gēge bǐ wǒ dà   (*Lit.* Elder brother/compared with/me/big)

        'Elder brother is older than me.'

The amount by which B is older or younger than A comes after *dà* or *xiǎo*:

Gēge bǐ jiějie xiǎo liǎng suì 'Elder brother is two years younger than elder sister.'

Gēge bǐ wǒ dà yí suì bàn 'Elder brother is 1½ years older than me.'

EXERCISE 7.1

Make each of the two statements below into one comparative sentence using *bǐ*:

Wǒ sānshí suì.
Wǒ péngyou èrshíliù suì. } → *Wǒ bǐ wǒ péngyou dà sì suì.*

1 *Érzi shísì suì.*
   Nǚ'ér jiǔ suì.

2 *Jiějie sānshíwǔ suì.*
   Mèimei èrshíjiǔ suì.

3 *Shǐ Àilì èrshíyī suì.*
   Wáng Yǒngshòu èrshísān suì.

4 *Lǐ tàitai sìshíqī suì.*
   Lǐ xiānsheng wǔshí suì.

5 *Zhōngguó chá hǎo hē.*
   Zhōngguó jiǔ bù hǎo hē.

6 *Zhōngguó cài hǎo chī.*
   Yīngguó cài bù hǎo chī.

7 *Tā de shēntǐ hǎo.*
   Nǐ de shēntǐ bù hǎo.

8 *Wǒ nán péngyou gāoxìng.*
   Wǒ bù gāoxìng.

6 *DÀ* AND *XIǍO*

With the basic meaning 'big' and 'small', respectively, *dà* and *xiǎo* are used here to express age, usually in the comparative sense even if this is not explicit. When asking a child his age the question form *Nǐ jǐ suì le?* is used but for adults it is:

Nǐ niánjì duō dà le? (Lit. You/year record/how/big/) or
Nǐ duō dà niánjì le? (Lit. You/how/big/year record/)

the modal particle *le* being used to convey the idea that the record of years has become big. *Duō* is used in a similar way with other adjectives such as *cháng* 'long', *kuān* 'wide' to ask the degree of length, width, etc. and is translated as 'how' in such cases as above: *Duō cháng?* 'How long?' Other compounds with *dà* and *xiǎo* are: *dàren* (big person) 'adult'; *dàxué* (big study) 'university'; *xiǎoxué* (small study) 'primary school'; *dàjiā* (big home) 'everybody'. NB *xiǎorén* (small person) 'a mean person'! As a verb, *dà* conveys the idea of growing up:

Háizi dà le 'The child(ren) has/have grown up (*Lit.* got big).

When stating that an adult is old or young in absolute terms then the adjectives *lǎo* (old) and *niánqīng* (years light) are used **not** *dà* and *xiǎo*.

7 *YI* + MEASURE WORD

When *yi* occurs with a measure word in the spoken language, the *yi* is often omitted:

Wǒ yǒu (yí) ge hǎo tóngshì 'I have a good colleague!'
Bàba…shì (yí) ge lǎo jiàoyuán 'Dad's been a teacher for many years.'

8 JOB + *YUÁN*

In post-1949 China many job descriptions were changed to convey a greater sense of equality. *-yuán* was added to the end of the description to indicate the person engaged in such an activity, e.g. *jiàoyuán* (teach/person) 'teacher'; *fúwùyuán* (serve/person) 'attendant'; *shòuhuòyuán* (sell/goods/person) 'shop assistant'; *shòupiàoyuán* (sell/ticket/person) 'bus conductor, booking office clerk, box-office clerk'. *Yuán* also has the meaning of 'member', e.g. *dǎngyuán* 'party member'.

9 INDIRECT OBJECT BEFORE DIRECT OBJECT

This basically follows English usage:

Bàba...zài Běijīng Yǔyán Xuéyuàn jiāo wàiguó liúxuéshēng (I.O)
Hànyú (D.O).

10 SENTENCE FINAL PARTICLE *LE*

Although used in the same position as the change of state *le* (see 4.6), i.e. at the end of a sentence, this *le* indicates that a certain state of affairs has already taken place. Some people call this the accomplished fact *le*. *Māma...xiànzài yǐjīng tuìxiū le*. Even the Chinese find it difficult to use *le* consistently so any pointers are invaluable. One such is that *le* is almost invariably found at the end of a clause with *yǐjīng* 'already' as in the example taken from the text. The question form is made by adding *ma* to the statement ending with *le* or by adding *méi yǒu* after it:

> *Māma tuìxiū le ma?*
> *Māma tuìxiū le méi you?** ⎫
> *Māma tuìxiū méi tuìxiū?* is also possible. ⎭ 'Has mum retired?'

(Light stress only on *méi* with *yǒu* becoming toneless.)

   * This is identical to the choice-type question form found in 1.5 except that the verb is not repeated. *Yǒu* is never omitted in this type of question form. The negative form is made with *méi yǒu* + verb where *yǒu* may be omitted.

> *Māma méi yǒu tuìxiū* ⎫
> *Māma méi tuìxiū.* ⎭ 'Mum hasn't retired.'

11 MORE ON THE TOPIC CONSTRUCTION

In the two sentences

> *Tāmen liǎ shēntǐ fēicháng hǎo* (*Lit.* [As for] they/two/body/ extremely/good) and
> *Wǒmen yì jiā rén gǎnqíng yě dōu hěn hǎo* (*Lit.* [As for] our/one/ family/people/feelings/also/all/very/good)

both *tāmen liǎ* and *wǒmen yì jiā rén* are acting as topics, the subject of the two sentences being *shēntǐ* and *gǎnqíng* respectively. The direct object can also be emphasised by putting it at the beginning of the sentence as a topic which is often 'resumed' with *dōu* before the verb. In this case, *dōu* refers **back** to the object and not to the subject. Note that *dōu* can never refer to a direct object which follows the verb:

> *Bīngxiāng、 xǐyījī wǒ dōu yǒu* (*Lit.* [As for] fridge/wash clothes machine/I/both/have) 'I've got a fridge and a washing machine'.

As was said in 2.5 this is a favourite construction of the Chinese with its own distinctive flavour.

12   *YŌU YÌDIĂN(R)* + ADJECTIVE

'A little + adjective'. When the adjective used conveys a negative or derogatory sense, even if this is only subjective on the part of the speaker, then *yǒu yìdiǎn(r)* is put in front of the adjective. If no such sense is implied then the order is adjective + *yìdiǎn(r)*:

> *Rè yìdiǎn(r) hǎo.* 'A bit hotter would be better.'
>
> *Yǒu yìdiǎn(r) rè.* 'It's a bit on the hot side.'

13   POTENTIAL RESULTATIVE VERBS

(For resultative verbs see 5.1.) A potential result is indicated by the insertion of *de* for the positive form ('can') and *bu* for the negative form ('cannot') between the verb of action and its resultative ending:

> *Guò qu* 'to pass' (as of one's days), *guò de qù* 'able to pass', *guò bu qù* 'unable to pass'; *kànjiàn* 'to see', *kàn de jiàn* 'can see', *kàn bu jiàn* 'can't see'.

The question form can either be made by adding *ma* to the positive form of the statement or by putting the positive and negative forms together as in 1.5:

> *Tā zhǎo de dào zhǎo bu dào duìxiàng?* ⎫ Can he/she find a
>
> *Tā zhǎo de dào duìxiàng ma?* ⎭ marriage partner?

(Note that the tone comes back onto simple directional endings and onto the first 'half' of compound directional endings when they form part of a potential resultative verb.)

14   *YĪ* + NOUN

In this context *yi* + noun conveys the idea of 'all', 'whole':

> *Yī jiā rén* 'the entire family', *yì shēn hàn* (*Lit.* all/body/sweat) 'covered in perspiration',
>
> *yì liǎn hóng* (*Lit.* whole/face/red) 'blush to the roots', etc.

More polite talk

A whole series of conventional formulae used to exist in pre-1949 China for asking and replying to such questions as one's name, the state and well being of one's wife and children (note wife not husband!), etc., even one's house was elevated to the rank of 'mansion' when its whereabouts were being ascertained! Perhaps the most common of these formulae is the question *Nín guǐ xìng?* (*Lit.* Your/expensive/ surname), often translated as 'Your honourable surname, sir?' The correct response used to be *Bǐ xìng* (*Lit.* Miserable/ humble surname) whatever it was. The question form is still quite widely used today but not the response. One may also be asked about one's 'expensive country' *guì guó* or one's 'expensive school' *guì xiào*! Such terms are commonly employed in letters for instance, where the language tends to be less idiomatic and more literary in style.

Brothers and sisters

A Chinese will always tell you whether his brother or sister is younger or older than himself by using the appropriate term. If he simply wishes to tell you that there are X number of sisters in the family without specifying how many are older and how many are younger he can simply use the term *jiěmèi* combining half of *jiějie* with half of *mèimei*, but this does imply that there is at least one of each. (An alternative to *jiěmèi* is *zǐmèi*.) Similarly there is a collective term for brothers, *xiōngdì*, although in this case a more literary term for elder brother is employed. Oriental inscrutability comes into play in that *xiōngdì* is equally acceptable as *dìxiōng* but *mèijiě* and *mèizǐ* are incorrect. Members of the congregation in the Chinese Protestant Church often refer to themselves as *dìxiōng、zǐmèi*.

EXERCISE 7.2

Fill in the blanks with the number supplied in the brackets:

Zhāng xiānsheng yǒu ____ ge jiějie (3) → *Zhāng xiānsheng yǒu sān ge jiějie.*

1   *Shǐ xiǎojie yǒu ____ ge gēge hé ____ ge mèimei.* (2, 1)
2   *Wǒ dìdi ____ suì.* (27)
3   *Lǎo jiàoyuán ____ suì, shēntǐ hěn hǎo.* (80)
4   *Zhè ge gōngrén bǐ nà ge gōngrén xiǎo ____ suì.* (5)
5   *Tā àiren bǐ ta māma dà ____ suì.* (4)
6   *____ ge fúwùyuán zài Běijīng Fàndiàn gōngzuò.* (99)
7   *Nà ge yīshēng hē ____ bēi jiǔ hé ____ bēi kāfēi.* (6, 2)

EXERCISE 7.3

Answer the following questions on the text:

1   *Zhāng Zhànyī de jiā zài nǎr?*
2   *Tā jiā yǒu jǐ kǒu rén?*
3   *Tā yǒu méi yǒu dìdì、mèimei?*
4   *Tā jiějie jié hūn lè méi you?*
5   *Tā gēge duō dà niánjì le?*
6   *Zhāng Zhànyī niánjì duō dà le?*
7   *Tā bàba zài nǎr jiāo Hànyǔ?*
8   *Tā jiāo shéi Hànyǔ?*
9   *Tā māma bǐ bàba dà ma? Māma niánjì duō dà le? Hái gōngzuò ma?*
10 *Tāmen liǎ shēntǐ zěnmeyàng?*
11 *Zhāng Zhànyī dāng gōngrén ma?*
12 *Tā de gōngzuò guò de qù guò bu qù?*
13 *Tāmen yì jiā rén gǎnqíng hǎo háishi bù hǎo?*

EXERCISE 7.4

Translate the following passages into colloquial English:

1   *Wǒ jiějie èrshíjiǔ suì, hái méi yǒu jié hūn ne. Tā zài Shànghǎi dāng yīshēng. Tā hěn xǐhuan tā de gōngzuò. Wǒ māma shuō tā yīnggāi jié hūn, yí ge nǚ háizi bù jié hūn bù xíng. Wǒ jiějie shuō, wǎn yìdiǎn(r) jié hūn méi yǒu guānxi dànshi wǒ māma bù tóngyì (agree).*
2   *Zhōu Gēngxīn shì Tiānjīn rén. Tā shì ge gōngrén. Tā jiā yǒu sì kǒu rén – bàba、māma、dìdi hé tā. Dìdi èrshíyī suì, bǐ tā xiǎo yí suì*

bàn. Dìdi zài Běijīng Dàxué xuéxí Yīngyǔ. Zhōu Gēngxīn yě xuéxí Yīngyǔ dànshi tā xuéxí de shíjiān hěn shǎo, suǒyǐ tā Yīngyǔ hěn bù hǎo.

EXERCISE 7.5

Translate into Chinese:

1 What's your name? My name is Shi Aili.
2 She has neither brothers nor sisters.
3 I invited two Chinese friends to come to my house for dinner (*wǎnfàn* 'late rice') tomorrow evening.
4 That chap (3)/studying Chinese (2)/at the Beijing Languages Institute (1)/hasn't come yet. (Follow the word order indicated. Link 2 and 3 with *de*.)
5 My friend is twenty-eight but she is still unmarried.
6 Has that American doctor in Shanghai already retired?
7 That British girl (3)/studying Chinese (2)/at Beijing University (1)/ is a fantastic cook. (Use complement of degree.)
8 My wife and her two younger sisters are very close.
9 Many Chinese speak English really well.
10 My girlfriend is one year older than I am but two years younger than my elder brother.
11 That person is not very nice so I haven't invited him for a drink.
12 We haven't got a washing machine or a colour TV but we still manage all right. (Use the topic construction with *dōu*.)

8

My Home

Zhang Zhanyi describes his family's living conditions.

Wǒmen zhùde hěn jiǎndān, zhǐ yǒu sān jiān fáng jiā shang chúfáng
We live very simply, we only have three rooms plus kitchen
hé cèsuǒ. / Fùmǔ de wòshì tóngshí yě dāng kètīng. /
and toilet. / My parents' bedroom also serves as the living-room. /

Wǒ hé gēge shuì(zài) yí ge fángjiān, wǒmen měi (ge) rén (dōu) yǒu
My elder brother and I sleep in one room, we each have
yì zhāng shūzhuō, zài nàr dú shū zǒng(shi) bǐ zài kètīng lǐ ānjìng
a desk, it's always much quieter studying there than in the living-room. /
de duō. /

Jiějie de fángjiān bǐ wǒmen xiōngdì liǎ de nà jiān hái xiǎo, zhǐ
My elder sister's room is even smaller than my brother's and mine, it can
fàng de xià yì zhāng chuáng、yì zhāng xiǎo xiǎo de zhuōzi hé yì bǎ
yǐzi. /
only hold a bed, a tiny table and a chair. /

Wǒmen xiōngdì、zǐmèi cānjiā gōngzuò yǐhòu, chúle xiūxi nà tiān
yǐwài,
After my brothers and sister and I started working, we're not at home
hěn shǎo zài jiā, suǒyǐ zhù de méi yǒu yǐqián nàme jǐ, fùmǔ yě bǐ
very much, apart from our day off, so we're not as cramped as we used to
be,

yǐqián zhù de shūfu yìxiē. /

and my parents are also somewhat more comfortable. /

Wǒ xiǎng zài Xīfāng yìbān zhùfáng bǐ wǒmen dà xiē. / *Nǐmen chúle*

I think accommodation in the West is generally more spacious than ours. / Apart

wòshì yǐwài hái yǒu kètīng, yǒude yǒu shūfáng, yǒude hái yǒu

from the bedroom(s), you also have a living room, some people have a study, others have a dining-room too

fàntīng, tīngshuō yǒu huāyuán de yě hěn duō. /

and there are also many with gardens. /

Wǒmen jiā jiājù bù duō, kètīng lǐ yǒu yì zhāng shuāngrénchuáng、yí ge

We haven't got much furniture in our house, there's a double bed, a

shāfā、yí ge yīguì、yì tái diànshì(jī). / *Hái yǒu yí tào zǔhéyīnxiǎng,*

settee, a wardrobe and a TV in the livingroom. / There is also a hi-fi

shì Rìběn huò. / *Féngrènjī shì guóchǎn huò.* /

which is Japanese. / The sewing-machine is made here (in China). /

Chī fàn de shíhou, dà yuánzhuō hé yǐzi dōu bān jìnlai. / *Dōngtiān*

We bring in the big round table and chairs when we eat. / In winter

tiānqì lěng de shíhou, dānwèi gěi wǒmen shāo nuǎnqì. / *Suīrán nǐmen*

when the weather is cold, the (work) unit turns on the central heating. / Although

fādá guójiā gōngzī bǐ women gāo de duō, dànshi wǒmen fángzū、

wages in (your) advanced countries are much higher than ours, our rents,

shuǐdiànfèi děng dōu bǐ nǐmen piányi duō le. /

water and electricity charges, etc. are all much cheaper than yours. /

Wǒmen jiā dìfang bú dà, kěshì àn Zhōngguó xiànzài de biāozhǔn,

Our home is quite small, but by present Chinese standards

wǒmen guò de hái búcuò. /

we're doing pretty well.

jiǎndān (adj.)	simple	zhùfáng (n)	housing, accommodation
jiā(shang) (v)	to add	yǒude (p.)	some
fùmǔ (n)	parents	shūfáng (n)	study
tóngshí (TW)	at the same time	tīngshuō (v)	be told, hear of
shuì(jiào) (v[-o])	to sleep, go to bed	jiājù (n)	furniture
měi (p./adj.)	each, every	shuāngrén-chuáng (n) [zhāng]	double bed
shūzhuō (n) [zhāng]	desk	zǔhéyīnxiǎng (n) [tào]	hi-fi
nàr	there	Rìběn (N)	Japan
zǒng(shi) (adv.)	always	huò (n)	goods
xiōngdì (n)	brothers	féngrènjī (n) [tái]	sewing-machine
-xià (RVE)	have the capacity to	guóchǎn (adj.)	made in one's country
chuáng (n) [zhāng]	bed	…de shíhou	when
zhuōzi (n) [zhāng]	table	yuán (adj.)	round
		bān (v)	to (re)move
yǐzi (n) [bǎ]	chair	-jìnlai (CDE)	verb + in (See 8.9)
zǐmèi (n)	sisters	dōngtiān (n)	winter
cānjiā (v)	to join; attend, take part in	tiānqì (n)	weather
		lěng (adj.)	cold
		dānwèi (n)	unit
yǐhòu (conj.; adv)	after; afterwards	shāo (v)	to burn
		suīrán… dànshi	although
chúle (…yǐwài)	except, apart from	fādá (adj.)	developed; advanced
xiūxi (v)	to rest	guójiā (n)	country
tiān (n)	day; sky, heaven	gōngzī (n)	wages
		fángzū (n)	rent
zhù (v)	to live (in, at)	shuǐdiànfèi (n)	water and electricity charges
jǐ (adv.; v)	crowded; to squeeze		
		děng (n)	etc.
shūfu (adj.)	comfortable	piányi (adj.)	cheap
(yì)xiē (adv; MW)	somewhat; some, a few	kěshì (conj.)	but
Xīfāng (n)	the West	àn (zhào) (prep.)	according to, on the basis of
yìbān (adv.; adj.)	generally; general	biāozhǔn (n; adj.)	criterion, standard

Grammar

1 ORDER OF ADVERBS

Where more than one adverb precedes the same verb a definite word order has to be observed (see 4.4 and 7.3). Generally speaking it is the monosyllabic adverb (*yě, dōu, jiù,* etc.) which directly precedes the verb, but if it occurs with *bù* or *méi* the order is:

(adverb +) monosyllabic adverb + *bù/méi* + verb.

Wǒmen yě dōu bú qù 'None of us is going either'

Tāmen jiù méi lái 'So they didn't come'

Thus *tóngshí* precedes *yě* in: *Fùmǔ de wòshì tóngshí yě dāng kètīng.*

2 MĚI...(DŌU)

One of the ways of expressing 'each, every' in Chinese is by using the pronoun *měi*. There is usually a measure word between *měi* and its noun but this may be omitted when the noun is *rén. Tiān* 'day' and *nián* 'year' act as measure words as well as nouns and therefore directly follow *měi*. The sentence with *měi* is often reinforced by the adverb *dōu* before the verb. In such cases *dōu* refers back to *měi*+noun which may or may not be the subject of the sentence:

Měi zhāng zhuōzi 'every table'.

Měi ge rén or *měi rén* 'everybody'.

Měi tiān 'every day'.

Měi bǎ yǐzi dōu hěn shūfu 'every chair/all the chairs is/are very comfortable'.

Tā měi tiān wǎnshang dōu qù 'He goes every evening'.

3 MORE ON THE COMPARATIVE

When we wish to extend the simple comparative (see 7.5) to denote 'much more' or 'even more' the constructions are as follows:

A *bǐ* B + appropriate adjective *de duō* (complement of degree *de,* see 4.8). Or A *bǐ* B + appropriate adjective *duō le.*

e.g. A *bǐ* B *hǎo de duō* or *hǎo duō le* means 'A is much better than B'.

The first example of this in the text is:

zài nàr dú shū zǒng(shì) bǐ zài kètīng lǐ ānjìng de duō (at/there/study/books/always/compared with/at/sitting room in/quiet/much). 'It's always much quieter studying there than in the living room.'

When we wish to say that A is 'even more' or 'still more' the quality of the adjective than B, the construction is:

A *bĭ* B *hái* (or *gèng*) + adjective.

e.g. A *bĭ* B *hái hăo* means 'A is even better than B'. The adverb *hái* has the basic meaning of 'still, in addition'. In this context it has the same meaning as the adverb *gèng* 'still more, even more'.

Jiĕjie de fángjiān bĭ wŏmen xiōngdì liă de nà jiān hái xiăo (*Lit.* elder sister/room/compared with/we/brothers/two/ that room/even more/small) 'Elder sister's room is even smaller than my brother's and mine'. Note that *hĕn* 'very' can **never** be used in the comparative.

When we wish to say that 'A is up to B's standard of whatever the adjective is' then the construction is:

A *yŏu* B (*nàme/zhème*) adjective 'A is as adjective as B'.

Zhè tào zŭhéyīnxiăng yŏu nà tái nàme piányi 'This hi-fi is as cheap as that one'. The negative form, which is used more frequently, depicts an inferior degree, i.e. that A is not up to B's standard of tallness, goodness, etc. See text:

suŏyĭ zhù de méi yŏu yĭqián (*zhù de* understood) *nàme jĭ* (*Lit.* therefore/live/ /not/have/previously(live)/so/crowded) 'so we're not as crowded as we used to be'. *Yŏu* may be omitted in the negative form.

4 *YĬHÒU, YĬQIÁN, DE SHÍHOU*

Yĭhòu 'after', *yĭqián* 'before' and *de shíhou* 'when' occur at the **end** of the clause to which they refer, the reverse of English word order:

xiūxi yĭhòu 'after having a rest'.

shuì jiào yĭqián 'before going to bed'.

dōngtiān tiānqì lĕng de shíhou 'when the weather is cold in winter'.

It is common practice for the subject not to appear until the following clause although there is no fixed rule about this:

Shàng cèsuŏ de shíhou wŏmen bù yīnggāi chī fàn. (*Lit.* get on/ toilet/when/we/not/ought to/) 'We ought not to be eating when we go to the toilet.' Note that *yĭqián* and *yĭhòu* can also act as adverbs with the meanings 'previously' and 'afterwards', respectively and as such they precede the verb.

Wŏ xiànzài qù, tā yĭhòu qù. 'I'm going now, she's going later'.

5 *TIĀN* AND *NIÁN*

As we mentioned in 8.2, *tiān* and *nián* act as measure words as well as nouns so that they directly follow numbers and demonstrative adjectives such as *zhè* 'this', *nà* 'that', *nǎ* 'which?' and *měi* 'every':

nà tiān 'that day'.

yì nián 'one year'.

liǎng tiān 'two days'.

6 (*YÌ*) *XIĒ*

When it occurs after an adjective, (*yì*)*xiē* (the *yì* may be omitted) has the meaning 'somewhat'. It usually appears in comparative sentences when used in this way as in the two examples from the text:

Fùmǔ yě bǐ yǐqián zhù de shūfu (*yì*)*xiē* (*Lit.* parents/also/compared with/previously/live/comfortable/somewhat) 'Father and mother are also somewhat more comfortable than they used to be.'

Wǒ xiǎng zài Xīfāng yìbān zhùfáng bǐ wǒmen dà xiē (*Lit.* I/think/in/West/generally/accommodation/compared with/us/big/somewhat) 'I think that accommodation in the West is generally somewhat more spacious than ours'.

Yìxiē has another more important function as a plural measure word meaning 'some, a few':

yìxiē fādá guójiā 'some developed countries'. The *yì* is sometimes omitted, particularly after the verb *yǒu*:

yǒu xiē rén 'there are some people...' When used with *zhè, nà* or *nǎ* the *yì* is dropped and we have *zhè xiē, nà xiē* or *nǎ xiē* which mean 'these', 'those' or 'which(ones)', respectively. As *xiē* is in itself a measure word they are used directly before a noun:

Zhè xiē Lúndūnrén 'These Londoners'.

Nà xiē Niǔyuērén 'Those New Yorkers'.

Nǎ xiē Rìběnrén? 'Which Japanese?'.

NB *Zhè, nà* and *nǎ* are also read as *zhèi, nèi* and *něi* respectively.

7 *YǑUDE*

Yǒude 'some' + noun (or noun understood) may occur once, twice or even three times in a sentence:

Yǒude yǒu shūfáng, yǒude hái yǒu fàntīng (*Lit.* Some/have/book room/some/in addition/have/rice-room).

Wŏ de shū hěn duō, yŏude yŏu yìsi yŏude méi yŏu yìsi (*Lit.* My/ books/very/many/some/have/meaning/some/not/have/meaning) 'I've got lots of books, some are very interesting, some aren't.'

Yŏu(de) rén xĭhuan kàn shū, yŏu(de) rén xĭhuan kàn diànshì, yŏu(de) rén xĭhuan kàn diànyĭng (*Lit.* Some/people/like/read/ book/some/people/like/watch/TV/some/people/like/watch/electric shadow) 'Some people like reading, some people like watching TV, while others like watching films'. (Note that when *yŏude* occurs with *rén*, the *de* may be omitted.)

Generally speaking *yŏude* + noun cannot be put in the object position. We cannot say *Wŏ bù xĭhuan yŏude shū*, the topic construction has to be used instead: *Yŏude shū wŏ bù xĭhuan* 'There are some books I don't like.'

8   X *YŎU* Y

Besides meaning 'to have' *yŏu* also means 'there is, there are'. The construction is normally word or phrase indicating position + *yŏu* + Noun or Nominal Phrase i.e. (*zài*) X *yŏu* Y 'there is/are Y at X'.

Lúndūn yŏu bù shăo gōngyuán (*Lit.* London has not few public enclosures) 'There are quite a few parks in London'.

Zài 'at, in' is often omitted when the adverbial word or phrase of place occurs at the beginning of a clause or sentence. Of course, the sentence above could also be translated as 'London has quite a few parks', the omission of *zài* making such an interpretation possible but it is important to understand how such sentences function grammatically otherwise it is easy to come unstuck when more precision is required as in the following example taken from the text:

Kètīng lĭ yŏu yì zhāng shuāngrénchuáng、yí ge shāfā… (*Lit.* Guest-room inside/have/1/MW/pair people bed/1/MW/sofa…). In this case *yŏu* has to be translated by 'there is' and not by 'have'.

9   COMPOUND DIRECTIONAL ENDINGS

In 5.1 we met the (simple) directional markers *lái* and *qù* which indicate direction towards or away from the speaker or point of reference. Compound directional endings show even greater precision and are formed by combining verbs such as *jìn* 'to enter', *chū* 'to come or go out' with *lái* or *qù* and attaching them to verbs of motion. Thus where in English we would say 'He came running in', the Chinese for this would be *Tā pǎo jìnlai le*, (*Lit.* He/run/enter/come/), 'we came running out', *wǒmen pǎo chūlai le*, 'they went running in' *tāmen pǎo jìnqu le*, etc. There is a good example of this construction in the text: ...*dà yuánzhuō hé yǐzi dōu bān jìnlai* (*Lit.* Big/round table/and/chair(s)/all/move/enter/come) (speaker is in the living-room).

NB Verbs with a compound directional ending (CDE) are often written as one word, e.g. *pǎochulai* and as such **both** parts of the CDE are usually indicated as toneless. For the sake of clarity I have split the verb and its CDE as above and indicated the tone on the first half of the CDE.

Where there is an object involved, this may go between the two parts of the compound directional ending or follow it:

Wǒ ná chū yīfu lai or *Wǒ ná chūlai yīfu* 'I take out clothes' (*ná* 'to take' [with the hand]).

Where there is a place-word involved, this may **only** go between the two parts of the compound directional ending:

...*dà yuánzhuō hé yǐzi dōu bān jìn kètīng lai* 'the big round table and chairs are all moved into the living room'.

Tāmen pǎo chū huāyuán qu 'They run/ran out of the garden'. For further examples of this construction see Chapter 12, p. 119–20.

EXERCISE 8.1

Make a sentence from the following groups of words using the compound directional ending indicated in brackets.

Yīshēng zǒu yīyuàn (*jìnqu*) → *Yīshēng zǒu jìn yīyuàn qu*.

1 *Fùmǔ zǒu kètīng* (*jìnlai*).
2 *Tāmen bān shūzhuō* (*chūqu*).
3 *Xiōngdì bān shuāngrénchuáng* (*jìnqu*).
4 *Xiǎoháir pǎo cèsuǒ* (*chūlai*).
5 *Jiàoyuán ná liǎng běn shū* (books) (*xiàlai* 'down', direction towards speaker).

10 VOICE

The sentence from the text given in 8.9, *dà yuánzhuō hé yǐzi dōu bān jìnlai* appears to suggest that the table and chairs are moving themselves insofar as no other subject is present. This is a reflection of the fact that Chinese verbs in themselves are neither active nor passive but that it is the **context** which makes them one or the other.

11   *ZHUŌZI* BUT *SHŪZHUŌ*

In 3.9 we saw that modern Chinese is becoming increasingly disyllabic and one feature of this is that some nouns which were originally monosyllabic such as *zhuō, bēi, yǐ, píng* have become disyllabic by the addition of a 'fill-in' *zi* to become *zhuōzi* 'table', *bēizi* 'cup' *yǐzi* 'chair' *'píngzi* 'bottle'. Other examples we have met are *érzi 'son'* and *háizi* 'child'. Another device to satisfy this need for disyllables is to repeat the original sound to give disyllabic nouns such as *gēge* 'elder brother', *dìdi* 'younger brother', *jiějie* 'elder sister', *mèimei* 'younger sister', etc. As soon as a noun becomes disyllabic in its own right then the *zi* or the reduplication is no longer necessary. Examples are: *shūzhuō* 'desk', *yuánzhuō* 'round table', *jiǔbēi* 'wine-glass', *dàgē* 'eldest brother' and *dàjiě* 'eldest sister'.

12   *SUĪRÁN...DÀNSHI*

Many conjunctions in Chinese occur in pairs as in *suīrán* 'although' ...*dànshi* 'but'.... There are many more which we shall meet as we progress through the book. Sometimes one of the pair, usually the first, is omitted. The last sentence of the text could well have started with a *suīrán* but it is obviously stylistically clumsy to have two consecutive sentences beginning in the same way so it has been omitted. Note that *kěshì* and *dànshi* 'but' are interchangeable.

The three wheels and the four machines

Until recent times it was the aspiration of every Chinese household to own at least one each of the 'three wheels' *sān lún*: 'sewing machine' *féngrènjī*, 'wristwatch' *shǒubiǎo* and 'bicycle' *zìxíngchē*. Now that the standard of living is rising the 'three wheels' have been replaced by the 'four machines' *sì jī*: *diànshìjī* 'TV', *féngrènjī* 'sewing machine', *shōuyīnjī* 'radio' and *xǐyījī* 'washing machine'. At one point in the not so distant past Chinese brides would demand '48 legs' *sìshíbā tiáo tuǐ* in their dowries, not more than four of which could belong to chairs! (Washing machines and televisions would count as having four legs a piece.) The Chinese language is particularly suited to creating new idioms such as these. As it is a language rich in homophones it also lends itself to punning which is a popular form of Chinese humour. Thus Mr King's given name in Chinese, *yǒngshòu*, means 'eternal' *yǒng*, 'longevity' *shòu*, but could also mean 'forever skinny' as the adjective for 'thin' has exactly the same pronunciation and tone as the noun for 'longevity'! (But of course they are two totally different characters.)

The 'unit'

The term *dānwèi* usually refers to one's work unit which plays a much more important role in daily life than in the West. It is normally 'the unit' which provides its employees with housing, organises excursions, provides them with cinema and theatre tickets, sometimes has its own holiday accommodation, buys essential train tickets, and even decides when the central heating should go on and off. Official forms almost always require you to state your work unit which, in a sense, is part of your identity, and without which everyday living is made more difficult.

EXERCISE 8.2

Answer the following questions on the text:

1 *Zhāng Zhànyī de jiā yǒu jǐ jiān fáng?*
2 *Zhè bāokuò* (include) *bu bāokuò chúfáng hé cèsuǒ?*
3 *Tā fùmǔ shuì zài nǎr?*
4 *Tā hé shéi* (who) *shuì yí ge fángjiān?*
5 *Tāmen xiōngdì de fángjiān dà háishi jiějie de fángjiān dà?*
6 *Jiějie de fángjiān fàng de xià shénme jiājù?*
7 *Tāmen xiōngdì、zǐmèi chángcháng zài jiā ma?*
8 *Shuāngrénchuáng zài nǎr?*
9 *Zǔhéyīnxiǎng shì bu shi Yīngguóhuò?*
10 *Chúle chī fàn de shíhou yǐwài, dà yuánzhuō hé yǐzi dōu zài kètīng lǐ ma?*

11   *Zhōngguó fángzū、shuǐdiànfèi piányi háishi fādá guójiā piányi?*
12   *Àn Zhōngguó xiànzài de biāozhǔn Zhāng Zhànyī hé tā yì jiā rén guò de zěnmeyàng?*

EXERCISE 8.3

Can you correct the following *bìngjù?*

Sì diǎn zhōng bú jiù xíng → Sì diǎn zhōng jiù bù xíng.

1   *Měi fādá guójiā, fángzū dōu hěn guì* (expensive).
2   *Zhōngguórén hǎo, Yīngguórén dōu yě hěn hǎo.*
3   *Féngrènjī bù yǒu zǔhéyīnxiǎng nàme guì.*
4   *Yǐqián shuì jiào, yīnggāi shuā yá* (brush teeth).
5   *Tā nà ge tiān xiūxi le.*
6   *Wǒ bú yuànyì xǐ yǒude yīfu* (clothes).
7   *Fúwùyuán pǎo fàndiàn jìn lai.*
8   *Yìxiē ge Rìběnrén gōngzī hěn gāo.*
9   *Sūgélán* (Scotland) *bǐ Měiguó ānjìng de hěn duō.*
10   *De shíhou tiānqì hǎo, yào hǎohāor wán(r).*

EXERCISE 8.4

Translate the following passage into colloquial English.

Nǐ zìjǐ de fángjiān zěnmeyàng? Jiājù duō bu duo? Chúle yì zhāng chuáng yǐwài nǐ hái yǒu shénme jiājù? Zǔhéyīnxiǎng、xǐyījī、diànshìjī dōu yǒu ma? Bīngxiāng ne? Nǐ xiànzài zhù de bǐ yǐqián shūfu yìxiē ma? Nǐ de gōngzī gāo bu gao? Fángzū、shuǐdiànfèi guì bu gui? Shéi gěi nǐ shāo nuǎnqì? Yídìng bú shi nǐ de dānwèi ba? Nǐ guò de hái hǎo ma? (Wǒ) Xīwàng (hope) *nǐ guò de hěn hǎo!*

EXERCISE 8.5

Translate the following into Chinese:

1   There are a table and six chairs in the dining room.
2   Although it's generally very quiet in a study, many people do not possess one.
3   When the weather is cold, everybody likes the central heating on.
4   When your wages are high, (1)/it doesn't matter (3)/(if) water and electricity charges are high too (2)/.
5   On the basis of existing criteria, Britain counts as (*suàn*) an advanced country.
6   It is not every sofa (which) is comfortable to sit on (*hǎo zuò*).

7 Hi-fis are not as expensive (*guì*) as they used to be.

8 The parents didn't go yesterday (*zuótiān*), my eldest sister and I are not going today either.

9 (A) single bed (*dānrénchuáng*) is even cheaper than a double one.

10 What else is there(3)/in life (1)/apart from eating (2)/?

11 Before (you) have a rest, please help (*bāngzhù*) me move the wardrobe out.

12 Although all (the) windows, doors (*mén*), etc. are very clean (*gānjìng*), (the) tables (and) chairs are all filthy (*zāng*).

9

Hotels

Zhang Zhanyi talks about Chinese hotels:

Běijīng de lǚguǎn dānrénfángjiān tèbié shǎo. / *Duōshù shi shuāng-rénfángjiān.* /
Single rooms in Beiging hotels are few and far between. /Most are double rooms. /

Yàoshi nǐ yuànyì yí ge rén zhù shuāngrén fángjiān, dāngrán yě
Of course if you wish to have a double room by yourself, you can,

kěyǐ, dànshi wǎngwǎng yào fù shuāngrénfángjiān de fángfèi. /
but you usually have to pay for a double. /

Wàiguó zhuānjiā hé liúxuéshēng píng gōngzuòzhèng huò (zhě)
Foreign experts and students can often enjoy preferential treatment

xuéshēngzhèng, píngcháng kěyǐ xiǎngshòu yōudài. /
on the strength of their (employer's) ID or student cards. /

Zhù wàibīn de dà bùfen fángjiān dōu bāokuò yùshì hé
Most of the rooms allocated to foreign guests include (a) bathroom and

cèsuǒ. / *Yùshì lǐ yǒu yùpén hé línyù pēntóu, yě dōu yǒu*
toilet. / The bathrooms have bath and shower and are also all equipped

máojīn、yùjīn、féizào、wèishēngzhǐ、bōlibēi děng. /
with towels, bath towels, soap, toilet paper, glasses etc. /

Měi ge fángjiān lǐ dōu yǒu diànhuà、diànshì、rèshuǐpíng、
Every room has a telephone, a TV, a Thermos,

cháyè、chábēi、liáng kāishuǐ shénmede. /
tea, teacups, cold boiled water and so on. /

(Dà)duōshù zhù wǒmen fàndiàn de wàibīn zǎoshang chī Xīcān. /
The (great) majority of foreign guests in our hotel eat Western food in the mornings. /

Yǒude rén xiǎng yòng Hànyǔ dìng cài. / *Nín yǐqián jiànguo*
Some people would like to order in Chinese. / Have you ever seen

Zhōngwén càidān méi you? / *Rúguǒ méi jiànguo de huà, jiù*
a Chinese menu before? / If you haven't, then take a look at the

kànkan kèwén xiàbian de càidān ba. / *Fúwùyuán cóngqián yòng*
one below the text. / Hotel staff used to use

suànpan suàn zhàng, dànshi xiànzài yòng jìsuànjī de yuè
an abacus to work out bills but more and more of them are now

lái yuè duō le. /
using calculators. /

Běijīng de fàndiàn hěn duō. / *Chúle chéng qiān shàng wàn de*
Beijing has many hotels. / Apart from thousands and thousands

yóukè yǐwài, yí bùfen wàiguó gōngsī de dàibiǎo
of tourists, a number of foreign company representatives

(jí shāngrén) yě zhù fàndiàn, suǒyǐ fàndiàn de shēngyì
(i.e. businessmen) also live in hotels, so business (for the hotels)

zǒngshi hěn búcuò de. / *Jiàqián què yuè lái yuè guì le,*
is always very good indeed. / Prices (in hotels) are becoming

érqiě fúwù 、 shèbèi hái bù yídìng gēn de shàng. /
increasingly expensive, however, and the service and facilities (offered)
cannot necessarily still keep pace (with them). /

Wǒ zài Běijīng Fàndiàn gōngzuò, jiēchùguo de wàiguórén
I work in the Beijing Hotel and have come into contact with

hěn duō. / *Wǒmen Zhōngguórén bùdé bù chéngrèn tāmen zài*
many foreigners. / We Chinese have to admit that in certain respects

mǒu xiē fāngmiàn xiǎngshòu yídìng de tèquán, jíshǐ zhè xiē
they enjoy definite privileges, even if these are sometimes

tèquán yǒu (de) shíhou zhǐ xiànyú suíshí dōu kěyǐ jìn
merely confined to being able to go into a hotel at any time

fàndiàn shàng cèsuǒ! / *Qíshí shéi yòngguo Zhōngguó gōnggòng*
and use the toilet! / Actually anybody who has used public toilets

cèsuǒ, shéi dōu huì tóngqíng tāmen zhè zhǒng zuòfǎ de! /
in China will sympathise with their doing this! /

Zǎocān Càidān
Breakfast Menu

Shuǐguǒzhī (*júzizhī、fānqiézhī*)
Fruit juice (orange juice, tomato juice)
Jīdàn (*chǎojīdàn、zhǔjīdàn jiānjīdàn wòjīdàn*)
Eggs (scrambled, boiled, fried or poached)
Huǒtuǐ
Ham (*Lit.* fire leg)
Kǎomiànbāo
Toast (*Lit.* roast bread)
Huángyóu
Butter (*Lit.* yellow oil)
Guǒjiàng
Jam
Suān (niú)nǎi
Yoghurt (*Lit.* sour milk)
Kāfēi、hóngchá、rè (niú)nǎi、kěkě
Coffee, tea (*Lit.* red tea), hot milk, cocoa

---

wàibīn (n)	*foreign guest, visitor*	**zhuānjiā** (n)	*expert, specialist*
lǚguǎn (n)	*hotel*	**píng** (v)	*to rely on, to depend on*
dānrén-fángjiān (n)	*single room*	**gōngzuò-zhèng** (n)	*(employee's) ID card*
tèbié (adv.; adj.)	*specially, special*	**huò(zhě)** (conj.; adv.)	*or; perhaps*
duōshù (n)	*majority*	**xuéshēng-zhèng** (n)	*student card*
yàoshi (conj.)	*if*		
dāngrán (adv.)	*of course, naturally*	**píngcháng** (adv.; adj.)	*usually; ordinary, commonplace*
wǎngwǎng (adv.)	*more often than not; frequently*	**xiǎngshòu** (v; n)	*to enjoy rights, etc.; treat*
fù (v)	*to pay*	**yōudài** (n)	*preferential treatment*
shuāngrén-fángjiān (n)	*double room*	**bùfen** (n)	*part, section*
fáng-fèi (n)	*room charge*	**bāokuò** (v)	*to include*

máojīn (n) [tiáo]	towel
yùjīn (n) [tiáo]	bath-towel
féizào (n) [kuài]	soap
wèishēngzhǐ (n) [juǎn]	toilet paper
chá-yè (n)	tea(-leaves)
chá-bēi (n)	teacup
kāishuǐ (n)	boiled water
shénmede	and so on
zǎoshang (TW)	morning
Xīcān (n)	Western food
dìng (v)	to order (in advance)
jiàn (v)	to see; to meet
-guo	verbal suffix (see 9.2)
Zhōngwén (n)	Chinese language (usually written form)
càidān (n)	menu
rúguǒ...(de huà), jiù	if...then
kèwén (n) [kè]	text
xiàbianr (PW)	under(neath), below
cóngqián (adv.)	previously, in the past
suànpan (n)	abacus
suàn zhàng (v-o)	to make/work out the bill (fig. 'settle accounts')
jìsuànjī (n) [jià]	calculating machine; computer
yuè lái yuè	more and more
chéng qiān shàng wàn	thousands and thousands
yóukè (n)	tourist, sightseer
xiāngdāng (adv.)	quite (a bit)
gōngsī (n)	company
dàibiǎo (n)	representative
jí (adv.)	that is, viz.

shāngrén (n)	businessman
shēngyì (n)	business
jiàqián (n)	price
què (adv.)	however
guì (adj.)	expensive
érqiě (conj.)	moreover
fúwù (n; v)	service; to serve
shèbèi (n)	equipment, facilities
gēn-shang (RV)	to keep pace with
jiēchù (v)	to come into contact with
bùdé bù	cannot but, have to
chéngrèn (v)	to admit
mǒu (adj.)	certain
fāngmiàn (n)	aspect, respect
tèquán (n)	privilege
jíshǐ (conj.)	even if, even though
yǒu (de) shíhou	sometimes
xiànyú (v)	to be confined to
suíshí (adv.)	at any time
jìn (v)	to enter
shàng cèsuǒ (v-o)	to go to the toilet
qíshí (adv.)	actually, as a matter of fact
shéi (QW)	who? (also read shuí)
gōnggòng (adj.)	public
huì (aux. v.)	will (showing possibility)
tóngqíng (v)	to sympathise with
zuòfǎ (n)	way of doing something

Grammar

1 *HUÒ(ZHĚ)*

Huò(zhě) 'or' is used to link statements or pronouns and nouns whereas *háishi* 'or' (see 5.2) is used to link questions:

Wàiguó zhuānjiā huò(zhě) liúxuéshēng píng gōngzuòzhèng huò (zhě) xuéshēngzhèng...(Lit. Outside country/special family/or/stay student/lean on/work proof/or/student proof...).

Wǒ xǐhuan kàn bào huòzhě kàn xiǎoshuō. (Lit. I/like/read/newspaper/or/read/small talk) 'I like reading the newspaper or novels'.

Huòzhě is used more in spoken Chinese whereas *huò* is more formal.

2 VERBAL SUFFIX *-GUO*.

In Chapter 5 we met *guò* as a verb meaning 'to pass' or 'to cross'. Put **after** the verb it indicates that something happened in the indefinite past, i.e. it emphasises a past experience and not completion as with verb + *le* (see 3.4):

Wǒ chīguo Yìndù fàn. 'I've eaten Indian food' (at sometime or other). The negative is formed by putting *méi* before the verb but the *-guo* is retained as there is no idea of completion or non-completion as with the verbal suffix *-le*:

Wǒ méi qùguo hěn duō guójiā. 'I haven't visited many countries.' (General statement about past experience).

Wǒ méi qù hěn duō guójiā. 'I didn't visit many countries' (on one specific occasion, e.g. last year). Adverbs such as *yǐqián*, *cónglái* 'hither to' often appear before the negated verb to emphasise the idea of never having done the action of the verb:

Wǒ cónglái méi chīguo Yìdàlì fàn. 'I've never eaten Italian food.' The question form is made by adding *ma* to the statement or by adding *méi you* after it:

Nín yǐqián jiànguo Zhōngwén càidān ma?
Nín yǐqián jiànguo Zhōngwén càidān méi you? }

'Have you ever seén a Chinese menu before?' (Note that *pinyin* convention always shows *guo* attached to the verb.)

3 *ZHŌNGWÉN, HÀNYŬ* AND *PŬTŌNGHUÀ*

Zhōngwén and *Hànyǔ* can both be translated as 'the Chinese language'. *Zhōngwén* is used more in connection with the written language whereas *Hànyǔ* (the language of the Han people, China's largest nationality) is used more for the spoken language. The Chinese language has eight major dialects but of the Chinese-speaking population, about 70% speak the northern dialect which is why it has been made the basis of *pǔtōnghuà*, 'the common spoken language' which is the *lingua franca* for the whole of China.

4 *RÚGUǑ...(DE HUÀ), JIÙ...*

As we said in 8.12 many conjunctions occur in pairs and here is another example of this, *Rúguǒ...(de huà), jiù...*, 'If..., then...':

Rúguǒ tā bù lái (de huà), wǒ jiù bú qù. 'If she doesn't come, I won't go.' ...*de huà* conveys the flavour of 'assuming that X is the case' (*tā bù lái*), then Y (*wǒ bú qù*)'. In the example from the text we have:

Rúguǒ méi jiànguo de huà, jiù kànkan kèwén xiàbian de càidān ba. (*Lit.* If/not/seen/assuming/then/look look//text/below/dish list//). In this construction, *rúguǒ* may be replaced by *yàoshi* which also means 'if' and is usually regarded as being the more colloquial of the two:

Yàoshi méi yǒu dānrénfángjiān, wǒ jiù zhù shuāngrénfángjiān ba. 'If there are no single rooms, then I'll have a double.' *Yàoshi* or *rúguǒ* may sometimes be omitted and in such cases it is the *jiù* (and the context) which convey the conditional flavour. It is important to be aware of the existence of these 'hidden if' sentences as they can influence the meaning a great deal.

5 *CÓNGQIÁN AND YǏQIÁN*

Both *cóngqián* and *yǐqián* can act as moveable adverbs or time-words meaning 'previously', 'in the past'. They normally occur before the verb and after the subject but they can be placed at the beginning of the sentence for extra emphasis:

Fúwùyuán cóngqián yòng suànpan suàn zhàng (*Lit.* Attendants/ in the past/use/calculate tray/calculate/bill). There is no sense of completed action or emphasis of a past experience, so no verbal suffix -*le* or -*guo* is required. The idea of the past tense is conveyed by using *cóngqián*. As we know from 8.4, *yǐqián* can also act as a conjunction, occurring at the end of the clause to which it refers; *cóngqián* cannot be used in this way. We can say *suàn zhàng yǐqián*, 'before making out the bill', but we cannot say *suàn zhàng cóngqián*.

6 YUÈ LÁI YUÈ + ADJECTIVE

This construction is relatively easy to use if you remember the basic formula that to express 'more and more of the adjective' is:

yuè lái yuè + adjective:

Shēngyì yuè lái yuè hǎo 'Business gets better and better'.

Yòng jìsuànjī de yuè lái yuè duō le. } Change of state *le* in both
Jiàqián què yuè lái yuè guì le. } cases.

If you wish to convey ideas such as 'the quicker the better' then the construction *yuè* adjective/verb *yuè* adjective/verb is used:

Yuè kuài yuè hǎo. 'The quicker the better'.

Wǒ yuè chī yuè pàng (le). 'The more I eat the fatter I get'. **But**

Wǒ yuè lái yuè pàng (le). 'I'm getting fatter and fatter'.

7 MORE ON *DE*

Apart from being able to nominalise a pronoun or adjective (see 5.12) and link two nouns (see 3.5), *de* may also be used to link quite complex clauses to their nouns. Again it is important to stress that it is the **main idea** which comes after *de*:

Zhù wàibīn de lǚguǎn (*Lit.* live/foreign guest//travel establishment).

Zhù wàibīn de dà bufen fángjiān (*Lit.* live/foreign guest/ /big/part/ rooms). NB *dà bùfen* is one idea, therefore no *de*.

Chéng qiān shàng wàn de yóukè (*Lit.* become/thousand(s)/go up/ ten thousand(s)//travelling guest).

Yí bùfen wàiguó gōngsī de dàibiǎo (*Lit.* one/part/foreign/company/ /representative).

8 THE DOUBLE NEGATIVE

Whereas in English the double negative is generally avoided, it is used quite freely in Chinese:

Bú qù bù xíng (*Lit.* Not/go/not/be all right) 'There is no alternative but to go.'

Wǒmen Zhōngguórén bùdé bù chéngrèn (*Lit.* We/China/people/ may not/not/admit).

9 *MǑU*

Mǒu is used with a measure word before a noun to indicate 'a certain':

mǒu zhǒng qíngkuàng 'a certain situation'.

mǒu xiē shāngrén 'certain businessmen'.

zài mǒu xiē fāngmiàn 'in certain respects'.

When *mǒu* is repeated before a title such as *xiānsheng*, etc. it takes on the meaning of 'so-and-so'. No measure word is required in this case:

mǒumǒu xiānsheng 'Mr So-and-So'.

mǒumǒu xiǎojie 'Miss So-and-So'.

10   QUESTION WORDS USED IN A NON-QUESTION WAY

(i)   Question words such as *shéi (shuí)*, *shénme*, *nǎ* and *nǎr* can be used in a non-question way to mean 'anybody', 'anything', 'any' and 'anywhere':

Wǒ bú qù nǎr. 'I'm not going anywhere'. (In response to *Nǐ qù nǎr?*, it seems, in addition, to convey a slight feeling of unwillingness to communicate with the questioner!)

(ii)   Only *jǐ* and *duōshao* can be used in the affirmative, to indicate 'several' and 'an indefinite number' respectively:

Tāmen yǒu jǐ běn Zhōngwén shū. 'They have several Chinese books.'

In this case, intonation and context tell the listener whether they are being used as question words or not.

(iii)   Question words can also be used to indicate inclusiveness in the affirmative, but exclusiveness in the negative. *Dōu* or *yě* must be added before the verb to reinforce this sense of inclusiveness or exclusiveness:

Shéi dōu bú suàn (Lit. Who/all/not/count) 'Nobody counts'.

In this construction, the direct object is moved to a position before the verb (but after the subject):

Wǒ shénme yě bú zuò (Lit. I/what/also/not/do) 'I'm not doing anything'.

Tā nǎr dōu qù (Lit. He/where/all/go) 'He goes everywhere'.

(Note that *jǐ* and *duōshao* cannot be used in this way.)

(iv)   Such concepts as 'whatever (one likes)', 'whoever (one likes)', 'wherever (one likes)' are expressed by repeating the question word and the verb in a second clause and putting *jiù* before the repeated verb in the second clause:

Nǐ yào qǐng shéi, nǐ jiù qǐng shéi (Lit. You/want/invite/who/you/ then/invite/who) 'Invite whoever you like'.

*Wŏmen yào măi **shénme**,* wŏmen *jiù măi **shénme** (Lit.* We/want/ buy/what/we/then/buy/what) 'We buy whatever we like'.

(v)   *Zĕnme,* 'how?' put before the verb roughly translates as 'no matter how' or 'to what degree'. *Dōu* or *yĕ* must be put before the verb in the following clause. *Bù zĕnme* + adjective translates as 'not particularly' + adjective:

Nà ge xuésheng hĕn rènzhēn ('conscientious'). *Tiānqì zĕnme lĕng, tā dōu lái shàng kè.* (v-o attend class) 'That student is very conscientious. He comes to class no matter how cold it is'.

Tā bù zĕnme niánqīng le. 'She's no longer particularly young'.

11   *HUÌ...DE*

The principal meaning of *huì* is 'to know how to (do), can' (Chapter 2), but it can also express the possibility or probability that something will happen and is translated as 'will': *Huì xià yŭ (Lit.* will/descend/rain) 'It will rain' or 'It's going to rain'. The addition of the modal particle *de* to such sentences introduces a note of affirmation or confirmation as well as slightly shifting the balance and rhythm of the sentence as a whole. Used in this way, it is generally to be found with such verbs as *huì, yào, shì,* etc. *Tā huì lái de.* 'He will come'. It is important to stress that *de* is not essential to the sentence but is used widely.

12   DEGREES OF 'MUCHNESS' (IN ASCENDING ORDER)

(hĕn)hăo	'(very) good'
tĭng hăo	'quite/rather good'
xiāngdāng hăo	'quite/rather good'
shífēn hăo	'very/rather good' (*Lit.* ten parts/good)
fēicháng hăo	'extremely good'
hăo jíle	'extremely good'
zuì hăo	'the best'.

In some ways the order is a little arbitrary but it will at least give you some idea.

EXERCISE 9.1

True or false?

1 *Běijīng de lǚguǎn yí ge rén zhù yí ge fángjiān bù kěyǐ.*
2 *Wàiguó zhuānjiā píng xuéshēngzhèng, píngcháng kěyǐ xiǎngshòu yōudài.*
3 *Zhù wàibīn de dà bùfen fángjiān lǐ dōu yǒu diànshì hé diànhuà.*
4 *Duōshù zhù fàndiàn de wàibīn zǎoshang chī Zhōngcān.*
5 *Fúwùyuán yǐqián yòng suànpan suàn zhàng, xiànzài yòng de yuè lái yuè shǎo le.*
6 *Méi yǒu shāngrén zhù fàndiàn.*
7 *Fàndiàn de shēngyì fēicháng hǎo dànshi fángfèi yuè lái yuè piányi le.*
8 *Suīrán zhù fàndiàn de jiàqián yuè lái yuè guì le dànshi fúwù ﹑ shèbèi bù yídìng gēn de shàng.*
9 *Zhōngguórén bùdé bù chéngrèn zài Zhōngguó de wàiguórén méi yǒu tèquán.*
10 *Zhōngguó gōnggòng cèsuǒ yìbān bù zěnme hǎo.*

EXERCISE 9.2

Fill in the blanks using the words given above each passage. Each word can only be used **once**.

Huòzhě bù cóngqián shuǐguǒzhī jiù shuì jiào kěkě háishi zěnme

(a) *Zǎoshang nǐ xǐhuan chī Xīcān _____ chī Zhōngcān? Wǒ xǐhuan chī Xīcān, hē _____. _____ yǐqián wǒ xǐhuan hē rè niúnǎi _____ _____. Wǒ _____ bù_____ xǐhuan hē kěkě, xiànzài hěn xǐhuan. Rúguǒ ràng* (have somebody do something) *wǒ wǎnshang hē kāfēi, wǒ _____ bù hē. Wǒ bùdé _____ chéngrèn, wǎnshang hē kāfēi shuì bu hǎo jiào.*

suīrán dōu jiù zěnme tǐng mǒu nǎr

(b) *Wǒ hěn xǐhuan wǒ gēge. Tā qù nǎr, wǒ _____ qù _____. Tā _____ huópo* (lively). *_____ tā zhǐ shísì suì, dànshi zài _____ xié fāngmiàn tā xiàng* (resemble) *(yí) ge dàren. Tiānqì _____ lěng, tā _____ qù gěi bàba ﹑ māma mǎi dōngxi* (v-o, buy things).

> **'Documents with everything'**
> In addition to the normal array of ID cards and passes of one sort or another, letters of introduction from one's work unit for example (or from one's embassy for foreigners) can be extremely useful in booking accommodation, securing tickets of various kinds, obtaining leave of absence and so on. It is probably true to say that headed notepaper with an official-looking stamp goes a long way in China! On the other hand, under certain (unspecified) circumstances, the Chinese can be *amazingly* flexible!

EXERCISE 9.3

Correct the word-order in the following sentences:

1 *Rúguǒ méi yǒu càidān, jiù wǒ bù kěyǐ dìng cài.*
2 *Nǐmen méi zhùguo lǚguǎn cóngqián.*
3 *Fādá guójiā shēnghuó yuè nán* (difficult) *yuè lái.*
4 *Suàn zhàng yòng jìsuànjī hěn fāngbiàn* (convenient) *yǒu shíhou.*
5 *Chéng qiān de shàng wàn yóukè qù yóulǎn Chángchéng* (visit the Great Wall) *měi nián.*
6 *Jīntiān bú è le. Shénme wǒ bù xiǎng chī yě.*
7 *Tā nà ge rén jíle hǎo, tā shuō zěnme tiānqì lěng, dōu méi guānxi.*

EXERCISE 9.4

Translate the following passages into colloquial English:

1 *Zhōngguórén hěn xǐhuan yòng rèshuǐpíng, yīnwèi* (because) *tāmen yìbān hěn xǐhuan hē chá. Dà bùfen Zhōngguórén bǐjiào xǐhuan hē lǜ chá dànshi yǒude shíhou hē hóng chá yě kěyǐ. Hē hóng chá de shíhou dàduōshù Zhōngguórén yào jiā niúnǎi hé táng* (sugar).
2 *Bēizi yǒu hěn duō zhǒng. Yǒu chábēi, yǒu kāfēibēi, yǒu bōlibēi, yě yǒu jiǔbēi. Píngzi yě shi yíyàng* (the same) *de. Yǒu huāpíng* (vase), *yǒu nǎipíng* (milk bottle), *yě yǒu rèshuǐpíng.*

EXERCISE 9.5

Translate the following into Chinese:

1 There's no yoghurt left. You can have either hot milk or cold (use *liáng*) milk.

2 Have you ever been to the Great Wall? Thousands of tourists go every year to visit (it).

3 If there's no toilet paper, it's very inconvenient (*bù fāngbiàn*) to go to the lavatory.

4 Everybody ought to enjoy the same rights (*quánlì*).

5 We have to admit that Swiss (*Ruìshì*) chocolate (*qiǎokèlì*) is excellent.

6 If you want to use a calculator to work out the bill, then go ahead.

7 Whom are you inviting to dinner tonight? I'm not inviting anyone.

8 (The) texts are becoming increasingly difficult.

9 As a matter of fact her way of doing things is the best.

10 That person living in (a) double room (use *de*), is a businessman from Tokyo (*Dōngjīng*).

11 Although it's raining, he says he will come.

12 In the past (*guòqù*) there were relatively few foreign company representatives in China, but they are now becoming more and more numerous.

10

Weather, Dates and Seasons

Zhang Zhanyi gives his views on Beijing's climate and describes recreational activities in the capital.

Jīnnián Běijīng de tiānqì hěn bú zhèngcháng. / Dōngtiān bù
The weather in Beijing has been very odd this year. / The winter
lěng, xiàtiān yě bú rè. / Yīnggāi xià xuě de shíhou bìng
has not been cold nor has the summer been hot. / When it should have
méi yǒu xià, yīnggāi xià yǔ de shíhou yě méi yǒu xià – zhēn
snowed it didn't, and when it should have rained it hasn't – it's
qíguài! /
really strange! /
Shì bu shi zhěnggè shìjiè de qìhòu zhèngzài biàn ne? /
Is it because the climate of the entire world is in the process of
Ōuzhōu píngcháng méi yǒu Běijīng nàme lěng dànshi
changing? / Europe is usually not as cold as Beijing, but
jīnnián fǎn'ér yǒude shíhou bǐ Běijīng hái lěng. /
this year on the contrary it has sometimes been even colder than Beijing. /
Chūntiān 、 qiūtiān shì Běijīng zuì hǎo de jìjié dànshi kěxī
The best seasons in Beijing are spring and autumn but it's a pity
tài duǎn le. / Yàoshi zài Zhōngguó lǚxíng de huà, wǔyuè hé
they're so short. / If you're travelling around in China, May and
jiǔyuè tiānqì zuì hǎo, qíngtiān duō, yīntiān shǎo. /
September have the best weather with many fine days and few cloudy
ones. /
Tiānqì yī hǎo, gōngyuán lǐ de rén jiù hěn duō. / Lǎorén xià

As soon as the weather brightens up, there are many people in the parks. /

qí de xià qí, dǎ pái de dǎ pái, liáo tiān(r) de liáo

There are some old people playing chess, others playing cards and some chatting to each other,

tiān(r), zǎoshang dǎ tàijíquán de yǒudeshì. / *Zhōngguó yǒu xiē*

and there's plenty of them doing taijiquan (a form of exercise) in the mornings. / In China

dìfang bǐrú Sìchuān 、 Guǎngdōng děng dì zài cháguǎn lǐ zuòzhe

there are some places such as Sichuan and Guangdong (Canton) where there are many of them sitting

hē chá de yě hěn duō. /

in teahouses drinking tea. /

Zhōngguórén yìbān yí ge xīngqī gōngzuò liù tiān, bú xiàng

The Chinese generally work a six-day week unlike

dà bùfen Ōuzhōu guójiā xīngqīliù yě xiūxi. / *Suīrán jīguān*

the greater part of Europe where Saturday is also a rest day. / Although cadres

gànbù xīngqītiān xiūxi, yǒude gōngchǎng xīngqītiān yě

in offices have Sundays off, some factories work as normal on

zhàocháng shēngchǎn, gōngrén lúnliú xiūxi. /

Sundays too, with workers taking time off in turn. /

Jīntiān shì xīngqītiān, tiānqì tèbié hǎo, nánnǚ lǎoshào yì

Today is Sunday and the weather is especially nice, one group after

qún yì qún dōu chū qu wánr. / *Gōngyuán lǐ sàn bù de sàn bù,*

another of men and women, old and young go out to enjoy themselves. /

zhào xiàng de zhào xiàng, yǒude xǐhuan guàng dà jiē,

Some people stroll in the parks or take photographs, some like to go

shāngdiàn lǐ zǒngshi hěn jǐ – zhěnggè Běijīng rènào jíle. /

window-shopping, the shops are always very crowded – the whole of Beijing is a hive of activity. /

Zài Zhōngguó yào(shi) xiǎng zhǎo yí ge ānjìng de dìfang, yí

If you wish to find a quiet place in China to be by yourself for

ge rén dāi yíhuìr, shì hěn nán bàn dào de. / *Nǐ yào xiǎng*

a while, it's extremely difficult to do so. / If you wish to

shài tàiyáng, jiù děi gēn chéng qiān shàng wàn de rén yìqǐ

sunbathe you have to do so with thousands of other people! /

shài! / *Fǎnzhèng xīngqītiān dàochù dōu shì rén!* /

In any case there are people everywhere on Sundays! /

Jīnnián dōngtiān jié bīng yǐhòu, wǒ jīngcháng qù huá bīng,
This winter after it fell below freezing I have been skating regularly,
yī xià bān jiù pǎo dào Běihǎi Gōngyuán qù huá. / Rúguǒ zài
as soon as I finish work I rush to Beihai Park to skate. / If
jiā jiù dào fùjìn de Yuánmíngyuán huò Yíhéyuán qù huá. /
I'm at home then I go to the old Summer Palace or the Summer Palace to
skate. /

zhèngcháng (adj.)	*normal, regular*	lǎorén (n)	*old people*
xiàtiān (n)	*summer*	xià qí (v-o)	*to play chess*
xià xuě (v-o)	*to snow*	dǎ pái (v-o)	*to play cards or mahjong*
bìng (adv.) + bù/méi	*see 10.1*	liáo tiān(r) (v-o)	*to chat*
xià yǔ (v-o)	*to rain*	dǎ tàijíquán (v-o)	*to do taijiquan*
qíguài (adj.)	*strange*		
zhěnggè (adj.)	*whole, entire*	yǒudeshì	*to have plenty of, there's no lack of*
shìjiè (n)	*world*		
qìhòu (n)	*climate*	bǐrú	*for example, such as*
zhèngzài...ne	*in the middle of -ing (see 10.3)*	Sìchuān (N)	*Sichuan*
biàn (v)	*to change*	Guǎngdōng (N)	*Canton (province)*
Ōuzhōu (N)	*Europe*		
fǎn'ér (conj.)	*on the contrary*	dì (n)	*locality, land (as used for farming); the earth*
chūntiān (n)	*spring*		
qiūtiān (n)	*autumn*		
jìjié (n)	*season*	cháguǎn (n)	*teahouse*
kěxī	*it's a pity that*	-zhe	*verbal suffix (see 10.11)*
duǎn (adj.)	*short (in length)*		
yào (shi)...(de huà), (jiù)...	*if...then...*	xīngqī (n)	*week*
		xiàng (v)	*to resemble, to be like*
lǚxíng (v)	*to travel*		
yuè (n)	*month*	jīguān (n)	*offices, organisation*
qíng (adj.)	*(of weather) fine, clear, bright*	gànbù (n)	*cadre*
		gōngchǎng (n)	*factory*
yīn (adj.)	*cloudy, overcast*	zhàocháng (adv.)	*as usual*
yī...jiù...	*no sooner... than...; as soon as*	shēngchǎn (v)	*to produce, to manufacture*
gōngyuán (n)	*park*	lúnliú (v)	*to take turns, in turn*

nánnǚ	*men and women,*	**gēn** (prep.;	*with; and*
lǎoshào	*old and young*	conj.)	
qún (MW)	*group, flock*	**yìqǐ** (adv.;	*together*
chū (v)	*to come* or *to go*	PW)	
	out	**fǎnzhèng**	*anyway, in*
sàn bù (v-o)	*to take a walk, to*	(adv.)	*any case*
	stroll	**dàochù** (PW)	*everywhere*
zhào xiàng	*to take a picture; to*	**jié bīng** (v-o)	*to freeze, to ice over*
(v-o)	*have one's picture/*	**jīngcháng**	*regularly, frequently*
	photo taken	(adv.)	
guàng dà jiē	*to go window-*	**huá bīng** (v-o)	*to skate (Lit.*
(v-o)	*shopping*		*slide ice)*
shāngdiàn (n)	*shop*	**xià bān** (v-o)	*to finish work*
rènào (adj.)	*bustling; exciting*	**pǎo** (v)	*to run*
dāi (v; coll.)	*to stay*	**Běihǎi**	
yíhuìr (TW)	*a short while,*	**Gōngyuán** (N)	*Beihai Park*
	(after) a moment	**dào...qù/lái**	*to go/come to; to*
nán (adj.)	*difficult*		*arrive*
bàn-dào (RV)	*to get something*	**fùjìn** (n)	*nearby*
	done, to accomplish	**Yuánmíng-**	*the Old Summer*
shài tàiyáng	*to sunbathe*	**yuán** (N)	*Palace*
(v-o)		**Yíhéyuán** (N)	*the Summer Palace*

Grammar

1 *BÌNG*

Bìng before *bù* or *méi* (*yǒu*) emphasises the negation and conveys the idea that it is not what might have been expected: *Yīnggāi xià xuě de shíhou bìng méi yǒu xià* (*Lit.* Ought to/descend/snow/when/ /not/have/descend).

2 *SHÌ BU SHÌ*

Shì bu shì is used to make the question form when you wish to indicate to the listener that you are seeking confirmation of something you believe to be the case. It can be put at the beginning or end of the sentence, or after the subject with the following slight shifts in emphasis:

Shì bu shì nǐ míngtiān qù yóuyǒng (swimming)?

Nǐ shì bu shì míngtiān qù yóuyǒng?

In both of the above sentences you are confident that I am going swimming tomorrow, but using *shì bu shi* softens the tone and indicates a wish on your part to discuss the matter with me. It in no way implies an order.

Nǐ míngtiān qù yóuyǒng shì bu shi?

At the **end** of the sentence *shì bu shi* seeks a more direct confirmation and conveys the idea of 'Am I right?' 'Is it true?'

All three sentences can probably be roughly translated as:

'You are going swimming tomorrow aren't you?'

...shì ma? or *...duì ma?* have the same meaning as *shì bu shi* used at the end of the sentence, and they too can only appear at the end of the sentence: *Sìchuān rén xǐhuan chī là de* (hot/spicy[food]), *shì ma?* 'People from Sichuan like spicy food, don't they?'. The answer to all three forms is *Shì(a)* or *Duì* if the listener agrees and *Bù* if he or she does not.

3   THE PROGRESSIVE ASPECT – 'TO BE IN THE MIDDLE OF DOING SOMETHING'

To show that an action is in progress, one of the adverbs *zhèngzài*, *zhèng* or *zài* is placed before the verb or *ne* is placed at the end of the sentence. However, *zhèngzài*, *zhèng* or *zài* often occur **together** with *ne* to indicate the progressive aspect:

Shòuhuòyuán (shop assistant) *zhèngzài liáo tiān(r)* (*ne*). 'The shop assistant is/was (in the middle of) chatting'.

Tā zài dǎ tàijíquán (*ne*). 'He is/was (in the middle of) doing taijiquan'.

Gōngchǎng zhèng shēngchǎn...(ne). 'The factory is/was (in the middle of) manufacturing...'.

Tāmen zhào xiàng ne. 'They are/were (in the middle of) taking photos.'

The negative is made by putting *méi* (*yǒu*) before the verb but if the verb is omitted then *yǒu* **must** be used:

Nǐmen zài shài tàiyáng ma? 'Are you sunbathing?'.

Wǒmen méi (*yǒu*) *shài tàiyáng, wǒmen kàn diànshì ne.* 'We're not sunbathing, we're watching TV'.

Méi yǒu, wǒmen kàn diànshì ne. 'No, we're watching TV'.

Méi yǒu. 'No'.

What the Chinese call 'aspect' is different from 'time' (past, present or future). An action in progress may take place in the past, present or future and it is the use of time-words (plus context) which tells us when the action actually takes place. (This is why it is also dangerous to think of the verb + *le* as indicating the past tense.) The following examples will illustrate this point:

Present – *Question: Nǐ xiànzài zuò shénme ne?* 'What are you doing now?'.

Answer: *Wǒ zài huá bīng ne* (*Lit.* I/ /slide/ice/). 'I'm skating'.

Past – *Zuótiān* (yesterday) *tā lái de shíhou, wǒ zhèng shuì jiào ne.* 'I was asleep when he came yesterday'. (Note the clause sequence, the 'when' clause comes first.)

Future – *Míngtiān xiàwǔ* (afternoon) *xià bān yǐhòu qù zhǎo tā, tā yídìng zài dǎ pái ne.* '(If) you go and look for her tomorrow afternoon after work, she'll certainly be playing cards'.

4 *KĚXĪ*

A whole range of adjectives are made up of *kě* + verb to give the literal meaning of 'being worth -ing', 'able to be -ed'. Some of the more common ones are given below:

kě'ài 'lovable, lovely' *kěkào* 'reliable'
kělián 'pitiable, pitiful' *kěpà* 'terrifying (able to be feared)'
kěxī 'it's a pity' *kěxiào* 'laughable, ridiculous'

5 MONTHS OF THE YEAR

yīyuè	*January*	**qīyuè**	*July*
èryuè	*February*	**bāyuè**	*August*
sānyuè	*March*	**jiǔyuè**	*September*
sìyuè	*April*	**shíyuè**	*October*
wǔyuè	*May*	**shíyīyuè**	*November*
liùyuè	*June*	**shí'èryuè**	*December*

Note that whereas *yī* + *yuè* means 'January' (some people say *yíyuè*), *yí* + *ge* + *yuè* means 'one month', *èryuè* means February, but *liǎng ge yuè* 'two months' and so on. If *-chū* 'at the beginning of' or *-dǐ* 'at the end of' is added to a specific month, April for instance, we get *sìyuèchū*, '(in) early April' and *sìyuèdǐ*, 'at the end of April'.

This also works with *nián*, 'year', *niánchū* meaning 'at the beginning of the year' and *niándǐ*, 'at the end of the year'.

6   OMISSION OF *HĚN* IMPLIES COMPARISON

This point has already been touched on in 4.8 but the example from the text illustrates it beautifully as well as providing another example of the balance which is such a feature of Chinese:

   qíngtiān duō, yīntiān shǎo.

7   *YĪ...JIÙ...*

Yī...jiù... are used to connect two actions which follow on closely one from another:

   Wǒ yī huá xuě (slide snow 'ski') *jiù gāoxìng le.* 'As soon as I get skiing, I'm happy'.

   Tiānqì yī hǎo, gōngyuán lǐ de rén jiù hěn duō....
   yī xià bān jiù pǎo dào Běihǎi Gōngyuán qù huá.

It may help you to remember this construction if you think of it as *yī* verb₁, *jiù* verb₂, 'as soon as verb₁ happens, then verb₂ happens'.

8 V_1-O *DE*, V_1-O

When we wish to convey the idea that amongst a specified group of people some are engaged in one activity, others in another and so on, each group and its activity is expressed by the construction V_1-O *de*, V_1-O. This is repeated as many times as there are activities, with the verb-object changing each time of course: *Lǎo(nián) rén xià qí de xià qí, dǎ pái de dǎ pái, liáo tiān(r) de liáo tiān(r)....* In other words, of the old people in the park, some are doing A (playing chess), some are doing B (playing cards) and some are doing C (chatting).

   Gōngyuán lǐ sàn bù de sàn bù, zhào xiàng de zhào xiàng.... 'Some people in the park are taking a stroll, others are taking photographs...'.

9   *DǍ* + OBJECT

In addition to the two examples from the text, *dǎ pái* and *dǎ tàijíquán, dǎ* (*Lit.* 'to hit' or 'to strike') can appear with a whole series of different objects, some of which are given below:

   dǎ diànbào   'to send a telegram' (*Lit.* hit electric newspaper)
   dǎ diànhuà   'to make a telephone call' (*Lit.* hit electric speech)

dǎ gē(r)	'to belch'
dǎ gǔ	'to beat a drum'
dǎ hān	'to snore'
dǎ hāqian	'to yawn'
dǎ hū(lu)	'to snore (coll.)'
dǎ pìgu	'to spank' (*Lit.* hit buttocks)
dǎ qì	'to pump, inflate'
dǎ qiú	'to play ball'
dǎ zhēn	'to give or have an injection' (*Lit.* hit needle)
dǎ zì	'to type' (*Lit.* hit characters)

10 *DĚNG* + NOUN

We met *děng* 'etc.' in Chapter 8 and this is an extension of that meaning. 'Such people as Mr Li, Mr Wang and Miss Scurfield' translates into Chinese as *Lǐ xiānsheng、Wáng xiānsheng、Shǐ xiǎojie děng rén* (*Lit.* etc./people). 'Such places as Sichuan and Guangdong (Canton)' translates as *Sìchuān、Guǎngdōng děng dì* (*Lit.* etc./ places).

11 VERBAL SUFFIX *-ZHE*

The verbal suffix *-zhe* is placed **after** the verb to show that the action of the verb goes on for some time. It may sometimes be thought of as indicating a continuous state: *Chuānghu guānzhe*. 'The window is shut'. *Mén kāi*zhe*. 'The door is open'. *-zhe* often appears with verbs such as *zuò* 'to sit', *zhàn* 'to stand' and *děng* 'to wait' which are often prolonged. In such cases the verb + *zhe* is often translated by a continuous tense in English, 'to be -ing':

Tā zuòzhe. 'He is/was sitting'.

The negative is made by putting *méi* (*yǒu*) in front of the verb with *-zhe*: *Mén méi kāi*zhe*. 'The door isn't/wasn't open (has not remained open)'.

The question form is made by adding *ma* to the statement or by adding *méi yǒu* after it, the implication being that the speaker wishes the state of affairs indicated in his question to continue: *Shōuyīnjī kāi*zhe ma?* 'Is the radio on?' *Lùyīnjī kāi*zhe méi you?* 'Is the record player on?'

* *kāi* 'to open' (of doors, windows); 'to turn on' (of lights, radio, TV and so on).

Note that:

1 An adverbial phrase of manner is often formed with a verb + *zhe* (+ object) which then precedes the main verb: *Tā xiàozhe shuō* (*Lit.* he/laughing/say) 'He says/said with a smile/laugh'. *Tā qízhe zìxíngchē qù gōngyuán wán(r)* (*Lit.* She/riding astride/self-propelling machine/go/park/have fun) 'She's going/gone on her bicycle to the park to enjoy herself'.

In the example from the text, the adverbial phrase of manner with *zhe* and the verb-object phrase which follows it have become a nominal phrase describing the people in tea-houses: *zài cháguǎn lǐ zuòzhe hē chá de yě hěn duō* (*Lit.* At/tea establishment inside/sitting/ drink/tea/ /also/very/many) 'There are also a lot of (old – understood from previous sentence) people who sit in teahouses drinking tea'.

2 The continuation of an action generally implies that the action is also in progress so that *-zhe* is often to be found together with *zhèngzài, zhèng, zài* or *ne* (see 10.3). *Xiàozhǎng lái de shíhou, wǒ zhèng dǎzhe diànhuà ne* (*Lit.* School head/come/when/I/in the middle of/hitting/electric speech/) 'I was on the phone when the headmaster/mistress came'.

3 Verbs with *-zhe* cannot take verb endings or complements of any sort. It would be incorrect to say, for instance, *Wǒ dǎzhe zi dǎ de hěn hǎo.* (Note that *pinyin* convention always shows *zhe* attached to the verb.)

12 ADVERBIAL PHRASES OF TIME ('TIME HOW LONG')

As we saw in 3.8, adverbs of 'time when' precede the verb, but adverbs of 'time how long' follow the verb:

Zhōngguórén yìbān gōngzuò liù tiān 'The Chinese generally work six days'. (Remember that *tiān* does not require a measure word, see 8.5.)

Jīguān gànbù měi tiān gōngzuò qī ge xiǎoshí (hour) 'Cadres in offices work a seven-hour day'. (Note that *měi tiān*, 'time when', precedes the verb.)

Where there is a direct object, the construction is:

1	S	V₁	O,	V₁	'time how long'
	Wǒ	*chàng*	*gēr,*	*chàng*	***liǎng ge xiǎoshí***.
(*Lit.*	I	sing	songs,	sing	two hours.)

'I sing for two hours'.

or

2	S	V	'time how long'	*de*	O
	Wǒ	*chàng*	***liǎng ge zhōngtóu***	*de*	*gēr.*
(*Lit.*	I	sing	two hours (worth of)	songs.)

'I sing for two hours'.

De is sometimes omitted but it is helpful to beginners to think of it as always being there. (*Zhōngtóu* 'hour' is interchangeable with *xiǎoshí*.)

EXERCISE 10.1

Change the following pattern (i) sentences into pattern (ii) sentences:

Tā kàn diànshì, kàn liǎng ge xiǎoshí → Tā kàn liǎng ge xiǎoshí de diànshì.

1 *Tā xī yān, xī shí fēn zhōng.*
2 *Lǎoshī* (teacher) *jiāo shū, jiāo yí ge xiǎoshí.*
3 *Gēge lù yīn, lù bàn ge zhōngtóu.*
4 *Wǒ àiren huà huàr, huà sān kè zhōng.*
5 *Chǎngzhǎng* (head of a factory) *kāi chē, kāi sān ge bàn* (three-and-a-half) *xiǎoshí.*

Change the following pattern (ii) sentences into pattern (i) sentences:

Tāmen xiě yí kè zhōng de zì → Tāmen xiě zì, xiě yí kè zhōng.

6 *Dìdi kàn bàn ge xiǎoshí de shū.*
7 *Lǎorén shuì yí ge bàn* (one-and-a-half) *xiǎoshí de jiào.*
8 *Wǒ yí ge péngyou zǒu qī ge zhōngtóu de lù.*
9 *Nà wèi xiānsheng shuō hěn cháng* (long) *shíjiān de huà le.*
10 *Nǎ wèi xiǎojie néng dǎ jiǔ ge xiǎoshí de zì?*

13 DAYS OF THE WEEK

Xīngqī (*Lit.* 'star period'), the Chinese word for 'week' precedes the numerals 1–6 to give the days of the week from Monday to Saturday. 'Sunday' is not *xīngqīqī*, however, but *xīngqītiān* or *xīngqīrì*. 'What day is it today?' is *Jīntiān xīngqījǐ?* (Note that no verb is necessary.)

xīngqīyī	*Monday*
xīngqī'èr	*Tuesday*
xīngqīsān	*Wednesday*
xīngqīsì	*Thursday*
xīngqīwǔ	*Friday*
xīngqīliù	*Saturday*
xīngqītiān/xīngqīrì	*Sunday*

Other useful vocabulary items are *běn xīngqī* or *zhè ge xīngqī*, 'this week', *shàng (ge) xīngqī*, 'last week' and *xià (ge) xīngqī*, 'next week'. The same system applies to *yuè*, 'month': *běn yuè* or *zhè ge yuè*, 'this month', *shàng (ge) yuè*, 'last month' and *xià (ge) yuè*, 'next month'. An alternative word for 'week' is *lǐbài*. The days of the week work in exactly the same way as for *xīngqī*. For example, 'Wednesday' would be *lǐbàisān* and 'Sunday' would either be *lǐbàitiān* or *lǐbàirì*. *Lǐbài* is often used by overseas Chinese rather than *xīngqī* and has religious connotations. *Zuò lǐbài* (v-o) means 'to go to church'.

EXERCISE 10.2

Fill in the blanks with the appropriate time word or phrase
Jīntiān xīngqījǐ? → *Jīntiān xīngqī'èr.*

1 *Jīntiān xīngqīsān. Míngtiān* _____.

2 *Zuótiān* (yesterday) *xīngqītiān. Jīntiān* _____*? Jīntiān* _____.

3 *Shàng ge yuè wǔyuè. Xià ge yuè jǐ yuè? Xià ge yuè* _____.

4 *Yì nián yǒu jǐ ge yuè? Yì nián yǒu* _____.

5 *Yí ge xīngqī yǒu jǐ tiān? Yí ge xīngqī yǒu* _____.

6 *Jiǔyuè yǒu duōshao tiān? Jiǔyuè yǒu* _____.

7 *Èryuè ne? Èryuè yǒu* _____ *huòzhě* _____.

8 *Yì nián yǒu duōshao tiān? Yì nián yǒu* _____ *huòzhě* _____(*bǎi* hundred).

14 REDUPLICATION OF MEASURE WORDS

Repeating *yi* + measure word after the noun gives the meaning 'one after another', whether it is 'one worker after another', *gōngrén yí ge yí ge...*, 'one sheet of paper after another', *zhǐ yì zhāng yì zhāng...*, or 'one group after another', *yì qún yì qún* (made up of 'men and women, old and young' in the text), etc.

15 POSITION OF CONJUNCTIONS

We have met *suīrán...dànshi...* in 8.12 and *rúguǒ... (de huà) jiù*; *yàoshi...jiù* in 9.4. Two other common pairs are *yīnwèi...suǒyǐ...*, 'because...(so)...'; and *búdàn...érqiě...* 'not only...but also...'. The first one of the pair can occur either at the beginning of the sentence or after the subject. *Jiù*, being a true adverb, immediately precedes the verb and therefore always comes **after** the subject if there is one: *Nǐ yào xiǎng shài tàiyáng, jiù děi gēn chéng qiān shàng wàn de rén yìqǐ shài!* Note that *yàoshi* can be reduced to *yào*. It is sometimes merely a matter of the sentence rhythm or of how it sounds which decides whether *yàoshi* or *yào* is used.

16 GĒN...YÌQǏ

Wǒ gēn nǐ qù means 'I'll go with you' (*Lit.* I/with/you/go). *Wǒ gēn nǐ yìqǐ qù* (*Lit.* I/with/you/together/go) may also be translated as above, but the addition of *yìqǐ* reinforces the idea of togetherness: *Wǒmen yìqǐ qù ba* 'Let's go together'.

17 DÀO...QÙ/LÁI

As a verb, *dào* means 'to go, to arrive (in), to reach'. *Tā dào le* 'he's arrived'. If there is a place-word after *dào*, the simple directional ending *lái* or *qù* is used at the end of the clause to indicate direction towards or away from the speaker (see 5.1).

As a compound directional ending with *qù* or *lái*, *dào* can translate simply as 'to' when used with such verbs as *pǎo*, 'to run', *zǒu*, 'to walk' and *bān*, 'to remove': *Wǒmen xiǎng míngnián* (next year) *bān dào Jiānádà qu* (*Lit.* We/fancy/next year/move to/Canada/go) 'We plan to move to Canada next year'.

...yī xià bān jiù pǎo dào Běihǎi Gōngyuán qù huá. (*Lit.* As soon as/descend/shift/then/run to/Beihai/Park/go/slide).

Chinese togetherness
The Chinese have developed various ways of handling their enforced 'togetherness' and in general they cope with crowd situations a great deal more good-humouredly than their Western counterparts. In spite of the fact that living accommodation is generally cramped, at least in the cities, most Chinese actually find it unthinkable or even undesirable to spend much time on their own and are often surprised by some Westerners' need for privacy.

EXERCISE 10.3
Mark the following sentences with (+) for the correct ones and (−) for the incorrect ones.

1   *Wǒ zhèng dǎ diànhuà, tā jīntiān lái de shíhou.*
2   *Shì ma, nǐ míngtiān qù huá xuě (to ski)?*
3   *Mèimei shuì jiào, shuì sān ge zhōngtóu.*
4   *Dìdi shuì jiào sì ge xiǎoshí.*
5   *Xià bān yǐqián, tā zhèngzài shài tàiyáng ne.*
6   *Zǒnglǐ (premier) xiǎng bāyuèdǐ qù Yàzhōu (Asia).*
7   *Wǒ péngyou zhēn qíguài, yī huí jiā, jiù tā dǎ tàijíquán.*
8   *Diànshì kāizhe méi ma?*
9   *Zǒngtǒng (president) xià ge yuè qù Fēizhōu (Africa), qù èr ge yuè.*
10 *Xiàtiān rúguǒ xià dà yǔ, qù lǚxíng jiù bù hǎo bàn le!*

EXERCISE 10.4
Translate the following passage into colloquial English:
Yǒu rén xiǎng Yīngguó tiānqì bù zěnmeyàng dànshi fǎnguòlái (conversely) yě yǒu yìxiē rén juéde (feel) Yīngguó tiānqì hěn búcuò, bù lěng yě bú rè, dōngtiān yě bù yídìng xià xuě, dànshi yǒu yì diǎn bùdé bù chéngrèn, Yīngguó bùguǎn (no matter) nǐ zài nǎr dōu jīngcháng xià yǔ. Zhōngguó yìbān qíngtiān duō, yīntiān shǎo dànshi Yīngguó xiāngfǎn (opposite), yīntiān dūo, qíngtiān shǎo. Yǒu rén shuō zhè ge gēn Yīngguórén de guài (strange) píqi (temperament) yǒu guānxi, yě yǒu rén shuō zhè ge gēn Yīngguórén kě'ài de píqi yǒu guānxi. Nǎ zhǒng shuōfǎ duì ne? Qǐng nǐ shuōshuo!

EXERCISE 10.5

Translate the following into Chinese:

1   I was in the middle of watching TV when my friend came on Sunday.

2   I'd like to go with you to the Summer Palace for a walk.

3   As soon as she starts (*kāishǐ*) snoring, I leave!

4   The windows were open but the door was closed.

5   There was a lot of activity (use *rènào*) going on in the park – some people were doing taijiquan, others were taking photographs and some people were sunbathing.

6   When the weather's fine, I sit outside and read a book (use *-zhe*).

7   We sing for half an hour every evening and then go to bed.

8   Because she didn't phone at all on Tuesday I don't know (*zhīdao*) whether I'm going or not (use *bìng*).

9   If I'm at my parents' home, I frequently go to the park nearby to play tennis (*wǎngqiú*) (use *dào...qù*).

10 She said with a smile that she was already married.

11 Are you listening to the radio? No, we're listening to a tape (use *lù yīn*).

12 You're going to see a play (*kàn xì*) tomorrow, aren't you? What a pity I can't go with you.

11

In the Restaurant

Zhang Zhanyi is now working in the Western dining-room (*Xī Cāntīng*) at the Beijing Hotel where one lunch-time he encounters Mr King and Miss Shaw.

Zhāng Have you ordered? *Nǐmen cài dìng hǎo le méi you?*

Shǐ *Dìng hǎo le, xièxie nǐ. Píjiǔ lái le – à, bú shi Běijīng píjiǔ ér shi Qīngdǎo píjiǔ.*

Zhāng *Méi guānxi, Qīngdǎo píjiǔ gèng hǎo hē. Nín pǔtōnghuà shuō de zhēn hǎo.*

Shǐ *Guòjiǎng, guòjiǎng, shuō de bù hǎo.*

Zhāng *Shuō de hěn hǎo. Nín shi nǎ guó rén?*

Shǐ *Nǐ cāicai ba.*

Zhāng *Bú shi Měiguórén jiù shi Yīngguórén.*

Shǐ *Wǒ shi Yīngguórén. Nǐ zěnme zhīdao ne?*

Zhāng *Yīnwèi gāngcái nín shi gēn nín péngyou shuō Yīngyǔ! Nín péngyou yě huì shuō Hànyǔ ma?*

Shǐ *Yě huì shuō.*

Wáng *Shuō de méi tā hǎo.*

Zhāng *À, nǐmen liǎ de Hànyǔ zhēn bàng, xué le jǐ nián le?*

Shǐ *Xué le liǎng nián le.*

Zhāng *Nín ne? (Zhǐ de shì Wáng Yǒngshòu).*

Wáng *Xué le sì nián le.*

Zhāng *Nǐmen zài Zhōngguó dāi le hěn cháng shíjiān le ba?*

Wáng *Bù cháng, lái le sān ge duō yuè le.*

Zhāng *Zhè shi nǐmen dì yí cì lái Zhōngguó ma?*

Wáng *Bù, tā shi dì yí cì, wǒ shi dì èr cì.*

Zhāng *Nǐmen zhēn xíng, fāyīn hěn qīngchu, méi shénme yángwèi(r), hěn biāozhǔn de pǔtōnghuà. Xué Zhōngwén bú shi hěn nán xué ma?*

Wáng *Nán shi nán, kěshì yě yǒu tā róngyì de dìfang, bǐfang shuō Zhōngwén fāyīn、yǔfǎ dōu bìng bù nán, nán de shi shēngdiào. Duì wǒmen Xīfāngrén lái shuō, Zhōngwén de sìshēng háishi xiāngdāng kùnnan de.*

Zhāng *Xiě Hànzì ne?*

Shǐ *Xiě Hànzì hěn bù róngyì, yīnwèi wǒmen wàiguórén yìbān shi chéngniánrén cái kāishǐ xué Zhōngwén, bú xiàng nǐmen liù、qī suì jiù kāishǐ le. Dāngrán hái yǒu yì diǎn, Zhōngwén jiùshì nǐmen de mǔyǔ.*

Zhāng *Nà dàoshì. Xiàng nǐmen zhè yàng de shuǐpíng, bàozhǐ kàn de dǒng ma?*

Shǐ *Kàn de dǒng.*

Zhāng *Xiǎoshuō ne?*

Shǐ *Yě xíng, dànshi bú rènshi de zì hái yào chá zìdiǎn. À, cài lái le, zhēn piàoliang a! Kàn qǐlai yídìng hěn hǎo chī.*

Zhāng *Nàme, nǐmen mànmānr chī ba, bú zài dǎrǎo nǐmen le. Yǒu shénme shì, suíshí kěyǐ jiào wǒ.*

Wáng *Hǎo le, xièxie nǐ, yǒu shénme shì yídìng zhǎo nǐ. Gēn nǐ liáo tiān(r) hěn yǒu yìsi.*

* * *

Zhang Have you ordered?

Shi Yes we have, thank you. Here comes the beer – oh, it's Qingdao beer not Beijing beer.

Zhang It doesn't matter, Qingdao beer is even better. You (pol.) speak really good Chinese.

Shi You're too kind, I don't speak it well at all.

Zhang Yes you do. Where are you from?

Shi Have a guess.

Zhang You're either American or British.

Shi I'm British. How did you know?

Zhang Because you (pol.) were speaking English with your friend just now! Can your (pol.) friend also speak Chinese?

Shi   Yes he can.

Wang   I'm not as good as she is.

Zhang   Oh, both of you have got brilliant Chinese. How many years have you been studying it?

Shi   Two years (so far).

Zhang   How about you? (*He is referring to Wang Yongshou.*)

Wang   I've been studying for four.

Zhang   I suppose you've been in China for a very long time?

Wang   No we haven't, we've only been here a little over three months.

Zhang   Is this your first time in China?

Wang   No, it's her first but my second.

Zhang   You're really great! Your pronunciation is very clear with no foreign overtones, it's good standard Chinese. Isn't Chinese awfully hard to learn?

Wang   Yes it is, but there are some easy things about it too – for example, neither Chinese pronunciation nor grammar is at all difficult, what is difficult are the tones. As far as we Westerners are concerned, the four tones in Chinese are still pretty difficult.

Zhang   How about writing Chinese characters?

Shi   Writing Chinese characters is very difficult because we foreigners generally do not start learning Chinese until we are adults, not like you people who start at six or seven. Of course the other thing is that Chinese happens to be your mother tongue.

Zhang   Yes indeed. With Chinese at a level like yours, can you read newspapers?

Shi   Yes.

Zhang   How about novels?

Shi   They're OK too, but we still have to look up characters we don't know in the dictionary. Oh, the food's here, it looks great. It certainly looks appetising.

Zhang   I'll leave you to get on with your meal in peace. Call me if you need anything.

Wang   Fine, thank you. If we need anything we'll certainly ask for you. It's been really interesting chatting with you.

-hǎo (RVE)	*to do the action of the verb satisfactorily*	**róngyì** (adj.)	*easy*
		bǐfang shuō	*for example*
		yǔfǎ (n)	*grammar*
píjiǔ (n)	*beer*	**shēngdiào** (n)	*tone*
bú shi...ér shi...	*not...but...*	**duì X lái shuō**	*as far as X is concerned*
Qīngdǎo (N)	*Qingdao*	**Xīfāngrén** (n)	*Westerner*
gèng (adv.)	*even more, still more*	**sì shēng** (n)	*the four tones*
		háishi (adv.)	*after all, still (emphatic)*
pǔtōnghuà (n)	*common spoken language (Modern Standard Chinese; Mandarin)*	**kùnnan** (adj.; n)	*difficult; difficulty*
		xiě (zì) (v(-o))	*to write (characters)*
guòjiǎng	*you flatter me*	**Hànzì** (n)	*Chinese character(s)*
cāi (v)	*to guess*		
bú shi A jiù shi B	*if it's not A then it's B*	**chéngniánrén** (n)	*an adult*
Měiguórén (n)	*(an) American*	**cái** (adv.)	*not...until...; only*
zěnme (QW)	*how*	**kāishǐ** (v)	*to begin*
zhīdao (v)	*to know*	**diǎn** (n)	*point, aspect*
yīnwèi (conj.)	*because (also read yīnwei)*	**jiùshì**	*(be) precisely*
		mǔyǔ (n)	*mother tongue*
gāngcái (TW)	*just now*	**dào(shì)** (adv.)	*indeed, as it happens (indicates something contrary to the general train of thought)*
Yīngyǔ (n)	*English language*		
bàng (adj.)	*excellent (coll.)*		
zhǐ (v)	*to refer to; to point at/to*		
cháng (adj.)	*long*	**zhè yàng** (dem. adj. +n)	*this kind of, such a*
duō (num.)	*used to express an approximate no.*		
dì	*ordinal prefix*	**shuǐpíng** (n)	*level, standard*
cì (MW)	*time, occasion*	**bào(zhǐ)** (n) [**zhāng** or **fēn**]	*newspaper*
fāyīn (n)	*pronunciation*		
qīngchu (adj.; RVE)	*clear; clearly*		
		-dǒng (RVE; v)	*-ing with understanding; to understand*
yángwèi(r) (n)	*foreign flavour*		
A shi A dànshi...	*it's A all right but...*	**xiǎoshuō** (n) [**běn**]	*novel*

chá (v)	to check	**-qǐlai** (RVE)	see 11.13
zìdiǎn (n)	dictionary	**dǎrǎo** (v)	to disturb
[**běn**]		**shì(qing)** (n)	matter, thing
chá zìdiǎn	to consult a	[**jiàn**]	
(v-o)	dictionary	**yǒu yìsi** (v-o)	to be interesting

Grammar

1 *BÚ SHI...ÉR SHI...*

If we wish to convey the idea that 'it is not A but B' we use the construction *bú shi A ér shi B*, where *shi* is the verb 'to be' and *ér* is a conjunction which has come into modern Chinese from the classical language meaning amongst other things, 'and', 'but':

Bú shi Běijīng píjiǔ ér shi Qīngdǎo píjiǔ.

Bú shi zhūròu ér shi niúròu (*Lit.* Not/be/pig meat/but/be/cattle meat) 'It's not pork but beef'.

2 *BÚ SHI... JIÙ SHI...*

'If it is not A then it is B', *bú shi A jiù shi B*. This construction is easily confused with the one above but by remembering that *jiù* means 'then' you should be able to distinguish them correctly:

Bú shi Měiguórén jiù shi Yīngguórén.

Bú shi niúròu jiù shi yángròu (*Lit.* Not/be/cattle/meat/then/be/ sheep meat) 'If it's not beef then it's mutton'.

Of course *bú shi...jiù shi...* could be translated as 'either...or...' but in doing so it somehow loses its flavour.

3 *ZĚNME* AND *ZĚNMEYÀNG*

Zěnme and *zěnmeyàng* can both be used adverbially before a verb to ask how something is done, although *zěnme* is used much more frequently in this way: *Nǐ zěnme zhīdao ne? Nǐ zěnmeyàng zhīdao?*

Zěnme can also be used to ask the reason why something happens but *zěnmeyàng* cannot be used in this way: *Tā zěnme méi gěi nǐ dǎ diànhuà ne?* (*Lit.* She/why/not (have)/for/you/hit/electric speech/) 'How come she hasn't phoned you?'.

Zěnme feels a little less formal than *wèi shénme*, 'why?', hence its translation as 'how come' in the previous example. Note that question words such as *zěnme*, *zěnmeyàng* and *wèi shénme* often take *ne* at the end of the sentence containing them (see 3.3). Only *zěnmeyàng* can be used after the complement of degree marker *de* (see 4.8) or to ask something about the subject of a sentence:

Tā de pǔtōnghuà zěnmeyàng? 'What's his (spoken) Chinese like?'.

4   MORE ON *LE*

(i)   We know that *le* used at the end of a sentence can indicate a change of state (see 4.6). We also know it can indicate that a certain state of affairs has already taken place (see 7.9):

(a)   *Píjiǔ lái le.*
(b)   *Nǐmen liù ⟍ qī suì jiù kāishǐ le.*
(c)   *Wǒ zuótiān xiě zì le* (*Lit.* I/yesterday/write/characters/) 'I did some writing yesterday'.
(d)   *Tā jīntiān zhōngwǔ zuò huǒchē le* (*Lit.* He/today/noon/sit/fire vehicle/). 'He took the train at noon today'.

In (c) and (d) the object is simple and unmodified. As soon as the object is modified in any way we have to use the verbal suffix *le* (see 3.4) and the sentence *le* is dropped: *Wǒ zuótiān xiě le hěn duō zì* 'I did a lot of writing yesterday'. By doing this, we focus our attention on what has been done rather than on what has simply taken place.

(ii)   If the object is quantified, then the use of the verbal suffix *le* and the sentence-final particle *le* generally indicates the continuation of some action or state of affairs. Of course this also involves 'time how long' (see 10.12) so the construction is as follows:

Wǒ xué Zhōngwén, xué le wǔ nián le.
or
Wǒ xué le wǔ nián (de) Zhōngwén le.

'I have been studying Chinese for five years (and still am)'.

Compare this with:

Wǒ xué le wǔ nián (de) Zhōngwén 'I studied Chinese for five years (and am no longer doing so, i.e. it's over and done with)'.

Another example may help to highlight this difference:

Tā zài Zhōngguó zhù le bàn nián le 'She has been living in China for six months (and still is)'.

Tā zài Zhōngguó zhù le bàn nián 'She lived in China for six months (and is no longer doing so)'.

(iii)   A sentence consisting of a verb + *le* followed by a simple object is regarded as being incomplete, something else is expected to follow. Thus *Wǒ chī le fàn* is not a complete sentence in Chinese and must be followed by another clause:

Wǒ chī le fàn jiù zǒu le 'I left after having eaten'.

Wǒ chī le fàn jiù zǒu 'I'll leave after eating'. (In the second example, *le* shows completed action in the future, further illustrating the point that *le* should not be thought of as a past tense marker.) Where the object is a simple one, the addition of the final particle *le* makes the sentence complete: *Wǒ chī le fàn le* 'I've eaten'.

(iv)   When a past action is a habitual one or there is no need to emphasise its completion, no *le* is used after the verb: *Qùnián tā chángcháng lái* 'He often used to come last year'. *Qùnián xiàtiān tā zài Běijīng Yǔyán Xuéyuàn gōngzuò* 'Last summer he worked at the Beijing Languages Institute'.

5 APPROXIMATE NUMBERS

There are several ways of indicating approximate numbers in Chinese:

(i)   When *duō* is placed after a whole number plus its measure word or after a whole number plus a noun acting as a measure word (*nián, tiān*), it represents a fraction of one unit: *sān ge duō xiǎoshí* 'three and a bit hours, over three hours', *yì tiān duō* 'one and a bit days'.

(ii)   When *duō* is placed after the whole number but before the measure word or noun acting as a measure word, it represents a whole number in itself: *sānshí duō nián* 'over thirty years' (anything from 31 to 39), *yì bǎi duō yè* 'one hundred-odd pages' (could be 110, 125, etc.).

(iii)   *Jǐ* can be used to indicate an indefinite number under ten: *Zhǐ shàng xiězhe jǐ ge Hànzì* 'There were several Chinese characters written on the paper'. *Lǎoshī yǒu shí jǐ běn zìdiǎn* 'The teacher has a dozen or so dictionaries' (any number from 11 to 19). *Xuésheng yǐjīng xué le jǐ bǎi ge shēngcí le* 'The students have already learnt several hundred new words (so far)'.

(iv)   Two consecutive numbers may be put together: *Wǒ zhǐ* (only) *qùguo liǎng、sān cì Měiguó* 'I've only been to the States two or three times'. NB the pause-mark (*dùnhào*), and not a comma, is used between 'two' and 'three'. *Xuéxiào yǒu bā、jiǔshí ge háizi* 'There are eighty or ninety children in the school'. *Nǐmen liù、qī suì jiù kāishǐ le*. If the object is a pronoun, it precedes *yí cì*, etc. *Wǒ kànguo tā yì ⟍ liǎng cì* 'I've seen him/her once or twice'.

(v)   *Zuǒyòu* (*Lit.* left right) may be put after a number to indicate 'around' or 'about': *yì bǎi ge rén zuǒyòu* 'about one hundred people', *liǎng diǎn bàn zuǒyòu* 'around 2.30'.

6   *DÌ* + NUMBER

Ordinal numbers (first, second, third) are made by putting *dì* in front of the number: *dì yī* 'first', *dì'èr* 'second', and *dì sān* 'third'. Thus *dì yí cì* means 'the first time'. In competitions of any sort, the Chinese are encouraged to remember *Yǒuyì dì yī, bǐsài dì èr*, 'Friendship first, competition second'. Make sure you distinguish between *èryuè*, 'February', *dì èr ge yuè*, 'the second month' and *liǎng ge yuè*, 'two months'.

7   *BÚ SHI ... MA?*

Bú shi ... ma? asks a question which expects the answer 'yes'.
   The word order is:
   (Topic +) subject *bú shi* (+ adverb) Verb (+ other elements) *ma?*
   Tā bú shi hěn lèi ma? 'Isn't she very tired?' (Yes, she is.)
   Xué Zhōngwén bú shi hěn nán xué ma? (Yes, it is.)

8   *A SHI A DÀNSHI / KĚSHÌ ...*

'It's A all right but...'. The main clause (A *shi* A) contains a positive or negative statement with some sort of a concession being made after *dànshi/kěshì*: *Guì shi guì, dànshi zhìliàng fēicháng hǎo* 'It's expensive all right, but the quality is excellent'. *Tā hǎo shi hǎo, kěshì píqi hěn huài* 'She is nice, but she's got a terrible temper (*Lit.* temperament very bad). *Nán shi nán, kěshì yě yǒu tā róngyì de dìfang.* 'Yes, it is difficult, but there are some easy things about it too!'

EXERCISE 11.1

Answer these questions using the A *shi* A construction followed by a suitable 'but' clause of your own devising:
1   *Tā de fāyīn bú shi hěn qīngchu ma?*
2   *Wáng xiānsheng de Hànyǔ shuǐpíng gāo ma?*
3   *Zhè běn xiǎoshuō yǒu méi you yìsi?*
4   *Duì wàiguórén lái shuō, Zhōngwén de sìshēng shì bu shi hěn nán?*
5   *Qīngdǎo píjiǔ hǎo hē ma?*

9 *CÁI* AND *JIÙ*

Both *cái* and *jiù* are adverbs indicating something about time. *Cái* indicates that something takes place later or with more difficulty than had been expected. It translates into English as 'not...until...', 'then and only then': *Tā sān diǎn zhōng cái lái* 'He didn't come until 3' (but I had asked him to come at 2.30).

It is a common mistake for students to try and translate the 'not' in English with a *bù* or *méi* in Chinese. Remember that 'not' is already contained in *cái*.

Jiù, on the other hand, indicates that something takes place earlier or more promptly than expected: *Tā sān diǎn zhōng jiù lái le* 'He came at 3/He was there by 3' (but I had asked him to come at 3.30).

Both *cái* and *jiù* must come **immediately before** the verb regardless of what other elements there are in the sentence. *Jiù* usually takes *le*, whereas *cái* does not, perhaps because the verb with *cái* does not convey any real sense of completion. The following examples should help to make the distinction between the two clearer:

(a) *Wǒ qǐng tā shàngwǔ bā diǎn bàn lái dànshi tā bā diǎn jiù lái le* 'I asked him to come at 8.30 am but he was there by 8' (i.e. too early).

(b) *Wǒ qǐng tā shàngwǔ bā diǎn bàn lái dànshi tā jiǔ diǎn bàn cái lái* 'I asked him to come at 8.30 am but he didn't come until 9.30' (i.e. too late).

(a) *Gēn nǐ liáo tiān(r) jiù zhīdao nǐ zhè ge rén hěn yǒu yìsi* 'As soon as I chatted to you I realised what a fascinating person you were'.

(b) *Gēn nǐ liáo tiān(r) cái zhīdao nǐ zhè ge rén hěn yǒu yìsi* 'It was not until I'd had a chat with you that I realised what a fascinating person you were'.

Cái and *jiù* can also be translated as 'only' in sentences such as:

Tā cái sān suì ⎫
Tā jiù sān suì ⎬ 'She's only three years old'.
　　　　　　　　 ⎭

EXERCISE 11.2

Fill in the blanks with the adverbs *jiù* or *cái*.

1 *Wǒ dào le Zhōngguó yǐhòu ＿＿＿ zhīdao Qīngdǎo píjiǔ hěn hǎo hē.*

2 *Wǒ dào Zhōngguó qù yǐqián* ＿＿＿ *zhīdao Qīngdǎo píjiǔ hěn hǎo hē.*

3 *Nà fēng* (MW) *xìn* (letter) *xiě hǎo le méi you? Xiě hǎo le, zuótiān* ＿＿＿ *xiě hǎo le.*

4 *Nà fēng xìn yǐjīng xiě hǎo le ma? Hái méi xiě hǎo ne, míngtiān* ＿＿＿ *xiě.*

5 *Tā kāishǐ xué Hànyǔ yǐhòu* ＿＿＿ *fāxiàn* (discover) *Hànyǔ yǔfǎ bìng bù nán.*

6 *Diànyǐng qī diǎn bàn kāishǐ, tā bā diǎn* ＿＿＿ *lái.*

7 *Qù Měiguó yǐqián* ＿＿＿ *cāi Měiguórén hěn kāilǎng* (open).

8 *Yīnwèi shìqing hěn zhòngyào* (important) *wǒ* ＿＿＿ *dǎrǎo nǐmen.*

10 *JIÙSHÌ*

Jiùshì 'to be precisely (something or somebody)', 'to be nothing else but' is used in the following way:

Question: *Wǒ zhǎo Yuàn lǎoshī. Nǐ rènshi tā ma?* 'I'm looking for Teacher Yuan. Do you know him?'

Answer: *Wǒ jiùshì tā* 'I am he (and no other)'.

11 *ZHÈ ZHǑNG* BUT *ZHÈ YÀNG DE*

Unlike *zhǒng* which is a true measure word and can therefore directly precede its noun, *yàng* acts as a noun with *zhè* and *nà* and must therefore take *de* before any noun which follows it: *zhè zhǒng qíngkuàng* 'this sort of situation' but *zhè yàng de shuǐpíng* 'this kind of level'. *Zhèyàng* and *nàyàng* can operate independently as adverbs to mean 'in this way' or 'in that way' ('like this' or 'like that'). *Zhèyàng zuò bù hǎo* 'It's no good doing it like this'. *Zhèyàng lěng, duì shēntǐ bù hǎo* 'Weather as cold as this is bad for the health'. *Tā xiě de zhèyàng kuài, zhēn méi xiǎng dào* 'I never expected him to write so quickly'.

12 MORE ON RESULTATIVE VERBS

Resultative verbs were first introduced in 5.1, potential resultative verbs in 7.13. In this chapter we meet two more resultative verb endings:

-*hǎo* meaning 'to do the action of the verb satisfactorily' (and therefore also expressing the idea of completion).

-*dǒng* meaning 'to do the action of the verb with understanding'.

-*hǎo* can be found with many different verbs such as *zuò, shuō,*

zhǔnbèi ('to prepare') and *xiě* but *-dǒng* is limited to *tīng* ('to listen')
and *kàn* ('to read'):

   Nǐmen cài dìng hǎo le méi you?
   Bàozhǐ kàn de dǒng ma?

-qīngchu can also act as a resultative verb ending meaning
'to do (the action of the verb) clearly'.

13   MORE ON DIRECTIONAL ENDINGS

We met simple directional endings in 5.1 and compound directional endings in 8.9. Apart from their more literal meaning, a
certain number of directional endings have extended or figurative
meanings: verb + *qǐlai* (*Lit.* 'up': *ná qǐlai* 'to pick up', *zhàn qǐlai* 'to
stand up').

   (i)   'to start to do' the action of the verb (and continue doing it)
or for a state of affairs to start (and continue): *tán qǐlai* 'start to
chat'. *Tiānqì nuǎnhuo qǐlai le* 'The weather's starting to get warm'.

   (ii)   To express a view or convey an impression: *kàn qǐlai* 'from
the look of things'. *Kàn qǐlai yào xià yǔ* 'It looks like rain'. *Tīng qǐlai
hěn yǒu dàolǐ* (*Lit.* Listen up/very/have/reason). 'It sounds very
reasonable'. *Shuō qǐlai róngyì, zuò qǐlai nán* 'It's easier said than
done'.

   (iii)   *Xiǎng qǐlai* is widely used to mean 'to remember', 'to
recall':

   A, wǒ xiǎng qǐlai le, tā xìng Chén 'I've got it, she was called Chen'.

   Another very useful directional ending used in a figurative way is
-xiàqu (*Lit.* '(go) down') which is used to mean 'to carry on' doing
the action of the verb: *zuò xiàqu* 'to carry on doing' (in a different
context it could mean 'to sit down'!). *Tīng xiàqu* 'to carry on
listening'.

EXERCISE 11.3

Fill in the blanks with the most appropriate resultative verb ending
(two brackets indicate a compound directional ending). You may
need to refer back to 5.1, 7.13 and 8.9 to refresh your memory.

1   *Zhè kè kèwén wǒ kàn bu* (   ), *néng bu neng* (be capable of/
   can) *bāngzhù wǒ yíxià?*
2   *Zhuōzi tài dà le, bān bu* (   ) (   ).
3   *Wǒ zài wàimiàn děngzhe nǐ. Qǐng nǐ zǒu* (   ) (   ), *hǎo bu
   hao?*

4 *Liànxí* (exercise) *wǒ hái méi zuò* ( ) *ne, jīntiān shìqing tài duō le.*

5 *Nǐ zěnme bù chī cài ne? Shì bu shi yǐjīng chī* ( ) *le?*

6 *Wǒ tài bèn* (stupid) *le, gēn bu* ( ) *nǐmen liǎng wèi.*

7 *Jīntiān de bàozhǐ méi kàn* ( ), *bù zhīdao zài nǎr.*

8 *Zuìjìn* (recently) *hǎishuǐ* (seawater) *rè* ( ) ( ) *le, míngtiān kěyǐ qù yóuyǒng* (swim).

9 *Nà ge shāfā tài xiǎo le, zuò bu* ( ) *sān ge rén.*

10 *Zhè ge zì xiě* ( ) *yìdiǎnr, yàobùrán wǒ zěnme kàn de* ( )?

11 *Duìxiàng shénme shíhou* (when?) *zhǎo de* ( ) *shì hěn nán shuō de.*

12 *Zhè běn xiǎoshuō suīrán méi yǒu yìsi, dànshi hái yào kàn* ( ) ( ).

Chinese classlessness
One of the delights of Chinese society is that on some levels, (as shown in the text for instance), people appear unaffected by apparent differences in social status, and natural curiosity and real friendliness win the day. In general it is much easier for foreigners, with or without the right 'credentials' or connections (*guānxi*) to meet relatively well-known public figures, particularly those in the arts, than it would be for them in the West. If you are one of those people who 'succeeds' in this direction, beware of a false sense of your own importance – it may be that your Chinese contacts are just being polite! That many famous people seem to remain relatively untouched by their own success is a measure of how civilized, in real terms, the Chinese are.

EXERCISE 11.4
Make up your own sentences using the following constructions:

1 *yī...jiù...*   5 *yuè lái yuè...*
2 *yòu...yòu...*   6 *rúguǒ...jiù...*
3 *bú shi...jiù shi ...*   7 *suīrán...dànshi...*
4 *bú shi...ér shi...*   8 *bú shi...ma?*

EXERCISE 11.5

Translate the following passage into colloquial English:

Zhāng Zhànyī shi ge fúwùyuán. Tā hěn xǐhuan tā de gōngzuò, yīnwèi tā yǒu jīhuì (opportunity) gēn hěn duō bù tóng (not same, different) de rén jiēchù. Bú shi Měiguórén jiù shi Yīngguórén, bú shi Zhōngguórén jiù shi Rìběnrén. Yǒude wàiguórén huì shuō hěn liúlì (fluent) de pǔtōnghuà, dànshi yángwèi(r) hěn zhòng (heavy), fāyīn, yǔfǎ dōu bú dà duì, kěshì hái tīng de dǒng. Yǒude wàiguórén yī shuō qǐ Hànyǔ lai jiù hěn hǎoxiào (funny), yīnwèi méi yǒu shénme shēngdiào. Yě yǒu yìxiē wàiguórén Hànyǔ shuǐpíng hěn gāo, zài Zhōngguó dāi le hěn cháng shíjiān le, Zhōngwén bàozhǐ, xiǎoshuō dōu kàn de dǒng, Hànzì yě huì xiě yìxiē. Chéngniánrén xué qǐ Hànyǔ lai bìng bù róngyì, zhíde (be worth) pèifú (admire) tāmen. Yǒude rén lián (even) tāmen zìjǐ de mǔyǔ yě shuō bu hǎo, gèng bú bì (not have to) shuō yì mén (MW) wàiyǔ le!

NB. *lián...yě...* go together in the same way as *rúguǒ...jiù...* (see 9.4).

EXERCISE 11.6

Translate the following into Chinese:

1 I guess that if she's not American, she must be English.
2 His tones are really excellent but his pronunciation is hopeless.
3 I've already been to (1)/China(3)/six times(2)/but (I) *still* can't understand what people are saying.
4 As far as my best friend is concerned, writing is even more interesting than reading.
5 His hair (*tóufa*) is really long. How come he hasn't got it cut (*jiǎn*) yet?
6 She mastered (use *xué hǎo*) modern standard Chinese after only two years.
7 He's been learning Chinese for three years so his standard is pretty good now.
8 I didn't know until yesterday that he does not know how to use a Chinese dictionary.
9 Everyone likes talking to interesting people but there aren't many of them around (use *zhè yàng*).
10 I'll only disturb you if it's something important (*zhòngyào*).

11 I liked him very much after only talking with him once or twice.

12 He is terribly lazy (*lǎn*). It took him until today to read one page.

The Guanxi network

Who knows whom in China is very important when the wheels of bureaucracy need a certain amount of oiling and certain goods and services are in short supply. Your personal relations network is known as your *guānxihù* 关系户 (*Lit.* relationship household) and some people seem to have very extensive ones. Your *guānxihù* will be made up of many of those *tóng* relationships explained in Chapter 21, as well as your relatives and other people you have met along life's path. Many educated young people from urban areas who were sent to the countryside during the Cultural Revolution established quite sizeable *guānxihù* during that time which still stand them in good stead. If for instance a friend, colleague or *lǎo tóngxué* (old classmate) gives you an introduction (whether personally or by phone or letter) to one of his/her *guānxi* it is quite usual to present your new '*guānxi*' with a suitable present of some sort, a carton of foreign cigarettes *yì tiáo wàiguó yān* used to be quite acceptable. It would, of course, be wonderful not to have to have recourse to the *guānxihù* system to buy air or rail tickets or other goods and services (this is a small part of what the students were protesting about in 1989) but in a country so densely populated as China, it is well nigh impossible *not* to use the *guānxihù* system on occasions.

12

Grammar Review

As this chapter is for reference, characters have been included where they may be helpful.

Common measure words

Pinyin	Character	Classification	Examples
bǎ	把	Objects with a handle, chairs	knife, umbrella, toothbrush; chair
bāo	包	packet (e.g. 20)	cigarettes
bēi	杯	cup	tea, coffee
běn	本	volume	books, magazines
bù	部		film
dǐng	顶		hats
fèn	份		newspaper
fēng	封		letter
fù	副		sunglasses
gè	个	used if you have forgotten the correct one!	man
jià or tái	架、台	machines	television, radio, computer
jiān	间		room
jiàn	件	piece, article	clothes, luggage
jù	句	phrase	remarks
juǎn	卷	reel, spool	toilet paper, camera film

Pinyin	*Character*	*Classification*	*Examples*
kē	棵		tree
kè	课		text, lesson
kǒu	口	family members	
kuài	块	piece	soap, land
liàng	辆	wheeled vehicles	car, bicycle
píng	瓶	bottles	
qún	群	crowd, group, flock	sheep, bees
shǒu	首		poem
tào	套	set	suite of furniture, set of stamps
tiáo	条	long and winding; carton (e.g. 200)	towel, fish, street, river; cigarettes
wèi	位	person (polite)	teacher, Mrs
zhāng	张	flat, rectangular objects	map, bed, table
zhī	枝、支	long and thin objects	pencil, cigarette (one)
zhī	只	animals, one of paired body parts	butterfly, cat, hand, leg
zuò	座	large, solid thing?	mountain, bridge, building

Denominations of money and time used like measure words

Pinyin	*Character*	*Meaning*
fēn	分	1/10 of a máo
máo	毛	1/10 of a kuài
kuài	块	basic unit of Chinese currency
fēn	分	minute
kè	刻	quarter
tiān	天	day
nián	年	year

Time words and expressions

Time words have two functions:

(a) As adverbs, they stand before a verb or another adverb to form a time background for the verb: *Wǒ jīntiān bú qù* 'I'm not going today'. *Shàng ge xīngqī tā méi qù gōngzuò* 'She didn't go to work last week'.

(b) As nouns, they may function as the subject or object of a verb or modify another noun (with *de* 的): *Jīntiān shì xīngqīsì* 'Today is Thursday'. *Zuótiān de bào, nǐ kàn le mei you?* 'Did you see yesterday's paper?'.

(a) Time words and phrases such as:

cóngqián formerly	*zuótiān wǎnshang*	yesterday evening
jīntiān today	*tiāntiān zhōngwǔ*	every day at noon
yè lǐ in the night	*qīyuè sì hào dì èr tiān*	July 4th the
nà tiān that day	second or next day	
zhè jǐ ge yuè these last few months	*měi (ge) xīngqītiān*	every Sunday

(b) Time clauses such as:
xiǎo de shíhou 'when one is young'.
xuéxí Zhōngwén de shíhou 'when one is learning Chinese'.
cóng xīngqīyī dào xīngqīwǔ 'from Monday till Friday'.

(c) Lapse of time **before** negated verbs
Wǒ sān tiān méi chī dōngxi 'I didn't eat a thing for three days'.
Sān tiān bù chī fàn bù xíng 'It won't do not to eat for three days'.
Wǒ hěn jiǔ méi yǒu hē jiǔ le 'I haven't touched alcohol for ages'.
Wǒ nà sì nián méi kànjiàn tāmen 'I didn't see them during those four years'.

3 TYPES OF 'TIME DURING WHICH' EXPRESSIONS (STANDING AFTER THE VERB)

(a) Num + MW + (*de* 的) and Num + MW + Noun + (*de* 的) such as: *liù tiān* 'six days', *liǎng ge xīngqī* 'two weeks', *shí nián de Zhōngwén* 'ten years of Chinese', *yí ge bàn yuè de Rìwén* 'a month and a half of Japanese'.

(b) Indefinite quantities of time

(*i*) *Tāmen zǒu le hěn jiǔ le* 'They've been gone for a long time'.

(*ii*) *Wǒ zhǔnbèi kèwén, zhǔnbèi hěn jiǔ le* 'I spent a lot of time on preparing the text'.

NB in (b) (*i*) two *le*s – action still going on; in (*ii*) one *le* – action happened in the past.

Resultative verbs (an introduction)

A resultative verb consists of a stem (an action verb) with a complement expressing the result of the action of the stem, e.g. *Tā kàn cuò le zhè ge zì* 'S/he read this character wrongly', *Nǐ de huà, wǒ tīng qīngchu le* 'I heard clearly what you said'. As can be seen from this, the ending or complement may be followed directly by an object.

A resultative ending is regularly followed by the perfective suffix *-le* 了 and is negated by *méi* (*you*) 没(有), e.g. *Nǐ de huà wǒ méi tīng qīngchu* 'I didn't hear clearly what you said'. If the result has not yet been achieved then of course the sentence is negated by *bù* 不: *Zhōngwén xiǎoshuō wo hái bù néng kàn dǒng* 'I can't read Chinese novels (i.e. novels written in Chinese) yet'.

When the sentence refers to future time or is in the imperative form, the suffix *-le* 了 is not normally used: *Wǒmen yídìng yào xué hǎo Zhōngwén* 'We certainly must/want to master Chinese', *Niàn shú kèwén* 'Read the text aloud until you're familiar with it'. Apart from common resultative endings such as *-hǎo* 好 and *-wán* 完 there are also directional endings which can function as resultative endings: *Yào kàn zhè bù diànyǐng de rén fēicháng duō, wǒ hái méi kàn shàng ne* 'Masses of people want to see this film, I (still) haven't managed to see it (yet)'. *Nǐ mǎi dào zhè běn shū méi you?* 'Did you manage to buy this book'?.

Table of resultative verb endings: common functional endings

Ending		Type of result	Used with (examples)	Limitations
wán	完	completion	*zuò* 作、做、 *shuō* 说、*xiě* 写、 *kàn* 看	
hǎo	好	satisfaction, completion	as above + bàn 办，*zhǔnbèi* 准 备	
huì	会	learning mastery	*xué* 学	
zháo	着	attainment	*zhǎo* 找、*mǎi* 买、*shuì* 睡	
liǎo	了	possibility	*zuò* 作、*ná* 拿、 *chī* 吃、*mǎi* 买、 *mài* 卖	potential form only actual form: -le 了
cuò	错	error	*shuō* 说、*xiě* 写、 *zuò* 作、*tīng* 听	
dào	到	arrival, attainment	*xiǎng* 想、*bān* 搬、*sòng* 送、 *pǎo* 跑、*zǒu* 走、 *xué* 学、*tán* 谈	
qǐ	起	(i) afford to (ii) respect for, self-respect	*mǎi* 买、*chī* 吃, *zhù* 住、*duì* 对	potential only potential only
bǎo	饱	satisfaction of appetite	*chī* 吃	
dǒng	懂	understanding, comprehension	*tīng* 听、*kàn* 看	

Ending	Type of result	Used with (examples)	Limitations
jiàn 见	perception (sensory)	*kàn* 看、*tīng* 听	
kāi 开	separation, leaving room for	*kāi* 开、*lí* 离、*zǒu* 走	
dòng 动	movement	*ná* 拿、*bān* 搬	potential only
gānjìng 干净	cleanness	*xǐ* 洗	

NB: The example verbs listed under 'used with' are far from an exhaustive list. Some endings such as -*bǎo* 饱, -*dǒng* 懂 and -*jiàn* 见 are limited by their essential meaning.

Directional endings or complements

Both intransitive action verbs of motion and transitive action verbs indicating the handling of objects commonly take directional endings or complements: *Tāmen cóng wàibian zǒu jìnlai le* 'They walked in from outside', *Wǒ jīntiān ná lai le hěn duō zhàopiàn* 'I've brought a lot of photos today'.

Directional endings are either: (1) simple or (2) compound. In (2) the second element is either *lái* 来 or *qù* 去. Only a small group of simple directional endings form compound directional endings with *lái* 来 or *qù* 去 as the second element. These are *shàng* 上、*xià* 下、*jìn* 进、*chū* 出、*qǐ* 起、*huí* 回、*guò* 过 and *kāi* 开.

If the object is a **place word** it must come **before** *lái* 来 or *qù* 去. If not it may either come before *lái* 来 or *qù* 去 or it may come after the verb + simple or compound ending:

Wǒ yào qù túshūguǎn **ná** *wǒ de bàozhǐ* **lai** 'I want to/must go to the library to fetch my newspaper'.

Tā cóng zhuōzi shang **ná qǐ** *tā de bào* **lai***, zuò* **xiàlai** *kàn* 'S/he picked up his/her newspaper from (on) the table and sat down and/to read it'. *Tā cóng zhuōzi shang* **ná qǐlai** *tā de bào.* 'She picked up his/her newspaper from (on) the table.' Other directional endings are *dǎo* 倒、*zǒu* 走 and *diào* 掉, but these and other similar directional endings cannot form compound endings with *lái* 来 or *qù* 去.

Auxiliary verbs

What is an auxiliary or modal verb? An auxiliary verb is a member of a limited class of verbs which occur before action verbs or verbal expressions, adding a semantic value of modality ('can, will, must') to the expression as a whole. They cannot take verbal complements or verbal suffixes, and are not used as modifiers before nominals. They usually express the modality of action verbs.

(a)   **Auxiliary verbs expressing capability,** e.g. *néng* 能, *huì* 会, *kěyǐ* 可以.

(i)   *Néng lái, jiù qǐng lái,* 'Please come if you can'.

(ii)   *Tā huì shuō Hànyǔ* 'S/he can speak Chinese'.

(iii)   *Nà ge gōngchǎng kěyǐ zhìzào hěn duō dà jīqì* 'That factory can produce a lot of heavy machinery'.

Huì 会 usually expresses an acquired capability, although *néng* 能 and *kěyǐ* 可以 can have a similar meaning.

(i)   *Nǐ huì huá xuě, wǒ bú huì* 'You know how to ski, but I don't'.

(ii)   *Tā néng kàn Zhōngwén xiǎoshuō* 'S/he is able to read Chinese novels'.

(b)   **Expressing permission or prohibition,** e.g. *néng* 能 and *kěyǐ* 可以.

(i)   *Zhèr kěyǐ* (or *néng*) *xī yān* 'Smoking is permitted here'. NB when *néng* 能 and *kěyǐ* 可以 express capability, the negated verb can only be *bù néng* 不能. When expressing prohibition, both *bù néng* 不能 and *bù kěyǐ* 不可以 can be used.

(c)   **Expressing possibility,** e.g. *huì* 会 (usually in relation to some future occurrence).

(i)   *Bú huì xià yǔ, nǐ qù ba* 'Off you go, it can't (possibly) rain/ won't rain'.

(ii)   *Tā huì lái bāngzhù nǐ* 'S/he may come to help you'.

(iii)   *Wǒ xiǎng zhènme jiǎngjiù de lǚguǎn bú huì tài piányi (de)* (*Lit.* I think such an elegant hotel can't be too inexpensive/I shouldn't think such an elegant hotel can be very cheap).

(d)   *Yào* 要 has three meanings as an auxiliary verb:

1 Expressing will, wish or 'wanting to'.
2 Expressing necessity 'must'.
3 Expressing the future likelihood of something happening.

Wǒ yào qù túshūguǎn 'I want to go to the library'. This sentence could also mean 'I'll be going to the library' or even 'I must go to the library'. Such ambiguities are removed if the sentence is negated. The negative counterpart of (1) is *bù xiǎng* 不想 and of (2) *bú yòng* 不用. *Yào* 要 is also used with '*le* 了' to indicate (3), e.g. *yào xià yǔ le* 'It's going to rain'. *Bú yào (bié)* 不要〔别〕is used for negative imperatives, e.g. *Nǐ bú yào/bié lái!* 'Don't (you) come!' and not 'You don't want to come'.

(e) **Expressing desire, inclination or preference**, e.g. *xiǎng* 想 or *xǐhuan* 喜欢.

(i) *Wǒ bù xiǎng qù kàn tā, wǒ xiǎng zài jiā lǐ kàn diànshì* 'I don't fancy going to see him, I fancy staying at home and watching TV' Note the overlap with *yào* 要 (1) in the negative.

(ii) *Háizi xǐhuan wánr* 'Children like to play'.

NB both these verbs can function as transitive verbs (as can *yào* 要).

(f) **Expressing willingness**, e.g. *yuànyì* 愿意 and *kěn* 肯.

(i) *Tā yuànyì cānjiā pīngpāngqiú bǐsài.* 'S/he's willing to/wishes to take part in the table-tennis competition'.

(ii) *Tā bú shi bù néng lái, ér shi bù kěn lái* 'It isn't that s/he can't come, but that s/he's unwilling to'.

(g) **Expressing 'ought to', 'should'**, e.g. *yīnggāi* 应该, *gāi* 该, *yīngdāng* 应当.

(i) *Nǐ bù yīnggāi nàme shuō* 'You shouldn't talk like that'.

(ii) *Wǒ xiànzài gāi zǒu le* 'I ought to go now'.

(h) **Expressing necessity** (other than *yào* 要), e.g. *děi* 得, *bìděi* 必得, *bìxū* 必须.

(i) *Wǒ děi zǒu le* 'I must go'.

(ii) *Wǒ jīntiān bìděi kàn wán nà běn shū* 'I must finish reading that book today'.

Their negative counterparts are *bú yòng* 不用, *bú bì* 不必 and *bù xūyào* 不需要.

(i) **Other modal verbs**, e.g. *gǎn* 敢 'to dare to', *pà* 怕 'to be afraid of' (*pà* 怕 can take a noun as its object), *hǎo yìsi* 好意思 'have the nerve to'.

(i) *Wǒ bù gǎn gēn tā shuō huà* 'I don't dare talk to him'.

(ii) *Zhè ge háizi hěn pà jiàn shēngrén* 'This child is very much afraid of meeting strangers'. NB some grammarians maintain that *pà* 怕 is not a real auxiliary verb because it can take *hěn* 很, *gèng* 更, etc.

(iii) *Zuò le zhè zhǒng shì, kuī tā hái hǎo yìsi shuō ne!* 'Fancy his doing that sort of thing and then having the nerve to talk about it!'

Remember that auxiliary verbs:

cannot take aspect markers, e.g. *le* 了, *-guo* 过, *-zhe* 着;

cannot be modified by intensifiers such as *hěn* 很, *gèng* 更;

cannot be nominalised;

cannot occur before the subject;

cannot take a direct object.

Auxiliary verbs *must* co-occur with a verb (or an 'understood' verb).

Table of common pairs of conjunctions

búdàn...érqiě (or yě/hái)... 不但　　而且（or 也/还）…	not only...but also
rúguǒ (de huà)...jiù... 如果（的话）　　就 *yàoshi...jiù...* 要是　　就	if...then
yào bù...jiù 要不　　就	if not...then
yào bú shì...jiù... 要不是　　就	if not that...then
jiǎrú...yě... 假如　也 *jiǎshǐ...yě...* 假使　也	supposing, in the event that...still
jíshǐ...yě (hái)... 即使　也（还） *jiùshì...yě (hái)...* 就是　也（还）	even if...still

jìrán...jiù... 既然　就	since...then
bùguǎn ... 不管 *búlùn*　...*yě (hái)...* 不论　　也（还） *wúlùn* ... 无论	no matter whether...still
suīrán...dànshi/kěshì... 虽然　但是/可是	although...but
yīnwèi...suǒyǐ... 因为　所以	because...therefore
yóuyú...(jiù) 由于　就	because, owing to, due to ...then
chúfēi...cái... 除非　才	unless...
zhǐyào...yě/jiù... 只要　也/就	if only, as long as...then
zhǐyǒu...cái 只有　才	only if...then
búshi...érshi... 不是　而是	it's not...but
búshi...jiùshi... 不是　就是	if it's not...then it's
fánshì...dōu... 凡是　都	all...
chúle...yǐwài... 除了　以外	besides...
lián...yě/dōu... 连　也/都	even...
fēi + verb...bùkě 非 + *verb*　不可	must (do the action of the verb)

Adverbs as conjunctions

(i)   Same element occurring in first and second clauses:

yòu...	*yòu...*	both...and
又	又	
yě...	*yě...*	not only...but also
也	也	
yuè...	*yuè...*	the more...the more...
越	越	
(yù)...	*(yù)...*	(more formal than *yuè*)
愈	愈	
yìbiān + V₁,*yìbiān* + V₂		doing V₁ at the same time as V₂
一边 + V₁, 一边 + V₂		

(ii)   Different element in second clause:

yī V₁,	*jiù* V₂	as soon as V₁ happens, then V₂ begins.
一 V₁,	就 V₂	

13

An Introduction to Chinese Characters

What are Chinese characters? These are the symbols used to write Chinese which you will have seen written over Chinese restaurants or takeaways. What on earth have they to do with 'China Garden' or 'Jade Cottage' you may well have asked yourself. Well, here's your chance to find out!

Written Chinese is understood by more people in the world than any other language and its earliest written records date back over 3500 years. These were the markings scratched onto tortoise shells and animal bones which were used to predict future events. These 'oracle bones' were used in divination rites during the Shang dynasty (c. 1500 BC). Even at that time, the Chinese had already developed quite a sophisticated language with an extensive vocabulary. From these ancient writings we can see that many of the earliest characters were pictures or *pictographs*. Below are a few examples showing the evolution of such characters into their modern day form. You should move from left to right, the character now in use being the one on the extreme right!

☉	⊖	⊟	日	*rì*	sun
☽	𝔻	𝖰	月	*yuè*	moon
🖑	𝒦	儿	人	*rén*	person
米	米	米	木	*mù*	tree

Abstract concepts could also be represented by symbols:

⌣ ⊥ Ž 上 *shàng* up

⌢ T Ƀ 下 *xià* down

As time went on and people needed to express more complex ideas or concepts, pictographs were extended or combined to form *ideographs*. A sun and a moon together mean 'bright', a woman under a roof means 'peace', a woman with a child beside her means 'good', a sun rising behind a tree means 'east'. A tree doubled forms the character for 'forest' and if tripled it means a 'dense forest'.

日	sun	+ 月	moon	= 明	bright
女	woman	+ 宀	roof	= 安	peace
女		+ 子	child	= 好	good
日		+ 木	tree	= 东	east
木		+ 木		= 林	forest
林		+ 木		= 森	dense forest

(Extensions of meaning were sometimes inherent in the character itself and required no further addition, thus 日 'sun' also means 'day', 月 'moon' also means 'month'.)

What a wonderful way of creating language this was, but of course only a limited number of ideas could be expressed in this way. Characters of this type which do not possess a phonetic element are relatively few and account for maybe 10% of all Chinese characters but many of them are still in common use today.

Most characters contain a phonetic element. Such characters are known as *phonograms* or *radical-phonetic* characters. They are made up of two components, one called the *radical* (the Chinese call these 'significs' or 'common heads') which indicates the classification of the character and the other the *phonetic*, which should give a clue to its pronunciation. Thus 青 *qīng* 'blue', 'green', 'black' is a character in its own right but it is the phonetic for such characters as 情 *qíng* 'emotion', 'feelings', 清 *qīng* 'pure', 'clear' and 请 *qǐng* 'ask', 'request' whereas the radical for these is heart 忄, 'water' 氵 and 'speech' 讠 (言), respectively.

青		=	blue, green, black
忄 heart	+ 青	= 情	emotion, feelings
氵 water	+ 青	= 清	pure, clear
讠 speech	+ 青	= 请	ask, request

Before you get too carried away with the neatness of this one, I should say that as a result of the gradual development of the language and the many changes that have occurred in pronunciation, many phonetics now only indicate the approximate sound: 工 *gōng* 'work' becomes 空 *kōng* 'empty' (穴 is a cave), silk + *gōng* becomes *hóng* 红 'red' and insect + *gōng* also becomes *hóng* 虹 'rainbow'.

工		=	gōng
穴 cave	+ 工	= 空	kōng
纟 silk	+ 工	= 红	hóng
虫 insect	+ 工	= 虹	hóng

Others are of even less assistance, but learning to recognise phonetics and radicals is of great help in learning characters. Fortunately there are not too many radicals to be learnt. Older dictionaries list 214, modern ones have reduced this to 189. If the forms in combination and/or full characters are listed separately, this can increase the number to around 250. A good many of these are very little used so I have listed 80 or so of the more common ones overleaf in the hope that they will serve as a useful reference point in your recognition and learning of characters.

Now look at the first column of the radical table which shows what each radical looks like on its own (not all of them appear as characters in their own right in modern Chinese). The second column shows what they look like when they are combined with a phonetic if there is any change (otherwise this column is left blank). The third gives the romanisation and the last column the meaning.

Radicals/significs

In isolation	In combination	Romanisation	Meaning
人	人 亻	*rén*	person
刀	刀 刂	*dāo*	knife
口	口	*kǒu*	mouth
土	土 土	*tǔ*	earth
女	女	*nǚ*	woman
宀		–	roof
山	山 山	*shān*	mountain
心	心 忄	*xīn*	heart
手	手 扌	*shǒu*	hand
日		*rì*	sun
木		*mù*	tree
水	水 氵	*shuǐ*	water
火	火 灬	*huǒ*	fire
疒		–	disease/sickness
目		*mù*	eye
禾		*hé*	grain
竹	⺮	*zhú*	bamboo
纟（糹/糸）		*sī*	silk
肉	月*	*ròu*	flesh
月	*	*yuè*	moon
艹（草）	艹 艹	*cǎo*	grass
言	讠	*yán*	speech
车（車）	车	*chē*	cart/carriage
辶		–	walking
金	钅	*jīn*	metal (gold)
食	饣	*shí*	food
马（馬）		*mǎ*	horse
鱼（魚）		*yú*	fish
鸟（鳥）		*niǎo*	bird (long-tailed)

* Characters with the 'moon' and 'flesh' radical are no longer differentiated and appear under the same 'radical' viz. 月.

In isolation	In combination	Romanisation	Meaning
亠		–	above
冰	冫	*bīng*	ice
厂		–	cliff
八	八, ˅	*bā*	eight
儿		*ér*	child, son
又		*yòu*	also, again
力		*lì*	strength
囗		–	an enclosure
大		*dà*	big, noble
子	子, 孑	*zǐ*	child, son
寸		*cùn*	inch
尸		*shì*	corpse
巾		*jīn*	napkin, towel, handkerchief
广		–	covering, roof
彳		*chì*	to step (with left foot)
攵		–	to tap, rap
阝 on left		–	abundant, mound
邑 on right	阝	*yì*	region
门 (門)		*mén*	door
小	小, ˅	*xiǎo*	small
犬	犬, 犭	*quǎn*	dog
示	礻	*shì*	an omen; express
玉		*yù*	jade
戈		*gē*	spear, lance
贝 (貝)		*bèi*	shell/object of value
丶		*diǎn*	dot
一		*héng*	horizontal
丨		*shù*	vertical

In isolation	In combination	Romanisation	Meaning
见（見）		jiàn	to see
爪	爫	zhuǎ	claw
穴		xué	cave, hole
立		lì	to stand
衣	衣 衤	yī	clothing
石		shí	stone, mineral
田		tián	field
矢		shǐ	arrow
羊	羊, 𦍌, 羊	yáng	sheep
米		mǐ	rice
耳		ěr	ear
页（頁）		yè	page/leaf
虫		chóng	insect
舟		zhōu	boat
走		zǒu	walk/travel
酉		yǒu	(i) 10th of Twelve Earthly Branches (ii) spirit made from ripe millet
足	𧾷	zú	foot/enough, satisfied
身	身	shēn	body
角 角		jiǎo	horn, angle
青		qīng	blue/green/black
雨	雨	yǔ	rain
佳		zhuī	short-tailed bird
革		gé	hide/leather/remove
骨/骨		gǔ	bone
黑		hēi	black/dark
羽（羽）		yǔ	feather/wing

Many of these radicals were originally pictographs but some of them have been simplified so much that the original picture has almost been lost. Any radicals which appear in brackets in the first column are so-called 'full' characters, which are still in use in Hong Kong, Taiwan, Singapore and other overseas Chinese communities. The Chinese, needless to say, have their own way of describing individual characters (and radicals) as you will see in Chapter 16 where Mr King explains to the box-office clerk how his name is written. If you really 'get into' characters you will go into this aspect in greater depth. For the moment, if we say that the water radical (氵) is described as being *sān diǎn shuǐ* 'three drops water', that characters with the speech radical (讠) on the left-hand side are described as having *yán zì páng(r)* 'yan character side', (i.e. the character *yán* at the side) and that characters with grass *cǎo* (⺿) on top are described as *cǎo zì tóu,* having 'a grass character head', you will have some idea of how this works.

Since the founding of the People's Republic of China in 1949, the Chinese have simplified a number of their characters (well over 2000) in an attempt to improve the literacy of the ordinary population. Until then, characters had remained essentially unchanged for about 2000 years. There is now a permanent committee responsible for the reform of Chinese characters. The majority of books, magazines and newspapers printed in the People's Republic are now written in simplified characters, as is this book. The main principles used in simplification are: (a) changing one part of a character, (b) striking out one or two parts of a character (c) substituting a 'simple' character for a difficult one and (d) reconstructing the whole character. The following examples are divided into these four categories. When you have done some more work on characters come back and see if you can work out what has happened in each case!

(a) Changing one part of a character

1	劉	刘	*liú*
2	禮	礼	*lǐ*
3	難	难	*nán*
4	環	环	*huán*
5	漢	汉	*hàn*

(b) Striking out one or two parts of a character

6	務	务	*wù*
7	處 (虙)	处	*chù*
8	開	开	*kāi*
9	標	标	*biāo*
10	醫	医	*yī*
11	習	习	*xí*
12	滅	灭	*miè*

13	號	号	*hào*
14	麗	丽	*lì*
15	婦	妇	*fù*
16	鄉	乡	*xiāng*
17	豐	丰	*fēng*
18	蟲	虫	*chóng*

(c) Substituting a 'simple' character for a 'difficult' one

19	鬱	郁	*yù*
20	穀	谷	*gǔ*
21	醜	丑	*chǒu*

(d) Reconstructing the whole character

22	頭	头	*tóu*
23	靈	灵	*líng*
24	龜	龟	*guī*
25	體	体	*tǐ*

How do the Chinese learn to write characters?

Official figures put illiteracy in China at 20–25%, but in reality it is likely to be much higher. Literacy in the towns is far higher than in the countryside for obvious reasons. With the introduction of the 'responsibility system' *zérènzhì* there is less incentive for rural children to study. How do Chinese children master such a complicated system of writing anyway? The answer is that they start at a very early age and spend a lot of time on it, both at home and in school, far more than we have to do in learning how to write English. At this point I shall introduce you to one or two learning aids which are widely used in China and may serve as an inspiration to you in your learning of characters. There are numerous little books entitled 看图识字, *kàn tú shí zì* 'Look at the picture and recognise the character' or 你认识吗? *Nǐ rènshi ma?* 'Do you know (it)? (i.e. the character)' which contain drawings of everyday objects, parts of the body, fruit, vegetables, different types of weather, common actions like singing, washing – you name it and it's there somewhere. The drawings below are extracts from one such little book.

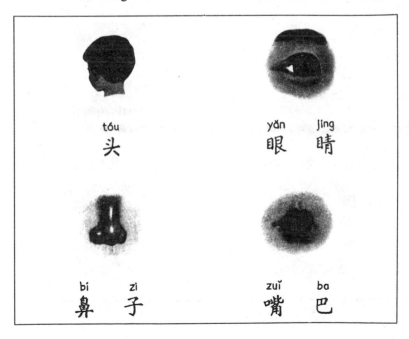

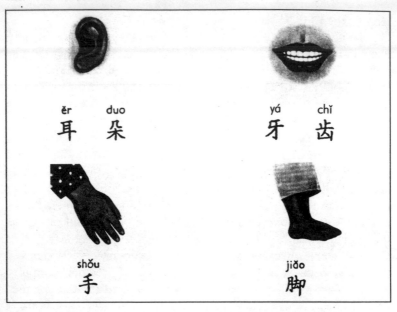

ěr   duo
耳   朵

yá   chǐ
牙   齿

shǒu
手

jiǎo
脚

guō
锅

wǎn
碗

hú
壶

pán
盘

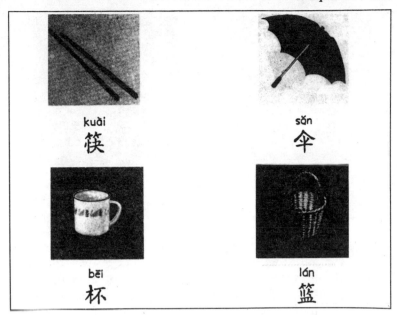

kuài

筷

sǎn

伞

bēi

杯

lán

篮

Another system is to have a small card with a drawing of the object on one side and the *pinyin* and characters for it on the other. You will see Chinese children from the age of three upwards shuffling these cards around. As most Chinese couples are only allowed one child, they usually encourage him/her to start learning to read and write as early as possible.

huǒ chē

火车

máo jīn

毛巾

Literal meanings: 'fire vehicle' (train) and 'hair cloth' (towel)

fēi jī

飞机

chàng gē

唱歌

Literal meanings: 'fly machine' (aeroplane) and 'sing song' (to sing)

You can make your own 'flash cards' as you work your way through the book from Chapter 14 onwards and you may decide to go back and make them for Chapters 1–11 also as these contain a lot of basic vocabulary. The characters for all the vocabulary items in the texts appear in the *Pinyin*-Chinese characters – English Vocabulary at the back of the book. Your flash cards will normally consist of the character or characters on one side and the *pinyin* and the English on the other. Work through them looking at the character side first, seeing how many of the characters you recognise. Check your answers with the *pinyin* and English on the back. Put the ones you get right on one side and then work your way through the ones you got wrong, again putting to one side the ones you get right this time. Carry on until you have mastered them all.

As your vocabulary (and pile of flash cards) increase, you may have to put the ones you are unfamiliar with the first time through on one side and tackle them again on another occasion. This exercise should be repeated constantly! Make your cards a handy size for taking around with you on buses, trains and the underground. Having worked through your flash cards 'recognising' the characters, do it the other way around. Look at the *pinyin* and English side and try writing out the Chinese character for it. This is much more difficult. Check your answer with the character on the other side. Adopt the same system as before, discarding the ones you get right and 'keeping' the ones you get wrong.

By deciding to learn Chinese you have made a decision that you will never be able to complain that you have nothing to do!

Chinese children also trace the characters in copybooks which may or may not contain material which we would regard as propaganda. Below is the first page from a copybook printed in 1970 (Cultural Revolution time) which contains Mao's famous speech on 'Serve the People' *Wèi Rénmín Fúwù* delivered by him at a memorial meeting for Zhang Side on 8 September 1944. When you have worked through a few of the chapters in characters come back and see if you can spot the date.

This extract illustrates the point that each individual Chinese character occupies the same amount of space, i.e. a square of the same proportions, whether it be in the mind or actually indicated as here (so as to help children keep their characters all the same size). Characters which go together and form a 'word' such as *àiqíng* 爱情 'love' are not written any closer together than the two characters for 'I love' *wǒ ài* 我爱 although 'love' is one word and 'I love' is two words. (At least this avoids the headache which we have with *pinyin* of deciding what should be joined and what should be split.) Because each character occupies the same amount of space, I always encourage beginners to start practising characters on squared paper, which forces you to observe this practice.

BASIC RULES FOR WRITING CHARACTERS

As you can imagine, there are some basic rules for writing characters which you need to master. This is important if you are to remember them, because in order to store them away so that it can reproduce them when you require it to, the brain needs to operate a kind of orderly filing system. To do this, it needs all the help it can get. Most characters are made up of two or more basic structural parts called 'character components' though of course some character components such as 日 *rì* 'sun' can stand by themselves as we have mentioned earlier. Although the total number of characters is quite large, (I won't put you off by telling you precisely *how* large), the number of character components is limited. These components are written with a number of basic strokes which are illustrated below:

Stroke	*Name*		
丶	点	*diǎn*	dot
一	横	*héng*	horizontal
丨	竖	*shù*	vertical
丿	撇	*piě*	left-falling
乀	捺	*nà*	right-falling
亅	提	*tí*	rising
丨乚乙丶	钩	*gōu*	hook
乛一	折	*zhé*	turning

These strokes are basically straight lines and were traditionally written in ink with a hair brush. The main directions are from top to bottom and from left to right. The arrows on the basic strokes below show how the characters are written by showing the direction each stroke takes:

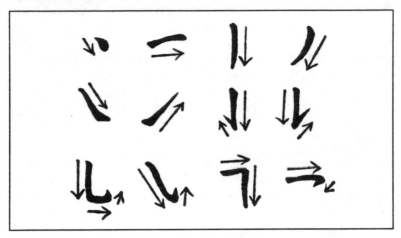

The rules of stroke order in writing Chinese characters and character components are as follows:

Example	*Stroke*	*Order*						*Rule*
十	一						十	First horizontal, then vertical
人	ノ						人	First left-falling, then right-falling
三	一	二					三	From top to bottom
州	丶	丿	丬	州	州		州	From left to right
月	ノ	刀	月				月	First outside, then inside
四	丨	冂	叼	四			四	Finish inside, then close
小	亅	小					小	Middle, then the two sides

There will be a table of the stroke-order of Chinese characters in Chapters 14–18 to help you practise writing characters correctly. When looking at a character decide whether it can be split into an upper and lower part, or perhaps a left and a right. Has it got some sort of a roof? Or a base? Is it symmetrical? Asking yourself these sorts of questions should give you a better chance of getting the stroke order right. Perhaps you may like to try and copy or trace the following public notices and signs. Numbers 14–18 are all in Beijing.

Some useful public notices and signs

Chinese characters	Pinyin transliteration and literal meaning	English translation
1 银行	*yínháng* silver business	Bank
2 汽车站	*qìchēzhàn* steam carriage stop	Bus stop
3 男厕所	*nán cèsuǒ* male lavatory place	Men's lavatory
4 女厕所	*nǚ cèsuǒ* female lavatory place	Women's lavatory
5 派出所	*pàichūsuǒ* assign/send place	Police Station (local)
6 邮局	*yóujú* post office	Post Office
7 饭馆	*fànguǎn* rice establishment	Restaurant
8 入口	*rùkǒu* enter mouth/opening	Entrance

Chinese characters	Pinyin transliteration and literal meaning	English translation
9 出口	*chūkǒu* come/go out mouth/opening	Exit
10 危险	*wēixiǎn!*	Danger
11 谢绝参观	*xièjué cānguān* refuse/decline visit	No admission
12 禁止吸烟	*jìnzhǐ* *xīyān* prohibit/ inhale forbid tobacco	No smoking
13 禁止照相	*jìnzhǐ* *zhàoxiàng* prohibit reflect appearance	Photography forbidden
14 天安门	*Tiān' ānmén* heaven peace gate	Tiananmen/ The Gate of Heavenly Peace
15 长安街	*Cháng'ān jiē* long peace street	Changan Street
16 北京饭店	*Běijīng Fàndiàn* north capital rice shop	Beijing Hotel
17 王府井	*Wángfǔjǐng* king residence well	Wangfujing (Street)
18 友谊商店	*Yǒuyì Shāngdiàn* friendship merchant shop	Friendship Store

Even today, the art of calligraphy (the writing of Chinese characters as an art form) is highly regarded in China and many educated Chinese will hang scrolls of characters, beautifully mounted, on their walls, just as we would hang a picture by, say, Turner or Picasso. Calligraphers all have their own individual styles and of course their admirers and critics, just as painters do. (As calligraphy is an art with its roots in the ancient past, these scrolls are always written in the traditional way from top to bottom and usually in their full form which is visually more pleasing.)

USING A CHINESE–ENGLISH DICTIONARY

Most of the dictionaries you will have access to, use *pinyin* to list the characters in alphabetical order according to their pronunciation. This is only of use if you know how a particular character is pronounced, otherwise you will have to look it up using the radical. (There are other systems but this is the most straightforward at this stage.) Having identified the radical, (not always so easy) and counted up the number of strokes it has, you look for it in the radical index at the front of the dictionary. Radicals are arranged according to the number of strokes they have – all the radicals with 'one stroke' 一画 *yī huà* come first, all the radicals with 'two strokes' 二画 *èr huà* next and so on. Each radical has a number assigned to it which may vary slightly from dictionary to dictionary so don't automatically assume it's the same. Having found which number radical it is (the number may be to the left or to the right of the radical itself), then look it up in the character index proper which immediately follows and which lists each radical in order. Under each radical are listed all the characters which have that radical in common. These are listed in turn according to the number of strokes they have when the radical has been taken away.

Thus 情 *qíng* 'emotions' is listed under the heart radical 忄 as having eight strokes 八画, but it will come after 恨 *hèn* 'hate' which has six. 吗 *ma* (question particle) will come under the mouth radical and be listed as having three strokes 三画 and will precede 哭 *kū* 'weep, cry' which has seven. I hope you have got the idea! Having found the character you are looking for in the index, you will either find a page number next to it or the *pinyin* and tonemark, either of which will enable you to look it up in the dictionary proper. It sounds hard work but it's not as bad as it looks once you get the hang of it and it can be quite satisfying. It is reckoned that there are around 4000 characters in daily use, of which approximately 2000 are needed to read a newspaper. Overleaf is the radical index from a popular dictionary (汉英词典 A Chinese–English Dictionary). It may prove useful to you as a reference. The number to the left of the radical indicates the order in which it appears.

When tackling the character exercises, don't expect to get them **all** right all at once. They are there for you to learn from as you go along and to go back to time and time again. Perhaps you will only recognise a few characters to start with (and be able to write even fewer), but you will gradually recognise more and more (and be able to write more). Be patient, stay with it – believe me, it can be a rewarding experience.

Whatever way you look at them, Chinese characters are fascinating, representing as they do the continuity of Chinese culture. Even if you decide not to spend too much time on them, appreciate their beauty and their long history. If you do decide you want to pursue this side of your Chinese studies there are many interesting books to read and enjoy. This chapter can only scratch the surface of what characters are all about but if it has kept your interest or better still, fired your imagination, it has served its purpose.

部 首 检 字
Radical Index

（一）部首目录

部首左边的号码表示部首的次序

#	部首	#	部首	#	部首	#	部首	#	部首	#	部首	#	部首
	一 画	35	又	70	彐(彐彑)	105	中	140	业	175	缶	209	金
1	、	36	廴	71	弓	106	贝	141	目	176	耒	210	鱼
2	一	37	厶	72	己(巳)	107	见	142	田	177	舌		九 画
3	丨	38	凵	73	女	108	父	143	由	178	竹(⺮)	211	音
4	丿	39	匕	74	子(孑)	109	气	144	申	179	臼	212	革
5	乛		三 画	75	马	110	牛(牛)	145	罒	180	自	213	是
6	亅	40	氵	76	幺	111	手	146	皿	181	血	214	骨
7	乙(乁乚)	41	忄	77	纟(糸)	112	毛	147	钅	182	舟	215	香
	二 画	42	丬(爿)	78	巛	113	攵	148	矢	183	羽	216	鬼
8	冫	43	亡	79	小(⺌)	114	片	149	禾	184	艮(艮)	217	食
9	亠	44	广		四 画	115	斤	150	白		七 画		十 画
10	讠	45	宀	80	灬	116	爪(爫)	151	瓜	185	言	218	高
11	二	46	门	81	心	117	尺	152	鸟	186	辛	219	髟
12	十	47	辶	82	斗	118	月	153	皮	187	辰	220	鬲
13	厂	48	工	83	火	119	殳	154	癶	188	麦		十一 画
14	ナ	49	土(士)	84	文	120	欠	155	矛	189	走	221	麻
15	匚	50	卄	85	方	121	风	156	疋	190	赤	222	鹿
16	卜(卜)	51	廾	86	户	122	氏		六 画	191	豆		十二 画
17	刂	52	大	87	礻	123	比	157	羊(⺶⺷)	192	束	223	黑
18	冖	53	尤	88	王	124	聿	158	关	193	酉		十三 画
19	冂	54	寸	89	主	125	水	159	米	194	豕	224	鼓
20	人	55	扌	90	天(夭)		五 画	160	齐	195	里	225	鼠
21	亻	56	弋	91	韦	126	立	161	衣	196	足		十四 画
22	厂	57	巾	92	耂	127	疒	162	亦(亦)	197	釆	226	鼻
23	人(入)	58	口	93	廿(卅)	128	穴	163	耳	198	豸		——
24	八(丷)	59	囗	94	木	129	衤	164	臣	199	谷	227	余类
25	乂	60	山	95	不	130	夹	165	戋	200	身		
26	勹	61	屮	96	犬	131	玉	166	西(西)	201	角		
27	刀(⺈)	62	彳	97	歹	132	示	167	束		八 画		
28	力	63	彡	98	瓦	133	去	168	亚	202	青		
29	儿	64	夕	99	牙	134	艹	169	而	203	卓		
30	几(⺇)	65	夂	100	车	135	甘	170	页	204	雨		
31	マ	66	丸	101	戈	136	石	171	至	205	非		
32	卩	67	尸	102	止	137	龙	172	光	206	齿		
33	阝(在左)	68	饣	103	日	138	戊	173	虍	207	黾		
34	阝(在右)	69	犭	104	曰	139	业	174	虫	208	隹		

14

Shopping

Mǎi dōngxi 买东西

Pattern one: 'Specific item' 多少 (*duōshao*) 钱? (*qián?*) How much is this/that item?

Question:	这本杂志多少钱？
	Zhè běn zázhì duōshao qián?
Answer:	这本杂志七毛六。
	Zhè běn zázhì qī máo liù.
Question:	那张地图多少钱？
	Nà zhāng dìtú duōshao qián?
Answer:	那张地图四毛九。
	Nà zhāng dìtú sì máo jiǔ.
Question:	这件衣服多少钱？
	Zhè jiàn yīfu duōshao qián?
Answer:	这件衣服十五块二。
	Zhè jiàn yīfu shíwǔ kuài èr.
Question:	那件衬衫多少钱？
	Nà jiàn chènshān duōshao qián?
Answer:	那件衬衫八块钱。
	Nà jiàn chènshān bā kuài qián.
Question:	这件毛衣多少钱？
	Zhè jiàn máoyī duōshao qián?
Answer:	这件毛衣四十一块零五分。
	Zhè jiàn máoyī sìshíyī kuài líng wǔ fēn.

买 [大]	**mǎi** (v)	*to buy*
东 [一] 西 [西]	**dōngxi** (n)	*thing(s)*
买东西	(v-o)	*to go shopping*
多 [夕] 少 [小]	**duōshao** (QW)	*how many?*
钱 [钅]	**qián** (n)	*money*
这 [辶]	**zhè** (dem. adj./p.)	*this*
本 [木]	**běn** (MW)	*for books, magazines*
杂 [木] 志 [心]	**zázhì** (n)	*magazine*
七 [一]	**qī**	*seven*
毛 [毛]	**máo** (MW; n)	*for money; wool*
六 [八]	**liù**	*six*
那 [阝]	**nà** (dem. adj./p.)	*that*
张 [弓]	**zhāng** (MW)	*for flat, rectangular objects*
地 [土] 图 [口]	**dìtú** (n)	*map*
四 [口]	**sì**	*four*
九 [丿]	**jiǔ**	*nine*
件 [亻]	**jiàn** (MW)	*piece, article, item*
衣 [衣] 服 [月]	**yīfu** (n)	*clothes*
十 [十] 五 [一]	**shíwǔ**	*fifteen*
块 [土]	**kuài** (MW)	*lump (for money, soap, etc.)*
二 [二]	**èr**	*two*
衬 [衤] 衫 [衤]	**chènshān** (n)	*shirt, blouse*
八 [八]	**bā**	*eight*
毛衣	**máoyī** (n)	*sweater, woolly*
一 [一]	**yī**	*one*
零 [雨]	**líng**	*zero*
分 [八]	**fēn** (MW)	*for money*

Table of stroke order of Chinese characters

买	⸋ ⸌ ⸍ 三 买 买
东	一 ⸊ 东 东 东
西	一 丆 丆 两 西 西
钱	钅 (丿 ⸌ ⸍ 钅 钅)
	戋 (一 二 戋 戋 戋)
杂	九 (丿 九) 木 (一 十 才 木)
志	士 (一 十 士) 心 (丶 心 心 心)
七	一 七
毛	一 二 三 毛
六	丶 亠 广 六
那	那 (刁 刁 刁 那) 阝 (阝 阝)
张	弓 (一 弓 弓) 长 (丿 ⸍ 长 长)
地	土 (一 十 土) 也 (一 也 也)
图	囗 冬 丨 冂 冂 図 图 图 图 图
四	丨 冂 冈 四 四
九	丿 九
件	亻 (丿 亻) 牛 (丿 ⸍ 牜 牛)
衣	丶 亠 广 衣 衣 衣
服	月 (丿 刀 月 月) 艮 (乛 尸 艮 艮)

十	一 十
五	一 丁 五 五
块	土 夬 (フ ユ ユ 夬)
二	一 二
衬	衤 (` ユ ラ 衤 衤 衤) 寸 (一 寸 寸)
衫	衤 彡 (´ ´ 彡)
八	丿 八
零	雨 (一 广 戸 雨 雨 雨 雨 雨) 令 (丿 人 人 今 令)
分	八 刀 (フ 刀)

Pattern two: Item 多少钱一 MW? How much per unit is item?

Question:	报多少钱一份儿?
	Bào duōshao qián yí fènr? (the 儿 *ér* on 份 *fèn* is optional but is often there).
Answer:	报一毛钱一份儿。
	Bào yì máo qián yí fènr.
Question:	香烟多少钱一包?
	Xiāngyān duōshao qián yì bāo?
Answer:	中国烟七、八毛钱一包。
	Zhōngguó yān qī、bā máo qián yì bāo.
Answer:	外国烟三块五一包。
	Wàiguó yān sān kuài wǔ yì bāo.
Question:	香皂多少钱一块?
	Xiāngzào duōshao qián yí kuài?
Answer:	香皂八、九毛钱一块。
	Xiāngzào bā、jiǔ máo qián yí kuài.
Question:	苹果多少钱一斤?
	Píngguǒ duōshao qián yì jīn?

Answer: 苹果一块二一斤。

Píngguǒ yí kuài èr yì jīn.

Question: 邮票多少钱一套?

Yóupiào duōshao qián yí tào?

Answer: 邮票四块钱一套。

Yóupiào sì kuài qián yí tào.

报 [扌]	**bào** (n)	*newspaper*
份 [亻]	**fèn** (MW)	*a copy; portion*
香 [禾] 烟 [火]	**(xiāng)yān** (n)	*cigarette*
包 [勹]	**bāo** (MW)	*packet (of),*
	(n)	*package*
中 [丨] 国 [囗]	**Zhōngguó**	*China*
外 [夕] 国	**wàiguó** (adj.)	*foreign*
三 [一]	**sān**	*three*
香皂 [白]	**xiāngzào** (n)	*toilet soap*
苹 [艹] 果 [木]	**píngguǒ** (n)	*apple*
斤 [斤]	**jīn** (MW)	*catty (½ kilogram)*
邮 [阝] 票 [示]	**yóupiào** (n)	*stamp*
套 [大]	**tào** (MW)	*set*

Table of stroke order of Chinese characters

报	扌 (一 十 扌) 艮	
香	禾 (一 二 千 禾 禾) 日 (丨 冂 日 日)	
烟	火 (丶 丷 ナ 火) 囗 丈 丨 冂 冂 冃 冈 因	
包	勹 (丿 勹) 巳 (丁 彐 巳)	
中	丨 囗 (丨 冂 口)	
国	囗 玉 丨 冂 冂 冃 冃 囯 国 国	

外	夕（ノ ク 夕） ト（丨 ト）
皂	白（ˊ 丿 冂 白 白）七
苹	艹（一 十 艹）平（一 丷 ヽ 立 平）
果	曰 木 ｜丨 冂 日 日 旦 甲 里 果
斤	一 厂 斤 斤
邮	由（丨 冂 月 日 由）阝
票	覀 示（一 二 于 亍 示）
套	大 長（一 ᐧ 厂 匚 匡 長 長 長）

Pattern three: 我要这 (*Wǒ yào zhè*) MW 'I would like this one'.

Dialogue:

售货员: 您要买什么?

Shòuhuòyuán: *Nín yào mǎi shénme?*

史爱理: 我要买丝绸, 多少钱一米?

Shǐ Àilǐ: *Wǒ yào mǎi sīchóu, duōshao qián yì mǐ?*

售货员: 十三块五。您要几米?

Shòuhuòyuán: *Shísān kuài wǔ. Nín yào jǐ mǐ?*

史爱理: 两米半。

Shǐ Àilǐ: *Liǎng mǐ bàn.*

售货员: 一共三十三块七毛五。这是四十块, 找您六块二毛五。

Shòuhuòyuán: *Yígòng sānshísān kuài qī máo wǔ. Zhè shì sìshí kuài, zhǎo nín liù kuài èr máo wǔ.*

史爱理: 好, 谢谢。

Shǐ Àilǐ: *Hǎo, xièxie.*

售货员: 没什么, 再见。

Shòuhuòyuán: *Méi shénme, zàijiàn.*

史爱理: 再见。

Shǐ Àilǐ: *Zàijiàn.*

售 [口] 货 [贝] 员 [口]	**shòuhuòyuán** (n)	*shop assistant*
您 [心]	**nín** (p.s)	*you* (polite)
要 [女]	**yào** (v)	*want*
什 [亻] 么 [丿]	**shénme** (QW)	*what?*
我 [戈]	**wǒ** (p.s)	*I, me*
丝 [一] 绸 [纟]	**sīchóu** (n)	*silk*
米 [米]	**mǐ** (MW)	*metre*
几 [几]	**jǐ** (QW/adj.)	*how many?; several*
两 [一]	**liǎng**	*two* (of a kind)
半 [丷]	**bàn**	*half*
一共 [一]	**yígòng** (adv.)	*altogether*
是 [是]	**shì** (v)	*to be*
找 [扌]	**zhǎo** (v)	*to give back* (as of change)
好 [女]	**hǎo** (adj.)	*good*
谢谢 [讠]	**xièxie** (v)	*to thank; thank you*
没 [氵]	**méi** (neg.)	*not*
再 [一] 见 [见]	**zàijiàn**	*goodbye*

Table of stroke order of Chinese characters

售	隹 (丿 亻 亻 广 产 阝 隹 隹) 口		
货	亻	匕	贝 (丨 冂 贝 贝)
员	口	贝	
您	亻	尔 (丿 ⺈ 忉 勺 尔) 心	
要	覀	女 (乀 女 女)	
什	亻	十	
么	丿	厶 (乚 厶)	
我	一 二 于 手 我 我 我		

丝	㇀ 纟 纟 纟 丝
绸	纟 (㇀ 纟 纟) 周 (丿 刀 月 门 月 月 周 周)
米	丶 丷 丷 半 米 米
几	丿 几
两	一 厂 厅 丙 丙 两 两
半	丶 丷 丷 半 半
共	一 十 卄 뀨 共 共
是	日 疋 (ㄒ 下 疋 疋)
找	扌 戈 (一 弋 弋 戈)
好	女 子 (㇇ 了 子)
谢	讠 (丶 讠) 身 (ノ ㇉ 勹 勹 勹 身 身) 寸
没	氵 (丶 丶 氵) 殳 (丿 几 𠬶 殳)
再	一 厂 冂 冂 冉 再
见	l 冂 𠃌 见

Grammar

MONEY

The Chinese currency is known as 'the people's currency', *rénmínbì* (RMB) 人民币. ('Foreign currency' is *wàibì* 外币). The largest single unit is the *yuán* 元 (represented by ￥ in many transactions). There are 10 *jiǎo* 角 in one *yuán* and 10 *fēn* 分 in one *jiǎo*. These are the characters used in the written language and printed on banknotes, tickets, etc. In spoken Chinese, *kuài* 块 'piece/lump' is used for *yuán* and *máo* 毛 for *jiǎo* but *fēn* remains unchanged. When two or more different units of currency are used together, the last one is usually omitted so it is *sān kuài wŭ* and not *sān kuài wŭ máo, sì máo liù* and not *sì máo liù fēn*. If a sum of money involves *kuài* and *fēn* but no *máo*, the absence of the latter is marked by a *líng*, 'zero':

27.05 元 *èrshíqī kuài **líng** wŭ fēn*.

Note that under these circumstances *fēn* cannot be omitted.

The word for 'money' *qián* is sometimes put after amounts expressed entirely in *kuài, máo* or *fēn*:

*jiŭ kuài **qián***	9.00 元
*qī máo **qián***	0.7 元
*bā fēn **qián***	0.08 元

Liăng is often used with *kuài* and *máo* (**liăng** *kuài,* **liăng** *máo*) but only with *fēn* when there are no *kuài* or *máo*:

liăng *kuài* **liăng** *máo èr*   2.22 元

but

liăng *fēn qián*   0.02 元

When the last number in a series is 'two' then *èr* is always used:

*liăng kuài **èr***   2.2 元

RMB (*Rénmínbì*)	*Spoken*	*Written*
0.01 *yuán*	*yì fēn (qián)*	*yì fēn*
0.1 *yuán*	*yì máo (qián)*	*yì jiăo*
1.00 *yuán*	*yì kuài (qián)*	*yì yuán*
3.5 *yuán*	*sān kuài bàn* ⎫ *sān kuài wŭ* ⎬	*sān yuán wŭ jiăo*
7.68 *yuán*	*qī kuài liù máo bā*	*qī yuán liù jiăo bā fēn*
12.09 *yuán*	*shí'èr kuài líng jiŭ fēn*	*shí'èr yuán líng jiŭ fēn*
20.00 *yuán*	*èrshí kuài (qián)*	*èrshí yuán*
99.99 *yuán*	*jiŭshíjiŭ kuài jiŭ máo jiŭ*	*jiŭshíjiŭ yuán jiŭ jiăo jiŭ fēn*

EXERCISE 14.1

Supply the missing MW (in *pinyin* and in characters):

*Wŏ măi zhè*____ *zázhì* → *Wŏ măi zhè **běn**/ 本 *zázhì*.

1 *Tā mǎi le sān* ____ *dìtú.*
2 *Wǒ zuótiān mǎi le yí* ____ *xīn (new) yīfu.*
3 *Liǎng* ____ *máoyī shì jiù (old) de.*
4 *Tā měi tiān xī (smoke) sì* ____ *yān.*
5 *Wǒmen yí ge xīngqī yòng yí* ____ *féizào.*
6 *Zuò zhè* ____ *chènshān yào mǎi liǎng* ____ *bù (cloth).*

EXERCISE 14.2

Write out in characters the sum of money in each sentence.
Nà jiàn máoyī wǔshí kuài qián → 五十块钱。

1 *Zhè jiàn yīfu èrshí kuài.*
2 *Yì mǐ bù sì kuài bā.*
3 *Sān jīn píngguǒ sān kuài jiǔ.*
4 *Yóupiào liù kuài qī yí tào.*
5 *Bào yì máo èr yì fèn.*
6 *Zhōngguó yān bā máo sì yì bāo.*

EXERCISE 14.3

Learn the following radicals, their romanisation and their meaning:

1	大	*dà*	'big'.
2	一	*héng*	'horizontal (line)'.
3	小	*xiǎo*	'small'.
4	钅(金)	*jīn*	'metal'.
5	辶	–	'walking radical' (always written last no matter what its position).
6	木	*mù*	'tree'.
7	心	*xīn*	'heart'.
8	口	*kǒu*	'mouth'.
9	囗	–	'enclosure'.
10	月	*yuè* or *ròu*	'moon' or 'flesh' (see Chapter 13).
11	土	*tǔ*	'earth'.
12	衤(衣)	*yī*	'clothing'.
13	扌(手)	*shǒu*	'hand'.
14	禾	*hé*	'grain'.
15	日	*rì*	'sun'.

EXERCISE 14.4

Write out each of the following characters in *pinyin* and say what the radical is: e.g. 国 → *guó* 'enclosure'. (Use Chapter 13 if you have any difficulties.)

1 苹 **2** 衬 **3** 没 **4** 谢 **5** 块
6 本 **7** 是 **8** 烟 **9** 志 **10** 买

EXERCISE 14.5
For each of the following characters take out the radical and then count up the number of strokes remaining. Indicate what the radical is: e.g. 钱 → 5 (钅)。
1 东 **2** 件 **3** 图 **4** 好 **5** 我
6 报 **7** 邮 **8** 套 **9** 您 **10** 找

The three Ms
Shopping in China requires a different set of skills from that in the West. Always buy whenever you see something you like – you may never see it again! Delay and you may well be greeted by one of the dreaded three Ms: *Méi yǒu le* 'It is no more!', *Mài wán le* 'sold out' and in answer to your query as to when the goods might again be on sale you may be told *Míngtiān* 'tomorrow' but tomorrows have a nasty habit of never coming so be warned! Avoid disappointment, buy now.

EXERCISE 14.6
Write the following sentences in Chinese characters and then translate them into English:
1 *Shòuhuòyuán shì Zhōngguórén* (人).
2 *Dìtú sān máo èr yì zhāng.*
3 *Nà běn zázhì bā máo jiǔ.*
4 *Nín méi mǎi dōngxi.*
5 *Píngguǒ yí kuài sì yì jīn.*

EXERCISE 14.7
Translate into Chinese characters:
1 I want to buy three magazines and a newspaper.
2 Yesterday (昨天) I bought (*le* 了) two shirts.
3 He (他) wants to go shopping.
4 How many metres of silk do you want?
5 Thank you. Goodbye.

15

Buying Tickets (i)

去影剧院买票 *Qù yǐngjùyuàn mǎi piào*

史爱理	十二月十三号的音乐会还有票吗？
Shǐ Àilǐ	*Shí 'èryuè shísān hào de yīnyuèhuì hái yǒu piào ma?*
售票员	还有。你要几张？
Shòupiàoyuán	*Hái yǒu. Nǐ yào jǐ zhāng?*
史爱理	要四张。楼下的还有吗？
Shǐ Àilǐ	*Yào sì zhāng. Lóuxià de hái yǒu ma?*
售票员	有。你看，第九排怎么样？
Shòupiàoyuán	*Yǒu. Nǐ kàn, dì jiǔ pái zěnmeyàng?*
史爱理	很好。多少钱一张？
Shǐ Àilǐ	*Hěn hǎo. Duōshao qián yì zhāng?*
售票员	一块三。四张五块二。
Shòupiàoyuán	*Yí kuài sān. Sì zhāng wǔ kuài èr.*
史爱理	给你六块。
Shǐ Àilǐ	*Gěi nǐ liù kuài.*
售票员	找你八毛，这是你的票。
Shòupiàoyuán	*Zhǎo nǐ bā máo, zhè shi nǐ de piào.*
史爱理	谢谢你。请问，《日出》这部电影怎么样，有意思吗？
Shǐ Àilǐ	*Xièxie nǐ. Qǐng wèn, 《Rìchū》 zhè bù diànyǐng zěnmeyàng, yǒu yìsi ma?*
售票员	挺好的。大家都说很有意思。你下个星期来看吧。
Shòupiàoyuán	*Tǐng hǎo de. Dàjiā dōu shuō hěn yǒu yìsi. Nǐ xià ge xīngqī lái kàn ba.*

去 [土]	qù (v)	*to go*
影 [彡] 剧 [刂] 院 [阝]	yǐngjùyuàn (n)	*cinema* and *theatre*
票 [示]	piào (n) [zhāng]	*ticket*
售票员	shòupiàoyuán (n)	*box office clerk*
月 [月]	yuè (n)	*month*
号 [口]	hào (n)	*number; date*
的 [白]	de	*see 3.5*
音 [音] 乐 [木] 会 [人]	yīnyuèhuì (n)	*concert*
还 [辶]	hái (adv.)	*still*
有 [月]	yǒu (v)	*to have; there is/are*
吗 [口]	ma	*question particle*
你 [亻]	nǐ (ps)	*you*
楼 [木] 下 [一]	lóuxià (n)	*downstairs*
看 [目]	kàn (v)	*to look, see*
第 [灬]	dì	*ordinal prefix*
排 [扌]	pái (n)	*row, line*
怎 [心] 么 样 [木]	zěnmeyàng	*what about it?*
很 [亻]	hěn (adv.)	*very*
给 [纟]	gěi (v)	*to give; for*
请 [讠]	qǐng (v)	*to invite*
问 [口]	wèn (v)	*to ask*
日 [日] 出 [丨]	Rìchū (N)	*Sunrise (film version of a play by Cao Yu)*
部 [阝]	bù (MW)	*for films*
电 [田] 影	diànyǐng (n)	*film*
意 [心] 思 [心]	yìsi (n)	*meaning*
有意思	yǒu yìsi (v-o)	*to be interesting*
挺 [扌]	tǐng (adj.)	*very, rather*
大 [大] 家 [宀]	dàjiā (p)	*everybody*
都 [阝]	dōu (adv.)	*all, both*
说 [讠]	shuō (v)	*to speak, say*
下 [一]	xià (adj.)	*next*
个 [人]	gè (MW)	*see 3.1*
星 [日] 期 [月]	xīngqī (n)	*week*
来 [一]	lái (v)	*to come*
吧 [口]	ba	*particle indicating suggestion*

Table of stroke order of Chinese characters

去	土	厶		
影	日	京 (丶 一 亠 宀 宀 亨 亨 京) 彡		
剧	尸 (一 コ 尸) 古 (一 十 古 古 古) 刂 (丨 刂)			
院	阝	宀 (丶 丶 宀) 元 (一 二 テ 元)		
号	口	丂 (一 丂)		
的	白 (丶 丨 白 白 白) 勺 (丿 勹 勺)			
音	立 (丶 一 亠 立 立) 日			
乐	一 匸 乐 牙 乐			
会	人 (丿 人) 云 (一 二 云 云)			
还	不 (一 フ 不 不) 辶 (丶 辶 辶) *this component is always written last			
有	𠂇 (一 𠂇) 月			
吗	口	马 (一 马 马)		
楼	木	米	女	
下	一 丅 下			
看	手 (一 二 三 手) 目 (丨 冂 冂 月 目)			
第	𥫗 (丿 𠂉 𠂉 𥫗 𥫗 𥫗) 弔 (一 弓 弓 弔 弔)			
排	扌	非 (丨 刂 刂 刂 刂 非 非 非)		
怎	乍 (丿 乍 乍 乍 乍) 心			

样	木	羊（丶 丷 ﹀ 兰 兰 羊）
很	彳	彳（彳 彳 彳）艮（フ ㄱ ㅋ 艮 艮 艮）
给	纟	合（丿 人 ᐱ 合 合 合）
请	讠	青（一 ⁼ ㇐ 主 丰 青 青 青）
问	门（丶 冫 门）口
出	丨 屮 屮 出 出
部	立	口	阝
电	田（丨 冂 冃 用 田）乚
意	立	日	心
思	田	心
挺	扌	廴（廴 廴）壬（丿 ⁼ 千 壬）
都	者（一 ㇏ 土 耂 耂 者 者 者）阝
说	讠	兑（丶 丷 ﹀ 䒑 台 台 兑）
个	人	丨
星	日	生（丿 ㇐ ⁼ 牛 生）
期	其（一 十 卄 世 甘 其 其 其）月
来	一 ㇐ 亍 亚 平 来 来
吧	口	巴（フ 丆 丏 巴）

Grammar

1 DATES

We have already covered months of the year and days of the week in 10.5 and 10.3 but we still do not know how to tackle dates. The order for a date is the reverse of that used in English: year, month, day, hour.

The year is read as single numbers followed by the word *nián* (年) 'year': 1949 *yījiǔsìjiǔnián* (*yī jiǔ sì jiǔ nián*), 1976 *yījiǔqīliùnián*, 1988 *yījiǔbābānián*.

When asking what the date is the Chinese use *jǐ yuè jǐ hào?* (*Lit.* how many months how many numbers):

Question: *Jīntiān (shì) jǐ yuè jǐ hào?*
Answer: *Jīntiān wǔyuè èrshí'èr hào.* (22 May)
Question: *Xīngqītiān jǐ hào?*
Answer: *Xīngqītiān sānshíyī hào.* (31st)

Equipped with this information we can now tackle such phrases as 9 am on Monday, 11 July 1936: *Yījiǔsānliùnián qīyuè shíyī hào (rì*) xīngqīyī shàngwǔ jiǔ diǎn.*

Note that in Chinese you move from the general to the particular. As we are on dates, the chart below should be of interest!

* *Rì* (日) is used more frequently in formal, written Chinese whereas *hào* is commonly used in the spoken language.

China's main dynasties

夏	*Xià*	c. 21st–16th century BC
商	*Shāng*	c. 16th–11th century BC
周	*Zhōu*	c. 11th–256 BC
秦	*Qín*	211–206 BC
汉	*Hàn*	206 BC–AD 220
三国	*Sānguó* Three Kingdoms	220–280
晋	*Jìn*	265–420
南北朝	*Nán-Běi Cháo* North/South Dynasties (see 17.1)	420–589
隋	*Suí*	581–618

唐	*Táng*	618–907
五代	*Wǔdài*	907–960
	Five Dynasties	
宋	*Sòng*	960–1279
辽	*Liáo*	970–1125
金	*Jīn*	1115–1234
元	*Yuán*	1279–1368
明	*Míng*	1368–1644
清	*Qīng*	1644–1911
中华民国	*Zhōnghuá Mínguó*	1912–1949
	Republic of China	
中华人民 共和国	*Zhōnghuá Rénmín* *Gònghéguó*	1949–
	People's Republic of **China**	

NB	公元前	*gōngyuán qián*	BC
	公元	*gōngyuán*	AD
	世纪	*shìjì*	century
	二十一世纪	*èrshíyī shìjì*	21st century

2 TITLES

As capital letters cannot exist in the Chinese script, except artificially in romanisation, the titles of books, films, plays, etc. are distinguished by placing them between 《　》marks: 《*Rìchū*》《日出》 'Sunrise'.

EXERCISE 15.1

Learn the following radicals, their romanisation and their meaning.

1 刂(刀)   *dāo*   'knife'.
2 示 (礻)   *shì*   'omen'.
3 ㇓
4 人 } *rén*   'person' (we used to call it 'the man' radical!).
5 目   *mù*   'eye'.
6 ⺮ (竹)   *zhú*   'bamboo'.
7 纟   *sī*   'silk'.
8 讠 (言)   *yán*   'speech'.

9 丨   *shù*   'vertical (line)'.
10 田   *tián*   'field'.

EXERCISE 15.2

Write out each of the following characters in *pinyin* and put the common component contained in the characters of each group in the brackets:

e.g. 谢 *xiè*、说、*shuō*、请 *qǐng* (讠).

1 意 ＿＿＿＿、志 ＿＿＿＿、怎 ＿＿＿＿   (   ).
2 报 ＿＿＿＿、挺 ＿＿＿＿、排 ＿＿＿＿   (   ).
3 号 ＿＿＿＿、员 ＿＿＿＿、问 ＿＿＿＿   (   ).
4 都 ＿＿＿＿、部 ＿＿＿＿、邮 ＿＿＿＿   (   ).
5 来 ＿＿＿＿、七 ＿＿＿＿、下 ＿＿＿＿   (   ).

EXERCISE 15.3

Write out the characters you have met containing each of the following components. (In each case, find the number of characters indicated by the dashes.)

e.g. 口: <u> 吧 </u>、<u> 吗 </u>。

1 土: ＿＿＿＿、＿＿＿＿、＿＿＿＿。
2 女: ＿＿＿＿、＿＿＿＿。
3 丨: ＿＿＿＿、＿＿＿＿。
4 木: ＿＿＿＿、＿＿＿＿、＿＿＿＿、＿＿＿＿、＿＿＿＿。
5 月: ＿＿＿＿、＿＿＿＿、＿＿＿＿。
6 囗: ＿＿＿＿、＿＿＿＿。
7 彡: ＿＿＿＿。
8 人: ＿＿＿＿、＿＿＿＿。
9 亻: ＿＿＿＿、＿＿＿＿、＿＿＿＿、＿＿＿＿。
10 辶: ＿＿＿＿、＿＿＿＿。

EXERCISE 15.4

Write the following *pinyin* sentences in Chinese characters and then translate them into English.

1 *Kàn diànyǐng zěnmeyàng?*
2 *Lóuxià yǒu rén ma?*
3 《*Rìchū*》 *zhè bù diànyǐng yǒu méi you yìsi?*
4 *Shàng* (上 last) *ge xīngqī nǐ méi lái.*
5 *Yīnyuèhuì jǐ yuè jǐ hào?*

EXERCISE 15.5

Translate into Chinese characters:

1 Today（今天）is 3 November.
2 Excuse me, what is the date today?
3 There is nobody upstairs (楼上 *lóushàng*).
4 Everybody says that shopping is very interesting.
5 Have you still got any money?/How much do you want?
6 I was in (在 *zài*) China in 1968.

16

Buying Tickets (*ii*)

打电话买票 *Dǎ diànhuà mǎi piào*

王永寿 *Wáng Yǒngshòu*	（拨五五．零九七八，过了一会儿才有人接） *(Bō wǔ wǔ líng jiǔ qī bā, guò le yíhuìr cái yǒu rén jiē)* 喂，首都剧场吗？ *Wèi, Shǒudū Jùchǎng ma?*
售票员 *Shòupiàoyuán*	是，您是哪里？ *Shì, nín shì nǎlǐ?*
王	我是北大的英国专家。请问，《上帝的宠儿》还在演吗？ *Wǒ shì Běidà de Yīngguó zhuānjiā. Qǐng wèn, 《Shàngdì de Chǒng'ér》 hái zài yǎn ma?*
售票员	还在演，可是快要不演了，大后天就不演了。 *Hái zài yǎn, kěshi kuài yào bù yǎn le, dàhòutiān jiù bù yǎn le.*
王	明天、后天都有票吗？ *Míngtiān, hòutiān dōu yǒu piào ma?*
售票员	明天客满了，后天的票不多了。 *Míngtiān kèmǎn le, hòutiān de piào bù duō le.*
王	后天星期五，能不能给我留两张好票？我今天下午去取。 *Hòutiān xīngqīwǔ, néng bu néng gěi wǒ liú liǎng zhāng hǎo piào? Wǒ jīntiān xiàwǔ qù qǔ.*
售票员	行，可是今天下午一定来取，因为票快卖完了，不好留。 *Xíng, kěshì jīntiān xiàwǔ yídìng lái qǔ, yīnwei piào kuài mài wán le, bù hǎo liú.*

王	您放心吧，我一定会去。
	Nín fàng xīn ba, wǒ yídìng huì qù.
售票员	您贵姓？
	Nín guìxìng?
王	我姓王，名字叫王永寿。
	Wǒ xìng Wáng, míngzi jiào Wáng Yǒngshòu.
	王是三横一竖的王，
	'Wáng' shì sān héng yí shù de 'Wáng',
	'永' 是 '永远' 的 '永'，'寿' 是 '长寿' 的 '寿'。
	'yǒng' shì 'yǒngyuǎn' de 'yǒng', 'shòu' shì 'chángshòu' de 'shòu'.
售票员	好了，我记下来了。
	Hǎo le, wǒ jì xiàlai le.
王	太谢谢您了，下午见。
	Tài xièxie nín le, xiàwǔ jiàn.
售票员	冉见。
	Zàijiàn.

打电话	**dǎ diànhuà** (v-o)	*to telephone*
拨	**bō** (v)	*to dial*
过	**guò**	
了	**le**	*modal particle*
一会儿	**yíhuìr**	
才	**cái**	
人	**rén** (n)	*person*
接	**jiē**	*take hold of, receive; to meet*
喂	**wèi**	*hello (on telephone)*
首都剧场	**Shǒudū Jùchǎng** (N)	*Capital Theatre*
北大	**Běidà**	
英国	**Yīngguó**	
专家	**zhuānjiā** (n)	*expert*
在	**zài**	*in the middle of doing*
演	**yǎn** (v)	*to perform; to act*
可是	**kěshì**	
快要……了	**kuài yào...le**	*(see 16.4)*

大后天	**dàhòutiān** (TW)	*the day after the day after tomorrow*
就	**jiù**	
后天	**hòutiān** (TW)	*the day after tomorrow*
客满	**kèmǎn** (adj.)	*sold out, full house*
星期五	**xīngqīwǔ**	
能	**néng** (aux. v.)	*to be able to, can*
留	**liú** (v)	*to reserve for someone; remain; let grow*
今天	**jīntiān** (TW)	*today*
下午	**xiàwǔ** (TW)	*afternoon*
取	**qǔ** (v)	*to get, fetch*
行	**xíng**	
一定	**yídìng**	
因为	**yīnwei** or **yīnwèi**	
卖	**mài** (v)	*to sell*
-完	**-wán**	
放心	**fàng xīn** (v-o)	*to set one's mind at rest*
会	**huì**	
贵姓	**guìxìng?** (*Lit.* expensive surname)	*may I ask your name?*
名字	**míngzi** (n)	*(given) name*
叫	**jiào**	*to be called; to call*
横	**héng** (adj.)	*horizontal*
竖	**shù** (adj.)	*vertical*
永远	**yǒngyuǎn** (adj.)	*forever*
长寿	**chángshòu** (n)	*long life, longevity*
记下夹	**jì xiàlai** (v + CDE)	*to note down; to record*
太	**tài**	*extremely; too*
见	**jiàn**	
《上帝的宠儿》	《**Shàngdì de Chǒng'ér**》(N)	*'Amadeus'* (*Lit.* God's favourite), *play by Peter Shaffer*

Table of stroke order of the more difficult characters

拨	扌	发（乛 ナ 步 发 发）
首	⸜（丶 ⸜）百（一 丆 一 厂 丆 百 百）
场	土	扬（𠃌 万 扬）
北	丨 一 丬 北 北	
专	一 二 专 专	
家	宀	豕（一 宀 丆 豕 豕 豕 豕）
演	氵	宀	寅（一 丆 宀 宀 寅 寅 寅 寅）
就	京	尤（一 ナ 尤 尤）
客	宀	各（丿 夂 夂 各 各 各）
满	氵	㶳（一 十 艹 艹 芹 芮 芮 芮 满 满）
能	厶	月	匕（乛 匕 匕 匕）
留	𠃌（丿 𠃌 𠃌 𠃌 𠃌）田
取	耳（一 丆 丌 耳 耳 耳）又（乛 又）
为	丶 丿 为 为	
放	方（丶 一 亠 方）攵（丿 𠂉 攵 攵）
贵	虫（丿 口 曰 曰 虫）贝
横	木	黄（一 十 艹 艹 芦 芦 苔 苗 黄 黄）
竖	收（丨 丨 收 收）立
永	丶 丁 方 永 永	

远	元	辶	Remember this component is always written last no matter what its position is in the character
寿	耂	(一 ̄ 三 耂) 寸	
记	讠	己 (フ ⊃ 己)	
太	大	太	
上	丨	卜 上	
帝	产	(丶 ̄ ̄ 产 产 产) 巾 (丨 冂 巾)	
宠	宀	龙 (一 ナ ナ 龙 龙)	

Grammar

1 TELEPHONE NUMBERS

A telephone number is written as a series of single numbers but in spoken Chinese the number of the exchange is often said first followed by the word *jú* (here meaning 'exchange', but normally 'office', 'bureau') and the rest of the number is said as single numbers as before: 55.0978 *wǔ wǔ líng jiǔ qī bā* or *wǔshíwǔjú líng jiǔ qī bā*.

2 WHERE ARE YOU?

Instead of asking *who* you are, the Chinese often ask *where* you are. (In actual fact the Chinese are really asking you for the name of your work unit.) In response to *Nín shì nǎlǐ?* Mr King could equally well have replied that he was Beijing University! (*Wǒ shì Běijīng Dàxué*). The idea being that you follow this up with the equivalent of your rank and number so that again you can be slotted into that imaginary filing system! Of course you may be asked who you are and the polite form would probably be *Nǐ (nín) shì nǎwèi?* (*Lit.* you are which polite MW for people?) In both *Nín shì nǎlǐ?* and *Nín shì nǎwèi?* the *shì* may be omitted. Don't be surprised if you are simply asked who you are without any frills: *Nǐ shì shéi?*

3 DESCRIBING YOUR 'CHARACTER'?

Mr King says he is 'the three horizontals and one vertical' King, that the *yǒng* in his name is the *yǒng* in *yǒngyuǎn* 'eternal' and the *shòu* is as the *shòu* in *chángshòu* 'longevity'! That leaves the box-office clerk in no doubt as to how to write his name. Because Chinese is so full of homophones it is common practice to describe one's name in this way so that there can be no misunderstanding as to what characters are used. Thus *Shǐ Àilǐ*'s name, literally 'history loves principle', could be described as *Shǐ shì lìshǐ de shǐ, ài shì ài guó de ài, lǐ shì dàolǐ de lǐ* 'the **shǐ** as in history , the **ài** as in patriotic and the **lǐ** as in principle (or truth)'.

4 (KUÀI) YÀO V...LE

To indicate imminent action or that the action of the verb is going to take place within a relatively short space of time we can put *yào* in front of the verb and the modal particle *le* at the end of the sentence. *Kuài* or *jiù* can be put before *yào* to make the imminence of the action even clearer:

Tā yào dǎ diànhuà le. 'She's going to phone'.

《*Rìchū*》 *kuài yào yǎn le* 'Sunrise is coming on soon'.

Wǒ xiàwǔ jiù yào zǒu le 'I'm leaving this afternoon'.

Note that an adverb or adverbial phrase of time may come before *jiù yào* V...*le* but not before *kuài yào* V...*le*.

As you can see, the concept of 'imminent' is a relatively elastic one but the juxtaposition of *míngtiān* and *kuài* as in *Wǒ péngyou míngtiān kuài yào chū guó le* does seem to be taking this too far (hence the rule) whereas *Wǒ péngyou míngtiān jiù yào chū guó le* 'My friend is going abroad tomorrow' is perfectly acceptable. This construction can also appear as

kuài V...*le*:

Piào kuài mài wán le.   'The tickets are almost sold out'.

but not

jiù V...*le*   which would be far too ambiguous as *jiù* can be used in so many different ways.

The question form is made by adding *ma* to the statement and *méi you* is used for an answer in the negative: *Huǒchē kuài yào kāi le ma?* 'Is the train about to leave?' *Méi you* 'No'.

The three Ps

Making a telephone call in China is not always as easy as it may appear in this chapter as many of us know to our cost. A whole morning can sometimes be spent making three or four long-distance calls so *p*atience and *p*ersistence are required. Apart from local calls, all calls have to go through the operator although this is slowly changing as more modern equipment is being installed. *Zhàn xiàn le* 'the line's engaged' (*Lit.* occupied line) is a phrase with which one soon becomes very familiar.

Buying tickets of any sort in China, given the vastness of the population, is no easy matter and it is often very difficult for individuals to buy tickets for any even moderately popular event. As we have said before, it is usually the work unit which performs this function. Foreigners are sometimes privileged in this respect. With *p*atience, *p*ersistence and *p*oliteness they can, on occasions, manage to obtain tickets which seem to be unavailable to the general public.

EXERCISE 16.1

Learn the following radicals, their romanisation and their meaning:

1	⺿ (草)	*cǎo*	'grass'.
2	氵 (水)	*shuǐ*	'water'.
3	忄 (心)	*xīn*	'heart'.
4	女	*nǚ*	'woman'.
5	耳	*ěr*	'ear'.
6	宀	–	'roof'.
7	贝	*bèi*	'shell, object of value'.
8	八 ⍀ (八)	*bā*	'eight'.
9	饣 (食)	*shí*	'food'.

Some characters appear to be made up of more than one recognisable radical. Which one do you choose to look up the character under? You will slowly learn that certain radicals seem to take precedence over others. The 'five elements' (wood, fire, earth, metal and water) for instance, but these are all defeated by 'heart'. If you are totally at sea, look at the left-hand side of the character first and see if you can spot a radical. The 'head' is another place to look (grass, bamboo, various kinds of roofs). In absolute dire straits try the horizontal or vertical lines or the dot!

EXERCISE 16.2

Write out each of the following characters in *pinyin* and say what its radical is; e.g. 喂 *wèi* 'mouth'.

1 演 **2** 行 **3** 记 **4** 打 **5** 取
6 过 **7** 英 **8** 接 **9** 卖 **10** 天.

EXERCISE 16.3

For each of the following characters take out the radical and then count up the number of strokes remaining. Indicate what the radical is: e.g. 行 → 3 (彳); 了 → 1 (乛)

1 话 **2** 剧 **3** 专 **4** 叫 **5** 今
6 满 **7** 星 **8** 贵 **9** 客 **10** 姓

EXERCISE 16.4

Fill in the square in the centre with a component or character which when combined with each of the components in the other squares forms a separate character:

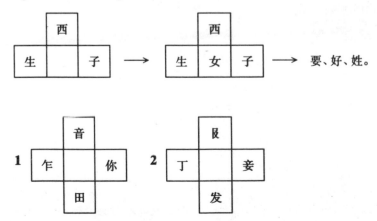

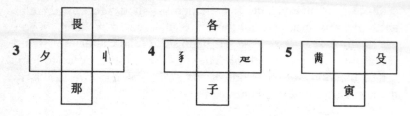

Write the following *pinyin* sentences in Chinese characters and then translate them into English:

1 *Jīntiān méi yǒu rén gěi wǒ dǎ diànhuà.*
2 *Shǒudū Jùchǎng zài nǎr?*
3 *Tā míngtiān xiàwǔ jiù yào qù Běijīng* (北京) *le.*
4 *Nǐ hòutiān néng bu neng lái jiē wǒ?*
5 *Xīngqīwǔ xíng bu xíng? Bù xíng, jiù xīngqīliù ba.*

Translate into Chinese characters:

1 I went to the Capital Theatre today. (了)
2 What is your (expensive) name? My name is Shi, Shi Aili.
3 He says he'll save two tickets for us.
4 They want to see that film this afternoon but it's sold out.
5 Would it be all right if I come and pick up the tickets next Friday?

17

Directions and Transport

问路、坐车 *Wèn lù zuò chē*

Famous places of interest in and around Tian'anmen Square

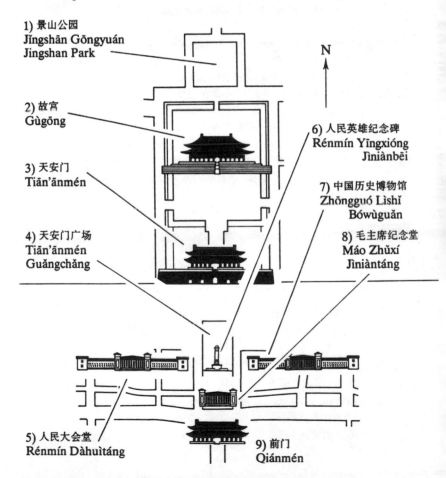

1) 景山公园
Jǐngshān Gōngyuán
Jingshan Park

2) 故宫
Gùgōng

3) 天安门
Tiān'ānmén

4) 天安门广场
Tiān'ānmén
Guǎngchǎng

5) 人民大会堂
Rénmín Dàhuìtáng

6) 人民英雄纪念碑
Rénmín Yīngxióng
Jìniànbēi

7) 中国历史博物馆
Zhōngguó Lìshǐ
Bówùguǎn

8) 毛主席纪念堂
Máo Zhǔxí
Jìniàntáng

9) 前门
Qiánmén

N

Pattern one: to taxi-driver, bus-conductor, etc.
我要去 PW   *Wǒ yào qù PW.*
我要去天坛   *Wǒ yào qù Tiāntán.*

Pattern two: you are in the vicinity of a place (PW) and ask a passer-by
PW 在哪儿? 怎么走?
PW zài nǎr? Zěnme zǒu?

Standing in Tiananmen Square
故宫在哪儿? 怎么走?
Gùgōng zài nǎr? Zěnme zǒu?

Pattern three: as for Pattern two, but slightly more formal
(a) 请问 PW 在哪儿? 怎么走?
Qǐng wèn, PW zài nǎr? Zěnme zǒu?
In the North   (b) 劳驾 PW 在哪儿? 怎么走?
Láojià, PW zài nǎr? Zěnme zǒu?
or   (c) 请问/劳驾 PW 怎么走?
Qǐng wèn/láojià PW zěnme zǒu?
请问，人民大会堂在哪儿? 怎么走?
Qǐng wèn, Rénmín Dàhuìtáng zài nǎr? Zěnme zǒu?

Pattern four: reply to a question asking for directions
往 direction 走   *Wàng Direction zǒu.*
往东走   *Wàng dōng zǒu.*

Linking question and answer

1   甲   请问，前门在哪儿? 怎么走?
  Jiǎ   *Qǐng wèn, Qiánmén zài nǎr? Zěnme zǒu?*
  乙   前门离这儿不远。往南走就到了。
  Yǐ   *Qiánmén lí zhèr bù yuǎn. Wàng nán zǒu jiù dào le.*

2   甲   劳驾，故宫在哪儿? 怎么走?
  Jiǎ   *Láojià, Gùgōng zài nǎr? Zěnme zǒu?*
  乙   (pointing) 离这儿很近，你看，就在那儿，
    你往北走就到了。

Yǐ *Lí zhèr hěn jìn, nǐ kàn, jiù zài nàr,*
     nǐ wàng běi zǒu jiù dào le.

甲 谢谢你。

Jiǎ *Xièxie nǐ.*

问路	**wèn lù** (v-o)	*ask the way*
坐车	**zuò chē** (v-o)	*go by transport*
天坛	**Tiāntán** (N)	*Temple of Heaven*
怎么	**zěnme**	
走	**zǒu**	
故宫	**Gùgōng** (N)	*the Forbidden City (the Imperial Palace)*
劳驾	**láojià**	*excuse me*
人民大会堂	**Rénmín Dàhuìtáng** (N)	*Great Hall of the People*
往	**wàng** (prep.)	*towards, to*
东	**dōng**	*east*
甲	**jiǎ**	*A (the first of the Ten Heavenly Stems)*
乙	**yǐ**	*B (the second of the Ten Heavenly Stems) (See Chapter 22)*
前门	**Qiánmén** (N)	*Qianmen*
离	**lí** (prep.)	*(distance) from*
这儿（这里）	**zhèr (zhèlǐ)**	
不	**bù**	
远	**yuǎn** (adj.)	*far*
南	**nán**	*south*
到	**dào**	*arrive, go to*
近	**jìn** (adj.)	*near*
你	**nǐ**	
那儿（那里）	**nàr (nàlǐ)** (PW)	*there*
北	**běi**	*north*

Table of stroke order of the more difficult characters

路	𧾷 (' ⼌ ⼝ ⼝ ⾜ ⾜ 𧾷) 各
坐	⼈⼈ (⼃ ⼂ ⼈ ⼈⼈) 土
车	一 ⿻ ⿻ 车
劳	⼗⼗ ⺈ (' ⺈) 力 (⼆ 力)
驾	⿰加 马
民	⼝ (⼌ ⼆ ⼝) 七 (一 七)
堂	⺌ (' ⺌ ⺌) 室 (' ⼀ ⼓ ⼀ ⼀ ⼀ ⼀ 室)
往	⼻ 主 (` ⼀ ⼆ ⼿ 主)
甲	⼁ ⼌ ⽇ ⽇ 甲
乙	乙
前	⺌ 月 刂
离	` ⼀ ⼡ ⼡ ⼛ ⽚ 产 离 离 离
这	文 (` ⼀ ⼧ 文) ⻌
里	⼁ ⼌ ⽇ ⽇ 旦 甲 里
南	⼗ 甬 (⼁ ⼌ ⼌ ⼌ ⼌ ⼌ 甬)

Dialogue

Mr King comes out of the Imperial Palace (*Gùgōng*) and asks the way to the Great Hall of the People (*Rénmín Dàhuìtáng*):

王   人民大会堂离故宫远吗?

      Rénmín Dàhuìtáng lí Gùgōng yuǎn ma?

路人   不远，离故宫很近，就在天安门广场西边儿。

Lùrén	***Bù yuǎn, lí Gùgōng hěn jìn, jiù zài Tiān'ānmén Guǎng-chǎng xībianr.***
王	中国历史博物馆也在西边儿吗？
	Zhōngguó Lìshǐ Bówùguǎn yě zài xībianr ma?
路人	不，中国历史博物馆和中国革命博物馆就在天安门东边儿，人民大会堂对面。
	Bù, Zhōngguó Lìshǐ Bówùguǎn hé Zhōngguó Gémìng Bówùguǎn jiù zài Tiān'ānmén dōngbianr, Rénmín Dàhuìtáng duìmiàn.
王	人民英雄纪念碑呢？
	Rénmín Yīngxióng Jìniànbēi ne?
路人	在天安门广场中间，在毛主席纪念堂前边儿。
	Zài Tiān'ānmén Guǎngchǎng zhōngjiān, zài Máo Zhǔxí Jìniàntáng qiánbianr.
王	那么，前门在毛主席纪念堂后边儿对不对？
	Nàme, Qiánmén zài Máo Zhǔxí Jìniàntáng hòubianr duì bu duì?
路人	对，这几个地方都很有意思，值得看一看。
	Duì, zhè jǐ ge dìfang dōu hěn yǒu yìsi, zhíde kànyikàn.

路人	**lùrén** (n)	*passer-by; stranger*
天安门广场	**Tiān'ānmén Guǎng-chǎng** (N)	*Tiananmen Square*
西边儿	**xībianr** (n)	*west (side)*
中国历史博物馆	**Zhōngguó Lìshǐ Bówùguǎn** (N)	*Museum of National History (Lit. China history museum)*
也	**yě**	
中国革命博物馆	**Zhōngguó Gémìng Bówùguǎn** (N)	*Museum of Revolution (Lit. China revolution museum)*
东边儿	**dōng(bianr)** (PW)	*east (side)*
对面	**duìmiàn** (PW)	*opposite*
人民英雄纪念碑	**Rénmín Yīngxióng Jìniànbēi** (N)	*Monument to the People's Heroes (Lit. people's hero monument)*

呢	**ne**	
中间	**zhōngjiān** (PW)	*middle; between*
毛主席纪念堂	**Máo Zhǔxí Jìniàn táng** (N)	*Mao Zedong (Chairman Mao) Mausoleum*
前边儿	**qiánbianr** (PW)	*front, in front of*
那么	**nàme**	
后边儿	**hòubianr** (PW)	*back, behind*
对	**duì**	
几	**jǐ**	
地方	**dìfang** (n)	*place*
值得	**zhíde** (v)	*to be worth, deserve*

Table of stroke order of the more difficult characters

广	丶 亠 广
边	𠃌 力 辶
历	厂 力
史	口 虫 史
博	十 甫 (一 厂 冂 冃 冒 甫 甫) 寸
物	牛 (丿 𠂉 牛) 勿 (丿 勹 勺 勿)
馆	饣 (丿 𠃌 饣) 官 (丶 𭕄 宀 宀 宁 官 官)
革	一 十 廿 莊 莊 苎 莒 苣 革
命	人 一 叩
面	一 𠃌 厂 帀 而 而 面 面
雄	厷 (一 十 左 厷) 隹
碑	石 (一 丆 不 石 石) 卑 (丿 白 鱼 甶 卑)

Welcome to Neva Lomason Memorial!
21057004449778 checked out the
following items:

1. Chinese
   Barcode: 31057101014135
   Due: 12/02/2017 11:59 PM

**Total fines/fees on this
account: $0.00**

WGRL-HQ 2017-11-18 16:12
To renew your items:
please call 770-836-6711
or online @ www.wgrl.net
Library cards are updated every 2
years.
Your card will be due for updating on:
2019-05-22

Cost of buying these items:$15.00
Cost of getting these items from your
library $FREE

席	广	茅 (一　十　廿　廿　芦　芦　茅)		
值	亻	直 (一　十　广　市　肖　肖　直　直)		
得	彳	日	寻 (一　二　寻　寻)	

Grammar

1 POINTS OF THE COMPASS

Perhaps as China is situated in the East, the important cardinal points for her are east and west (in that order!) rather than north and south. Whereas when listing the cardinal points we say north, south, east, west, the Chinese say *dōng, nán, xī, běi* (E, S, W, N).

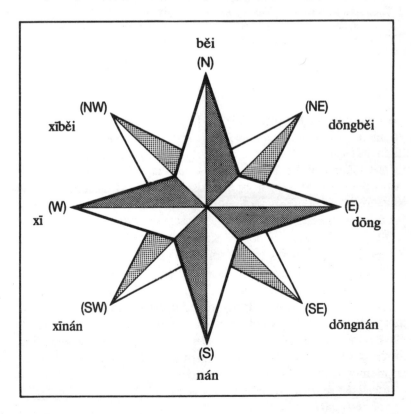

Instead of south-east they say 'east-south' (*dōngnán*), instead of north-west, 'west-north' (*xīběi*) and so on. NB The figure above shows the western representation of the compass. The Chinese version always shows **South** at the top.

The Chinese are more likely to give you directions in terms of north, south, etc. than left and right. This stems from the fact that old Chinese cities (Beijing is a good example) are laid out on a north-south, east-west axis, so in these cases, this is the most helpful way for someone to orientate him/herself.

2 PLACE WORDS

*qiánbiān	*front, in front of, before*	*lǐbiān	*inside*
*hòubiān	*back, at the back of, behind*	*wàibiān	*outside*
*shàngbiān	*top, on, over, above*	zhōngjiān	*middle, between*
*xiàbiān	*bottom, below, under*	duìmiàn	*opposite*
zuǒbiān	*left*	pángbiān	*side*
yòubiān	*right*		

(All these words are often followed by '-*ér*' which renders the *biān* toneless: *qiánbianr*, *hòubianr*, etc. and I have generally glossed them as such.)

NB -*biān* may be replaced by -*miàn* or -*tóu* in the examples asterisked above. Which one is used seems to depend on the speaker, with Southerners tending to use -*tóu* more, and -*biān* and -*miàn* being interchangeable.

Place words such as those listed above function as **nouns** in Chinese. When such a place word is used to tell us more about another noun it is usually followed by *de*: *qiánbiān de rén* 'the person/people in front'.

Conversely, when it is itself preceded by another noun or pronoun the *de* is normally omitted: *zhuōzi pángbiān* 'beside the table'. The same rule applies to *dōngbiān*, *xībiān*, etc. and as students often put these place words in the wrong position it may be helpful to memorise the following 'pair' of examples:

dōngbiān de xuéxiào 'the school to the east'
xuéxiào dōngbiān 'to the east of the school'.

In the first example we are talking about the **school**, in the second example we are talking about what exists to the **east** of it. This is exactly the same rule as in 3.5 but the frequent omission of *de* before the place word when used in this way tends to obscure this fact. Think of the *de* as being there when working out where the place word should come in such cases.

When the place word *lǐbiān* or *shàngbiān* is attached to a noun, *biān* is very often omitted:

zài jiā lǐ	'at home'
zài chéng lǐ	'in town'
zài yǐzi shàng	'on the chair'.

This also works with **xià** in such expressions as:

yǐzi xià	'beneath the chair'
zhuōzi xià	'beneath the table'.

The *biān* in other place words is seldom omitted, however, and where it is, the phrase should be learnt separately: *guówài* 'overseas, abroad'.

If these phrases occur at the beginning of the sentence, the use of *zài* is optional:

Jiālǐ yǒu rén 'there's somebody at home' but it is compulsory **after** the verb: *Wǒ yào fàng zài yǐzi shàng* 'I want to put (it) on the chair'.

Some adverbial phrases do not take *zài* wherever they occur in the sentence. Examples include:

chūntiān lǐ	'in the spring'
jiàqī zhōng	'in the holidays'
sānyuè zhōng	'mid-March'

Note that *lǐ* is used in the first example and *zhōng* in the second, although both are translated into English as 'in'.

Conversely, other adverbial phrases may take an optional *zài* but no other place word:

(**zài**) *zhōumò*	'at the weekend'
(**zài**) *yìjiǔjiǔlíngnián*	'in 1990'

Some take neither *zài* or any other place word: *èryuè fēn(r)* 'in February' although *èryuè* by itself is also possible.

All the above examples should be noted and added to as your studies progress. Listen carefully to Chinese speakers and imitate them as far as possible. The cassette will help you do this.

The verbs *shì* 'to be' and *yǒu* 'to have' are both used to denote existence and are often to be found with the place words described above. The basic difference is that the object of a sentence with *yǒu* is usually indefinite whereas the object of a sentence with *shì* may be either definite or indefinite and usually implies a judgement that something is so (and not something else):

Gùgōng qiánbianr yǒu yì tiáo dà jiē 'There's a big street in front of the Forbidden City' (indicating existence, position).

Gùgōng qiánbianr shì Tiān'ānmén Guǎngchǎng 'In front of the Forbidden City is Tiananmen Square' (not the Temple of Heaven for instance).

EXERCISE 17.1

Look at the map at the the beginning of this chapter and answer the following questions using the points of the compass. (Use the point of reference given in brackets after the question.)

Gùgōng zài nǎr? (Jǐngshān Gōngyuán) → *Gùgōng zài Jǐngshān Gōngyuán nánbianr.*

1 *Jǐngshān Gōngyuán zài nǎr? (Gùgōng.)*
2 *Qiánmén zài nǎr? (Máo Zhǔxí Jìniàntáng.)*
3 *Rénmín Dàhuìtáng zài nǎr? (Rénmín Yīngxióng Jìniànbēi.)*
4 *Zhōngguó Lìshǐ Bówùguǎn zài nǎr? (Rénmín Yīngxióng Jìniànbēi.)*
5 *Máo Zhǔxí Jìniàntáng zài nǎr? (Rénmín Dàhuìtáng.)*

3 JIǍ AND YǏ

Jiǎ and *yǐ* are the first and second of the ten Heavenly Stems just like alpha, beta in Greek. They are also often used in the same way as we use 'A' and 'B' in English.

4 A LÍ B

When we wish to express how far A is from B where the positions of A and B are fixed, the construction is as follows:

A *lí* B distance in time or space.

Gōngyuán lí shāngdiàn hěn yuǎn 'The park is a long way from the shops'.

Hòutiān lí jīntiān hái yǒu liǎng tiān 'The day after tomorrow is still two days away (from today)'.

Niújīn lí Lúndūn yǒu jiǔshíyī gōnglǐ 'Oxford is 91 kilometres (public *lǐ*) from London'.

EXERCISE 17.2

Using the map again, answer the following questions.

Gùgōng lí Qiánmén yuǎn ma? → *Gùgōng lí Qiánmén yuǎn.*

1 *Jǐngshān Gōngyuán lí Qiánmén yuǎn ma?*
2 *Rénmín Dàhuìtáng lí Rénmín Yīngxióng Jìniànbēi jìn bu jìn? Zěnme zǒu?*
3 *Máo Zhǔxí Jìniàntáng lí Tiān'ānmén yuǎn bu yuan? Zěnme zǒu?*
4 *Rénmín Yīngxióng Jìniànbēi lí Zhōngguó Lìshǐ Bówùguǎn hěn jìn, shì bu shi?*
5 *Niújīn lí Lúndūn yǒu duō yuǎn?*
6 *Sānshí hào lí èrshíqī hào hái yǒu jǐ tiān?*
7 *Yuándàn* (New Year's Day) *lí Shèngdànjié* (Christmas Day) *yǒu jǐ ge xīngqī?*

EXERCISE 17.3

Write out the characters you have met with the following radicals or character components. (Go through Chapters 14–17 to find the answers.)

e.g. 艹 → 苹 ____ ____

1	宀	11	土
2	刂	12	女
3	禾	13	丨
4	门	14	木
5	阝 (RHS)	15	月
6	氵	16	口
7	纟	17	彡
8	目	18	人 or 亻
9	心/忄	19	辶
10	灬	20	火

EXERCISE 17.4

Write out your answers to Exercises 17.1 and 17.2 (1–4 only) in characters.

EXERCISE 17.5

Translate into Chinese characters:

1 Excuse me, where is the Temple of Heaven? How do I get there?
2 Is the Great Hall of the People a long way from here? No, it's just opposite.

3   The Monument to the People's Heroes is to the east of the
    Great Hall of the People but to the west of the Museum of
    National History.

Regional differences

Given China's vastness, it is not surprising that there are a
number of major dialects in China and countless minor ones.
These do not include the languages of the minority peoples
such as Tibetan (*Xīzàngwén*), Thai (*Tàiwén*), Vietnamese
(*Yuènánwén*), Uighur (*Wéiwú'ěrwén*), etc. Some expressions
which you will hear frequently in the North such as *láojià*
are hardly heard in the South. Although *pǔtōnghuà* has
standardised much of the vocabulary you will still find
regional differences. Examples include:

	North	South*
'potato'	*tǔdòu*	*mǎlíngshǔ*
'tomato'	*xīhóngshì*	*fānqié*
'pineapple'	*bōluó*	*fènglí*
'taxi'	*chūzūqìchē*	*jìchéngchē*
'bicycle'	*zìxíngchē*	*jiǎotàchē*

* plus Taiwan and overseas Chinese communities

18

At the Post Office
在邮电局 *Zài yóudiànjú*

Mr King goes to the post office to send a parcel of books back home, and post two letters.

王	请问，寄包裹是在这儿吗？
	Qǐng wèn, jì bāoguǒ shì zài zhèr ma?
营业员	不，在隔壁。
Yíngyèyuán	*Bù, zài gébì.*
王	这儿能买邮票吗？
	Zhèr néng mǎi yóupiào ma?
营业员	能。
	Néng.
王	这两封信多少钱？
	Zhè liǎng fēng xìn duōshao qián?
营业员	寄哪儿？
	Jì nǎr?
王	重的寄上海，另（外）一封寄美国。
	Zhòng de jì Shànghǎi, lìng (wài) yì fēng jì Měiguó.
营业员	上海的要寄航空还是寄平信？
	Shànghǎi de yào jì hángkōng háishi jì píngxìn?
王	寄航空。
	Jì hángkōng.
营业员	（把信放在天平上）寄美国的两块四，寄上海的三毛。一共两块七。
	(Bǎ xìn fàng zài tiānpíng shàng) Jì Měiguó de liǎng kuài sì, jì Shànghǎi de sān máo. Yígòng liǎng kuài qī.

（王先生给他十块）

(Wáng xiānsheng gěi tā shí kuài)

营业员　找你七块三。

Zhǎo nǐ qī kuài sān.

王　谢谢。(走到邮寄包裹的地方)

Xièxie. (Zǒu dào yóujì bāoguǒ de dìfang)

王　同志，请问，把这包书寄到英国要多少钱？

Tóngzhì, qǐng wèn, bǎ zhè bāo shū jì dào Yīngguó yào duōshao qián?

营业员　(把书放在天平上)重五公斤，三十六块七毛钱。要不要挂号？

(Bǎ shū fàng zài tiānpíng shàng) Zhòng wǔ gōng jīn, sānshíliù kuài qī máo qián. Yào bu yào guà hào?

王　嗯，挂号吧。

Ng, guà hào ba.

营业员　再加上挂号费六毛钱，一共三十七块三。请把邮票贴上，再填一张包裹单，把收件人、寄件人的地址和姓名填写清楚。

Zài jiā shang guàhàofèi liù máo qián, yígòng sānshíqī kuài sān. Qǐng bǎ yóupiào tiē shang, zài tián yì zhāng bāoguǒdān, bǎ shōujiànrén 、 jìjiànrén de dìzhǐ hé xìngmíng tiánxiě qīngchu

（过了一会儿）

(Guò le yíhuìr)

王　邮票贴好了，包裹单也填好了。

Yóupiào tiē hǎo le, bāoguǒdān yě tián hǎo le.

营业员　把书给我吧。这是收据，请收好。

Bǎ shū gěi wǒ ba. Zhè shì shōujù, qǐng shōu hǎo.

王　谢谢你。请问，这儿可以打长途电话吗？

Xièxie nǐ. Qǐng wèn, zhèr kěyǐ dǎ chángtú diànhuà ma?

营业员　可以。你去 '电报、电话' 柜台问一问。

Kěyǐ. Nǐ qù 'diànbào, diànhuà' guìtái wènyiwèn.

王　好，麻烦你了。

Hǎo, máfan nǐ le.

营业员　没什么。

Méi shénme.

邮电局	yóudiànjú (n)	*post and telecommunications office*
寄	jì (v)	*to post, mail*
包裹	bāoguǒ (n)	*parcel, package*
营业员	yíngyèyuán (n)	*clerk, shop employee*
隔壁	gébì (PW)	*next door*
这儿		
封	fēng (MW)	*for letters*
信	xìn (n)	*letter*
寄	jì (v)	*to post, mail*
哪儿		
重	zhòng (adj.)	*heavy*
上海	Shànghǎi (PW)	*Shanghai*
另（外）	lìng(wài) (adj.; adv)	*another; separately*
美国	Měiguó (PW)	*USA, America*
航空（信）	hángkōng (xìn)	*airmail*
还是		
平信	píngxìn (n)	*surface mail*
把	bǎ (prep.)	*a preposition showing disposal*
放（在）	fàng (zài) (v)	*to put (on)*
天平	tiānpíng (n)	*scales*
到	-dào (DE)	*-to*
邮寄	yóujì (v)	*to send by post or mail*
同志	tóngzhì (n)	*comrade*
书	shū (n) [běn]	*book*
公斤	gōngjīn (n)	*kilogram (Lit. public catty)*
挂号	guà hào (v-o)	*to register (Lit. hang number)*
嗯	ǹg	*uh-huh, hm*
加（上）	jiā (shang) (v)	*to add (on)*
挂号费	guàhàofèi (n)	*registration charge*
先	xiān (conj.)	*first*
贴（上）	tiē (shang) (v)	*to stick (on)*

填（写）	**tián (xiě)** (v)	*to fill in*
包裹单	**bāoguǒdān** (n)	*parcel form*
收件人	**shōujiànrén** (n)	*addressee, recipient*
寄件人	**jìjiànrén** (n)	*sender*
地址	**dìzhǐ** (n)	*address*
姓名	**xìngmíng** (n)	*full name*
清楚	**qīngchu**	
收据	**shōujù** (n)	*receipt*
收（好）	**shōu (hǎo)** (v)	*to put away; to receive*
长途电话	**chángtú diànhuà** (n)	*long distance telephone call*
可以	**kěyǐ**	
电报	**diànbào** (n)	*telegram*
柜台	**guìtái** (n)	*counter*
麻烦	**máfan**	

Table of stroke order of the more difficult characters

局	尸 尸 厅 局 局 局
寄	宀 大 可（一 亠 亓 亓 可）
裹	亠 果 厽（ノ 厸 厸 厽）
营	艹 宀 吕
业	丨 刂 业 业 业
隔	阝 冂 呙
壁	辟 月 辛（丶 亠 亠 立 立 立 辛） 土
书	丨 亅 书 书
重	一 一 一 一 一 盲 盲 重 重
费	弗（一 一 弓 弔 弗） 贝

先	ノ	ー	⺧	生	牛	先						
填	土	真 (一 十 广 卢 占 峀 峀 直 真 真)										
写	⼍	与 (一 ㇉ 与)										
单	⺌	甲 (丨 冂 冃 日 旦 甲)										
址	土	止 (丨 卜 ⺊ 止)										
楚	林	疋										
据	扌	居										
以	㇄	⼄	㠯	以								
柜	木	巨 (一 ㇕ 彐 巨)										
烦	火	页 (一 ⺄ 厂 厉 页 页)										

Grammar

1 THE *Bǎ* CONSTRUCTION (I)

By using *bǎ*, the direct object is brought forward to a position in front of the verb instead of after it so the sentence order becomes:

Subject *bǎ* object verb + other element(s)

Wǒ bǎ bāoguǒ fàng zài tiānpíng shàng

'I put the parcel on the scales'.

It is important to note that:

1 The verb cannot stand on its own after *bǎ* and that something else has to come after it even if it is only *le* or the verb is simply reduplicated. *Tā bǎ zìxíngchē mài le*. 'He sold the bicycle.'

Qǐng nǐ bǎ chuānghu kāikai. 'Please open the window.'

2 The object of a *bǎ* sentence is normally a *specific* person or thing(s) even when no specification is overtly expressed in the Chinese; it cannot refer to people or things in general: *Tā bǎ shū jì zǒu le* 'She posted *the* books'.

3 Negatives, auxiliary verbs, adverbial phrases of 'time when' and 'time within which' go before *bǎ*. When *dōu* refers to the subject it comes directly after the subject and before *bǎ*, but when it refers to the object it comes directly after the object and before the verb.

*Wǒ jīntiān **méi bǎ** diànhuà hàomǎ jì xiàlai* 'I didn't note down *the* telephone number(s) today'.

*Yíngyèyuán **yào bǎ** shōujù gěi wǒ* 'The clerk wants/wanted to give me *the* receipt'.

Nǐ zhè liǎng ge xīngqī zěnme méi bǎ zhè běn shū kàn wán ne? 'How come you haven't finished this book during the last two weeks?'.

*Wǒmen **dōu bǎ** yīfu chuān shang le* (*chuān*: to wear) 'We **all** put the clothes on'.

*Wǒmen **bǎ** yīfu **dōu** chuān shang le* 'We put **all** the clothes on'.

4 Although *bǎ* cannot be translated into English it does contain a sense of disposal, i.e. to hold or take an object and do something with it (hence the hand radical), which is why it cannot be used with verbs which contain no such idea of disposal such as *shì*, *yǒu*, *zhīdao*, *juéde*, *xǐhuan*, *zài*, *lái*, *qù* and *huí*. These points are summarised in the following table:

Subj. (N or pr.)	Adv. time	Neg.	Aux. v.	Prep.	Obj.	Verb	Other elements
Wǒ				*bǎ*	*shìqing*	*zuò*	*wán*
Wǒ			*néng*	*bǎ*	*shìqing*	*zuò*	*wán*
Wǒ		*bù*	*néng*	*bǎ*	*shìqing*	*zuò*	*wán*
Wǒ	*jīntiān*	*bù*	*néng*	*bǎ*	*shìqing*	*zuò*	*wán*
Tā				*bǎ*	*xìn*	*xiě*	*wán le*
Tā		*méi*		*bǎ*	*xìn*	*xiě*	*wán*
Tā	*hái*	*méi*		*bǎ*	*xìn*	*xiě*	*wán ne*

SOME USES OF THE *BǍ* CONSTRUCTION (II)

1 When the main verb is followed by the resultative ending *zài* or *dào* plus a place word:

Qǐng nǐ bǎ dìtú fàng zài zhuōzi shàng 'Please put the map on the table.'

Wǒ yǐjīng bǎ tā sòng dào (*sòng* 'to see somebody off') *fēijīchǎng* ('airport') *le* 'I've already seen her off to the airport'.

2 When the verb is reduplicated:

Qǐng nǐ bǎ zhè jiàn shìqing hǎohāor xiǎngyixiǎng 'Please think over this matter carefully'.

3 When the main verb is followed by the resultative ending *gěi* and takes both a direct and an indirect object (note that *gàosu* 'to tell' also comes into this category although it does not take *gěi*):

Wǒmen bǎ qián huán gěi (*huán* 'to give or pay back') *lǎobǎn* ('the boss') *le* 'We've paid back the money to the boss'.

Tā zǎo jiù ('long ago') *bǎ nà jiàn shìqing gàosu wǒ le* 'He told me about that matter ages ago.'

4 When verbs of movement take the directional endings *lái* or *qù, huí, zǒu*, etc.:

Tāmen zuótiān bǎ zhàopiàn ('photograph') *dài huílai le* 'They brought the photos back yesterday'.

Xuésheng bǎ lùyīnjī jiè zǒu (*jiè* 'to borrow; lend') *le* 'The student borrowed the tape-recorder (and went off with it)'.

5 When there is a quantified expression in the sentence such as *yí cì*:

Wǒ bǎ kèwén kàn le yí cì 'I('ve) read the text once'.

(If *bǎ* were not used then the sentence would read *Wǒ kàn le yí cì kèwén*. Note that if the object were a pronoun, the word order would be reversed, i.e. *Wǒ kàn le tā yí cì*.)

6 When the main verb is followed by the resultative ending *chéng* (*Lit.* 'to become') or *zuò* (*Lit.* 'to regard as') *Wàiguórén jīngcháng bǎ 'shǒudū'* ('capital') *liǎng ge zì niàn chéng 'shǒudōu'*. 'Foreigners often read "*shǒudū*" as "*shǒudōu*"':

Nǐ wèi shénme bǎ wǒ dāng zuò (*dāng* 'to be, work as') *nǐ de dírén* (enemy) *ne?* 'Why do you regard me as your enemy?'.

EXERCISE 18.1

Turn the following sentences into *bǎ* sentences:

Yíngyèyuán zài xìnfēng (envelope) *shàng tiē yóupiào* → *Yíngyèyuán bǎ yóupiào tiē zài xìnfēng shàng.*

1 *Qǐng nǐ shōu hǎo shōujù.*
2 *Bāoguǒdān shàng yào xiě qīngchu jìjiànrén de dìzhǐ hé xìngmíng.*
3 *Jiā shang guàhàofèi yígòng yào duōshao qián?*
4 *Tā méi tián hǎo bāoguǒdān.*
5 *Yóukè* (tourist) *méi hǎohāor kànyikàn Gùgōng.*

Turn the following *bǎ* sentences into sentences without *bǎ*: *Wǒ jīntiān yào bǎ zhè fēng xìn jì zǒu* → *Wǒ jīntiān yào jì zǒu zhè fēng xìn.*

6 *Shòupiàoyuán bǎ liǎng zhāng hǎo piào liú gěi Wáng xiānsheng le.*
7 *Wàiguó zhuānjiā yīnggāi bǎ jùchǎng de diànhuà hàomǎ* (number) *jì xiàlai.*
8 *Shòuhuòyuán bú yuànyì bǎ sīchóu chènshān mài gěi tā.*
9 *Dàifu* (doctor) *yào bǎ bìngrén* (patient) *sòng* (send) *dào yīyuàn* (hospital).
10 *Wǒ yí ge Zhōngguó péngyou yì tiān néng bǎ liǎng bāo yān xī wán* (*xī* 'to inhale, smoke').

2 SAME CHARACTER DIFFERENT PRONUNCIATION

Several characters have two or more different readings depending on context. 都 *dōu* is read as *dū* in 首都; 大夫 'doctor' is read as *dàifu* not *dàfu*; 还 is read *huán* as a verb meaning 'to give or pay back' but as *hái* when it is an adverb meaning 'still'; 和 is read as *huo* in *nuǎnhuo* 'warm'; 行 is read as *háng* in *yínháng* 'bank' and so on. Some characters have the same pronunciation but different tones but they do not lie within the scope of this book!

3 *-SHANG*

As a resultative verb ending, *-shang* is often used to indicate:
(a) that the object has become attached to something else as a result of the action of the verb:

*Qǐng xiān bǎ yóupiào tiē **shang*** 'Please stick the stamps on first'. (i.e. to the wrapping paper).

*Tiānqì lěng le, yīnggāi chuān **shang** máoyī* 'It's turned cold, you ought to put a sweater on'.

(b)   Or that the completion of the action of the verb has resulted in something being closed or brought together:

Qǐng nǐ bǎ mén guān shang 'Please close the door'.

Jì bāoguǒ děi yòng bù (cloth) *bāo shang* (wrap up)、*féng shang* (sew up), *zài bǎ shōujiànrén de xìngmíng hé dìzhǐ xiě zài bù shàng.* 'In China when you send a parcel, you have to wrap it up in a piece of cloth, sew it up and then write the name and address of the recipient on the cloth.' (This is absolutely normal practice when sending small items except for books – the sender must also write her/his name and address on the cloth too.)

4   *XIĀN* V₁ *ZÀI* V₂

The construction *xiān* V₁ *zài* V₂ shows a sequence of actions, first V₁ has to be done, then V₂. This means that you can only carry out the action of the second verb when you have carried out the action of the first:

Qǐng xiān bǎ yóupiào tiē shang, zài tián yì zhāng bāoguǒdān.

'Please stick the stamps on first and then fill out a parcel form'. (Note that the *xiān* is sometimes omitted in this construction, leaving only the *zài* before the second verb. This *zài* is written 再 as in 再见 *zàijiàn* not as in 在, 'at, in'.)

Comrade and others

Although the term 同志 *tóngzhì* is still used, it is less common than it was and will presumably eventually become even less so. Terms of address which were regarded as 'feudal' before the Great Proletarian Cultural Revolution (now written in Chinese with inverted commas to express political disapproval) are coming back into fashion. It is quite common to address youngish women as *xiǎojie.* The once universal *àiren* 'love person' for husband or wife is also slowly being replaced with the more conventional and less intimate *xiānsheng* or *zhàngfu* for 'husband' and *tàitai* or *qīzi* for 'wife'. These 'new/old' terms are particularly in favour with some people who live in the coastal provinces or come into contact with foreigners.

Receipts

Most Chinese hang onto their receipts like mad as there is a tremendously widespread system of 报销 *bàoxiāo* 'reimbursement of expenses'. Many of the Chinese people travelling on the little mini-buses 小公共汽车 *xiǎo gōnggòng qìchē* (usually called 面包车 *miànbāochē* [lit bread vehicle because of their shape] when they belong to a work unit) or on trains, planes or in taxis are on business (出差 *chū chāi*) and consequently can claim back all expenses. Hence the loudhailers used by minibus drivers and conductors encouraging prospective passengers to take advantage of the fact that *piào kěyǐ bàoxiāo* and to use the mini-buses, which are a more expensive but much more efficient means of transport. For a Chinese, his/her grade or position in the ranking order determines whether he/she travels hard or soft class on the train (see next chapter).

EXERCISE 18.2

Write out each of the following characters in *pinyin* and put their common component or radical in brackets afterwards.

e.g. 把、挂、打 → *bǎ、guà、dǎ* (扌)

1 想、您、怎、意、思、志。

2 请、说、谢、话。

3 喂、售、员、吗、问、号。

4 近、还、过、这、远、边。

5 部、那、邮、都。

Repeat this exercise for yourself in subsequent chapters.

EXERCISE 18.3

Write a character for each of the following phonetic transcriptions so as to make a word with the character given.

e.g. 北 *biān*, 北 *jīng* → 北边, 北京.

1 东 *xi*, 东 *biān*.

2 *wài* 国, *Zhōng* 国.

3 售 *huò* 员, 售 *piào* 员.

4 *máo* 衣, 衣 *fu*.

5　电 *yǐng*, 电 *huà*, 电 *bào*.
6　星期 *èr*, 星期 *sì*.
7　地 *tú*, 地 *fang*, 地 *zhǐ*.
8　*shōu* 件人, *jì* 件人.

EXERCISE 18.4

Translate this passage into colloquial English and then into Chinese characters.

Wáng xiānsheng rén hěn hǎo dànshi tā yǒu yí ge xiǎo máobìng (毛病 'defect') *tā hěn xǐhuan huā* (花 'spend') *qián. Qù mǎi yí jiàn chènshān, tā jiù mǎi sān jiàn, nǐ yào tā mǎi yì běn zázhì jiù gěi nǐ mǎi shí běn. Tā shuō dōu hěn yǒu yìsi suǒyǐ dōu mǎi le. Ràng* (让 'let') *tā qù mǎi dōngxi, nǐ zěnme néng fàng xīn ne?*

EXERCISE 18.5

Translate the following into *pinyin* and then into Chinese characters:

1　You can make long distance phone-calls in Chinese post and telecommunications offices.
2　This is your receipt, please put (it) away carefully.
3　Please fill in this parcel form. Write the names and addresses of the recipient and sender clearly. (NB the name comes after the address in Chinese so reverse the order.)
4　Have you stuck the stamps on? Not yet.
5　Posting books is a hassle but worth it.

19

At the Railway Station

在火车站 *Zài huǒchēzhàn*

Foreigners are very fortunate in being able to buy their train tickets in a special office at Beijing Railway Station (*Běijīng Huǒchēzhàn*) otherwise they would have to queue (*pái duì* v-o) for a very long time. Miss Shaw and Mr King wish to go to Tai'an (*Tài'ān*) over the mid-Autumn Festival (*Zhōngqiūjié*) in order to climb Mount Tai (*Tàishān*). Miss Shaw goes to buy the tickets.

史　　九月二十七、八号幺六幺次还有硬卧吗?

售票员　要几张?

史　　要两张。

售票员　对不起,只剩一个上铺。软卧行吗?

史　　软卧太贵了,那么我看看(拿出火车时刻表查一下)。星期六一百二十五次几点开?啊,上午十点三十八分,晚上八点一刻到泰安——可以。星期六一百二十五次有软座吗?

售票员　一百二十五次没有软座,只有硬座、硬卧和软卧。您买硬卧下铺就等于软座了。

史　　好,那就这样吧。

售票员　您有学生证或者专家证吗?如果有,票价就跟中国人一样,要不,贵百分之七十五。

史　　有学生证,也有优待证所以就可以付人民币,是不是?

售票员　是的。(付钱以后,就接着问)您是第一次来中国吧?

史　　是啊,我刚来几个月。

售票员　您中国话讲得不错。您为什么要去泰安而不去一个比较好玩儿的地方呢?

史　　　我非常想爬泰山，中秋节那天晚上在泰山顶上看日落，又在月光下吃月饼，第二天还希望能看到日出。

售票员　你这个人真有意思呀！您跟谁一起去？

史　　　跟我男朋友一起去。

售票员　他是中国人还是外国人？

史　　　是外国人，他是我的未婚夫。

售票员　啊，你们已经订婚了。难怪你们愿意在泰山上看日落，你们够浪漫的！

史　　　年轻的时候不浪漫一阵子还等到老了才浪漫吗？我的未婚夫很喜欢唐诗，他选了好几首，准备在泰山顶上给我朗诵。这些诗都是描写月光的。

售票员　真逗你们！

史　　　请问，我有一个朋友快要回国了，想坐火车经过莫斯科，能在这里买票吗？

售票员　不行，要去国际饭店中国旅行社订票。

史　　　你帮了我不少忙，太谢谢你了。

售票员　没什么。祝你们中秋节玩儿得愉快。

* * *

This is the same dialogue, this time in *pinyin*:

Shǐ　　　*Jiǔyuè èrshíqī、bā hào yāo liù yāo cì hái yǒu yìngwò ma?*

Shòupiàoyuán　*Yào jǐ zhāng?*

Shǐ　　　*Yào liǎng zhāng.*

Shòupiàoyuán　*Duìbuqǐ, zhǐ shèng yí ge shàngpù. Ruǎnwò xíng ma?*

Shǐ　　　*Ruǎnwò tài guì le. Nàme wǒ kànkan (ná chū huǒchē shíkèbiǎo chá yíxià). Xīngqīliù yìbǎi'èrshíwǔ cì jǐ diǎn kāi? À, shàngwǔ shí diǎn sānshíbā fēn, wǎnshang bā diǎn yíkè dào Tài'ān – kěyǐ. Xīngqīliù yìbǎi'èrshíwǔ cì yǒu ruǎnzuò ma?*

Shòupiàoyuán　*Yìbǎi'èrshíwǔ cì méi yǒu ruǎnzuò, zhǐ yǒu yìngzuò、yìngwò hé ruǎnwò. Nín mǎi yìngwò xiàpù jiù děngyú ruǎnzuò le.*

Shǐ　　　*Hǎo, nà jiù zhèyàng ba.*

Shòupiàoyuán　*Nín yǒu xuéshēngzhèng huòzhě zhuānjiāzhèng ma?*

	Rúguǒ yǒu, piàojià jiù gēn Zhōngguórén yíyàng, yàobù, guì bǎifēn zhī qīshíwǔ.
Shǐ	*Yǒu xuéshēngzhèng, yě yǒu yōudàizhèng suǒyǐ jiù kěyǐ fù rénmínbì, shì bu shì?*
Shòupiàoyuán	*Shìde. (Fù qián yǐhòu, jiù jiēzhe wèn) Nín shì dì yí cì lái Zhōngguó ba?*
Shǐ	*Shì a, wǒ gāng lái jǐ ge yuè.*
Shòupiàoyuán	*Nín Zhōngguóhuà jiǎng de búcuò. Nín wèi shénme yào qù Tài'ān ér bú qù yí ge bǐjiào hǎowánr de dìfang ne?*
Shǐ	*Wǒ fēicháng xiǎng pá Tàishān, Zhōngqiūjié nà tiān wǎnshang zài Tàishān dǐng shàng kàn rìluò, yòu zài yuèguāng xià chī yuèbǐng. Dì èr tiān hái xīwàng néng kàn dào rìchū.*
Shòupiàoyuán	*Nín zhè ge rén zhēn yǒu yìsi ya! Nín gēn shéi yìqǐ qù?*
Shǐ	*Gēn wǒ nán péngyou yìqǐ qù.*
Shòupiàoyuán	*Tā shì Zhōngguórén háishi wàiguórén?*
Shǐ	*Shì wàiguórén, tā shì wǒ de wèihūnfū.*
Shòupiàoyuán	*À, nǐmen yǐjīng dìnghūn le. Nánguài nǐmen yuànyì zài Tàishān shàng kàn rìluò, nǐmen gòu làngmàn de!*
Shǐ	*Niánqīng de shíhou bu làngmàn yìzhénzi hái děng dào lǎo le cái làngmàn ma? Wǒ de wèihūnfū hěn xǐhuan Táng shī, tā xuǎn le hǎo jǐ shǒu, zhǔnbèi zài Tàishān dǐng shàng gěi wǒ lǎngsòng. Zhè xiē shī dōu shì miáoxiě yuèguāng de.*
Shòupiàoyuán	*Zhēn dòu nǐmen!*
Shǐ	*Qǐng wèn, wǒ yǒu yí ge péngyou kuài yào huí guó le, xiǎng zuò huǒchē jīngguò Mòsīkē, néng zài zhèlǐ mǎi piào ma?*
Shòupiàoyuán	*Bù xíng, yào qù Guójì Fàndiàn Zhōngguó Lǚxíngshè dìng piào.*
Shǐ	*Nǐ bāng le wǒ bù shǎo máng, tài xièxie nǐ le.*
Shòupiàoyuán	*Méi shénme. Zhù nǐmen Zhōngqiūjié wánr de yúkuài.*

火车站	**huǒchēzhàn** (n)	*railway station*
幺	**yāo** (num.)	*one (used orally only)*
次	**cì** (MW)	*time*
硬卧	**yìngwò** (n.)	*hard sleeper*
对不起	**duìbuqǐ**	*sorry; excuse me*
剩（下来）	**shèng (xiàlai)** (v)	*be left (over); remain*
上铺	**shàngpù** (n)	*upper berth*
软卧	**ruǎnwò** (n)	*soft sleeper*
拿出	**ná chū** (v)	*to take out*
火车	**huǒchē** (n)	*train*
时刻表	**shíkèbiǎo** (n)	*timetable, schedule*
一百	**yì bǎi**	*one hundred*
开	**kāi** (v)	*to start; to open; to drive*
上午	**shàngwǔ** (TW)	*morning*
软座	**ruǎnzuò** (n)	*soft seat (train)*
硬座	**yìngzuò** (n)	*hard seat (train)*
下铺	**xiàpù** (n)	*bottom berth*
等于	**děngyú** (v)	*to be equal to; be equivalent to*
这样	**zhèyàng**	*like this, in this way*
专家证	**zhuānjiāzhèng** (n)	*expert card*
如果	**rúguǒ** (conj.)	*if*
票价	**piàojià** (n)	*ticket price*
跟 A 一样	**gēn A yíyàng**	*the same as A*
百分之 X	**bǎifēn zhī X**	*X per cent*
优待证	**yōudàizhèng** (n)	*preferential card (often known as white card) (see pages 202–203)*
人民币	**rénmínbì** (n)	*RMB (Chinese currency)*
接着	**jiēzhe** (v)	*to carry on; follow*
刚	**gāng** (adv.)	*just*
中国话	**Zhōngguóhuà**	*Chinese language (older term)*
讲	**jiǎng** (v)	*to speak; to explain*
为什么	**wèi shénme** (conj.)	*why*
而	**ér** (conj.)	*but; and*

好玩（儿）	hǎowán(r) (adj.)	*entertaining, enjoyable*
爬	pá (v)	*to climb*
顶	dǐng (n)	*top, peak; MW for hat*
日落	rìluò (n)	*sunset*
月光	yuèguāng (n)	*moonlight*
月饼	yuèbǐng (n)	*mooncake*
希望	xīwàng (v and n)	*to hope; hope*
未婚夫	wèihūnfū (n)	*fiancé*
订婚	dìnghūn (v-o)	*to be or get engaged*
难怪	nánguài (conj.)	*no wonder*
够	gòu (adv.)	*rather, quite; enough (adj.)*
浪漫	làngmàn (adj.)	*romantic*
年轻	niánqīng (adj.)	*young*
一阵子	yízhènzi (n)	*a period of time, spell*
等	děng (v)	*wait*
唐	Táng (N)	*the Tang Dynasty (AD 618–907)*
诗（首）	shī (n) [shǒu]	*poem*
选	xuǎn (v)	*to choose*
好几	hǎo jǐ (adj.)	*a good many*
准备	zhǔnbèi (v)	*to prepare*
朗诵	lǎngsòng (v)	*to recite, read about with expression*
描写	miáoxiě (v)	*to describe*
逗	dòu (adj.)	*funny*
回国	huí guó (v-o)	*to return to your own country*
经过	jīngguò (v)	*to go through, pass*
莫斯科	Mòsīkē (N)	*Moscow*
国际饭店	Guójì Fàndiàn (N)	*the International Hotel*
中国旅行社	Zhōngguó Lǚxíngshè (N)	*China Travel Service*
订	dìng (v)	*to book, reserve, subscribe to*
帮忙	bāng máng (v-o)	*to help, do a favour*
不少	bù shǎo	*quite a bit, quite a few*
祝	zhù (v)	*to offer good wishes*
愉快	yúkuài (adj.)	*happy, pleased*

On trains

In China one does not buy a single or return ticket to X but asks for a seat on a certain number train on a certain day to X! In general, trains with one or two figure numbers are express, those with three figures semi-fast or ordinary stopping trains. The ordinary method of notation (see 2.11) is used when expressing train numbers of 100 or less, numbers over 100 may be expressed as three individual digits. To avoid possible confusion with *qī* ('seven'), *yāo* is used instead of *yī* ('one') as in the example in the dialogue or in telephone numbers. On long distance trains (and I mean long distance) you can travel soft or hard sleeper or hard seat. On shorter distance main routes you can travel soft or hard seat, on 'minor' routes hard seat only. Soft sleepers are arranged in small compartments of four (two-up two-down). Hard sleepers are arranged in blocks of six (two *shàngpù*, two *zhōngpù* and two *xiàpù*) in huge compartments. Each block of six has its own Thermos flask of hot water (as does each soft sleeper compartment) which is filled at intervals by the *chéngwùyuán* ('train attendant') responsible for that part of the train. Everybody in hard class usually brings her/his own tea-cup with lid and her/his own supply of tea-leaves. (Cups with lids are normally provided free of charge in soft class.) A rail runs the length of the hard sleeper compartment at roughly eye-level and everybody wraps a thin face towel over it, folding the towel into a narrow strip (if it hangs down too far, the *chéngwùyuán* will usually adjust it). There is usually a *cānchē* ('restaurant car') on all long- and medium-distance trains where you generally get an indifferent meal; so bring your own supplies to fill in the gaps. Try the cardboard boxes of *kuàicān* ('fast food'). Use your own chopsticks at all times. When you start your journey, a disembodied voice over the loudspeakers announces that your new life on the train is about to begin and lists the various rules and regulations you should adhere to to make the journey a happy one. Early to bed, early to rise are the general principles to be observed on

Chinese trains. It has hitherto been impossible to buy return tickets in China so as soon as you get to a place you have to start thinking of how and when you are going to get out of it! Travelling on Chinese trains is well worth the effort however and a way of experiencing Chinese society in miniature.

Zhengs of all sorts

As in most socialist countries, IDs of all kinds are *de rigueur* in China. All Chinese have a *gōngzuòzhèng* ('work ID card'), foreign experts have a *zhuānjiāzhèng* ('expert's ID card'), students have a *xuéshēngzhèng* ('student card') and so on. These cards entitle the bearer to special privileges or allow her/him access to places which would otherwise be barred to her/him. Chinese visiting foreign friends or colleagues who live in foreigners' compounds or hotels have to show their *gōngzuòzhèng* and possibly fill out a form saying whom they are going to visit, his/her room number, etc. before being allowed in by their Chinese compatriots at the door or gate. Handled sensitively, this issue is not quite as formidable as it appears. You can always go to the main door/gate of your building to meet your friends to save them any embarrassment. The Chinese authorities, for their part, claim it is to ensure the safety of their foreign guests and that of their possessions.

A *yōudàizhèng* ('superior treatment card'), now known as *gòuwùzhīfùzhèng* (购物支付证) and yellow in colour, is another animal altogether. It entitles the bearer to pay in *rénmínbì* (RMB) where the ordinary foreigner would normally be required to pay in FEC (foreign exchange certificates – *wàihuìquàn** in Chinese), e.g. for accommodation, food and entertainment in some hotels and 'official' guest-houses, taxi fares and goods purchased in Friendship Stores (*Yǒuyì Shāngdiàn*) or hotels. However, imported goods such as foreign cigarettes, alcohol, chewing gum, and chocolates have to be paid for in FEC whether or not you have a *yōudàizhèng* or a *gòuwùzhīfúzhèng*. (This also applies to many joint venture hotels now where payment has to be in FEC). Amongst those issued with a *yōudàizhèng* or a *gòuwùzhīfúzhèng* are foreign experts and teachers recruited by the Chinese *dānwèi*. There is a considerable difference in status and salary between these two groups. The foreign experts have part of their salary paid in RMB and part in hard currency, the foreign teachers have all their salary (which is much lower) paid in RMB. Chinese government sponsored students also have their scholar- ships paid in RMB so are entitled to a *gòuwùzhīfúzhèng (yōudàizhèng)*. People who use them are regarded by some Chinese as 'second class *wàiguórén*', business people and diplomats come into the first class category. Please note that terms such as *gòuwùzhīfúzhèng (yōudàizhèng)* are subject to constant revision as to their terms of reference and are thus liable to change in the future. NB: FEC abolished 1994.

* Most people appear to pronounce this *wàihuìjuàn*.

Grammar

1 MORE ON THE COMPARATIVE

We have already met the comparative in 7.5 and again in 8.3. To express that 'A is the same as B' we say *A gēn B yíyàng*. In the text *piàojià gēn Zhōngguórén yíyàng* stands for *piàojià gēn Zhōngguórén de piàojià yíyàng* 'The price is the same as for Chinese'. This can be taken a step further using the formula:

'A is as adjective as B', *A gēn B yíyàng adjective:*
A gēn B yíyàng guì 'A is as expensive as B'.
Niúròu gēn yú yíyàng guì 'Beef is as expensive as fish'.

EXERCISE 19.1

Write out the following sentences in characters and then translate them into English. Look up any characters you don't know in the index.

1 *Yìngwò gēn ruǎnwò yíyàng ma?*
 Bù yíyàng, ruǎnwò bǐ yìngwò guì duōle.

2 *Yìngwò gēn yìngzuò yǒu shénme bù yíyàng?*
  Yìngzuò bǐ yìngwò piányi de duō.
3 *Nǐ gēn tā yíyàng bù xǐhuan tīng yīnyuè ma?*
  Bù, wǒ hěn xǐhuan tīng gǔdiǎn yīnyuè.
4 *Wǒ gēn wǒ de wèihūnqī* (未婚妻 fiancée) *yíyàng làngmàn, dōu
  xǐhuan xiě shī.*
5 *Zài Ōuzhōu Rìběn diànshì gēn zài Zhōngguó yíyàng nán mǎi ma?*

2 PERCENTAGES AND FRACTIONS

As stated in 15.1, the Chinese move from the general to the
particular, so in line with this principle instead of saying 75%, the
Chinese say 100 parts classical possessive marker *zhī* 75, i.e. *bǎifēn
zhī qīshíwǔ*. Sixty per cent would be *bǎifēn zhī liùshí* and so on.

To say something is 10% more expensive than something else
the adjective for 'expensive' *guì* is placed in front of the percentage:
guì bǎifēn zhī shí so 'this video-recorder is 20% more expensive
than that one' would be:

  Zhè tái lùxiàngjī bǐ nà tái (lùxiàngjī) guì bǎifēn zhī èrshí.

'How many per cent' is expressed as *bǎifēn zhī duōshao*?

Fractions work in exactly the same way. Three quarters (3/4) is
expressed as four parts *zhī* three, i.e. *sìfēn zhī sān*; 7/8 *bāfēn zhī qī*,
etc. 'How many eighths' would therefore be *bāfēn zhī jǐ* (not
duōshao as the answer has to be less than 10.)

If you want to say something is 'twice as expensive as something
else' the formula is'. *A bǐ B guì yí bèi*, where *bèi* 倍 means 'times or
-fold'.

EXERCISE 19.2

Write out each sentence in characters including translating the
percentage, fraction or -fold contained in the brackets:

  Wàiguórén de piàojià bǐ Zhōngguórén guì (75%).
  → 外国人的票价比中国人贵**百分之七十五**。

1 *Guójì Fàndiàn bǐ Běijīng Fàndiàn guì* (50%).
2 *Shuǐdiànfèi bǐ qùnián guì* (10%).
3 *Xiàpù bǐ shàngpù guì* (20%).
4 *Dǎ chángtú diànhuà bǐ dǎ diànbào guì bǎifēn zhī duōshao? Guì*
  (200%).
5 *Rìběn yīfu bǐ Zhōngguó yīfu guì* (300%).

6 *Píngguǒ bù hǎo chī, wǒ zhǐ chī le* (1/4).

7 *Wàiguó yān hǎo chōu* (抽 to smoke), *zhè bāo yǐjīng chōu le* (2/3).

8 *Yīnyuèhuì de piào zuótiān mài le* (7/8).

9 *Guóchǎn diànshì bǐ wàiguó diànshì piányi* (one-fold).

10 *Zài Zhōngguó Měiguó zhuānjiā bǐ Yīngguó zhuānjiā duō* (ten-fold).

3 USE OF *ÉR*

Ér 而 is another reminder of how much classical Chinese is contained in the modern language. It is not just used by educated people either, which shows how deeply engrained it is in the linguistic memories of the Chinese. *Ér* is a conjunction roughly meaning 'and' if the sentence is made up of two complementary halves and 'but', 'whereas' if they are contrasting. It combines with *qiě* 且 to mean 'moreover' and in this context often appears with *búdàn* 不但 to form a pair of conjunctions, viz. *búdàn...érqiě* 'not only...but also...': *Tā **búdàn** méi lái **érqiě** hái gàosu wǒ tā yǒngyuǎn bú huì zài lái* 'Not only did she not come but she also told me that she would never come again'.

4 MORE ON *YÒU*

We met the construction *yòu...yòu* in 5.11 meaning 'both...and...'. The most common meaning for *yòu* (又) is 'again' but it is to be distinguished from *zài* (再) in that *yòu* means 'again' in the past, whereas *zài* means 'again' in the present or future. It may be useful to memorise the following sentences:

*Tā zuótiān lái le. Tā jīntiān **yòu** lái le. Tā shuō tā míngtiān **zài** lái* 'She came yesterday. She came *again* today. She says she's coming *again* tomorrow'. In the text, however, *yòu* has yet another meaning of 'in addition'.

*Zhōngqiūjié nà tiān wǎnshang zài Tàishān dǐng shàng kàn rìluò, **yòu** zài yuèguāng xià chī yuèbǐng.*

It can also be translated as something like 'but', 'yet', and 'at the same time' in a sentence where it links two contradictory states of mind:

*Wǒ yào chū qu, **yòu** pà xià yǔ* 'I want to go out but I'm afraid it's going to rain'.

*Wǒ ài nǐ, **yòu** hèn nǐ* 'I love and hate you at the same time'.

5 EXTENSIONS OF PLACE WORDS

Zài yuèguāng xià 'Beneath the light of the moon' is to be taken literally, but what about: *Zài nǐ bāngzhù zhī* (classical possessive marker) *xià*? Does it literally mean 'underneath your help'? Of course not, it is just the Chinese way of saying 'with your help'. Another good example of this is: *Zài gòngchǎndǎng de lǐngdǎo* (leadership) *(zhī) xià* 'Under the leadership of the Communist Party'. If we replace *xià* with *zhōng* we may get a sentence such as *wǒmen péngyou zhī zhōng* (之中) or *wǒmen péngyou zhī jiān* (之间), both of which mean 'between or amongst friends'.

6 USE OF *GÒU*

Gòu (够) literally means 'sufficient' or 'enough' but it is combined with a wealth of adjectives or nouns to form expressive colloquial phrases such as:

gòugé	'up to standard'
gòu péngyou	'really friendly'
gòu yìsi	'fascinating'
gòuqiàng	'hard to bear, terrible'.

Here *gòu làngmàn* means 'really romantic'.

7 TO SIT, TO DRIVE, TO SIT ASTRIDE

The Chinese language is much more precise than is English when it comes to expressing how or by what form of transport one goes somewhere. One sits (*zuò*) in a car, bus, train, plane or boat:

zuò (坐) *qìchē* (汽车)	'by car' (*Lit.* steam vehicle)
zuò gōnggòngqìchē (公共汽车)	'by bus' (*Lit.* public together steam vehicle)
zuò fēijī (飞机)	'by plane' (*Lit.* fly machine)
zuò chuán (船)	'by boat'

but 'sits astride' a bicycle, a horse or a motorbike:

qí (骑) *zìxíngchē* (自行车)	'by bicycle' (*Lit.* self-propelling machine)
qí mǎ (马)	'on horseback'
qí mótuōchē (摩托车)	'on a motorbike'.

Note the horse radical (马) employed in the character for *qí*. *Qí* (奇) is used to provide the phonetic element for the character as a whole. We have met the verb *kāi* (开) meaning 'to open' (as of doors) or 'to turn on' (as of lights, radios, etc.). The same verb also means 'to drive' as of cars, trains, planes and buses.

EXERCISE 19.3

Choose the correct verb from *zuò*, *qí* and *kāi* to fill the blank in each sentence and then write out the whole sentence in characters.
Nǐ huì bu huì ____ *mǎ?* → 你会不会骑马？

1 ____ *huǒchē bǐ* ____ *gōnggòngqìchē kuài duō le.*
2 ____ *fēijī de rén gōngzī hěn gāo.*
3 *Zài Zhōngguó* ____ *zìxíngchē de rén fēicháng duō.*
4 *Yǒude rén xǐhuan* ____ *mótuōchē yīnwei hěn zìyóu* (自由 'free/freedom')
5 *Yīngguórén shíqī suì cái kěyǐ* ____ *chē.*

8 *ZHĒN DÒU NǏMEN*

Not all colloquial expressions are grammatical as can be seen from the above example. The normal word order has been reversed, giving a fresher, more casual effect, or the impression that the sentence was perhaps an afterthought. Listen out for such expressions and learn them.

9 FOREIGN NAMES (II)

Foreign names can be expressed in Chinese in two principal ways, *viz.* by rendering the sounds with disregard to the meaning; by translating the meaning. *Mòsīkē* (莫斯科) 'Moscow' falls into the first of these categories as 'no then science' does not appear to have a great deal of significance.

Niújīn (牛津) 'Oxford' on the other hand, falls into the second category as *niú* ('ox') and *jīn* ('ford') precisely express the meaning of the English Ox-ford. Of course there are further refinements in that when rendering the sounds, care can be taken to find characters with a 'good' meaning (if that is the intention of course!). Thus Hyde Park is translated as *Hǎi* (海) *dé* (德) *gōngyuán* (公园) 'Sea virtue public enclosure' (park), but it could have been translated as *Hài* (害) *dé* (德) *gōngyuán* 'Harm(s) virtue park'.

Mozambique was originally translated into Chinese as *Mò* (莫) *sān* (三) *bí* (鼻) *jǐ* (给) 'No three nose(s) provide' but was later changed to *Mò* (莫) *sāng* (桑) *bǐ* (比) *kè* (克) 'No mulberry tree compare overcome' which was obviously an improvement as *sāng* has poetic overtones which I won't go into here and *kè* is suitably strong.

Kennedy fared much worse. In Chinese *xiàngshēng* ('cross talk') his name was translated as *kěn* (啃) *ní* (泥) *de* (的) 'gnaw mud person' but officialdom saw fit to change it to *Kěn* (肯) *ní* (尼) *dí* (迪) 'willing Buddhist nun enlighten'!

EXERCISE 19.4

Translate the following Chinese renderings of foreign words back into English by (a) looking at the pronunciation and/or (b) finding out the meaning in a Chinese–English dictionary.

e.g. 罗马尼业 *Luómǎníyà* → Romania.

1 热狗包　*règǒubāo*.

2 汉堡牛肉包　*hànbǎoniúròubāo*.

3 可口可乐　*kěkǒukělè*.

4 雅马哈　*Yā __ __*.

5 加拿大　*Jiānádà*.

6 古巴　*Gǔbā*.

7 剑桥　*Jiànqiáo*.

8 华沙　*Huáshā*.

9 华盛顿　*Huáshèngdùn*.

10 撒切尔夫人　*Sāqiē'ěr fūrén*.

EXERCISE 19.5

Translate the following sentences into colloquial English:

1 中国的中秋节是阴历 (*yīnlì* 'lunar calendar') 八月十五日。
那天晚上大家要看月亮 (*yuèliàng* 'the moon')、吃月饼。

2 唐诗很有名 (*yǒu míng* 'to be famous') 也很有意思，
都值得学中文的人看一看。

3 跟朋友一起去买东西一定很好玩 (儿)。

4 您贵姓? 您叫什么名字? 我都要记下来好吗?

5 要是你有学生证和优待证，火车票价跟中国人一样，同时 (*tóngshí* 'moreover') 也可以付人民币。

On festivals and mooncakes

Prior to 1949, the Chinese followed the lunar calendar which is said to have been in existence for almost 4000 years and is still used to calculate China's traditional festivals. The most important ones are: 春节 *Chūnjié* 'the Spring Festival' or 'Lunar New Year' which falls on the first day of the first lunar month. The Lunar New Year itself may occur as early as 21 January and as late as 21 February. It is the major festival in China when most Chinese have at least 3–4 days' holiday and everybody tries to get back home to celebrate. (Avoid travelling in China at this time if possible.) Couplets wishing the household happiness, prosperity and longevity are written in the old way, i.e. vertically not horizontally, on red paper and pasted on either side of the door. The children normally get new clothes, everybody consumes vast quantities of food (noodles at midnight on New Year's Eve ensure long life). Firecrackers which ensure a deafening sound are set off, mainly on New Year's Eve and on New Year's Day supposedly to warn off evil spirits, hence the need for a big noise.

元宵节 *Yuánxiāojié* 'the Lantern Festival' or 'the Feast of the First Full Moon' falls on the 15th day of the first lunar month. People (or more usually work-units in the cities) make lanterns (灯 *dēng*) which are then exhibited at colourful lantern fairs, usually held in a park. The lanterns were apparently used as torches to help people see the good spirits which were flying in the sky by the light of the first full moon. Dragon dances and lion dances are performed to the noisy accompaniment of gongs and drums. *Yuánxiāo* are the special food associated with the Lantern Festival. They are small round dumplings made of glutinous rice, usually with a sweet filling. Their roundness symbolises the full moon.

清明节 *Qīngmíngjié* 'the Pure Brightness Festival' falls during the first few days of the third lunar month. This is the day on which the Chinese traditionally 'sweep' the graves of their dead and pay them their respects. This used to involve making offerings of food and wine, burning incense, candles and paper money. This may still happen in the countryside but people in the towns generally confine themselves to tidying up the graves and laying flowers (white is for mourning in China, so don't give people white flowers).

端午节 *Duānwǔjié* 'the Dragon Boat Festival' falls on the fifth day of the fifth lunar month and commemorates 屈原 *Qū Yuán* a great poet and patriot of the state of Chu during the Warring States period (475–221 BC). Qu Yuan's story is too long to be told here. Why not find it out for yourself? Why *do* the Chinese hold dragon boat races and eat 粽子 *zòngzi* (pyramid shaped dumplings made of glutinous rice wrapped in bamboo or reed leaves) on *Duānwǔjié*?

中秋节 *Zhōngqiūjié* 'the Mid-Autumn Festival' falls on the 15th day of the eighth lunar month. People traditionally admire the full moon which is said to be at its brightest and clearest on this day of the year, and eat mooncakes 月饼 *yuèbǐng*, special pastries with savoury or sweet fillings of various kinds. Find out who or what lives on the moon in Chinese mythology. Who was *Cháng'é* (嫦娥) and why did she fly to the moon?

After the founding of the People's Republic in 1949, the solar calendar was adopted in China. The main holidays according to the solar calendar are:

元旦	*Yuándàn* 'New Year's Day'
国际劳动妇女节	*Guójì Láodòng Fùnǚjié* 'International Working Women's Day' (8 March)
国际劳动节	*Guójì Láodòngjié* 'International Labour Day' (1 May)
青年节	*Qīngniánjié* 'Youth Day' (4 May)
国际儿童节	*Guójì Értóngjié* 'International Children's Day' (1 June)
	(1 July is the Anniversary of the Founding of

	the Communist Party of China but there is no set phrase for it with -*jié*)
建军节	*Jiànjūnjié* 'Anniversary of the Founding of the People's Liberation Army' (1 August)
国庆节	*Guóqìngjié* 'National Day' (1 October)

20

Change Money?

The ordinary foreigner will find him or herself conducting all his or her money matters through the Bank of China (*Zhōngguó Yínháng*). Business people may well find themselves conducting business through various branches of the China International Trust and Investment Corporation (CITIC) (*Zhōngguó Guójì Xìntuō Tóuzī Gōngsī*).

凡是外国人存钱、取钱、换钱都要通过中国银行。熊先生去北京语言学院的中国银行分行打听一下情况。

熊	请问一下，活期存款和定期存款有什么不一样？
营业员甲	活期存款和定期存款样式不同，利率也不同。定期的利息当然比活期要高得多。
熊	定期存款还有一些什么规定？
营业员甲	定期存款有三个月的，有半年的，也有一、两年的，利（息）率都不同。存的时间越长，利息越高。如果取钱的时候存钱的时间没到期，那就只能按照活期利息计算。
熊	啊，我明白了，跟英国大同小异。在中国可以开一个外币帐户吗？
营业员甲	当然可以。这样就可以从国外直接存钱，是英镑就存英镑，是美元就存美元，依此类推。
熊	那就很方便。我想打听一下，把旅行支票换成外汇卷非在中国银行办理不可吗？
营业员甲	对了，但是你尽管放心，基本上所有接待外国人的大旅馆都有中国银行的点儿，大城市的友谊商店里也有。
熊	牌价是一样吗？

营业员甲	不管你在什么地方换，牌价都是一模一样的，你甭操心了。别忘了，一定要把外汇兑换证明好好儿保存，千万别丢了，否则出境的时候不能把剩下来的人民币再换成外汇。
熊	现在换钱可以吗？
营业员甲	可以。请先填这张取钱表。护照带来了吗？
熊	哎呀，真没想到，怎么办？
营业员甲	护照号码还记得吗？
熊	还记得。
营业员甲	那就算了。按规定换钱的时候应该出示护照，但是除非我们怀疑有什么问题，想对照本人的签字，填上护照号码就行了。(接过熊先生填好的表) 你是十一号 (给他一个号码牌) 请等一会儿吧。
营业员乙	十一号。
熊	欸，在这儿呢。
营业员乙	请把钱点一点。
熊	(点好了) 正好。谢谢 (对营业员甲说) 今天给你添了不少麻烦。
营业员甲	没什么麻烦。欢迎你再来。
	(熊出门的时候正好碰到另外一种换钱的!)
换钱的	Change money?

* * *

Fánshì wàiguórén cún qián、qǔ qián、huàn qián dōu yào tōngguò Zhōngguó Yínháng. Xióng xiānsheng qù Běijīng Yǔyán Xuéyuàn de Zhōngguó Yínháng fēnháng dǎtīng yíxià qíngkuàng.

Xióng	*Qǐng wèn yíxià, huóqī cúnkuǎn hé dìngqī cúnkuǎn yǒu shénme bù yíyàng?*
Yíngyèyuán Jiǎ	*Huóqī cúnkuǎn hé dìngqī cúnkuǎn yàngshì bù tóng, lìlǜ yě bù tóng. Dìngqī de lìxī dāngrán bǐ huóqī yào gāo de duō.*
Xióng	*Dìngqī cúnkuǎn hái yǒu yìxiē shénme guīdìng?*
Yíngyèyuán Jiǎ	*Dìngqī cúnkuǎn yǒu sān ge yuè de, yǒu bànnián de, yě yǒu yì、liǎng nián de, lì(xī)lǜ dōu bù tóng. Cún de shíjiān yuè cháng, lìxī yuè gāo. Rúguǒ qǔ qián de shíhou cún qián de shíjiān méi dàoqī, nà jiù zhǐ néng ànzhào huóqī lìxī jìsuàn.*
Xióng	*À, wǒ míngbai le, gēn Yīngguó dàtóng-xiǎoyì. Zài Zhōngguó kěyǐ kāi yí ge wàibì zhànghù ma?*

Yíngyèyuán Jiǎ   *Dāngrán kěyǐ. Zhèyàng jiù kěyǐ cóng guówài zhíjiē*
cún qián, shì Yīngbàng jiù cún Yīngbàng, shì
Měiyuán jiù cún Měiyuán, yīcǐ lèituī.

Xióng   *Nà jiù hěn fāngbiàn. Wǒ xiǎng dǎtīng yíxià, bǎ*
lǚxíng zhīpiào huàn chéng wàihuìquàn fēi zài
Zhōngguó Yínháng bànlǐ bùkě ma?

Yíngyèyuán Jiǎ   *Duìle, dànshi nǐ jǐnguǎn fàng xīn, jīběnshang suǒyǒu*
jiēdài wàiguórén de lǚguǎn dōu yǒu Zhōngguó
Yínháng de diǎnr, dà chéngshì de Yǒuyì Shāngdiàn
lǐ yě yǒu.

Xióng   *Páijià shì yíyàng ma?*

Yíngyèyuán Jiǎ   *Bùguǎn nǐ zài shénme dìfang huàn, páijià dōu shì*
yìmó-yíyàng de, nǐ béng cāo xīn le. Bié wàng le,
yídìng yào bǎ wàihuì duìhuàn zhèngmíng hǎohāor
bǎocún, qiānwàn bié diū le, fǒuzé chūjìng de shíhou
bù néng bǎ shèng xiàlai de rénmínbì zài huàn chéng
wàihuì.

Xióng   *Xiànzài huàn qián kěyǐ ma?*

Yíngyèyuán Jiǎ   *Kěyǐ. Qǐng xiān tián zhè zhāng qǔqiánbiǎo. Hùzhào*
dài lai le ma?

Xióng   *Āiyā, zhēn méi xiǎng dào, zěnme bàn?*

Yíngyèyuán Jiǎ   *Hùzhào hàomǎ hái jìde ma?*

Xióng   *Hái jìde.*

Yíngyèyuán Jiǎ   *Nà jiù suàn le. Àn guīdìng huàn qián de shíhou*
yīnggāi chūshì hùzhào, dànshi chúfēi wǒmen huáiyí
yǒu shénme wèntí, xiǎng duìzhào běnrén de qiān zì,
tián shang hùzhào hàomǎ jiù xíng le. (Jiē guò Xióng
xiānsheng tián hǎo de biǎo) Nǐ shì shíyī hào. (Gěi tā
yí ge hàomǎ pái) Qǐng děng yíhuìr ba.

Yíngyèyuán Yǐ   *Shíyī hào.*

Xióng   *Èi, zài zhèr ne.*

Yíngyèyuán Yǐ   *Qǐng bǎ qián diǎnyidiǎn.*

Xióng   *(Diǎn hǎo le) Zhèng hǎo. Xièxie. (Duì yíngyèyuán*
Jiǎ shuō) Jīntiān gěi nǐ tiān le bù shǎo máfan.

Yíngyèyuán Jiǎ   *Méi shénme máfan. Huānyíng nǐ zài lái.*
(Xióng chū mén de shíhou zhèng hǎo pèng dào
lìngwài yì zhǒng huàn qián de!)

Huàn qián de   Change money?

凡是	**fánshì** (adv.)	*every, any, all*
存钱	**cún qián** (v-o)	*deposit money*
取钱	**qǔ qián** (v-o)	*withdraw money*
换钱	**huàn qián** (v-o)	*change money*
通过	**tōngguò** (v)	*to pass through*
中国银行	**Zhōngguó Yínháng** (N)	*Bank of China*
分行	**fēnháng** (n)	*branch (bank)*
打听	**dǎtīng** (v)	*to enquire*
活期存款	**huóqī cúnkuǎn** (n)	*current account*
定期存款	**dìngqī cúnkuǎn** (n)	*deposit account*
一样	**yíyàng** (adj.)	*the same, alike*
样式	**yàngshì** (n)	*form, pattern*
不同	**bù tóng** (adj.)	*different*
利（息）率	**lì(xī)lǜ** (n)	*rate of interest*
利息	**lìxī** (n)	*interest*
规定	**guīdìng** (n)	*rule, regulation*
到期	**dàoqī** (v-o)	*become due, expire*
计算	**jìsuàn** (v)	*to count, calculate*
明白	**míngbai** (v; adj.)	*to understand; clear*
大同小异	**dàtóng-xiǎoyì** (adj.)	*similar in major areas but different on minor points*
外币	**wàibì** (n)	*foreign currency*
帐户	**zhànghù** (n)	*account*
国外	**guówài** (adj.)	*overseas, abroad*
直接	**zhíjiē** (adj.; adv.)	*direct, directly*
英镑	**Yīngbàng** (n)	*pound Sterling*
美元	**Měiyuán** (n)	*US dollar*
依此类推	**yīcǐ lèituī**	*others can be deduced similarly*
方便	**fāngbiàn** (adj.)	*convenient*
旅行支票	**lǚxíng zhīpiào** (n)	*traveller's cheque*
V + 成	**V + chéng**	*see 20.2*
外汇（卷）	**wàihuì(quàn)** (n)	*foreign exchange (certificate)*
非…不可	**fēi…bùkě**	*see 20.3*

办理	bànlǐ (v)	to conduct, handle, transact
尽管	jǐnguǎn (adv.; conj.)	feel free to; even though, despite
基本(上)	jīběn (shang) (adj.)	basic(ally)
所有	suǒyǒu (de) (adj.)	all
接待	jiēdài (v)	to receive, admit
点儿	diǎnr (n coll.)	spot, small branch
城市	chéngshì (n)	city, town
友谊商店	Yǒuyì Shāngdiàn (N)	Friendship Store
牌价	páijià (n)	market quotation (exchange rate)
不管…都/也	bùguǎn....dōu/yě	see 20.6
一模一样	yìmó-yíyàng	exactly alike
甭	béng (v)	bú yòng, 'needn't'
操心	cāo xīn (v-o)	to worry about
忘(记)	wàng (jì) (v)	to forget
兑换	duìhuàn (v)	to exchange
证明	zhèngmíng (n; v)	certificate; to prove
保存	bǎocún (v)	to keep, preserve
千万	qiānwàn (adv.)	whatever you do (Lit. ten million)
丢	diū (v)	to lose
否则	fǒuzé (conj.)	otherwise, or else
出境	chūjìng (v-o)	leave the country
取钱表	qǔqiánbiǎo (n)	cash withdrawal form
护照	hùzhào (n)	passport
带	dài (v)	to bring, take
哎呀	āiyā (interj.)	oh dear (expressing surprise)
怎么办?	zěnme bàn?	what's to be done?
号码	hàomǎ (n)	number
记得	jìde (v)	to remember
算了	suàn le	forget it, let it pass
出示	chūshì (v)	to show, produce
除非	chúfēi (conj.)	unless (see 20.7)
怀疑	huáiyí (v)	to suspect
问题	wèntí (n)	question, problem

对照	**duìzhào** (v)	*to compare*
本人	**běnrén** (n)	*in person, oneself*
签字	**qiān zì** (v-o; n)	*to sign; signature*
牌	**pái** (n)	*plate (here disc); brand; card*
	èi (interj.)	*yes (verbal response to enquiry)*
点	**diǎn** (v)	*to check, count (e.g. money)*
正好	**zhènghǎo** (adv.; v)	*just right; to happen to*
碰到	**pèng (dào)** (v)	*to bump (into)*
另外	**lìng(wài)** (adj.; adv.)	*another; separately*

Grammar

1 *FÁNSHÌ...DŌU*

One way of expressing that everyone of a certain category of person, creature or inanimate object possesses the same kind of characteristic is to use the construction: *Fánshì* + identification of group + *dōu* ('all') + characteristic:

Fánshì xiǎoháir dōu xǐhuan chī táng 'All children like eating sweets'.

Fánshì Yìdàlì júzi dōu hěn tián 'All Italian tangerines are very sweet'.

In the text we have *Fánshì wàiguórén...dōu yào tōngguò Zhōngguó Yínháng* 'All foreigners...have to go through the Bank of China'.

2 VERB + *CHÉNG*

When *chéng*（成）('to become') is attached to certain verbs such as *xiě*（写）'write', *fānyì*（翻译）'translate', *niàn*（念）'to read aloud', *biàn*（变）'to change' or 'transform' and *huàn*（换）'to exchange' (or change clothes, buses, money), it functions like a resultative verb ending (see 5.1). It differs from resultative verb endings like *-hǎo*, *wán*, etc. in that it must be followed by a noun which shows what the subject or object has turned into or become. This construction is often to be found together with *bǎ*（把）but not invariably so, as can be seen from the second example:

*Wǒ **bǎ** gùshi fānyì **chéng** Xībānyáwén* 'I translated the story into Spanish'.

*Tā mànmānr de biàn **chéng** yí ge hǎo rén* 'He slowly turned into a good person'.

*Lǎoshī **bǎ** nuǎnhuo de 'huó' niàn **chéng** 'hé'.* 'The teacher read the "huo" in "nuǎnhuo" as "he"'...*bǎ lǚxíng zhīpiào huàn **chéng** wàihuìquàn...*'to change travellers cheques into FEC'.

EXERCISE 20.1

Choose a suitable verb to fill the blank in each sentence. Each verb to be used once only. Choose from *biàn, fānyì, huàn, niàn* and *xiě*.

1　*Xuésheng niàn kèwén* (text) *de shíhou bǎ 'dàifu'* ＿＿＿ *chéng 'dàfu'.*

2　*Kuài sǐ* (die) *de shíhou, hěn duō rén yào gǎnkuài* (hastily)＿＿＿ *chéng hǎo rén!*

3　*Bǎ kèwén* ＿＿＿ *chéng Yīngwén róngyì bu róngyì?*

4　*Lǎoshī* (teacher) *bìng méi yǒu zhùyì, zài hēibǎn* (blackboard) *shàng bǎ 'hái' zì* ＿＿＿ *chéng 'bù' zì.*

5　*Wǒ yào bǎ mǎkè* (DM) ＿＿＿ *chéng Rìyuán* (yen).

3　*FĒI* VERB...*BÙKĚ*

This is an emphatic expression meaning 'must', 'have to'. *Fēi* comes from classical Chinese and means *bú shì*（不是）, *bùkě* is a shortened form of *bù kěyǐ* 'not permissible' so the whole phrase means 'not to do the action of the verb is not permissible'!

*Wǒ **fēi** qù **bùkě*** 'I absolutely have to go'.

*Tā **fēi** yào jié hūn **bùkě*** 'She insists on getting married'.

*...**fēi** zài Zhōngguó Yínháng bànlǐ **bùkě** ma?* 'Does (it) have to be done (transacted) at the Bank of China?'.

4　ADJECTIVE/NOUN + *SHANG*

A neat and easy way of forming an adverb from adjectives, such as *jīběn*（基本）'basic' and nouns such as *shíjì*（实际）'reality' is simply to add *-shang*（上）so that *jīběnshang* becomes 'basically' and *shíjìshang* becomes 'in reality'. Other examples are:

yìshùshang（艺术上）	'artistically'
zhèngzhìshang（政治上）	'politically'
jīngjìshang（经济上）	'economically'

lǐlùnshang (理论上)	'theoretically'
shìshíshang (事实上)	'in actual fact' (an alternative to *shíjìshang*)
shēnghuóshang (生活上)	'in life'
lìshǐshang (历史上)	'historically'

5 ALL AND ALL

There are several ways of expressing 'all' in Chinese and it is important to distinguish their different grammatical functions. *Dōu* is an adverb and therefore precedes the verb, *suǒyǒu (de)* is an adjective and precedes the noun it is referring to and *yíqiè* is a noun:

Tāmen dōu bù xǐhuan tā. 'None of them likes him.

Suǒyǒu de rén bù xǐhuan tā. Nobody likes him' (*Lit.* all people don't like him).

Tāmen bù xǐhuan yíqiè 'They like nothing' (*Lit.* they not like all).

Chinese would be more likely to say, however, *Tāmen yíqiè dōu bù xǐhuan* (see 21.11). It sounds so much better balanced and in the end that's what distinguishes the beginner from a fluent speaker of the language.

6 *BÙGUǍN...DŌU/YĚ*

Guǎn has several meanings but two of its principal meanings as a verb are 'to be in charge of / to run' and 'to bother about' or 'to mind': *Tā guǎn fángzi* 'He's in charge of the house (or housing)', *Wǒ guǎn háizi* 'I'm in charge of the children', *Nǐ bié guǎn wǒ!* 'Don't bother about me!' Taking this one step further, *bùguǎn* can be used as a verb to express the idea of 'regardless of', 'no matter' (what, how, etc.). *Bùguǎn zěnmeyàng* 'no matter what, in any case'.

Expanded into full sentences it expresses the idea that no matter what happens in the first clause, the state of affairs in the second clause will continue to be so:

Bùguǎn nǐ qù bu qu, wǒ dōu/yě yào qù 'No matter whether you're going or not, I am'.

Bùguǎn jǐngchá ('police') *zěnme mà* ('curse' berate) *shìwēizhě* ('demonstrator'), *tāmen dōu bù chéngrèn cuòwu* ('acknowledge one's mistake'). Work this one out for yourself:

Bùguǎn nǐ zài shénme dìfang huàn, páijià *dōu* shì yìmó-yíyàng de...
'No matter where you change (money), the exchange rate (*Lit.*
plate price) is exactly the same...'.

Búlùn...(*dōu*) and *wúlùn*...(*dōu*) are used very much like
bùguǎn...*dōu* but are to be found more in the written language:

Búlùn xìngbié ('gender')、 niánlíng ('age') 'regardless of sex and
age'.

Wúlùn nánnǚ lǎoshào 'No matter whether male or female, young
or old'. *Wúlùn rúhé* is a set adverbial phrase meaning 'whatever
happens':

Wúlùn rúhé wǒmen yě yào jìxù ('continue') dǐkàng ('resist').

7   *CHÚFĒI...CÁI*

As used in the text, *chúfēi* simply means 'unless' or 'only if'...*chúfēi*
wǒmen huáiyí yǒu shénme wèntí '...unless we suspect there is a
problem...'. In a more complicated construction usually coupled
with *cái* , it still has this meaning but you have to remember when
translating that *cái* already contains the negative. The following
examples will hopefully make this point clear:

Chúfēi míngtiān chū tàiyáng, wǒmen *cái* qù 'We *won't* go *unless*
it's sunny tomorrow' (chū tàiyáng *Lit.* 'come out excessive' yáng 'to
be sunny').

Chúfēi yǒu rén bāngmáng, wǒ *cái* zuò de wán 'I *can't* finish (it)
unless somebody helps (me)' or 'I can *only* finish (it) *if* somebody
helps me'.

8   MORE ON THE NOMINALISER *DE*

From 5.12 we see that *de* placed after a pronoun or adjective makes
it into a noun. Likewise if *de* is placed after a verb-object the whole
phrase becomes nominal:

Huàn qián *de* (*rén* 'understood')	'money changer' (person who changes money)
Zuò fàn *de*	'cook' (person who makes food)
Hē jiǔ *de*	'drinker' (person who drinks alcohol)
Jiāo shū *de*	'teacher' (person who teaches books)
Kāi chē *de*	'driver' (person who drives vehicles)

Waiting! More waiting! And yet more waiting!

A lot of time is spent in the big cities in China just waiting. Waiting to attract the attention of the shop assistant, waiting (not queuing note, although it is getting better) to buy tickets, waiting for one's number to come up at the bank (roughly four people check each transaction). This activity (waiting) ties in with my 3 Ps (see Chapter 16) but don't always hope to be rewarded – the 3 Ms (see Chapter 14) sometimes prevail. Keep trying, or rather keep waiting!

Change money?

A cry you will hear all over China from the lips of babes to women beautifully dressed in National Minority (*shǎoshù mínzú* 少数民族) costumes. Let me stress that it is illegal to change money (*huàn qián*) outside the banking system in China but that the existence of two monetary systems with vastly differing purchasing powers is a great temptation for many people, Chinese and non-Chinese alike. It is a way of controlling the supply of a limited number of goods and services. RMB is not a convertible currency so however rich a Chinese is in local currency it will do her/him no good if s/he wants to go abroad and study but has no scholarship. S/he will probably have to rely on friends and relatives abroad as well as finding some part-time work. It is possible under some circumstances to change RMB into FEC on the official market but the rate is very high, at least double. The flourishing black market works the other way, the moneychangers want your FEC or US dollars for RMB, again at high rates of exchange, but I repeat, it *is* illegal and you can get badly burnt.

EXERCISE 20.2

Using the text, say whether the following statements are true or false.

1 *Fánshì wàiguórén cún qián、qǔ qián、huàn qián dōu yào tōngguò Zhōngguó Guójì Xìntuō Tóuzī Gōngsī.*

2 *Zài Zhōngguó, huóqī cúnkuǎn hé dìngqī cúnkuǎn lìlǜ yíyàng.*

3 *Dìngqī cúnkuǎn yǒu bù tóng shíjiān de.*

4 *Cún de shíjiān yuè cháng, lìxī yuè gāo.*

5 *Zài Zhōngguó bù néng kāi yí ge wàibì zhànghù.*

6 *Bǎ lǚxíng zhīpiào huàn chéng wàihuìquàn fēi zài Zhōngguó Yínháng bànlǐ bùkě.*

7 *Dà chéngshì de Yǒuyì Shāngdiàn méi yǒu Zhōngguó Yínháng de diǎnr.*

8 *Huàn qián de shíhou bù tóng de dìfang yǒu bù tóng de páijià.*

9 *Wàihuì duìhuàn zhèngmíng diū le, chūjìng de shíhou jiù bù néng bǎ shèng xiàlai de rénmínbì zài huàn chéng wàihuì.*

10 *Huàn qián de shíhou zuìhǎo bǎ hùzhào dài qu.*

11 *Zài Zhōngguó zhǐ yǒu yì zhǒng huàn qián de bànfǎ* (method).

EXERCISE 20.3

Put the following sentences into characters and then translate them into colloquial English. The relevant grammar points in the sentence are printed in bold.

1 *Fánshì Zhōngguórén* **dōu** *xǐhuan chī Zhōngguó cài.*

2 *Fánshì Zhōngguó Yínháng huàn qián de páijià* **dōu** *yíyàng.*

3 *Huóqī cúnkuǎn hé dìngqī cúnkuǎn lìxīlǜ bù tóng.*

4 *Wǒ jīntiān* **fēi** *bǎ lǚxíng zhīpiào huàn chéng Měiyuán* **bùkě.**

5 *Qù guówài,* **fēi** *dài hùzhào* **bùkě,** *fǒuzé bù néng chūjìng.*

6 *Lìshǐshang Yàzhōu* (亚洲 'Asia') *hé Fēizhōu* (非洲 'Africa') *hěn bù yíyàng.*

7 *Tā de diànhuà hàomǎ hái jìde ma? Qiānwàn bié wàng le míngtiān gěi tā dǎ diànhuà.*

8 *Ōuzhōu guójiā* (国家 'country') **zhèngzhìshang** *dàtóng-xiǎoyì.*

9 **Bùguǎn** *nǐ qiān le zì méi you, wǒ* **dōu** *yào kàn hùzhào.*

10 **Bùguǎn** *yíngyèyuán diǎn le jǐ cì qián, tā yě yào diǎn yí cì.*

11 *Nǐ de yìsi shì* **chúfēi** *pèng dào tā* **cái** *rènshirènshi, duì bu dui?*

12 **Chúfēi** *yǒu guīdìng, wǒ* **cái** *zhèyàng bàn.*

EXERCISE 20.4

Translate the following sentences into *pinyin* and then into Chinese characters:

1 'I've caused you a lot of trouble today'. *Yíngyèyuán*: 'Not at all, please come back tomorrow'.

2 She originally (本来 *běnlái*) wanted to go to the bank and change money today but she's forgotten to bring the traveller's cheques.

3 'What do you suspect him of?' 'I don't know, but I don't like the way he looks.' (样子 *yàngzi.*)

4 The rate of interest (from) a deposit account (use 的) is much higher than that (from) a current account.

5 Those who drive shouldn't drink. (Use v-o construction.)

21

Traveller's Notes

旅途见闻 *Lǚtú jiànwén*

在中国旅行可以了解中国人生活的各个方面，比如说中国人放假、出差等情况。

王永寿和史爱理正在杭州玩儿，坐在世界闻名的西湖旁边儿，一边吃着三明治，一边聊天儿。

史	来杭州旅行的可真多呀！
王	可不是吗！没想到中国旅游事业发展得那么快。
史	你知道吗？中国有一句俗话：'上有天堂，下有苏、杭'，所以来杭州找人间乐园的人总是很多！
王	那倒是，你注意了没有？中国人喜欢照相。
史	是的。他们的照相机有老式的，也有新式的。'佳能'、'尼空'等日本货好象特别受欢迎。听说照相机也是可以租的。
王	对了，但是凡是有游客的地方都有职业照相的。
史	中国人还有一点不太象我们，他们很喜欢合伙儿出去玩儿，或者是同学或者是同事或者是同乡。(说着就有一个戴着太阳镜的年轻小伙子走过来)。
张锡群	(坐下就问) 你们是哪国人？是来杭州玩儿的吗？
史	是的，我们是英国人。你是本地人吗？
张锡群	不是，我是苏州人，来杭州办一点事。
王	苏州地方不错，有人叫它中国的威尼斯。也有人说'苏州出美人'。 (他正在说话的时候有一个小孩儿拉着他妈妈的手指着王永寿和史爱理大声喊着'老外老外！')

史	（笑着说）'老外'听起来还是有一种亲密的感觉，但是听到什么'洋鬼子'、'高鼻子'，心里就有一点不自在。
张锡群	这些称呼平常并没有什么坏的意思，主要是因为一些中国人没有跟外国人接触过，所以第一次碰到觉得十分新鲜。他们不懂这样称呼很不礼貌。你们听过这句话吗？'天不怕，地不怕，就怕洋鬼子说中国话'！
王	没听说过，真好玩儿！我想问你一个问题，可以吗？
张锡群	当然可以。什么问题？
王	你觉得中国人有种族偏见吗？
张锡群	这怎么说呢？我们受过教育的人，中国人也好，外国人也好，一般来说，都不认为自己有什么偏见，但是坦率地说，下意识肯定还是会有一点的。
王	一点也不错。咱们应该承认是有偏见的，要不很容易'自欺欺人'。承认错误等于改了一半儿了。
张锡群	太对了，我完全同意。

Zài Zhōngguó lǚxíng kěyǐ liǎojiě Zhōngguórén shēnghuó de gègè fāngmiàn, bǐrú shuō Zhōngguórén fàng jià、chū chāi děng qíngkuàng. Wáng Yǒngshòu hé Shǐ Àilǐ zhèngzài Hángzhōu wánr, zuò zài shìjiè wénmíng de Xīhú pángbiānr, yìbiān chīzhe sānmíngzhì, yìbiān liáo tiānr.

Shǐ	*Lái Hángzhōu lǚyóu de kě zhēn duō ya!*
Wáng	*Kěbúshì ma! Méi xiǎng dào Zhōngguó lǚyóu shìyè fāzhǎn de nàme kuài.*
Shǐ	*Nǐ zhīdao ma? Zhōngguó yǒu yí jù súhuà: 'Shàng yǒu tiāntáng, xià yǒu Sū、Háng', suǒyǐ lái Hángzhōu zhǎo rénjiān lèyuán de rén zǒngshi hěn duō!*
Wáng	*Nà dàoshì. Nǐ zhùyì le méi you: Zhōngguórén xǐhuan zhào xiàng.*
Shǐ	*Shì de. Tāmen de zhàoxiàngjī yǒu lǎoshì de, yě yǒu xīnshì de. 'Jiānéng'、'Níkòng' děng Rìběn huò hǎoxiàng tèbié shòu huānyíng. Tīngshuō zhàoxiàngjī yě shi kěyǐ zū de.*
Wáng	*Duìle, dànshi fánshì yǒu yóukè de dìfang dōu yǒu zhíyè zhàoxiàng de.*
Shǐ	*Zhōngguórén hái yǒu yìdiǎn bú tài xiàng wǒmen, tāmen hěn xǐhuan héhuǒr chū qu wánr huòzhě shì*

tóngxué huòzhě shì tóngshì huòzhě shì tóngxiāng!
(Shuōzhe jiù yǒu yí ge dàizhe tàiyángjìng de niánqīng
xiǎohuǒzi zǒu guòlai)

Zhāng Xīqún   *(zuò xià jiù wèn) Nǐmen shì nǎ guó rén? Shì lái*
Hángzhōu wánr de ma?

Shǐ   *Shì de. Wǒmen shì Yīngguórén. Nǐ shì běndìrén ma?*

Zhāng Xīqún   *Bú shì, wǒ shì Sūzhōurén, lái Hángzhōu bàn yìdiǎn*
shì.

Wáng   *Sūzhōu dìfang búcuò, yǒu rén jiào tā Zhōngguó*
de Wēinísī. Yě yǒu rén shuō 'Sūzhōu chū
měirén'....

(Tā zhèngzài shuō huà de shíhou yǒu yí ge xiǎoháir
lāzhe tā māma de shǒu zhǐzhe Wáng Yǒngshòu hé
Shǐ Àilì dà shēng hǎnzhe 'Lǎowài, lǎowài'!)

Shǐ   *(xiàozhe shuō) 'Lǎowài' tīng qǐlai háishi yǒu yì zhǒng*
qīnmì de gǎnjué, dànshi tīng dào shénme 'yángguǐzi、'
'gāo bízi', xīnlǐ jiù yǒu yìdiǎn bú zìzài.

Zhāng Xīqún   *Zhè xiē chēnghū jīngcháng bìng méi yǒu shénme huài*
de yìsi, zhǔyào shì yīnwei yìxiē Zhōngguórén méi yǒu
gēn wàiguórén jiēchùguo suǒyǐ dì yí cì pèng dào juéde
shífēn xīnxiān. Tāmen bù dǒng zhèyàng chēnghū hěn
bù lǐmào. Nǐmen tīngguo zhè jù huà ma? 'Tiān bú pà,
dì bú pà, jiù pà yángguǐzi shuō Zhōngguóhuà'!

Wáng   *Méi tīngshuōguo, zhēn hǎo wánr! Wǒ xiǎng wèn nǐ yì*
ge wèntí, kěyǐ ma?

Zhāng Xīqún   *Dāngrán kěyǐ. Shénme wèntí?*

Wáng   *Nǐ juéde Zhōngguórén yǒu zhǒngzú piānjiàn ma?*

Zhāng Xīqún   *Zhè zěnme shuō ne? Wǒmen shòuguo jiàoyù de rén,*
Zhōngguórén yě hǎo, wàiguórén yě hǎo, yìbān lái
shuō, dōu bú rènwéi zìjǐ yǒu shénme piānjiàn, dànshi
tǎnshuài de shuō, xiàyìshí kěndìng háishi huì yǒu
yìdiǎn de.

Wáng   *Yìdiǎn yě bú cuò. Zánmen yīnggāi chéngrèn shì yǒu*
piānjiàn de, yàobù hěn róngyì 'zì qī qī rén'. Chéngrèn
cuòwù děngyú gǎi le yíbàn(r) le.

Zhāng Xīqún   *Tài duìle, wǒ wánquán tóngyì.*

旅途	**lǚtú** (n)	*journey, trip*
见闻	**jiànwén** (n)	*what one sees and hears*
了解	**liǎojiě** (v)	*to find out, understand, know*
各个	**gègè** (adj.)	*each, every*
放假	**fàng jià** (v-o)	*have a holiday or vacation*
出差	**chū chāi** (v-o)	*be on a business trip*
杭州	**Hángzhōu** (N)	*Hangzhou*
闻名	**wénmíng** (adj.)	*well known, famous*
西湖	**Xīhú** (N)	*West Lake*
旁边儿	**pángbianr** (n)	*side*
一边…一边…	**yìbiān…yìbiān**	*see 21.1*
三明治	**sānmíngzhì** (n)	*sandwich*
旅游	**lǚyóu** (n; v)	*tourism, to tour*
可	**kě** (adv.)	*emphasises tone of speaker*
呀	**yā** (interj.)	*indicating surprise*
可不是吗	**kěbúshì ma?**	*exactly; that's just the way it is*
事业	**shìyè** (n)	*undertaking, cause*
发展	**fāzhǎn** (v)	*to develop*
俗话 [句]	**súhuà** (n) [jù]	*common saying, proverb*
天堂	**tiāntáng** (n)	*heaven, paradise*
苏杭	**Sū、Háng** (N)	*Suzhou and Hangzhou*
人间乐园	**rénjiān lèyuán** (n)	*paradise on earth*
注意	**zhùyì** (v)	*to pay attention to*
照相机	**zhàoxiàngjī** (n) [tái]	*camera*
老式	**lǎoshì** (adj.)	*old-fashioned*
新式	**xīnshì** (adj.)	*latest type, new-style*
佳能	**'Jiānéng'** (N)	*'Canon'*
尼空	**'Níkòng'** (N)	*'Nikon'*
好象	**hǎoxiàng** (v)	*to seem (see 21.4)*
受	**shòu** (v)	*to receive, be subjected to (see 21.6)*

租	zū (v)	*to rent, hire*
职业	zhíyè (n)	*occupation, profession*
合伙(儿)	héhuǒ(r) (v-o)	*form a company or partnership*
同学	tóngxué (n)	*fellow student*
同乡	tóngxiāng (n)	*person who was born in the same place as oneself*
戴	dài (v)	*to wear (see 21.8)*
太阳镜 [副]	tàiyángjìng (n) [fù]	*sunglasses*
小伙子	xiǎohuǒzi (n)	*young fellow*
本地	běndì (n)	*this locality*
办事	bàn shì (v-o)	*to arrange for something to be done*
它	tā (p.s.)	*it*
威尼斯	Wēinísī (N)	*Venice*
美人	měirén (n)	*beautiful woman*
拉	lā (v)	*to pull; to play (of stringed instruments)*
手	shǒu (n)	*hand*
大声(地)	dàshēng(de) (adv.)	*loudly*
喊	hǎn (v)	*to shout, cry out*
老外	lǎowài (n)	*'old foreigner'*
听起来	tīng qǐlai (v)	*to sound, ring*
亲密	qīnmì (adj.)	*close, intimate*
感觉	gǎnjué (n)	*feeling, sense*
洋鬼子	yángguǐzi (n)	*foreign devil*
高鼻子	gāo bízi (adj. + n)	*big nose (Lit. tall nose)*
心里	xīnlǐ	*in the heart or mind*
自在	zìzài (adj.)	*at ease, comfortable*
称呼	chēnghū (n; v)	*form of address; to address*
坏	huài (adj.)	*bad; broken*
主要	zhǔyào (adj.; adv.)	*principal(ly)*
觉得	juéde (v)	*to feel*
十分	shífēn (adv.)	*extremely, very*
新鲜	xīnxiān (adj.)	*fresh*
礼貌	lǐmào (adj.; n)	*courteous; manners*

话 [句]	huà (n) [jù]	remark, word(s)
怕	pà (v)	to fear, be afraid of
种族	zhǒngzú (n)	race
偏见	piānjiàn (n)	prejudice, bias
教育	jiàoyù (n; v)	education; to educate
A 也好 B 也好	A yě hǎo B yě hǎo	see 21.10
一般来说	yìbān lái shuō	generally speaking
认为	rènwéi (v)	to think, consider
坦率(地)	tǎnshuài(de) (adj.; adv.)	frank(ly)
下意识	xiàyìshí (n)	subconsciousness
肯定	kěndìng (adj.; adv.; v)	definite(ly); affirm
咱们	zánmen (p.p.)	we (see 21.12)
自欺欺人	zì qī qī rén	deceive yourself as well as others
错误	cuòwù (n)	mistake, error
改	gǎi (v)	to alter, change, correct
完全	wánquán (adj.; adv.)	complete(ly)
同意	tóngyì (v)	to agree with

Grammar

1 *YÌBIĀN* V₁...*YÌBIĀN* V₂

When we want to indicate that two actions are going on simultaneously we can use the construction *yìbiān* V₁, *yìbiān* V₂:

Tāmen yìbiān kàn fēngjǐng, yìbiān liáo tiānr. 'They chatted whilst looking at the scenery.' *Yǒude rén yìbiān kàn diànshì, yìbiān chī fàn.* 'Some people have their meals watching the TV.'

Tāmen yìbiān chīzhe sānmíngzhì, yìbiān liáo tiānr. 'They chatted while eating (their) sandwiches.'

When expressing the continuous past or present, one of the two verbs may be followed by *zhe* to emphasise the continuity of that verb (see the example above).

2 CHINESE PROVERBS

Chinese proverbs or idioms are known as *chéngyǔ* (成语) (*Lit.* become language) which are usually set phrases made up of four characters, although they are not necessarily limited to four, or *súhuà* (*Lit.* custom talk, i.e. 'old saying') which can be of any length. Both are an integral part of the Chinese language. All Chinese of whatever educational level seem to know and use some *chéngyǔ* or *súhuà* and the higher their level the more they are likely to use them. *Chéngyǔ* have their origins in classical poetry which was traditionally regarded in China as the highest medium of artistic expression (as opposed to the novel which is translated as *xiǎoshuō* 'small talk'). Many Chinese are now unaware of which poem a particular *chéngyǔ* comes from and who it was written by, but this cultural inheritance gives weight and beauty to the modern language and a pithiness which it would otherwise lack. The text has some good examples of different proverbs:

Shàng yǒu tiāntáng, xià yǒu Sū、Háng

'Above there is heaven, below there is Suzhou and Hangzhou' (i.e. these two places are regarded as being very beautiful).

Sūzhōu chū měirén

'Beautiful women come from Suzhou.'

Tiān bú pà, dì bú pà, jiù pà yángguǐzi shuō Zhōngguóhuà

'I'm not afraid of heaven or earth, only of foreign devils speaking Chinese'.

Zì qī qī rén

'Deceive oneself as well as others' (*Lit.* self cheat cheat people).

Four character phrases are particularly concise and contain a wealth of meaning.

3 MORE ON ABBREVIATIONS

We looked briefly at abbreviations in 4.5 and can now take things a step further. As you can see in the proverb: *Shàng yǒu tiāntáng, xià yǒu Sū、Háng* the *zhōu* of *Sūzhōu* and *Hángzhōu* has been dropped, so that the famous balance that the Chinese love so much can be retained, giving four characters in each phrase. Try saying it with the two *zhōu*s back in place and you'll see what I mean. Not the same effect at all, is it? The same thing is done when referring to two countries one after another.

Zhōng、Yīng liǎng guó   'the two countries China and the UK' (note the reversed word order in Chinese)

Sū、Ōu (Sūlián Ōuzhōu) 'the Soviet Union and Europe'.

This practice gives a much smoother rhythm to the sentence. How unpleasing to the ear it would be to say *Zhōngguó、Yīngguó liǎng guó*.

4 TO RESEMBLE OR NOT? (*XIÀNG AND HǍOXIÀNG*)

Students often confuse *xiàng* (象) and *hǎoxiàng* (好象) and of course they do appear to be very similar. Memorise a model sentence for each to avoid confusion. *Xiàng* means 'to resemble' in the sense of 'to look like somebody or something' whereas *hǎoxiàng* means 'to seem' or 'to look like something has happened or is going to happen':

Nǐ xiàng nǐ māma   'You look like your mum'
Tā bú xiàng wǒ   'She's not like me'
Nà ge xuésheng   'It seems that student is ill'
hǎoxiàng bìngle
Hǎoxiàng yào xià yǔ   'It looks like rain'.

'*Jiānéng*'、'*Níkòng*' *děng Rìběnhuò hǎoxiàng hěn shòu huānyíng*
'Japanese makes such as "Canon" and "Nikon" seem very popular' (*Lit.* 'Canon', 'Nikon', etc. Japanese goods seem very receive welcome).

Zhōngguórén hái yǒu yìdiǎn bú tài xiàng wǒmen.
The Chinese have another way in which they are very different from us' (*Lit.* Chinese people still have one point not too resemble us).

EXERCISE 21.1

Choose *xiàng* or *hǎoxiàng* to fill the blank space in each sentence. You can rewrite the exercise in characters for extra practice. Check your answers using the Vocabularies at the back of the book. Please take this instruction as read for subsequent exercises.

1 *Xiǎohuǒzi ____ lái Hángzhōu bàn shì.*
2 *Wǒ jiějie hěn ____ wǒ bàba, wǒ bǐjiào ____ wǒ māma.*
3 *Fǎguórén* (the French) *____ bu ____ Yìdàlìrén* (Italians)?
4 *Zhōngguó lǚyóu shìyè ____ fāzhǎn de hěn kuài.*
5 *Tā tài ____ nǐ, jīntiān ____ yòu bǎ zhàoxiàngjī wàng le!*

5 BALANCE WITH OPPOSITES

Balance in Chinese is very important. This sometimes makes for what looks at first sight to be a slightly wordy sentence as the verb is often repeated, but with further study you will appreciate this feeling of balance and harmony within the sentence. Compare the difference in feeling between *Lǎoshī jiāo Zhōngwén hé Yīngwén* and *Lǎoshī jiāo Zhōngwén yě jiāo Yīngwén*. Both are grammatically correct and mean 'The teacher teaches (both) Chinese and English' but the second somehow feels better. This can be taken one step further in the use of opposites, or contrasting ideas within the same sentence:

Wǒ yǒu cháng de, yě yǒu duǎn de 'I have both long ones and short ones'

Tāmen de zhàoxiàngjī yǒu lǎoshì de, yě yǒu xīnshì de 'They have both modern and old-fashioned cameras' (*Lit.* as for their cameras have old-fashioned ones, also have new style ones).

6 *SHÒU* AND THE PASSIVE

We have already seen in 8.10 that verbs in Chinese are neither active nor passive although some verbs of motion *appear* to be passive, even in Chinese, without changing their form or having anything added to them:

Bào mǎi lái le   'The newspaper has been bought' (by you, me, etc.)

However, the passive is usually expressed by using one of the following constructions:

(i)   to express the idea of 'receiving' or 'accepting', 'suffering' or 'being subjected to something' we use *shòu* (受) + verbal noun. For example:

shòu fá 受罚	'be punished' (suffer punishment)
shòu hài 受害	'be injured or killed' (suffer harm)
shòu huānyíng 受欢迎	'be welcomed' (receive welcome)
shòu jiàoyù 受教育	'be educated' (receive education)
shòu jīng 受惊	'be frightened' (suffer fright)
shòu piàn 受骗	'be fooled or taken in' (suffer cheat)
shòu shāng 受伤	'be wounded' (suffer wound)
shòu tuō 受托	'be commissioned' (accept entrust)

shòu yǐngxiǎng 受影响 'be influenced' (accept influence).
This group should be memorised before use and new ones added
to your mental list only when you have read or heard them. Do not
make up your own.

   (ii)   This construction follows the pattern:

     Subject +   *bèi* (被) + *agent* + verb (+ other elements)

              ràng (让)

              jiào (叫)

*Wǒ **bèi** tā dǎ le* 'I was hit by him/her'
*Tā **ràng** gǒu yǎo le* 'He was bitten by the dog'
*Nǐ **jiào** xuésheng xuǎn le dāng xuésheng dàibiǎo.* 'You have
been chosen by the students as student representative.'

If it is not clear who (or what) the agent is, an indefinite *rén*
(人) may be used instead:

*Dīng lǎoshī **jiào*** ⎤ *rén qǐng qù hē chá le.*

       ràng ⎬

       bèi ⎦

'Mr Ding was invited (by somebody) to have tea'. *Bèi, ràng* and *jiào*
can be used interchangeably but *bèi* is used more in the formal
written language, *ràng* and *jiào* in the spoken.

NB when no agent is marked in the sentence, only *bèi* can be
used: *Wǒ **bèi** jǐnggào le* 'I was warned'.

The negative adverb and/or auxiliary verb go before *bèi*, etc.
Other adverbs such as *zuótiān* (昨天) and *yǐjīng* (已经) normally precede *bèi* (*ràng, jiào*) too.

EXERCISE 21.2

Select *jiào, ràng, bèi* or *shòu* to fill the blank spaces in the following
sentences. Where there is more than one alternative, please give all
of them.

1 *Zhōngguó xuésheng zài 1989 nián liùyuè sān、sì hào* _____ *zhèngfǔ*
   (government) *hài le.*

2 _____ *jiàoyù de rén piānjiàn yīnggāi shǎo yìxiē.*

3 *Wǒ gàosu* (tell) *tā bié zhèyàng zuò, suǒyǐ* _____ *tā mà* (swear at,
   curse) *le yíxià.*

4 *Kěxī, xiǎoháir dōu hěn róngyì* _____ *piàn.*

5 *Tā* _____ *mìmì jǐngchá* (secret police) *bǔ* (arrest) *le.*

7 *TÓNG* WITH EVERYONE?

Tóng is an adjective with the meaning 'same', 'alike', 'similar' and has given rise to a whole series of useful expressions of which some of the more common are listed below:

tóngbāo (n) 同胞 (same parents)	'compatriot'
tóngháng (n) 同行 (same profession)	'person in the same profession'
tóngjū (v) 同居 (same live)	'cohabit'
tóngnián (n) 同年 (same year)	'of the same age'
tóngqíng (v) 同情 (same emotion)	'to sympathise with'
tóngshí (adv.) 同时 (same time)	'at the same time, in the meantime'
tóngshì (n) 同事 (same job)	'colleague'
tóngxiāng (n) 同乡 (same native place)	'person who comes from the same birth place
tóngxìng (adj.; n) 同姓 (same surname)	'of the same surname'
tóngxìngliàn (adj.; n) 同性恋 (same sex love)	'homosexual'
tóngxué (n) 同学 (same study)	'fellow student'
tóngyì (v) 同意 (same meaning)	'to agree with'
tóngzhì (n) 同志 (same aspiration)	'comrade'

8 *DÀI* OR *CHUĀN*?

Both these verbs mean 'to wear'. *Chuān* is the more widely used whereas *dài* is confined to items worn on extremities (but *not* shoes on feet!):

dài màozi	'wear a hat' (also 'to be labelled', e.g. counter-revolutionary)
dài yǎnjìng	'wear glasses'
dài lǐngdài	'wear a tie'
dài shǒutào	'wear gloves'
dài shǒubiǎo	'wear a watch'
dài érhuán	'wear ear-rings'
dài jiézhǐ	'wear a ring'
dài shǒuzhuó	'wear a bracelet'.

The only exceptions to this 'rule' appear to be 'shoes' and 'socks' which are *chuān*-ed rather than *dài*-ed. NB this *dài* 戴 is not the same *dài* as the verb meaning 'to take' or 'to bring' which is written 带.

EXERCISE 21.3

Choose *dài* or *chuān* to fill the blank space in each sentence.

1 *Yǐqián zài jiàotánglǐ* (in church) *fùnǚ yào*___*màozi* (hat), *xiànzài bù yídìng dài le.*

2 *Dōngtiān, tiānqì lěng*___*hěn hòu* (thick) *de shǒutào* (gloves) *hěn yǒu yòng.*

3 *Chū qu de shíhou, fēi*___*shang xié* (shoes) *bùkě yīnwei jiē* (street) *shàng tài zāng* (dirty) *le.*

4 *Yǒu yìxiē jùlèbù* (social club), *chúfēi nánrén*___*lǐngdài* (tie) *cái néng jìn qu.*

5 *Nǐ jūntiān*___*de máoyī hěn hǎo kàn. Shì zìjǐ zhī* (knit, weave) *de ma?*

9 *YĪN* AND *YÁNG* PLEASE!

Any of you who have dabbled in Chinese philosophy or traditional Chinese medicine will have some idea of the concept of *yīn* and *yáng*. It all comes back to balance in the end! *Yīn* 阴, written with the moon radical, is the feminine or negative principle in nature whereas *yáng* 阳, written with the sun radical, is the masculine or positive principle. To the Chinese way of thinking each individual (and on a much larger scale the universe) is made up of *yīn* and *yáng* and only when the right balance is achieved between the two will s/he be in good mental and physical health. *Yīn* characteristics include sensitivity, softness, feelings centred around home, family and friends; *yáng* characteristics centre around work, competitiveness, assertion, hence the traditional division into male and female. This is a fascinating subject to explore which could give you a whole different outlook on life – go for it!

Vocabulary items associated with *yīn* and *yáng*:

yīnlì 阴历	'lunar calendar' (the Chinese New Year or Spring Festival is based on the lunar calendar)
yánglì 阳历	'solar calendar'
yīntiān 阴天	'cloudy, overcast'
tàiyáng 太阳	(excessive *yáng*) 'the sun'
tàiyángjìng 太阳镜	(excessive *yáng* mirror) 'sunglasses'
yángdiàn 阳电	'positive electricity'
yīndiàn 阴电	'negative electricity'.

In traditional Chinese medicine a deficiency of *yáng* (*yáng xū* 阳虚) is associated with a lack of vital energy; a deficiency of *yīn* (*yīn xū* 阳虚) with an insufficiency of body fluid, irritability, thirst and constipation being its symptoms.

These are but a few examples, for a much fuller list consult any medium-sized Chinese–English dictionary.

10 A *YĚ HǍO*, B *YĚ HǍO*

This is a useful expression, meaning 'no matter whether A or B, something is still the case':

Xuéxí Hànyǔ yě hǎo, xuéxí Ālābóyǔ yě hǎo, tā dōu hěn gǎn xìngqù (*gǎn xìngqù* 'be interested in something') 'He's very interested in studying both Chinese and Arabic'.

Zhōngguórén yě hǎo, wàiguórén yě hǎo, yìbān lái shuō, dōu bú rènwéi zìjǐ yǒu shénme piānjiàn 'Generally speaking, neither Chinese nor foreigners think they have any prejudices'.

11 (*LIÁN*) *YÌDIǍN YĚ/DŌU BÙ*

This construction shares some similarities with 9.10(iii), question words used to indicate inclusiveness or exclusiveness. The pattern here is: (*lián*) *yìdiǎn yě/dōu bù* + adjective/verb (*Lit.* even little bit also not adj./v), (*lián*) *yìdiǎn yě bú cuò* 'absolutely right', *Wǒ* (*lián*) *yìdiǎn yě bù tóngyì* 'I don't agree at all', 'I disagree entirely'.

If the action took place in the past then *méi* is used instead of *bù*: *Zhè běn xiǎoshuō tā* (*lián*) *yìdiǎn yě méi kàn* 'He hasn't read a word of this novel'. The *yìdiǎn* may be replaced by such expressions as *yì fēn zhōng* ('one minute') *yì fēn qián* ('one cent/penny'), any expression indeed consisting of *yī* (one) MW + noun:

Jiějie yì fēn qián yě méi huā 'My (elder) sister didn't spend any money at all'

Kāi huì de shíhou, wǒ de tóngshì yí jù huà yě bù shuō 'My colleague never says a word at meetings' (*kāi huì* v-o 'hold a meeting').

In such cases the construction can also be used in the affirmative, i.e. without *bù* in which case *lián* is normally retained.

Tā lián xìn dōu kàn le 'She even read the letter'.

Wèile dádào (达到 'achieve, reach') *tāmen de mùbiāo* (aim), *lǐngdǎo lián zìjǐ de rénmín dōu huì xīshēng* (sacrifice). 'In order to achieve their objective, leaders will even sacrifice their own people'.

12 ZÁNMEN AND WǑMEN

Both these personal pronouns mean 'we' but *zánmen* specifically includes both the speaker and the person or persons spoken to, so if you want to make this point use *zánmen*. You will find several examples of *zánmen* in the texts of Chapters 21 and 22.

13 FALSE FRIENDS?

As I have already tried to indicate in 21.7. *tóngqíng* 'to sympathise with' and *tóngyì* 'to agree with' already contain the idea of 'with' in the verb and so there is no need to add anything else. This means that the direct object follows on directly after the verb:

Wo tóngyì nǐ de yìjiàn   'I agree with your opinion'
Tóngqíng ta méi yǒu yòng   'There's no point in
                              sympathising with him'.

By the way, 'wear one's hair long' does not use *chuān* or *dài* as the verb but *liú* 留 'let grow'.

Doing your own thing?

In Chinese society, particularly since Liberation, the emphasis has been on the collective, not on the individual, although the advent of the responsibility system *zérènzhì* (责任制) the open-door policy and the economic reforms of the Eighties have led to more people thinking for themselves and making their own decisions about their future. The Democratic Movement *mínzhǔ yùndòng* (民主运动) of 1989 has also to be seen in this light. Nevertheless, the general trend is still for everyone to know everyone else's business. The ever resourceful Chinese have devised various methods of coping with this social phenomenon, one of which is the use of the term *bàn shì* (办事) 'to go and get something done'. When asked why you are late for work or why you are leaving early or why you happen to be in a particular place, the answers might be, respectively:

> *Duìbuqǐ, lái wǎn le, wǒ bàn le yìdiǎn shì.*
> *Wǒ yào qù bàn yìdiǎn shì.*
> *Wǒ lái bàn yìdiǎn shì.*

Curiously enough, people rarely ask what the *shì* is. I suspect everybody needs to use this let-out clause from time to time and therefore respects other people's right to use it too.

Foreign devils and 'old' foreigners

Non-Chinese used to be classified as 'devils' *guǐ(zi)* 鬼(子) which is generally regarded as a term of abuse in China, *guǐ* traditionally being regarded as unhappy spirits who have to be placated in some way by those still on earth. In Imperial times Westerners were called *yángguǐzi* 'devils from across the sea' or 'foreign devils', while the Japanese were called *Rìběn guǐ(zi)*. Mr Qian's eldest son in Lu Xun's famous novel *The True Story of Ah Q* is called Imitation Foreign Devil *Jiǎ yángguǐzi* because he came back from Japan with straight legs, i.e. he walked differently and had had his pigtail cut off. I have not heard the term *yángguǐzi* for many years but I can't say the same for the term involving the Japanese who have a more recent unhappy history with China. Another expression still in use to refer to caucasian non-Chinese is *gāo bízi* 'tall noses'. Some Chinese might cite their noses not being sufficiently 'tall', *bízi bú gòu gāo* as a reason for not being able to enjoy certain privileges accorded to foreigners – funny, but not without irony you might say. We have discussed the use of *lǎo* 'old' and *xiǎo* 'young' in 5.10 and it is in this light that I have never found the term *lǎowài* offensive. Children and adolescents use it most, but it has always seemed to me to express active curiosity rather than any animosity. *Wài* is, of course, an abbreviation for *wàiguórén* 'foreigner'.

EXERCISE 21.4

Answer the following questions based on the text: Work in *pinyin* or characters.

1 *Zài Zhōngguó lǚxíng kěyǐ liǎojiě shénme ne?*
2 *Wáng Yǒngshòu hé Shǐ Àilǐ zài shénme dìfang?*
3 *Tāmen yìbiān chīzhe sānmíngzhì, yìbiān zuò shénme?*
4 *Zhōngguórén xǐhuan bu xǐhuan zhào xiàng? Tāmen de zhàoxiàngjī zěnmeyàng?*
5 *Rìběn zhàoxiàngjī shòu huānyíng ma?*
6 *Zhíyè zhàoxiàng de duō bu duō?*
7 *Zhōngguórén xǐhuan yí ge rén chū qu wánr ma?*
8 *Zhāng Xīqún shì shénme dìfang rén?*
9 *Shǐ Àilǐ tīng dào yángguǐzi、 gāo bízi zhè yàng de chēnghū tā xīnlǐ gāoxing bu gāoxing?*
10 *Wǒmen shòuguo jiàoyù de rén yě yǒu zhǒngzú piānjiàn ma?*
11 *Wáng Yǒngshòu tóngyì bu tóngyì Zhāng Xīqún de shuōfǎ (way of saying things)?*
12 *Wǒmen wèi shénme yào chéngrèn cuòwù ne?*

EXERCISE 21.5

Translate the following passage into colloquial English:

1 *Zài yǒuxiē fāngmiàn Zhōngguórén hé wàiguórén dàtóng-xiǎoyì, dōu xǐhuan chū qu wánr, zhǎo rénjiān lèyuán! Shéi bú yuànyì zhù de hǎo, chuān de hǎo, chī de hǎo ne? Zhōngguórén yě bú shì shénme lìwài (exception). Yǐqián zài Zhōngguó lǚyóu de Zhōngguórén hěn shǎo, xiànzài yì nián bǐ yì nián duō le.*
   在有些方面中国人和外国人大同小异，都喜欢出去玩儿，找人间乐园！谁不愿意住得好，穿得好，吃得好呢？中国人也不是什么例外。以前在中国旅游的中国人很少，现在一年比一年多了。

2 *Liǎojiě lìngwài yí ge mínzú hěn bù róngyì, lián liǎojiě zìjǐ de mínzú yě bù róngyì. Zhōngguó rénmín shì ge gǔlǎo (ancient) de rénmín. Tā de lìshǐ, wénhuà (culture) gēn wǒmen de hěn bù yíyàng, gèng*

bú bì shuō tā de wénzì (script) *ne! Xué qǐ Zhōngwén lai búdàn* (not only) *hěn yǒu yìsi érqiě* (but also) *duì wǒmen gèrén* (individual) *hěn yǒu yòng.*

了解另外一个民族很不容易，连了解自己的民族也不容易。中国人民是个古老的人民。它的历史、文化跟我们的很不一样，更不必说它的文字呢！学起中文来不但很有意思而且对我们个人很有用。

EXERCISE 21.6

Translate the following sentences into *pinyin* and then into Chinese characters:

1 Let's (use *zánmen*) talk about education whilst watching the sunset.

2 'Deceiving oneself as well as others' is a proverb well worth paying attention to.

3 Because of the Hong Kong (香港 *Xiānggǎng*) question, relations between Britain and China have become very complex (复杂 *fùzá*).

4 He is my colleague so of course that influences my opinion (意见 *yìjiàn*). (Use the passive.)

5 You haven't had a single day's holiday this year, so no wonder you're so tired.

6 She hasn't even eaten a sandwich today, so how come she's not starving?

22

Farewell to All That!

Mr King and Miss Shaw are preparing to return to the UK, the former after teaching one year at Beida, the latter after completing her compulsory year of study abroad. The Lis have invited them for a farewell dinner.

王永寿和史爱理打算回英国。前者在北大教了一年书，后者在中国学了一年必修课程。李先生和夫人为他们饯行。

李	欢迎，欢迎。请进。
李太太	外面冷吗？
史	有一点。风很大，我们是顶着风骑车来的，真费劲儿。
王	这是我们的一点心意（给李太太几个罐头和一些水果）。
李	你们太客气了，又让你们破费。
史	没什么，一点小意思吧。
李	那就谢谢你们了。不过，好朋友之间是不讲客气的。
李太太	别老站在外面厅里，请屋里坐，暖和暖和。
李	喝茶还是喝咖啡？
王	还是喝茶吧。
李太太	唉，爱理，你要回国了，今天可算是‘最后的晚餐’了，多遗憾哪！
史	别这么说，听了，心里不是滋味。
李太太	东西收拾好了没有？
史	差不多都收拾好了。
李太太	你们需要帮忙，尽管说吧，千万别客气。
史	我不会客气，不过真的没什么事儿。大部分书已经寄走了，邮费挺贵的，但是不寄不行。
李	行李会不会超重？

史　　一般超重两、三公斤没什么关系，我打算把一些重的东西放在手
　　　提包里。象磁带什么的，我已经分给朋友了。贝多芬、莫扎特等古
　　　典音乐磁带就送给你们吧。

李　　好极了！谢谢你。(转向王永寿)永寿，你教书教了一年了，有什么
　　　感想呢？听说有一点儿想留在中国是吗？

王　　这叫做'流连忘返'，但是最近父母身体不怎么样，想回去看一看
　　　再说。啊——一年过得真快，'光阴似箭，日月如梭'！

李　　你真是地地道道的中国通，跟中国人打成一片。难怪你的学生那
　　　么喜欢你，又认真又能干，又富于幽默感。爱理，你也舍不得走，
　　　是不是？

史　　是的。今年收获很大，可惜不能多留。

李　　你可算是'满载而归'了！

史　　也可以这么说。

李太太　来吃饭吧。饺子包好了。正在煮。先喝酒吧，这儿有冷盘。文华，
　　　把酒打开吧！

李　　这瓶酒不错，是白葡萄酒，合资企业的产品。中国酒一般是甜的，
　　　但是我们知道你们不太喜欢喝甜的。好，干杯！祝你们一路平安，
　　　早日回来！

史　　祝你们身体健康，万事如意！

李　　咱们来照几张相吧。不过，等饺子来了再照，更有中国味道。啊，
　　　饺子来了！

王　　你有闪光灯吗？

李　　有。准备好了吗？请笑一笑！哦，我忘了把镜头盖打开了。

李太太　你这个人太糊涂，浪费人的表情，快一点儿吧！

王　　我也来照几张，洗好了就给你们寄来。有没有我们在英国的地址？

李　　没有。

王　　我给你们写下来，爱理，有笔吗？我的圆珠笔坏了。

史　　有，给你。周德津，你的饺子真好吃，下一次一定要教我怎么包。

李太太　好吧，欢迎你们尽早回来……酱油和醋都在这儿。

史　　谢谢你。我放一点酱油。我这个人是绝对不会吃醋的，哈哈！

李太太　永寿，你看，你要多留一年，一点问题都没有！

王　　我比爱理安静，稳定。她朋友满天下，要有一个人吃醋的话，肯定
　　　是我！

史　　胡说 my dear！你的多少女生跟我说你这个人真帅！

李　　来，再喝一杯。祝咱们之间的友谊万古长存！干杯！

王　　李老师，下个星期五是你的生日，可惜那个时候我们已经离开中
　　　国了，所以我们现在要再敬你一杯，提前祝你'寿比南山，福如东
　　　海'！我们还给你准备了一点小东西。

李　　那怎么行？来的时候已经送东西了，怎么又送了？

史	那是给你们两个人的，这是生日礼物。希望你能为虎年添点虎气！
李	你们实在太客气了。
李太太	爱理，你怎么了？别哭了，'后会有期'，毕业以后再来吧。
史	别管我。没事儿。我是一个伤感主义者！跟朋友告别的时候，总会想起'相见时难，别亦难'这句话来。
李太太	那倒是。你们'不远万里而来'，确实不容易。但是你们来中国的机会还是会很多的。
李	等你们再来，我们开一个联欢会，怎么样？为了明、后年我们再相会，来，再干一杯！
李太太	这次不能不回去，爱理，你还要读一年书。但是以后机会多得很。
李	飞机几点钟起飞？
王	下午四点四十。应该三点钟到。
李	我们去送送你们吧。
史	不用了，机场太远了，太不方便了。今天晚上就算告别了吧。要不，我受不了，还要告一次别！
李	看情况吧。如果能早一点儿下课，我们一定去。好，不谈这个了。再干最后一杯吧。
李太太	我不行了，再喝，我就要醉了！你们看，脸都红了！
李	没关系，你不是开车的！来，为了大家幸福、快乐，干杯！
李太太、 史、 王	干杯！

Wáng Yǒngshòu hé Shǐ Àilǐ dǎsuàn huí Yīngguó. Qiánzhě zài Běidà jiāo le yì nián shū, hòuzhě zài Zhōngguó xué le yì nián bìxiūkèchéng. Lǐ xiānsheng hé fūrén wèi tāmen jiànxíng.

Lǐ	*Huānyíng, huānyíng. Qǐng jìn.*
Lǐ (t)	*Wàimiàn lěng ma?*
Shǐ	*Yǒu yìdiǎn. Fēng hěn dà, wǒmen shì dǐngzhe fēng qí chē lái de, zhēn fèijìnr.*
Wáng	*Zhè shì wǒmen de yìdiǎn xīnyì. (Gěi Lǐ tàitai jǐ ge guàntóu hé yìxiē shuǐguǒ.)*
Lǐ	*Nǐmen tài kèqi le, yòu ràng nǐmen pòfèi.*
Shǐ	*Méi shénme, yìdiǎn xiǎoyìsi ba.*
Lǐ	*Nà jiù xièxie nǐmen le. Búguò, hǎo péngyou zhī jiān shì bu jiǎng kèqi de.*
Lǐ (t)	*Bié lǎo zhàn zài wàimian tīng lǐ, qǐng wūlǐ zuò, nuǎnhuo nuǎnhuo.*

Lǐ	*Hē chá háishi hē kāfēi?*
Wáng	*Háishi hē chá ba.*
Lǐ (t)	*Ài, Àilǐ, nǐ yào huí guó le, jīntiān kě suàn shì 'zuìhòu de wǎncān' le, duō yíhàn na!*
Shǐ	*Bié zhème shuō, tīng le, xīnlǐ bú shì zīwèi.*
Lǐ (t)	*Dōngxi shōushi hǎo le méi you?*
Shǐ	*Chàbuduō dōu shōushi hǎo le.*
Lǐ (t)	*Nǐmen xūyào bāngmáng, jǐnguǎn shuō ba, qiānwàn bié kèqi.*
Shǐ	*Wǒ bú huì kèqi, búguò zhēnde méi shénme shìr. Dà bùfēn shū yǐjīng jì zǒu le, yóufèi tǐng guì de, dànshi bú jì bù xíng.*
Lǐ	*Xínglǐ huì bu huì chāozhòng?*
Shǐ	*Yìbān chāozhòng liǎng、 sān gōngjīn méi shénme guānxi. Wǒ dǎsuàn bǎ yìxiē zhòng de dōngxi fàng zài shǒutíbāo lǐ. Xiàng cídài shénmede, wǒ yǐjīng fēn gěi péngyou le. Bèiduōfēn、 Mòzhātè děng gǔdiǎn yīnyuè cídài jiù sòng gěi nǐmen ba.*
Lǐ	*Hǎo jíle! Xièxie nǐ. (Zhuǎn xiàng Wáng Yǒngshòu.) Yǒngshòu, nǐ jiāo shū jiāo le yì nián le, yǒu shénme gǎnxiǎng ne? Tīngshuō yǒu yìdiǎnr xiǎng liú zài Zhōngguó shì ma?*
Wáng	*Zhè jiàozuò 'liúlián wàng fǎn', dànshi zuìjìn fùmǔ shēntǐ bù zěnmeyàng, xiǎng huí qu kànyikàn zài shuō. Ā— yì nián guò de zhēn kuài, 'guāngyīn sì jiàn, rìyuè rú suō'.*
Lǐ	*Nǐ zhēn shì dìdìdàodào de Zhōngguótōng, gēn Zhōngguórén dǎchéng yípiàn. Nánguài nǐ de xuésheng nàme xǐhuan nǐ, yòu rènzhēn yòu nénggàn, yǒu fùyú yōumògǎn. Àilǐ, nǐ yě shěbude zǒu, shì bu shì?*
Shǐ	*Shì de. Jīnnián shōuhuò hěn dà, kěxī bù néng duō liú.*
Lǐ	*Nǐ kě suàn shì 'mǎn zài ér guī' le!*
Shǐ	*Yě kěyǐ zhème shuō.*
Lǐ (t)	*Lái chī fàn ba. Jiǎozi bāo hǎo le, zhèngzài zhǔ. Xiān hē jiǔ ba. Zhèr yǒu lěngpán. Wénhuá, bǎ jiǔ dǎkāi ba.*
Lǐ	*Zhè píng jiǔ búcuò, shì bái pútáojiǔ, hézī qǐyè de chǎnpǐn. Zhōngguó jiǔ yìbān shì tián de, dànshi wǒmen zhīdao nǐmen bú tài xǐhuan hē tián de. Hǎo, gān bēi! Zhù nǐmen yílù píng'ān, zǎorì huí lai!*
Shǐ	*Zhù nǐmen shēntǐ jiànkāng, wànshì rú yì!*
Lǐ	*Zánmen lái zhào jǐ zhāng xiàng ba. Búguò děng jiǎozi lái le zài zhào, gèng yǒu Zhōngguó wèidao. Ā, jiǎozi lái le!*

Wáng *Nǐ yǒu shǎnguāngdēng ma?*

Lǐ *Yǒu. Zhǔnbèi hǎo le ma? Qǐng xiàoyixiào! Ò, wǒ wàng le bǎ jìngtóugài dǎkāi le.*

Lǐ (t) *Nǐ zhè ge rén tài hútu, làngfèi rén de biǎoqíng, kuài yìdiǎnr ba!*

Wáng *Wǒ yě lái zhào jǐ zhāng. Xǐ hǎo le jiù gěi nǐmen jì lai. Yǒu méi yǒu wǒmen zài Yīngguó de dìzhǐ?*

Lǐ *Méi yǒu.*

Wáng *Wǒ gěi nǐmen xiě xiàlai. Àilǐ, yǒu bǐ ma? Wǒ de yuánzhūbǐ huài le.*

Shǐ *Yǒu, gěi nǐ. Zhōu Déjūn, nǐ de jiǎozi zhēn hǎo chī, xià yí cì yídìng yào jiāo wǒ zěnme bāo.*

Lǐ (t) *Hǎo ba, huānyíng nǐ jǐnzǎo huí lai…jiàngyóu hé cù dōu zài zhèr.*

Shǐ *Xièxie nǐ. Wǒ fàng yìdiǎn jiàngyóu. Wǒ zhè ge rén shì juéduì bú huì chī cù de, hāhā!*

Lǐ (t) *Yǒngshòu, nǐ kàn, nǐ yào duō liú yì nián, yìdiǎn wèntí dōu méi yǒu!*

Wáng *Wǒ bǐ Àilǐ ānjìng, wěndìng. Tā péngyou mǎn tiānxià, yào yǒu yí ge rén chī cù de huà, kěndìng shì wǒ!*

Shǐ *Húshuō my dear! Nǐ de duōshao nǚshēng gēn wǒ shuō nǐ zhè ge rén zhēn shuài!*

Lǐ *Lái, zài hē yì bēi. Zhù zánmen zhī jiān de yǒuyì wàngǔ chángcún! Gān bēi!*

Wáng *Lǐ lǎoshī, xià ge xīngqīwǔ shì nǐ de shēngrì, kěxī nà ge shíhou wǒmen yǐjīng líkāi Zhōngguó le, suǒyǐ wǒmen xiànzài yào zài jìng nǐ yì bēi, tíqián zhù nǐ 'Shòu bǐ Nánshān, fú rú Dōnghǎi'! Wǒmen hái gěi nǐ zhǔnbèi le yìdiǎn xiǎo dōngxi.*

Lǐ *Nà zěnme xíng? Lái de shíhou yǐjīng sòng dōngxi le, zěnme yòu sòng le?*

Shǐ *Nà shì gěi nǐmen liǎng ge rén de, zhè shì shēngrì lǐwù. Xīwàng nǐ néng wèi hǔnián tiān diǎn hǔqì!*

Lǐ *Nǐmen shízài tài kèqi le.*

Lǐ (t) *Àilǐ, nǐ zěnme le? Bié kū le, 'hòu huì yǒu qī', bìyè yǐhòu zài lái ba.*

Shǐ *Bié guǎn wǒ. Méishìr. Wǒ shì yí ge shānggǎnzhǔyìzhě! Gēn péngyou gàobié de shíhou, zǒng huì xiǎng qǐ 'Xiāng jiàn shí nán, bié yì nán' zhè jù huà lai.*

Lǐ (t)   *Nà dàoshì. Nǐmen 'bù yuǎn wàn lǐ ér lái', quèshí bù róngyì. Dànshi nǐmen lái Zhōngguó de jīhuì háishi huì hěn duō de.*

Lǐ   *Děng nǐmen zài lái, wǒmen kāi yí ge liánhuānhuì, zěnmeyàng? Wèile míng、hòunián wǒmen zài xiānghuì, lái, zài gān yì bēi!*

Lǐ (t)   *Zhè cì bù néng bù huí qu, Àilǐ, nǐ hái yào dú yì nián shū. Dànshi yǐhòu jīhuì duō dehěn.*

Lǐ   *Fēijī jǐ diǎn zhōng qǐfēi?*

Wáng   *Xiàwǔ sì diǎn sìshí...Yīnggāi sān diǎn zhōng dào.*

Lǐ   *Wǒmen qù sòngsong nǐmen ba.*

Shǐ   *Bú yòng le, jīchǎng tài yuǎn le, tài bù fāngbiàn le. Jīntiān wǎnshang jiù suàn gàobié le ba. Yàobù wǒ shòu bù liǎo, hái yào gào yí cì bié!*

Lǐ   *Kàn qíngkuàng ba. Rúguǒ néng zǎo yìdiǎnr xià kè, wǒmen yídìng qù. Hǎo, bù tán zhè ge le. Zài gān zuìhòu yì bēi ba.*

Lǐ (t)   *Wǒ bù xíng le, zài hē, wǒ jiù yào zuì le! Nǐmen kàn, liǎn dōu hóng le!*

Lǐ   *Méi guānxi, nǐ bú shi kāi chē de! Lái, wèile dàjiā xìngfú、kuàilè, gān bēi!*

Lǐ (t)
Shǐ   } *Gān bēi!*
Wáng

打算	**dǎsuàn** (v)	*to intend, plan*
前者	**qiánzhě** (n)	*the former*
后者	**hòuzhě** (n)	*the latter*
必修课程	**bìxiūkè(chéng)** (n)	*obligatory or required course*
夫人	**fūrén** (n)	*Mrs; Madame (formal)*
为	**wèi** (prep.)	*for, for the sake of*
饯行	**jiànxíng** (n)	*give a farewell dinner*
风	**fēng** (n)	*wind*
顶	**dǐng** (v)	*to go against*
骑	**qí** (v)	*to ride (as of horse, bicycle)*
费劲（儿）	**fèijìn(r)** (adj.)	*strenuous, energy consuming*
心意	**xīnyì** (n)	*kindly feelings, regard*

水果	**shuǐguǒ** (n)	*fruit*
让	**ràng** (v)	*to let, allow*
破费	**pòfèi** (v-o)	*to go to some expense*
小意思	**xiǎoyìsi** (n)	*small token, mere trifle*
之间	**zhī jiān**	*between, amongst*
老	**lǎo** (adj.)	*always*
站	**zhàn** (v)	*to stand; station, stop (bus. etc)*
屋里	**wūlǐ** (PW)	*in the room*
暖和	**nuǎnhuo** (adj.)	*warm*
算	**suàn** (v)	*to regard as, count as*
最后	**zuìhòu** (adj., adv.)	*the last, finally*
晚餐	**wǎncān** (n)	*supper, dinner*
多	**duō**	*how*
遗憾	**yíhàn** (v; n)	*to regret, be a pity; regret*
哪	**na**	*particle showing mood*
这么	**zhème**	*so, this way, like this*
滋味	**zīwèi** (n)	*(good) taste, flavour*
收拾	**shōushi** (v)	*to pack, tidy up, put in order*
差不多	**chàbuduō** (adv.)	*almost, nearly*
需要	**xūyào** (v; n)	*to need, require; needs*
不过	**búguò** (conj.)	*but, however, only*
邮费	**yóufèi** (n)	*postage*
行李	**xínglǐ** (n)	*luggage, baggage*
超重	**chāozhòng** (v-o)	*overweight*
手提包	**shǒutíbāo** (n)	*bag, handbag*
磁带	**cídài** (n)	*tape*
分	**fēn** (v)	*to divide, distribute, distinguish*
贝多芬	**Bèiduōfēn** (N)	*Beethoven*
莫扎特	**Mòzhātè** (N)	*Mozart*
古典	**gǔdiǎn** (adj.)	*classical*
音乐	**yīnyuè** (n)	*music*
送	**sòng** (v)	*to give as a present; see somebody off*
转	**zhuǎn** (v)	*to turn, transfer*
向	**xiàng** (prep.; v)	*towards; to face*
感想	**gǎnxiǎng** (n)	*reflections, thoughts*

叫做	**jiàozuò** (v)	*be called, be known as*
流连忘返	**liúlián wàng fǎn**	*enjoy oneself so much as to forget to go home*
最近	**zuìjìn** (adv.; adj.)	*recently, nearest, latest*
再说	**zài shuō** (v; conj.)	*not tackle a problem until some other time; what's more*
光阴似箭,	**guāngyīn sì jiàn,**	*time flies (see 22.5)*
日月如梭	**rìyuè rú suō**	
地道	**dìdào** (adj.)	*genuine*
中国通	**Zhōngguótōng** (n)	*an old China hand, expert on China*
打成一片	**dǎchéng yípiàn** (v-o)	*to become one with, identify with*
认真	**rènzhēn** (adj.)	*conscientious*
能干	**nénggàn** (adj.)	*capable, competent*
富于	**fùyú** (adj.)	*full of*
幽默感	**yōumògǎn** (n)	*sense of humour*
舍不得	**shěbude** (v)	*be unwilling to part with, grudge*
收获	**shōuhuò** (n)	*gains, results, harvest*
满载而归	**mǎn zài ér guī**	*return with fruitful results*
饺子	**jiǎozi** (n)	*a kind of ravioli, dumpling*
包	**bāo** (v)	*to make (**jiǎozi**); to wrap; to include*
煮	**zhǔ** (v)	*to boil, cook*
冷盘	**lěngpán** (n)	*cold dish; hors d'oeuvres*
打开	**dǎkāi** (v)	*to open (up); switch on*
瓶	**píng** (MW)	*for bottles*
白	**bái** (adj)	*white; blank*
葡萄酒	**pútáojiǔ** (n)	*wine*
合资企业	**hézī qǐyè** (n)	*joint venture*
产品	**chǎnpǐn** (n)	*product*
甜	**tián** (adj.)	*sweet*
干杯	**gān bēi** (v-o)	*drink a toast*
一路平安	**yílù píng'ān**	*Bon voyage, have a pleasant journey*
早日	**zǎorì** (TW)	*at an early date; soon*
健康	**jiànkāng** (adj.)	*healthy, sound*
万事如意	**wànshì rúyì**	*your heart's desire*

味道	**wèidao** (n)	*flavour, taste*
闪光灯	**shǎnguāngdēng** (n)	*flash(light)*
笑	**xiào** (v)	*to smile, laugh*
哦	**ò** (inter.)	*oh!*
镜头盖	**jìngtóugài** (n)	*lens cap*
糊涂	**hútu** (adj.)	*muddle-headed*
浪费	**làngfèi** (v)	*to waste, squander*
表情	**biǎoqíng** (n; v)	*expression; to express one's feelings*
(冲)洗	**(chōng)xǐ** (v)	*to develop (as of film); to wash*
圆珠笔	**yuánzhūbǐ** (n)	*ballpoint pen*
尽早	**jǐnzǎo** (adv.)	*as soon as possible, at the earliest possible date*
醋	**cù** (n)	*vinegar; jealousy (as in love affairs)*
绝对	**juéduì** (adj.; adv.)	*absolute(ly)*
吃醋	**chī cù** (v-o)	*to feel jealous*
哈哈	**hāhā** (onom.)	*haha*
稳定	**wěndìng** (adj.; v)	*stable, steady; to stabilise*
满	**mǎn** (adj.; v)	*full; to reach the limit, expire*
天下	**tiānxià** (n)	*land under heaven – the world or China*
胡说	**húshuō** (n; v)	*nonsense; to talk nonsense*
女生	**nǚshēng** (n)	*female student(s)*
帅	**shuài** (adj. coll; adv.)	*handsome; beautifully*
友谊	**yǒuyì** (n)	*friendship*
万古长存	**wàngǔ chángcún**	*last forever, be everlasting*
生日	**shēngrì** (n)	*birthday*
离开	**líkāi** (v)	*to leave*
敬	**jìng** (v)	*to propose (a toast), toast*
提前	**tíqián** (v)	*bring forward a date*
寿比南山，福如东海	**shòu bǐ Nánshān, fú rú Dōnghǎi**	*May you live as long as the Southern Mountain and be as blessed as the Eastern Sea*
礼物	**lǐwù** (n)	*present, gift*
虎年	**hǔnián** (n)	*the year of the Tiger*

虎气	**hǔqì** (n)	*vigour (Lit. tiger energy)*
实在	**shízài** (adv.; adj.)	*really, honestly; true, real*
怎么了	**zěnme le?**	*what's the matter?*
哭	**kū** (v)	*to weep, cry*
后会有期	**hòu huì yǒu qī**	*we'll meet again some day*
毕业	**bìyè** (v)	*to graduate*
管	**guǎn** (v)	*bother about; be in charge of*
没事儿	**méishìr**	*it's OK, it's nothing; have nothing planned*
伤感主义者	**shānggǎnzhǔyìzhě** (n)	*sentimentalist*
告别	**gàobié** (v-o)	*to take leave of*
想起来	**xiǎng qǐlai** (v)	*to remember, call to mind*
相见时难，别亦难	**xiāng jiàn shí nán, bié yì nán**	*meeting and parting are both difficult (see Ch. 22, p. 255)*
不远万里而来	**bù yuǎn wàn lǐ ér lái**	*not considering 10 000 li too far to come*
确实	**quèshí** (adv.; adj.)	*really, indeed; true, certain*
机会	**jīhuì** (n)	*opportunity, chance*
联欢会	**liánhuānhuì** (n)	*get-together, party*
明年	**míngnián** (TW)	*next year*
后年	**hòunián** (TW)	*the year after next*
相会	**xiānghuì** (v)	*meet one another*
多得很	**duō dehěn** (adj.)	*very many*
飞机[架]	**fēijī** (n) **[jià]**	*aeroplane*
起飞	**qǐfēi** (v)	*to take off (of aircraft)*
不用	**bú yòng** (v)	*need not*
飞机场	**fēijīchǎng** (n)	*airport*
受不了	**shòu bù liǎo** (v)	*be unable to bear or endure*
醉	**zuì** (adj.)	*drunk*
脸	**liǎn** (n)	*face*
红	**hóng** (adj.)	*red*
开车的	**kāi chē de** (n)	*a person who drives, driver*
为了	**wèile** (prep.)	*for the sake of, in order to*
幸福	**xìngfú** (adj.; n)	*enjoy good fortune, happy; well-being*
快乐	**kuàilè** (adj.)	*happy, joyful*

Grammar

1 EXCLAMATIONS!

The Chinese language has an infinite variety of its own particular version of ahs, oohs and ohs but it is perhaps the modal particles which occur at the end of the sentence which are of particular interest. Some of these have been scattered throughout the various texts in this book. In this chapter, we have 哪 *na,* 呢 *ne* and the all-time favourite 吧 *ba.* Apart from the few guidelines you have been given, for instance that 呢 *ne* tends to appear with the question words *shénme, zěnme, wèi shénme,* etc. and set-phrases such as *Nǐ zěnme le?* you should rely on your 'feel' of the language as to whether a *ya,* a *na,* or a *ne,* etc. is needed. Chinese has a lot to do with feeling rather than specific rules so start with your exclamations and expressions of surprise. If you have the opportunity, listen to Chinese speakers and imitate them as far as possible. Failing that, just remember that such things are the icing on the cake rather than the cake itself.

2 EATING BITTERNESS?

I have always teased Chinese friends about the emphasis that Chinese culture puts on food. Chinese people can talk for hours (and I mean hours) about the merits of various dishes, how to make them and how difficult (or expensive) it is to find such and such an ingredient. We can speculate endlessly on the reasons for this, which could vary from peasant poverty to magnificent Imperial banquets. Whatever the reason, it has left the Chinese language with a rich heritage based on eating. Note the following phrases which are just some of the ones in common usage:

吃醋	*chī cù*	'be jealous' (*Lit.* eat vinegar)
吃惊	*chī jīng*	'be shocked, amazed' (*Lit.* eat alarm)
吃苦	*chī kǔ*	'bear hardship' (*Lit.* eat bitterness)
吃亏	*chī kuī*	'stand to lose', 'come to grief', 'get the worst of it' (*Lit.* eat loss)
吃力	*chī lì*	'strenuous, difficult' (*Lit.* eat strength)
吃软不吃硬	*chī ruǎn bù chī yìng*	'be open to persuasion but not to coercion' (*Lit.* eat soft not eat hard)
吃闲饭	*chī xiánfàn*	'lead an idle life, be a sponger' (*Lit.* eat idle rice)

| 吃香 | *chī xiāng* 'be popular' (coll.) (*Lit*. eat spice) |
| 吃药 | *chī yào* 'take medicine' (*Lit*. eat medicine). |

The Chinese zodiac

The existence of the **Ten Heavenly Stems** was mentioned in the vocabulary of Chapter 17, but not elaborated upon further. They are 甲 *jiǎ*, 乙 *yǐ*, 丙 *bǐng*, 丁 *dīng*, 戊 *wù*, 己 *jǐ*, 庚 *gēng*, 辛 *xīn*, 壬 *rén* and 癸 *guǐ* in that order, 甲 *jiǎ* being the first. The Ten Heavenly Stems also combine in pairs, each pair corresponding to each of the five elements used in traditional Chinese medicine, *viz*. wood, fire, earth, metal and water. Thus *jiǎ* and *yǐ* are associated with 木 *mù* 'wood', *bǐng* and *dīng* with 火 *huǒ* 'fire' and so on.

In addition to the Ten Heavenly Stems, there are also the **Twelve Earthly Branches**, each of which is associated with a different animal which occurs in twelve-year cycles. Each of us is born in the lunar year of a particular animal. 1950 was the Year of the Tiger, therefore everyone born in 1950, 1962, 1974 and 1986 is a tiger. 1951 was the Year of the Rabbit so all those born in 1951, 1963, 1975 and 1987 are rabbits. Of course each Animal Year is said to possess certain characteristics and in the old days this played a role in deciding whether or not you were a suitable bride or bridegroom for somebody. Tiger women were thought of as being particularly difficult to handle! The order is as follows:

Earthly branches			*Symbolical animals*		
1	子	*zǐ*	鼠	*shǔ*	rat
2	丑	*chǒu*	牛	*niú*	ox
3	寅	*yín*	虎	*hǔ*	tiger
4	卯	*mǎo*	兔	*tù*	rabbit/hare
5	辰	*chén*	龙	*lóng*	dragon
6	巳	*yǐ*	蛇	*shé*	snake
7	午	*wǔ*	马	*mǎ*	horse
8	未	*wèi*	羊	*yáng*	ram
9	申	*shēn*	猴	*hóu*	monkey
10	酉	*xī*	鸡	*jī*	cockerel

11 戌 *xū*　　　　犬 *quǎn* dog
12 亥 *hài*　　　　猪 *zhū* pig

Astrology books are now being produced combining the
Chinese zodiac with our own Western one. A Tiger who is
also a Scorpio probably presents quite a challenge wouldn't
you say? What are you? (NB the Chinese have traditionally
used the Ten Heavenly Stems and the Twelve Earthly
Branches in a sequential order of two-character combinations
to denote different years, months and days.)

The Chinese Zodiac

3 ZHĚ AS NOMINALISER

Zhě 者 used after an adjective or verb (or adjectival or verbal phrase) serves to nominalise it or make it into a noun phrase. This is considerably more stylish than merely adding *de rén* 的人 ('the person who...') or *de shì* 的事 ('the thing/matter which...') after the character(s) involved and is in keeping with the fact that modern Chinese has managed to retain elements of its classical past. Certain collocations have become virtually set phrases and a few are listed below:

ruòzhě	弱者	'the weak'
qiángzhě	强者	'the strong'
qiánzhě	前者	'the former'
hòuzhě	后者	'the latter'
dúzhě	读者	'reader' (there is a popular newspaper column in some newspapers entitled *Dúzhě lái xìn* 'Readers' Letters')
xuézhě	学者	'scholar'.

Note the much more formal register of the introduction to this chapter which uses terms such as *qiánzhě* and *hòuzhě*. *Zhě* is commonly used after 工作 *gōngzuò* 'work' to indicate a person engaged in the profession under discussion. It is also used to change an -ism (*-zhǔyì* 主义) into an -ist. Hence *shèhuì* 'society', *shèhuìzhǔyì* 'socialism' and *shèhuìzhǔyìzhě* 'socialist': *Mǎkèsī* 'Marx', *Mǎkèsīzhǔyì* 'Marxism' and *Mǎkèsīzhǔyìzhě* 'Marxist'; '*gòngchǎnzhǔyìzhě*' 'communist' (*Lit.* together property-ism person); *fǎxīsīzhǔyìzhě* 'fascist'. We have the word for 'sentimentalist' *shānggǎnzhǔyìzhě* in the text and it is also used when referring to gays and lesbians *tóngxìngliànzhě* (*Lit.* same sex love person).

4 ADJECTIVE + *DEHĚN*

This is a simple construction meaning 'very much' of the adjective:

duō dehěn	'very many'
hǎo dehěn	'very good'
yǒu yìsi dehěn	'very interesting'.

It is different from *hěn duō* and *hěn hǎo* insofar as the *hěn* in the latter phrases does not really carry the force of 'very' (see 4.8.4) or is put there merely for balance.

5 MORE ON PROVERBS (II)

To put proverbs in their historical context we are going to trace the origins of two of the proverbs that occur in this text.

(i) *Guāngyīn sì jiàn, rìyuè rú suō*. A similar phrase *guāng liú sì jiàn* (time flows like (an) arrow) first appeared in a Tang poem by Wei Zhuang but it was the famous Song Dynasty (960–1279) poet Su Shi (also known as Su Dongpo) who used *guāngyīn sì jiàn* in one of his poems. The complete proverb *guāngyīn sì jiàn, rìyuè rú suō* occurred in Chapter 9 of the Ming dynasty novel *Xīyóujì* 西游记 translated variously as *Journey to the West* or *Monkey*, written by one Wu Cheng'en.

(ii) *Bù yuǎn wàn lǐ ér lái*. An alternative version *bù yuǎn qiān lǐ ér lái* may sometimes be found but *wàn* (10 000) makes it sound more of a big thing than *qiān* (1000) so I have used the former rather than the latter. (NB *lǐ* 'half a kilometre'.) This phrase first appeared in one of the books of Mencius, the famous Chinese Confucian philosopher of the fourth century BC who believed in the intrinsic goodness of human nature.

To end on a really positive note, particularly appropriate for aspiring students of Chinese, there is *Yǒu zhìzhě shì jìng chéng* 'Where there's a will there's a way' (*Lit.* have aspiration person, matter finally achieve). This occurred in a chapter of the *Hànshū* 'A History of the Han Dynasty' (in 120 volumes) written by 班固 Ban Gu who died in AD 92. As you can see, Chinese history is still alive and well today if we know where to go and look for it.

On Chinese poetry

To understand the Chinese, you also have to understand their poetry. People who regularly use poetry in their language also have poetry in their hearts.

Xiāng jiàn shí nán, bié yì nán quoted in the text comes from an untitled poem by Li Shangyin (812?–868). This line has come to symbolise in seven brief characters, the difficulties often involved in meeting someone and the pain involved in parting. (*Nán* means *kùnnan* 'difficult' in the first case, *nánkān* 'unbearable' in the second.)

Perhaps if I quote a poem written by Li Yu (937–978), the last emperor of the Southern Tang, you will get a taste of the beauty I am referring to. Li Yu was captured by the Song army and taken north to Kaifeng. This poem was written during his captivity, shortly before his death and laments his grievous loss and heavy heart.

无言独上西楼，
月如钩。
寂寞梧桐深院锁清秋。
剪不断，
理还乱，
是离愁，
别是一般滋味在心头。

Wú yán dú shàng Xīlóu
No word(s) alone climb West Tower
Yuè rú gōu.
moon like sickle
Jìmò wútóng shēn yuàn suǒ qīng qiū.
Lonely wútóng dark (deep?) courtyard lock clear autumn
Jiǎn bú duàn,
cut not sever
Lǐ hái luàn,
reason still disorderly
Shì lí chóu
Is separation melancholy
Bié shì yìbān zīwèi zài xīntóu.
Parting is just like (bitter) taste in heart.

Even after more than a 1000 years, the lines still rhyme, an incredible comment on the nature of the Chinese language. The visual impact of the characters is very important in poetry. *Chóu*, the character for 'sorrow' or 'melancholy' is made up of an autumn over a heart (愁), with all the symbolism which that conjures up.

The fact that classical Chinese poetry does not have a grammatical subject makes it seem so much more universal and heightens its effect. Let us look at the content of the poem more closely. Whoever it is, climbs the Western Tower, (the west – the setting sun, the end of one's life?) alone and in silence, the moon like a sickle overhead. (A new moon to heighten his grief, or the last sliver of a waning one?) The *wútóng* (it has a straight trunk of a beautiful shade of green and is said to be the only tree on which the phoenix will rest) is 'lonely' and the clear autumn is as though locked into the dark, deep courtyard. There is a great deal to be got from this line if you only think about it carefully.

The next four lines are truly famous and speak of the pain of parting and separation. Had you ever thought of this pain as being like a skein of wool which refuses to be disentangled and cannot be cut off cleanly? Or of the word 'parting' as leaving 'a taste in the heart'? These four lines are known to millions of Chinese and written as they were, by an emperor, prisoner in a foreign land, who had lost everything and was soon to die (forced to take poison by his captors), they take on a particular poignancy. May they say something to you as they have done to me over a period of many years.

Chinese language and culture are rich treasure-troves for us to explore. My hope is, that through this book, as well as learning some useful Chinese, you have been able to catch glimpses of them and are eager for more.

EXERCISE 22.1

Answer the following questions based on the text.

1　*Wáng xiānsheng hé Shǐ xiǎojie lái de shíhou guā bu guā fēng?*
2　*Wáng xiānsheng gěi Lǐ tàitai shénme xiǎo lǐwù?*
3　*Shǐ Àilǐ juéde bǎ shū jì dào Yīngguó guì bu guì?*
4　*Rúguǒ xínglǐ chāozhòng Shǐ Àilǐ dǎsuàn zěnme bàn?*
5　*Wáng xiānsheng juéde tā zài Zhōngguó de yì nián guò de kuài bu kuài? Tā yòng shénme chéngyǔ lái miáoxiě zhè diǎn?*

6 *Lǐ xiānsheng yòng shénme huà lái shuōmíng* ('show, explain')
   Wáng Yǒngshòu hěn liǎojiě Zhōngguórén?

7 *Shǐ Àilǐ zài Zhōngguó xué de zěnmeyàng? Nǐ zěnme zhīdao ne?*

8 *Tāmen hē de jiǔ shì guóchǎn de ma?*

9 *Lǐ xiānsheng wèi shénme kāishǐ zhào bu liǎo xiàng ne?* (see
   Chapter 12, p 118 for *liǎo*)

10 *Wáng xiānsheng wèi shénme xiàng Shǐ Àilǐ yào bǐ?* (*xiàng* Y *yào*
   X: 'to want X from Y')

11 *Chī jiǎozi de shíhou hái kěyǐ fàng shénme?*

12 *Wáng xiānsheng zěnme huì chī cù ne?*

13 *Lǐ xiānsheng shénme shíhou guò shēngrì? Nà ge shíhou Wáng
   Yǒngshòu hé Shǐ Àilǐ dàgài* ('probably') *zài nǎr?*

14 *Lǐ lǎoshī shǔ* (属 'belong to') *shénme* ('animal sign')?

15 *Shǐ Àilǐ wèi shénme kū qǐlai ne?*

16 *Lǐ xiānsheng dǎsuàn shénme shíhou kāi yí ge liánhuānhuì?*

17 *Tāmen fēijī shénme shíhou qǐfēi? Tāmen yīnggāi jǐ diǎn zhōng
   dào jīchǎng?*

18 *Shǐ Àilǐ wèi shénme bú ràng Lǐ xiānsheng hé Lǐ tàitai qù sòng
   tāmen ne?*

19 *Lǐ tàitai zěnme zhèngmíng* (证明 'prove') *tā kuài yào zuì le?*

20 *Lǐ xiānsheng wèi shénme shuō Lǐ tàitai duō hē yìdiǎn jiǔ méi yǒu
   guānxi?*

1 王先生和史小姐来的时候刮不刮风?

2 王先生给李太太什么小礼物?

3 史爱理觉得把书寄到英国贵不贵?

4 如果行李超重史爱理打算怎么办?

5 王先生觉得他在中国的一年过得快不快?他用什么成语来描写这点?

6 李先生用什么话来说明王永寿很了解中国人?

7 史爱理在中国学得怎么样? 你怎么知道呢?

8 他们喝的酒是国产的吗?

9 李先生为什么开始照不了相呢?

10 王先生为什么向史爱理要笔?

11 吃饺子的时候还可以放什么?

12 王先生怎么会吃醋呢?

13 李先生什么时候过生日? 那个时候王永寿和史爱理大概在哪儿?

14 李老师属什么?

15 史爱理为什么哭起来呢?

16   李先生打算什么时候开一个联欢会？

17   他们飞机什么时候起飞？他们应该几点钟到机场？

18   史爱理为什么不让李先生和李太太去送他们呢？

19   李太太怎么证明她快要醉了？

20   李先生为什么说李太太多喝一点酒没有关系？

EXERCISE 22.2

Translate the text into colloquial English.

EXERCISE 22.3

Correct the following *bìngjù* ('sick sentences'). Give the correct version (This exercise is based on the grammar of Chapters 16–22.)

Běijīng cóng Tiānjīn hěn jìn → Běijīng lí Tiānjīn hěn jìn.

1   *Zhǔnbèi hǎo le ma? Wǒ liǎng diǎn zhōng kuài yào zǒu le.*

2   *Yúnnán zài Zhōngguó de nánxī bù.*

3   *Bǎ zhàoxiàngjī bù kěyǐ jiè* ('lend; borrow') *gěi tā.*

4   *Wǒ yǒu sìshí zhī bǎi fēn de bǎwò* (把握 'certainty').

5   *Yīngguó de shēnghuófèi bǐ Zhōngguó hěn guì.*

6   *Gǔdiǎn yīnyuè gēn xiàndài* (现代 'modern') *yīnyuè hǎo tīng yíyàng.*

7   *Fánshì lǎoshī cái xǐhuan jiāo shū.*

8   *Chúfēi nǐ yuánliàng* (原谅 'forgive') *wǒ, wǒ jiù bù kū le.*

9   *Zài guówài shíjiān hěn cháng, kǒngpà* (恐怕 'be afraid') *huàn qián fēi bùkě.*

10   *Shàngjí* (上级 'superiors') *xiàng bù xǐhuan tā, bù zhīdao shénme yuányīn* (原因 'reason, cause').

11   *Nǐ chuān shang tàiyángjìng qù cānjiā* (参加 'take part in') *liánhuānhuì tài bù héshì* (合适 'suitable') *ne.*

12   *Tā jiào dǎ le yì tā hútu* (一塌糊涂 'a terrible mess').

13   *Shèhuìzhǔyìyuán yīnggāi tóngqíng qióng rén* (穷人 'poor person').

14   *Wǒ gēn nǐ bú tóngyì – tā bìng bú shi ge huài rén.*

15   *Qǐng nǐ bǎ èrshí'èr kè de kèwén fānyì Yīngwén.*

Key to the Exercises

Exercise 1.1

1 *Wǒ bú zuò.* 2 *Nǐ bù hǎo.* 3 *Wǒ bù hē chá.* 4 *Nǐ bù xǐhuan Zhōngguó.* 5 *Lǐ xiānsheng bú xièxie wǒ.* 6 *Wáng xiānsheng bù qǐng nǐ hē Zhōngguó chá.*

Exercise 1.2

1 *Wǒ xǐhuan bu xǐhuan hē kāfēi? Wǒ xǐhuan hē kāfēi. Wǒ bù xǐhuan hē kāfēi.* 2 *Nǐ xièxie bu xièxie wǒ? Nǐ xièxie wǒ. Nǐ bú xièxie wǒ.* 3 *Wáng xiānsheng qǐng bu qǐng wǒ zuò? Wáng xiānsheng qǐng wǒ zuò. Wáng xiānsheng bù qǐng wǒ zuò.* 4 *Lǐ xiānsheng xǐhuan bu xǐhuan hē shuǐ? Lǐ xiānsheng xǐhuan hē shuǐ. Lǐ xiānsheng bu xǐhuan hē shuǐ.*

Exercise 1.3

1 Mr King invites me to drink Chinese tea. 2 Mr Li greatly dislikes Mr King. (Mr Li can't stand Mr King.) 3 Mr King doesn't like Mr Li much either. 4 You don't thank me so I don't thank you either.

Exercise 1.4

1 *Wáng xiānsheng, nǐ hǎo. Qǐng zuò.* 2 *Wǒ bù hē chá.* 3 *Nàme, kāfēi xíng ma? (Nàme, kāfēi xíng bu xíng?)* 4 *Xièxie, kāfēi hěn hǎo.* 5 *Wǒ hěn xǐhuan nǐ.* 6 *Qǐng hē Zhōngguó chá.* 7 *Tā yě bù xǐhuan wǒ.*

Exercise 2.1

1 F 2 T 3 T 4 F 5 F.

Exercise 2.2

1 *Lǐ tàitai, rènshi nín wǒ zhēn gāoxìng.* 2 *Nàme, júzizhī hǎo ba?*

3 *Wǒ hěn xǐhuan hē jiǔ.* **4** *Nín bú huì hē sì bēi pútáojiǔ.* **5** *Wǒ gěi Lǐ xiānsheng jièshào wǒ àiren.*

Exercise 2.3

Mr King invites Mr Li for a drink. Mr Li is very pleased. He's a great drinker. What about his wife Zhou Dejin? His wife doesn't drink. She drinks orange juice. She is also very much against Mr Li drinking.

Exercise 2.4

1 *Nǐ hē jiǔ ma?* **2** *Wǒ bú huì hē jiǔ. Nín ne?* **3** *Zhōu xiānsheng, wǒ gěi nǐ jièshào wǒ àiren.* **4** *Tā rènshi tā ma? (Tā rènshi bu rènshi tā?)* **5** *Wǒ àiren xī yān, wǒ hěn bù gāoxìng.* **6** *Kāfēi hǎo ba?* **7** *Zhāng xiānsheng bú huì Yīngyǔ.* **8** *Nǐ bú huì hē qī bēi jiǔ.*

Exercise 3.1

1 *Wǒmen hē* **shénme?** **2** *Lǐ xiānsheng hé Lǐ tàitai yǒu* **jǐ** *ge xiǎoháir?* **3** *Pútáojiǔ* **zěnmeyàng?** **4** *Wáng xiānsheng de nǚ péngyou zài* **nǎr?** **5** *Tāmen míngtiān wǎnshang jǐ diǎn zhōng qù chī fàn?* **6** *Wáng xiānsheng qǐng* **shéi** *chī fàn?*

Exercise 3.2

1 *Jiǔ diǎn (zhōng)* **2** *Shíyī diǎn bàn* **3** *Liǎng diǎn èrshíwǔ fēn* **4** *Sān diǎn wǔshí fēn* or *Chà shí fēn sì diǎn* **5** *Yì diǎn yí kè* or *yì diǎn shíwǔ fēn* **6** *Bā diǎn (líng) wǔ fēn* **7** *Wǔ diǎn sìshíwǔ fēn* or *wǔ diǎn sān kè* or *chà yí kè liù diǎn* **8** *Shí'èr diǎn shí fēn.*

Exercise 3.3

1 *Wǒ yǒu liǎng ge xiǎoháir.* **2** *Tā méi yǒu nǚháir.* **3** *Nǐmen yǒu liù ge péngyou.* **4** *Zhōngguó zài nǎr?* **5** *Tāmen jǐ suì?* **6** *Wǒmen shí diǎn zhōng qù.* **7** *Hē lǜ chá zěnmeyàng?* **8** *Zhōu Déjūn méi yǒu jié hūn.* **9** *Wáng tàitai wǎnshang bù chī fàn.* **10** *Zhāng xiānsheng xiǎng qǐng wǒmen, wǒmen jiù bù qǐng tā.*

Exercise 3.4

We have four children, three girls and a boy. I have many friends. I have invited two friends to come to our house tomorrow evening for a meal. My wife is very put out because she doesn't know them.

Exercise 3.5

1 *Nǚháir sān suì, nánháir liǎng suì.* **2** *Tā jié hūn le ma? / Tā jié hūn le méi you? / Tā jié hūn méi jié hūn / Méi yǒu.* **3** *Nǐmen míngtiān wǎnshang qù tā jiā chī fàn ma?* **4** *Tā xiànzài zài nǎr? Tā zài Lúndūn.* **5** *Nǐ yǒu duìxiàng ma? / Nǐ yǒu mei yǒu duìxiàng? Méi* *yǒu, wǒ cái shíwǔ suì.* **6** *Wǒmen liǎ hěn xǐhuan hē kāfēi.* **7** *Nǐ jǐ diǎn zhōng zài jiā? / Qī diǎn zěnmeyàng? / Hǎo, jiù qī diǎn ba.* **8** *Wǒ àiren hěn hǎo dànshi tā bú tài xǐhuan shuō huà.* **9** *Nǐ de péngyou zài nǎr? Wǒ xiǎng qǐng tā chī fàn.*

Exercise 4.1

1 *Zhè* **wèi** *xiǎojie zài Běijīng Dàxué xuéxí Hànyǔ.* **2** *Nǎ* **wei** *xiānsheng shì nǐ àiren?* **3** *Wáng tàitai yǒu jǐ* **ge** *xiǎoháir?* **4** *Nà wǔ* **ge** *rén dōu shì nǐ péngyou ma?* **5** *Tāmen jǐ* **diǎn** *zhōng lái wǒmen jiā chī fàn?*

Exercise 4.2

1 *Wǒmen xuéxí de hěn shǎo.* **2** *Nǐmen shuō Hànyǔ, shuō de búcuò. Nǐmen Hànyǔ shuō de búcuò. Hànyǔ nǐmen shuō de búcuò.* **3** *Tā shēnghuó de bù zěnmeyàng.* **4** *Nà ge rén zuò Zhōngguó cài zuò de hěn hǎo. Nà ge rén Zhōngguó cài zuò de hěn hǎo. Zhōngguó cài nà ge rén zuò de hěn hǎo.* **5** *Zhè ge péngyou shuō huà shuō de bù duō. Zhè ge péngyou huà shuō de bù duō. Huà zhè ge péngyou shuō de bù duō.*

Exercise 4.3

1 *Tā shuō Hànyǔ shuō de hǎo ma? Tā shuō Hànyǔ shuō de hǎo bu hǎo? Tā shuō Hànyǔ shuō de zěnmeyàng? Tā shuō Hànyǔ shuō de bù hǎo.* **2** *Wǒ yí ge péngyou hē jiǔ hē de duō ma? Wǒ yí ge péngyou hē jiǔ hē de duō bu duō? Wǒ yí ge péngyou hē jiǔ hē de zěnmeyàng? Wǒ yí ge péngyou hē jiǔ hē de bù duō.* **3** *Shǐ xiǎojie xuéxí de màn ma? Shǐ xiǎojie xuéxí de màn bu màn? Shǐ xiǎojie xuéxí de zěnmeyàng? Shǐ xiǎojie xuéxí de bú màn.* **4** *Gōngrén jīntiān lái de shǎo ma? Gōngrén jīntiān lái de shǎo bu shǎo? Gōngrén jīntiān lái de zěnmeyàng? Gōngrén jīntiān lái de bù shǎo.* **5** *Yīngguórén zuò Yīngguó cài, zuò de hǎo ma? Yīngguórén zuò Yīngguó cài, zuò de hǎo bu hǎo? Yīngguórén zuò Yīngguó cài, zuò de zěnmeyàng? Yīngguórén zuò Yīngguó cài, zuò de bù hǎo.*

Exercise 4.4

1 *Wáng xiānsheng de nǚ péngyou shì Shǐ xiǎojie.* **2** *Shǐ xiǎojie shì Yīngguórén.* **3** *Shǐ xiǎojie zài Zhōngguó xuéxí Hànyǔ.* **4** *Zài Běijīng Dàxué shēnghuó hěn búcuò (hěn hǎo).* **5** *Tāmen jīntiān wǎnshang chī Zhōngguó cài.* **6** *Wáng xiānsheng hé Shǐ xiǎojie kuàizi yòng de búcuò (hǎo).* **7** *Lǐ tàitai zuò cài zuò de hěn hǎo.* **8** *Shǐ xiǎojie huì zuò Yīngguó cài.*

Exercise 4.5

1 I can cook but not very well. My girlfriend says I'm a very plain cook. We have many Chinese friends, they cook Chinese food very well. They use chopsticks very well too. What about you?

2 A friend of mine went to France to work. French food is delicious – he ate a lot of it. Now he's very fat. His wife says 'How about your eating less and working more?' My friend says 'Eating less is OK but not working more!'.

Exercise 4.6

1 *Wǒ zìjǐ bú huì zuò cài dànshi wǒ àiren zuò cài zuò de fēicháng hǎo.*
2 *Nǐ shì Fǎguórén ma? Wǒmen liǎ yě (dōu) shì Fǎguórén.* **3** *Nà wèi xiānsheng shì liǎng diǎn bàn lái de ma? Bù, tā shì sān diǎn lái de.*
4 *Nǐ zài nǎr xuéxí Hànyǔ? Xuéxí de zěnmeyàng?* **5** *Tā shì cóng Měiguó lái de. Tā zài zhèr gōngzuò.* **6** *Xiànzài jǐ diǎn? Nǐ(men) yídìng hěn è le!* **7** *Wǒ jīntiān méi yǒu kòng dànshi (wǒ) míngtiān bù gōngzuò. Shí diǎn (zhōng) xíng ma?* **8** *Tā yòng kuàizi yòng de bú tài hǎo dànshi (tā) zuò Zhōngguó cài zuò de hǎo jíle (hěn hǎo/fēicháng hǎo).*

Exercise 5.1

1 *Dèng xiǎojie yào huí Zhōngguó* **qu.** **2** *Érzi jìn kètīng* **lai** *le.* **3** *Tā jìn wòshì* **qu** *le.* **4** *Nǐmen yīnggāi huí jiā* **lai.** **5** *Wǒ xiǎng huí Yīngguó* **qu.**

Exercise 5.2

1 *Tāmen xǐhuan chī fàn háishi xǐhuan shuō huà?* **2** *Dèng tàitai yào mǎi bīngxiāng háishi yào mǎi xǐyījī?* **3** *Zhōu xiānsheng qù Fǎguó háishi Zhōu xiānsheng qù (Fǎguó)?* **4** *Shíjiān guò de kuài háishi guò de màn?* **5** *Wǒ péngyou de fángzi méi yǒu chúfáng háishi méi yǒu yùshì?* **6** *Nǐ xuéxí Hànyǔ háishi xuéxí dìlǐ?*

Exercise 5.3

1 *Dìfang xiǎo, bīngxiāng、xǐyījī dōu fàng zài zhèr.* **2** *Xiǎoháir xiànzài zài chúfáng hē niúnǎi.* **3** *Tā yuànyì zǎozāo qù.* **4** *Wǒ gěi nǐmen tiān le bù shǎo máfan.* **5** *Lǐ lǎoshī gāogāoxìngxìng de huí dàxué qu le.* **6** *Wàimiàn de rén dōu shì nánde.*

Exercise 5.4

The kids are going to my mum's place this evening. She's got a lot of space and has both a washing machine and a fridge. The children like to enjoy themselves, my mum also likes to take them to the cinema but she has neither the time nor the money so she has to let them play in the big garden. When they stop playing they can sit in the kitchen and chat and have something to eat. After the meal they can watch the (colour) TV.

Exercise 5.5

1 *Wǒ hé wǒ péngyou xiǎng qù Měiguó.* 2 *Tā zài nǎr kàn diànshì? Zài wòshì háishi zài kètīng?* 3 *Fùqīn shuō tā bú rènshi nǐ le.* 4 *Lǎo le, tā jiù bù hē jiǔ le.* 5 *Tā yòu xǐhuan jiāo shū yòu xǐhuan dú shū.* 6 *Tā zhǐ hǎo zhàn zài nàr.* 7 *Wǒ bùzhì wán kètīng, jiù ānānjìngjìng de kàn shū.* 8 *Xièxie nǐ de rèqíng zhāodài, wǒ yídìng zài lái.*

Exercise 7.1

1 *Érzi bǐ nǚ'ér dà wǔ suì.* 2 *Jiějie bǐ mèimei dà liù suì.* 3 *Shǐ Àilǐ bǐ Wáng Yǒngshòu xiǎo liǎng suì.* 4 *Lǐ tàitai bǐ Lǐ xiānsheng xiǎo sān suì.* 5 *Zhōngguó chá bǐ Zhōngguó jiǔ hǎo hē.* 6 *Zhōngguó cài bǐ Yīngguó cài hǎo chī.* 7 *Tā de shēntǐ bǐ nǐ (de shēntǐ) hǎo.* 8 *Wǒ nán péngyou bǐ wǒ gāoxìng.*

Exercise 7.2

1 *Shǐ xiǎojie yǒu liǎng ge gēge hé yí ge mèimei.* 2 *Wǒ dìdi èrshíqī suì.* 3 *Lǎo jiàoyuán bāshí suì, shēntǐ hěn hǎo.* 4 *Zhè ge gōngrén bǐ nà ge gōngrén xiǎo wǔ suì.* 5 *Tā àiren bǐ tā māma dà sì suì.* 6 *Jiǔshíjiǔ ge fúwùyuán zài Běijīng Fàndiàn gōngzuò.* 7 *Nà ge yīshēng hē liù bēi jiǔ hé liǎng bēi kāfēi.*

Exercise 7.3

1 *Zhāng Zhànyī de jiā zài Běijīng.* 2 *Tā jiā yǒu wǔ kǒu rén.* 3 *Tā méi yǒu dìdi、(yě méi yǒu) mèimei.* 4 *Tā jiějie méi yǒu jié hūn.* 5 *Tā gēge èrshíbā suì.* 6 *Zhāng Zhànyī èrshíliù suì bàn.* 7 *Tā bàba zài Běijīng Yǔyán Xuéyuàn jiāo Hànyǔ.* 8 *Tā jiāo wàiguó liúxuéshēng Hànyǔ.* 9 *Bù, tā māma bǐ bàba xiǎo. Māma wǔshíbā suì le. Bù gōngzuò, yǐjīng tuìxiū le.* 10 *Tāmen liǎ shēntǐ fēicháng hǎo.* 11 *Zhāng Zhànyī bù dāng gōngrén.* 12 *Tā de gōngzuò hái guò de qù.* 13 *Tāmen yì jiā rén gǎnqíng (dōu) hěn hǎo.*

Exercise 7.4

1 My elder sister is 29 years old and is still not married. She is a doctor in Shanghai. She really likes her job. My mum says she ought to get married – that it's not OK for a girl not to. My sister says it doesn't matter if she gets married a bit later on (in life) but my mum doesn't agree.

2 Zhou Gengxin is from Tianjin. He is a worker. There are four people in his family – his dad, mum, his younger brother and himself. His (younger) brother is 21, one and a half years younger than him. His brother is studying English at Beijing University. Zhou Gengxin is also studying English but he has very little time to study so his English is very bad.

Exercise 7.5

1 *Nǐ jiào shénme míngzi? Wǒ jiào Shǐ Àilǐ.* 2 *Tā méi yǒu xiōngdì, yě méi yǒu jiěmèi.* 3 *Wǒ qǐng liǎng ge Zhōngguó péngyou míngtiān wǎnshang lái wǒ jiā chī wǎnfàn.* 4 *Zài Běijīng Yǔyánxuéyuàn xuéxí Hànyǔ de nà ge rén hái méi yǒu lái ne.* 5 *Wǒ péngyou èrshíbā suì hái méi yǒu jié hūn ne.* 6 *Zài Shànghǎi de nà ge Měiguó yīshēng yǐjīng tuìxiū le ma?* 7 *Zài Běijīng Dàxué xuéxí Hànyǔ de nà ge Yīngguó nǚ háizi zuò cài zuò de hǎo jíle (fēicháng hǎo).* 8 *Wǒ àiren hé tā liǎng ge mèimei gǎnqíng (dōu) hěn hǎo.* 9 *Hěn duō Zhōngguórén shuō Yīngyǔ shuō de fēicháng hǎo.* 10 *Wǒ nǚ péngyou bǐ wǒ dà yí suì dànshi bǐ wǒ gēge xiǎo liǎng suì.* 11 *Nà ge rén bú tài hǎo suǒyǐ wǒ méi qǐng tā hē yì bei.* 12 *Xǐyījī hé cǎisè diànshì (cǎidiàn) dōu méi yǒu dànshi wǒmen hái guò de búcuò (rìzi guò de hái kěyǐ).*

Exercise 8.1

1 *Fùmǔ zǒu **jìn** kètīng **lai**.* 2 *Tāmen bān **chū** shūzhuō **qu**.* 3 *Xiōngdì bān **jìn** shuāngrénchuáng **qu**.* 4 *Xiǎoháir pǎo **chū** cèsuǒ **lai**.* 5 *Jiàoyuán ná **xià** liǎng běn shū **lai**. Jiàoyuán ná **xiàlai** liǎng běn shū.*

Exercise 8.2

1 *Zhāng Zhànyī de jiā yǒu sān jiān fáng.* 2 *Zhè bù bāokuò chúfáng hé cèsuǒ.* 3 *Tā fùmǔ shuì zài kètīng (lǐ).* 4 *Tā hé tā gēge shuì yí ge fángjiān.* 5 *Tāmen xiōngdì de fángjiān dà.* 6 *Jiějie de fángjiān fàng de xià yì zhāng chuáng、yì zhāng xiǎo zhuōzi hé yì bǎ yǐzi.* 7 *Tāmen xiōngdì、zǐmèi bù cháng(cháng) zài jiā.* 8 *Shuāngrénchuáng zài kètīng lǐ.* 9 *Bú shì, shì Rìběn huò.* 10 *Dà yuánzhuō hé yǐzi (dōu) bú zài kètīng lǐ.* 11 *Zhōngguó fángzū、shuǐdiànfèi piányi.* 12 *Àn Zhōngguó xiànzài de biāozhǔn Zhāng Zhànyī hé tā yì jiā rén guò de hái búcuò.*

Exercise 8.3

1 *Měi ge fādá guójiā fángzū dōu hěn guì.* 2 *Zhōngguórén hǎo, Yīngguórén yě dōu hěn hǎo.* 3 *Fēngrènjī méi yǒu zǔhéyīnxiǎng*

nàme guì.   4 *Shuì jiào yǐqián yīnggāi shuā yá.*   5 *Tā nà tiān xiūxi le.*   6 *Yǒude yīfu wǒ bú yuànyì xǐ.*   7 *Fúwùyuán pǎo jìn fàndiàn lai.*   8 *Yìxiē Rìběnrén gōngzī hěn gāo.*   9 *Sūgélán bǐ Měiguó ānjìng de duō.*   10 *Tiānqì hǎo de shíhou, yào hǎohāor wán(r).*

Exercise 8.4

What's your own room like? Do you have much furniture? What is there besides a bed? Do you have a hi-fi, a washing machine and a TV? What about a fridge? Do you live more comfortably than you used to? Do you have high wages? Are (your) rent, water and electricity dear? Who turns on your central heating for you? I bet it's not your boss? Is life OK for you? I hope things are going well for you!

Exercise 8.5

1 *Fàntīng lǐ yǒu yì zhāng zhuōzi hé liù bǎ yǐzi.*   2 *Suīrán shūfáng lǐ yìbān hěn ānjìng, dànshi hěn duō rén dōu méi yǒu.*   3 *Tiānqì lěng de shíhou, dàjiā (dōu) xǐhuan shāo nuǎnqì.*   4 *Gōngzī gāo de shíhou, shuǐdiànfèi guì yě méi (yǒu) guānxi.*   5 *Àn xiànzài de biāozhǔn, Yīngguó suàn shì (yí) ge fādá guójiā.*   6 *Bú shi měi ge shāfā dōu hǎo zuò.*   7 *Zǔhéyīnxiǎng méi yǒu yǐqián nàme guì.*   8 *Fùmǔ zuótiān méi qu, wǒ hé jiějie jīntiān yě bú qù.*   9 *Dānrénchuáng bǐ shuāngrénchuáng hái (gèng) piányi.*   10 *Shēnghuó chúle chī fàn yǐwài, hái yǒu shénme?*   11 *Xiūxi yǐqián, qǐng bāngzhù wǒ bàn chū yīguì qu.*   12 *Suīrán chuānghu、mén děng dōu hěn gānjìng, dànshi zhuōzi、yǐzi dōu hěn zāng.*

Exercise 9.1

1 F   2 F   3 T   4 F   5 T   6 F   7 F   8 T   9 F   10 T.

Exercise 9.2

(a) *háishi; shuǐguǒzhī; shuì jiào; huòzhě kěkě; cóngqián; zěnme; jiù; bù.*   (b) *jiù; nǎr; tǐng; suīrán; mǒu; zěnme; dōu.*

Exercise 9.3

1 *Rúguǒ méi yǒu càidān, wǒ jiù bù kěyǐ dìng cài.*   2 *Nǐmen cóngqián méi zhùguo lǚguǎn.*   3 *Fādá guójiā shēnghuó yuè lái yuè nán.*   4 *Yǒu shíhou suàn zhàng yòng jìsuànjī hěn fāngbiàn.* or *Suàn zhàng yòng jìsuànjī yǒu shíhou hěn fāngbiàn.*   5 *Chéng qiān shàng wàn de yóukè měi nián qù yóulǎn Chángchéng* or *Měi nián chéng qiān shàng wàn de yóukè qù yóulǎn Chángchéng.*   6 *Jīntiān bú è le. Wǒ shénme yě bù xiǎng chī.*   7 *Tā nà ge rén hǎo jíle, tā shuō tiānqì zěnme lěng, dōu méi guānxi.*

Exercise 9.4

1 The Chinese like using Thermos flasks a lot because they're generally very keen on drinking tea. Most Chinese prefer drinking green tea (China tea) but Indian tea is OK too on occasions. When they drink Indian tea the vast majority of Chinese drink it with milk and sugar (add milk and sugar).

2 There are many types of cups – teacups, coffee cups, glass cups and cups for wine. It's the same for bottles. There are bottles for flowers, milk and for hot water.

Exercise 9.5

1 *Suān niúnǎi méi yǒu le. Nǐ kěyǐ hē rè niúnǎi huòzhě liáng niúnǎi.*
2 *Nǐ qùguo Chángchéng ma? Chéng qiān shàng wàn de yóukè měi nián qù yóulǎn.* 3 *Yàoshi méi yǒu wèishēngzhǐ, shàng cèsuǒ jiù hěn nán (bù fāngbiàn).* 4 *Dàjiā yīnggāi xiǎngshòu yíyàng de quánlì.*
5 *Wǒmen bùdé bù chéngrèn Ruìshì qiǎokèlì fēicháng hǎo chī.*
6 *Rúguǒ nǐ yuànyì yòng jìsuànjī suàn zhàng, jiù qǐng ba.* 7 *Jīntiān wǎnshang nǐ qǐng shéi chī fàn? Wǒ shéi dōu bù qǐng.* 8 *Kèwén yuè lái yuè nán (le).* 9 *Qíshí tū de zuòfǎ zuì hǎo.* 10 *Zhù shuāngrénfángjiān de nà ge rén shì Dōngjīng shāngrén.* or *shì cóng Dōngjīng lái de shāngrén.* 11 *Suīrán xià yǔ, tā shuō tā (hái) huì lái.*
12 *Guòqù wàiguó gōngsī zhù Zhōngguó de dàibiǎo hěn shǎo, (dànshi) xiànzài yuè lái yuè duō le.*

Exercise 10.1

1 *Tā xī shí fēn zhōng de yān.* 2 *Lǎoshī jiāo yí ge xiǎoshí de shū.*
3 *Gēge lù bàn ge zhōngtóu de yīn.* 4 *Wǒ àiren huà sān kè zhōng de huàr.* 5 *Chǎngzhǎng kāi sān ge bàn xiǎoshí de chē.* 6 *Dìdi kàn shū, kàn bàn ge xiǎoshí.* 7 *Lǎorén shuì jiào, shuì yí ge bàn xiǎoshí.*
8 *Wǒ yí ge péngyou zǒu lù, zǒu qī ge zhōngtóu.* 9 *Nà wèi xiānsheng shuō huà, shuō hěn cháng shíjiān le.* 10 *Nǎ wèi xiǎojie néng dǎ zì, néng dǎ jiǔ ge xiǎoshí?*

Exercise 10.2

1 *Xīngqīsì* 2 *xīngqīyǐ? xīngqīyī* 3 *qīyuè* 4 *shí'èr ge yuè* 5 *qī tiān*
6 *sānshí tiān* 7 *èrshíbā tiān; èrshíjiǔ tiān* 8 *sānbǎiliùshíwǔ tiān; sānbǎiliùshíliù tiān.*

Exercise 10.3

1 (–) 2 (–) 3 (+) 4 (–) 5 (+) 6 (+) 7 (–) 8 (–) 9 (–)
10 (+)

Exercise 10.4

Some people think (that) British weather is pretty awful but conversely there are also some people who feel that British weather is pretty good – neither hot nor cold, nor does it always snow in winter but there's no getting away from one thing and that's no matter where you are, it often rains (in Britain). In China there are normally many sunny days and few cloudy ones but Britain is just the opposite with lots of cloudy days and few sunny ones. Some say this ties in with British people's peculiar temperament but others say it is related to their lovable character. Which view is right? Over to you!

Exercise 10.5

1 *Xīngqītiān wǒ péngyou lái de shíhou, wǒ zhèngzài kàn diànshì ne.*
2 *Wǒ xiǎng gēn nǐ yìqǐ qù Yíhéyuán sàn (san) bù.*   3 *Tā yī kāishǐ dǎ hūlu wǒ jiù zǒu!*   4 *Chuānghu kāizhe dànshi mén guānzhe.*
5 *Gōngyuán lǐ rènào jíle, dǎ tàijíquán de dǎ tàijíquán, zhào xiàng de zhào xiàng, shài tàiyáng de shài tàiyáng.*   6 *Tiānqì hǎo de shíhou, wǒ zài wàimiàn zuòzhe kàn shū.*   7 *Wǒmen měi tiān wǎnshang chàng bàn ge xiǎoshí de gēr jiù shàng chuáng. Wǒmen měi tiān wǎnshang chàng gēr chàng bàn ge xiǎoshí jiù qù shuì jiào.*   8 *Yīnwèi tā xīngqī'èr bìng méi yǒu dǎ diànhuà, suǒyǐ wǒ bù zhīdao wǒ qù bu qù.*
9 *Yàoshi zài fùmǔ jiā, wǒ chángcháng dào fùjìn de gōngyuán qù dǎ wǎngqiú.*   10 *Tā xiàozhe shuō tā yǐjīng jié hūn le.*   11 *Nǐmen zài tīng shōuyīnjī ma? Méi yǒu, wǒmen tīngzhe lù yīn.*   12 *Nǐ míngtiān qù kàn xì shì bu shì? Kěxī wǒ bù néng gēn nǐ yìqǐ qù.*

Exercise 11.1

1 *Tā de fāyīn qīngchu shi qīngchu dànshi...*   2 *Wáng xiānsheng de Hànyǔ shuǐpíng gāo shi gāo kěshì...*   3 *Zhè běn xiǎoshuō yǒu yìsi shi yǒu yìsi kěshì...*   4 *Duì wàiguórén lái shuō, Zhōngwén de sìshēng nán shi nán dànshi...*   5 *Qīngdǎo píjiǔ hǎo hē shi hǎo hē kěshì...*

Exercise 11.2

1 *cái* 2 *jiù* 3 *jiù* 4 *cái* 5 *cái* 6 *cái* 7 *jiù* 8 *cái.*

Exercise 11.3

1 *dǒng* 2 *chūqu/chūlai* or *jìnqu/jìnlai* 3 *chūlai* 4 *wán* 5 *bǎo*
6 *shàng* 7 *jiàn* 8 *qǐlai* 9 *xià* 10 *qīngchu; dǒng* 11 *dào/zháo*
12 *xiàqu.*

Exercise 11.5

Zhang Zhanyi is an attendant. He likes his job a lot because he has the chance to meet lots of different people. They may be American or British or then again Chinese or Japanese. Some foreigners can speak very fluent Chinese (*putonghua*) but with a strong foreign accent, their pronunciation and grammar are not very accurate but you can still understand them. It's very funny when some foreigners start speaking Chinese because they don't use tones. There are also some foreigners, with a very high level of Chinese who have been living in China for ages and can read (and understand) Chinese newspapers and novels and can also write Chinese more or less. It's not at all easy for adults to learn Chinese (start learning Chinese), you have to take your hat off to them. Some people can't even speak their own language properly let alone a foreign one!

Exercise 11.6

1 *Wǒ cāi bú shi Měiguórén jiù shi Yīngguórén.*   **2** *Tā de shēngdiào fēicháng hǎo dànshi tā de fāyīn bù xíng.*   **3** *Wǒ yǐjīng qù le liù cì Zhōngguó kěshì wǒ háishi tīng bu dǒng Zhōngguórén shuō shénme.*   **4** *Duì wǒ zuì hǎo de péngyou lái shuō, xiě zì bǐ kàn shū gèng (hái) yǒu yìsi.*   **5** *Tā (de) tóufa zhēn cháng. Tā zěnme hái méi jiǎn ne?*   **6** *Tā zhǐ yòng le liǎng nián (de shíjiān) jiù xué hǎo (zhǎngwò) le pǔtōnghuà.*   **7** *Tā xué Zhōngwén xué le sān nián le suǒyǐ tā de shuǐpíng xiāngdāng gāo.*   **8** *Wǒ (shì) zuótiān cái zhīdao tā bú huì chá Zhōngwén cídiǎn/zìdiǎn (de).*   **9** *Dàjiā dōu xǐhuan gēn yǒu yìsi de rén jiǎng huà dànshi zhè yàng de rén bù duō.*   **10** *Chúfēi yǒu zhòngyào (de) shìqing wǒ cái dǎrǎo nǐ.*   **11** *Wǒ cái gēn tā shuō le yì、 liǎng cì huà, jiù hěn xǐhuan tā le.* (This one is difficult!)   **12** *Tā tèbié lǎn. Tā jīntiān cái kàn wán yí yè.*

Exercise 14.1

1 *zhāng* 张.   **2** *jiàn* 件.   **3** *jiàn* 件.   **4** *bāo* 包.   **5** *kuài* 块.   **6** *jiàn* 件, *mǐ* 米.

Exercise 14.2

1 二十块.   **2** 四块八.   **3** 三块九.   **4** 六块九.   **5** 一毛二.   **6** 八毛四

Exercise 14.4

1 *píng* 'grass'.   **2** *chèn* 'clothing'.   **3** *méi* 'water'.   **4** *xiè* 'speech'.   **5** *kuà* 'earth'.   **6** *běn* 'tree'.   **7** *shì* 'sun'.   **8** *yān* 'fire'.   **9** *zhì* 'heart'.   **10** *mǎi* 'big'.

Exercise 14.5

1 4（一）. 2 4（亻）. 3 5（口）. 4 3（女）. 5 3（戈）. 6 4（扌）.
7 5（阝）. 8 7（大）. 9 7（心）. 10 4（扌）.

Exercise 14.6

1 售货员是中国人。The shop assistant is Chinese. 2 地图三毛二一
张。Maps are 0.32 yuan each. 3 那本杂志八毛九。That magazine
costs 0.89 yuan. 4 您没买东西。You haven't bought anything.
You haven't been shopping. 5 苹果一块四一斤。Apples are 1.4
yuan a catty.

Exercise 14.7

1 我要买三本杂志和一份报。(张 is used as the MW for newspaper if
there are only 4 pages!) 2 我昨天买了两件衬衫。 3 他要买东西。
4 你（您）要几米丝绸? 5 谢谢。再见。

Exercise 15.2

1 *yì, zhì, zěn*（心）。 2 *bào, tǐng, pái*（扌）。 3 *hào, yuán, wèn*（口）。
4 *dōu, bù, yóu*（阝）。 5 *lái, qī, xià*（一）。

Exercise 15.3

1 地、块、去。2 要、好。3 中、出。4 杂、本、果、乐、样。
5 服、有、期。6 图、四、国。7 影。8 会、个。9 件、份、什、你。
10 这、还。

Exercise 15.4

1 看电影怎么样? How about seeing a film? 2 楼下有人吗? Is anybody downstairs? Are there people downstairs? 3《日出》这部电影
有没有意思? Is the film *Sunrise* any good? (interesting). 4 上个星
期你没来。You didn't come last week. 5 音乐会几月几号? When
is the concert? (What day of what month).

Exercise 15.5

1 今天十一月三号（日）。 2 请问, 今天几月几号? 3 楼上没有人。
4 大家说买东西很有意思。 5 你还有钱吗? 你要多少? 6 我一九六八
年在中国。

Exercise 16.2

1 *yǎn* 'water'. 2 *xíng* 'to step with left foot'. 3 *jì* 'speech'. 4 *dǎ*
'hand'. 5 *qǔ* 'ear'. 6 *guò* 'walking'. 7 *yīng* 'grass'. 8 *jiē*
'hand'. 9 *mài* 'ten'. 10 *tiān* 'horizontal line'.

Exercise 16.3

1 6（讠）. 2 8（刂）. 3 3（一）. 4 2（口）. 5 2（人）. 6 10（氵）.
7 5（日）. 8 5（贝）. 9 6（宀）. 10 5（女）.

Exercise 16.4

1 心 → 意、您、思、怎。 2 扌 → 报、接、拔、打。 3 口 → 喂、叫、哪、名。 4 宀 → 客、定、字、家。 5 氵 → 没、演、满。

Exercise 16.5

1 今天没有人给我打电话。Nobody phoned me today. 2 首都剧场在哪儿? Where is the Capital Theatre? 3 他明天下午就要去北京了。He's going to Beijing tomorrow afternoon. 4 你后天能不能来接我? Can you come and meet me the day after tomorrow? 5 星期五行不行? 不行，就星期六吧。Is Friday OK? If not, then how about Saturday?

Exercise 16.6

1 我今天去首都剧场了。 2 您贵姓? 我姓史，名字叫史爱理。 3 他说他给我们留两张票。 4 他们要今天下午看那部电影可是客满了。 5 我下个星期五来取票行吧?

Exercise 17.1

1 *Jǐngshān Gōngyuán zài Gùgōng běibianr.* 2 *Qiánmén zài Máo Zhǔxí Jìniàntáng nánbianr.* 3 *Rénmín Dàhuìtáng zài Rénmín Yīngxióng Jìniànbēi xībianr.* 4 *Zhōngguó Lìshǐ Bówùguǎn zài Rénmín Yīngxióng Jìniànbēi dōngbianr.* 5 *Máo Zhǔxí Jìniàntáng zài Rénmín Dàhuìtáng dōngnánbianr.*

Exercise 17.2

1 *Jǐngshān Gōngyuán lí Qiánmén bǐjiào yuǎn.* 2 *Rénmín Dàhuìtáng lí Rénmín Yīngxióng Jìniànbēi hěn jìn. Wàng dōng zǒu jiù dào le.* 3 *Máo Zhǔxí Jìniàntáng lí Tiān'ānmén bú tài yuǎn wàng běi zǒu jiù dào le.* 4 *Shì, jiù zài Zhōngguó Lìshǐ Bówùguǎn duìmiàn. (jiù zài Zhōngguó Lìshǐ Bówùguǎn hé Rénmín Dàhuìtáng zhōngjiān)* 5 *Niújīn lí Lúndūn yǒu jiǔshíyī gōnglǐ.* 6 *Sānshí hào lí èrshíqī hào yǒu sān tiān.* 7 *Yuándàn lí Shèngdànjié yǒu yí ge xīngqī.*

Exercise 17.4

EXERCISE 17.1

1 景山公园在故宫北边儿。 2 前门在毛主席纪念堂南边儿。 3 人民大会堂在人民英雄纪念碑西边儿。 4 中国历史博物馆在人民英雄纪念碑东边儿。 5 毛主席纪念堂在人民大会堂东南边儿。

EXERCISE 17.2

1 景山公园离前门比较远。 2 人民大会堂离人民英雄纪念碑很近，往东走就到了。 3 毛主席纪念堂离天安门不太远，往北走就到了。 4 是，就在中国历史博物馆对面。(就在中国历史博物馆和人民大会堂中间。)

Exercise 17.5

1 请问，天坛在哪儿？怎么走？　**2** 人民大会堂离这儿远吗？不（远），就在对面。　**3** 人民英雄纪念碑在人民大会堂东边儿，中国历史博物馆西边儿。

Exercise 18.1

1 *Qǐng nǐ bǎ shōujù shōu hǎo.* **2** *Bāoguǒdān shàng yào bǎ jìjiànrén de dìzhǐ he xìngmíng xiě qīngchu.* **3** *Bǎ guàhàofèi jiā shang yígòng yào duōshao qián?* **4** *Tā méi bǎ bāoguǒdān tián hǎo.* **5** *Yóukè méi bǎ Gùgōng hǎohāor kànyikàn.* **6** *Shòupiàoyuán liú gěi le Wáng xiānsheng liǎng zhāng hǎo piào.* **7** *Wàiguó zhuānjiā yīnggāi jì xiàlai jùchǎng de diànhuà hàomǎ.* **8** *Shòuhuòyuán bú yuànyì mài gěi tā sīchóu chènshān.* **9** *Dàifu yào sòng bìngrén dào yīyuàn.* **10** *Wǒ yí ge Zhōngguó péngyou yì tiān néng xī wán liǎng bāo yān.*

Exercise 18.2

1 *xiǎng, nín, zěn, yì, sī, zhì*（心）。　**2** *qǐng, shuō, xiè, huà*（讠）。
3 *wèi, shòu, yuán, ma, wèn, hào*（口）。　**4** *jìn, hái, guò, zhè, yuǎn, biān*（辶）。　**5** *bù, nà, yóu, dōu*（阝）。

Exercise 18.3

1 东西、东边。　**2** 外国、中国。　**3** 售货员、售票员。　**4** 毛衣、衣服。
5 电影、电话、电报。　**6** 星期二、星期四。　**7** 地图、地方、地址。　**8** 收件人、寄件人。

Exercise 18.4

Mr King is a very nice person but he has one small defect, he really likes spending money. If he goes to buy a shirt, he ends up with three, if you want him to buy a magazine he buys you ten. He says they were all very interesting so he bought them all. How can you feel relaxed if you let him go and do the shopping?

王先生人很好但是他有一个小毛病，他很喜欢花钱。去买一件衬衫，他就买三件，你要他买一本杂志就给你买十本。他说都很有意思，所以都买了。让他去买东西，你怎么能放心呢？

Exercise 18.5

1 *(Zài) Zhōngguó yóudiànjú kěyǐ dǎ chángtú diànhuà.* **2** *Zhè shì shōujù, qǐng shōu hǎo.* **3** *Qǐng tián zhè zhāng bāoguǒdān. Bǎ shōujiànrén hé jìjiànrén de dìzhǐ hé xìngmíng (tián) xiě qīngchu.* **4** *Yóupiào tiē hǎo le ma? Hái méi yǒu ne.* **5** *Jì shū hěn máfan dànshi (hěn) zhíde.*

1（在）中国邮电局可以打长途电话。　**2** 这是收据，请收好。　**3** 请填这张包裹单，把收件人和寄件人的地址和姓名（填）写清楚。　**4** 邮票贴好了吗？还没有呢。　**5** 寄书很麻烦但是（很）值得。

Exercise 19.1

1 硬卧跟软卧一样吗？不一样，软卧比硬卧贵多了。 **2** 硬卧跟硬座有什么不一样？硬座比硬卧便宜得多。 **3** 你跟他一样不喜欢听音乐吗？不，我很喜欢听古典音乐。 **4** 我跟我的未婚妻一样浪漫，都喜欢写诗。 **5** 在欧洲日本电视跟在中国一样难买吗？

1 Is a hard sleeper the same as a soft sleeper? No, a soft sleeper is much more expensive than a hard sleeper. **2** What's the difference between a hard seat and a hard sleeper? A hard seat is much cheaper than a hard sleeper. **3** Are you and she alike in not enjoying listening to music? No, I like listening to classical music very much. **4** I am as romantic as my fiancée, we both like writing poetry. **5** Are Japanese TVs as hard to buy in Europe as they are in China?

Exercise 19.2

1 国际饭店比北京饭店贵百分之五十。 **2** 水电费比去年贵百分之十。 **3** 下铺比上铺贵百分之二十。 **4** 打长途电话比打电报贵百分之多少？贵百分之二百。 **5** 日本衣服比中国衣服贵百分之三百。 **6** 苹果不好吃，我只吃了四分之一。 **7** 外国烟好抽，这包已经抽了三分之二。 **8** 音乐会的票昨天卖了八分之七。 **9** 国产电视比外国电视便宜一倍。 **10** 在中国美国专家比英国专家多十倍。

Exercise 19.3

1 坐火车比坐公共汽车快多了。 **2** 开飞机的人工资很高。 **3** 在中国骑自行车的人非常多。 **4** 有的人喜欢骑摩托车因为很自由。 **5** 英国人十七岁才可以开车。

Exercise 19.4

1 Hot dog. **2** Hamburger. **3** Coca Cola. **4** Yamaha. **5** Canada. **6** Cuba. **7** Cambridge. **8** Warsaw. **9** Washington. **10** Mrs Thatcher.

Exercise 19.5

1 The Chinese mid-Autumn Festival falls on the 15th day of the 8th lunar month. On that evening everybody will look at the moon and eat mooncakes(!). **2** Tang poems are very famous and also very interesting. Students of Chinese will find them all worth looking at. **3** It's certainly fun to go shopping with friends. **4** What is your surname? And what is your Christian name? I'll make a note of them both if that's OK with you. **5** If you have a student card and a preferential card (yellow card), you pay the same price as the Chinese on the train, plus you can pay in RMB.

Exercise 20.1

1 *niàn.* 2 *biàn.* 3 *fānyì.* 4 *xiě.* 5 *huàn.*

Exercise 20.2

1 F 2 F 3 T 4 T 5 F 6 T 7 F 8 F 9 T 10 T 11 F

Exercise 20.3

1 凡是中国人都喜欢吃中国菜。 2 凡是中国银行换钱的牌价都一样。
3 活期存款和定期存款利息率不同。 4 我今天非把旅行支票换成美元不
可。 5 去国外，非带护照不可否则不能出境。 6 历史上亚洲和非洲很不
一样。 7 他（她）的电话号码还记得吗？千万别忘了明天给他（她）打电
话。 8 欧洲国家政治上大同小异。 9 不管你签了字没有，我都要看护
照。 10 不管营业员点了几次钱，他也要点一次。 11 你的意思是除非
碰到他才认识认识对不对？ 12 除非有规定，我才这么办。

1 All Chinese like eating Chinese food. 2 Any branch of the
Bank of China has the same exchange rate for changing money.
3 Current accounts and deposit accounts have different rates of
interest. 4 I have to change my traveller's cheques into US
dollars today. 5 When you go abroad you have to take your passport (with you) otherwise you can't leave the country. 6 Asia and
Africa are very different from a historical point of view. 7 Do you
still remember his (her) telephone number? Don't forget to give
him (her) a call tomorrow whatever you do. 8 Politically speaking
European countries are pretty much the same with a few minor
differences. 9 Regardless of whether you've signed (your name)
or not, I want to look at your passport. 10 No matter whether the
bank clerk had counted the money several times or not, he wanted
to (had to) count it (once). 11 What you're saying is that you'll
only get to know him if you happen to bump into him, is that it?
12 I won't do it like this unless there are regulations (to that
effect).

Exercise 20.4

1 *Wǒ jīntiān gěi nǐ tiān le bù shǎo máfan. Yíngyèyuán: Méi shénme,
huānyíng nǐ míngtiān zài lái.* 2 *Tā jīntiān běnlái yào qù yínháng
huàn qián dànshi tā wàng le bǎ lǚxíng zhīpiào dài lai.* 3 *Nǐ huáiyí tā
shénme? Wǒ bù zhīdao, kěshì wǒ bù xǐhuan tā nà ge yàngzi.*
4 *Dìngqī cúnkuǎn de lì(xī)lǜ bǐ huóqī cúnkuǎn (yào) gāo de duō.*
5 *Kāi chē de bù yīnggāi hē jiǔ.*

1 我今天给你添了不少麻烦。营业员：没什么，欢迎你明天再来。2 她今
天本来要去银行换钱但是她忘了把旅行支票带来。 3 你怀疑他什么？我

不知道，可是我不喜欢他那个样子。 **4** 定期存款的利(息)率比活期存款(要)高得多。 **5** 开车的不应该喝酒。

Exercise 21.1

1 *hǎoxiàng.* **2** *xiàng, xiàng.* **3** *xiàng, xiàng.* **4** *hǎoxiàng.* **5** *xiàng, hǎoxiàng.*

Exercise 21.2

1 *bèi, jiào, ràng.* **2** *shòu.* **3** *bèi, ràng, jiào.* **4** *shòu.* **5** *bèi, ràng, jiào.*

Exercise 21.3

1 *dài.* **2** *dài.* **3** *chuān.* **4** *dài.* **5** *chuān.*

Exercise 21.4

1 *Kěyǐ liǎojiě Zhōngguórén shēnghuó de gègè fāngmiàn.* **2** *Tāmen zài Hángzhōu.* **3** *Tāmen yìbiān chīzhe sānmíngzhì, yìbiān liáo tiān (r).* **4** *Zhōngguórén xǐhuan zhào xiàng. Tāmen de zhàoxiàngjī yǒu lǎoshì de, yě yǒu xīnshì de.* **5** *Rìběn zhàoxiàngjī tèbié shòu huānyíng.* **6** *Zhíyè zhàoxiàng de hěn duō.* **7** *Zhōngguórén bù xǐhuan yí ge rén chū qu wán(r).* **8** *Zhāng Xīqún shì Sūzhōurén. Tā lái Hángzhōu bàn shì(!).* **9** *Tā xīnlǐ bú tài gāoxìng.* **10** *Wǒmen shòuguo jiàoyù de rén yě yǒu yìdiǎn zhǒngzú piānjiàn.* **11** *Tā wánquán tóngyì tā de shuōfǎ.* **12** *Yīnwèi chéngrèn cuòwù děngyú gǎi le yíbàn(r) le.*

1 可以了解中国人生活的各个方面。 **2** 他们在杭州。 **3** 他们一边吃着三明治一边聊天（儿）。 **4** 中国人喜欢照相。他们的照相机有老式的，也有新式的。 **5** 日本照相机特别受欢迎。 **6** 职业照相的很多。 **7** 中国人不喜欢一个人出去玩（儿）。 **8** 张锡群是苏州人。他来杭州办事。 **9** 她心里不太高兴。 **10** 我们受过教育的人也有一点种族偏见。 **11** 他完全同意他的说法。 **12** 因为承认错误等于改了一半（儿）了。

Exercise 21.5

1 In some ways Chinese and foreigners are pretty similar – they both like to go out and enjoy themselves and seek paradise on earth! Who doesn't want to live comfortably, wear nice clothes and eat well? The Chinese are no exception. In the past there were very few Chinese tourists but now they are getting more and more numerous every year.

2 It is very difficult to understand another nationality (ethnic group), it's not even easy to understand your own! The Chinese people are a very ancient people. Their history and culture are very different from our own, let alone their script! Learning

Chinese is not only very interesting but also of use to us as individuals.

Exercise 21.6

1 *Zánmen yìbiān tán jiàoyu yìbiān kàn rìluò ba.*　2 *'Zì qī qī rén' shì yí jù hěn zhíde zhùyì de chéngyǔ.*　3 *Yīnwei Xiānggǎng wèntí, Zhōng、Yīng guānxi biàn de hěn fùzá.*　4 *Tā shì wǒ de tóngshì suǒyǐ wǒ de yìjiàn dāngrán (huì) shòu yǐngxiǎng.*　5 *Nǐ jīnnián lián yì tiān jià dōu méi yǒu (fàng), nánguài nǐ nàme (or zhème) lèi.*　6 *Tā jīntiān lián yí ge sānmíngzhì dōu méi chī, tā zěnme bú è ne?*

1 咱们一边谈教育，一边看日落吧。　2 "自欺欺人"是一句很值得注意的成语。　3 因为香港问题，中、英关系变得很复杂。　4 他是我的同事，所以我的意见当然（会）受影响。　5 你今年连一天假都没有（放），难怪你那么（or 这么）累。　6 她今天连一个三明治都没吃，她怎么不饿呢？

Exercise 22.1

1 *Tāmen lái de shíhou guā dà fēng.*　2 *Tā gěi tā jǐ ge guàntóu hé yìxiē shuǐguǒ.*　3 *Tā juéde bǎ shū jì dào Yīngguó hěn guì.*　4 *Tā dǎsuàn bǎ yìxiē zhòng de dōngxi fàng zài shǒutíbāo lǐ.*　5 *Tā juéde tā zài Zhōngguó de yì nián guò de hěn kuài. Tā yòng 'guāngyīn sì jiàn, rìyuè rú suō' zhè jù chéngyǔ lái miáoxiě zhè diǎn.*　6 *Tā shuō Wáng Yǒngshòu shì dìdìdàodào de Zhōngguótōng, gēn Zhōngguórén dǎchéng yípiàn.*　7 *Tā xué dào le hěn duō dōngxi (tā xué de hěn hǎo) yīnwei tā shuō 'jīnnián shōuhuò hěn dà'.*　8 *Shì guóchǎn de.*　9 *Yīnwei tā wàng le bǎ jìngtóugài dǎkāi (le).*　10 *Yīnwei tā de yuánzhūbǐ huài le.*　11 *Hái kěyǐ fàng jiàngyóu hé cù.*　12 *Yīnwei tā juéde Shǐ Àilǐ de péngyou tài duō le.*　13 *Lǐ xiānsheng xià ge xīngqīwǔ guò shēngrì. Nà ge shíhou tāmen dàgài zài Yīngguó.*　14 *Tā shǔ hǔ.*　15 *Yīnwei tā bù xǐhuan gēn péngyou gàobié.*　16 *Tā dǎsuàn děng Shǐ Àilǐ hé Wáng Yǒngshòu zài lái Zhōngguó kāi yí ge liánhuānhuì.*　17 *Tāmen (de) fēijī xiàwǔ sì diǎn sìshí qǐfēi. Tāmen yīnggāi sān diǎn (zhōng) dào.*　18 *Yīnwei tā bù xiǎng zài gào yí cì bié. (NB bù **xiǎng** not bú yào)*　19 *Tā ràng tāmen kàn tā de liǎn, dōu hóng le.*　20 *Yīnwei Lǐ tàitai bú (shi) kāi chē (de).*

1 他们来的时候刮大风。　2 他给她几个罐头和一些水果。　3 她觉得把书寄到英国很贵。　4 她打算把一些重的东西放在手提包里。　5 他觉得他在中国的一年过得很快。他用"光阴似箭"，"日月如梭"这句成语来描写这点。　6 他说王永寿是地地道道的中国通，跟中国人打成一片。　7 她学到了很多东西（她学得很好）因为她说"今年收获很大"。　8 是国产的。

9 因为他忘了把镜头盖打开（了）。 **10** 因为他的圆珠笔坏了。 **11** 还可以放酱油和醋。 **12** 因为他觉得史爱理的朋友太多了。 **13** 李先生下个星期五过生日，那时候他们大概在英国。 **14** 他属虎。 **15** 因为她不喜欢跟朋友告别。 **16** 他打算等史爱理和王永寿再来中国开一个联欢会。 **17** 他们（的）飞机下午四点四十起飞。他们应该三点（钟）到。 **18** 因为她不想再告一次别。 **19** 她让他们看她的脸，都红了。 **20** 因为李太太不（是）开车（的）。

Exercise 22.2

Li	There you are (welcome, welcome). Come in.
Mrs Li	Is it cold outside?
S	A bit. It's very windy, we were cycling against the wind, it was really strenuous.
K	This is a little token of our regard. *(He gives Mrs Li several tins and some fruit.)*
Li	You're too kind, you've gone to too much expense again.
S	It's nothing, it's just a small token.
Li	Well thank you both, but good friends shouldn't stand on ceremony.
Mrs Li	Stop hanging about (don't keep standing) in the hall, come inside and sit down and warm up.
Li	Would you like tea or coffee?
K	Tea I think.
Mrs Li	Ah, Aili, you're going back soon, so today is really your 'last supper', what a (great) shame.
S	Don't say that. When I hear that I feel really uncomfortable.
Mrs Li	Have you finished packing?
S	Almost.
Mrs Li	If you need any help don't hesitate to say so, for goodness sake don't stand on ceremony.
S	I wouldn't, but really there isn't anything. I've posted (mailed) off most of the books, (gosh) the postage cost a fortune but there was no way round it.
Li	Will you (your luggage) be overweight?
S	Normally it doesn't matter if you're two or three kilos over. I'm planning to put some of the heavy things in my

hand luggage. I've already shared out tapes and things amongst friends. I'll give you the classical tapes of Beethoven, Mozart and so on.

Li   Great! Thanks. (*Turning to King*) Yongshou, you've been teaching for a year now, what thoughts do you have on it all? I've heard that in a way you'd like to stay on in China, is that true?

K   This is called 'enjoying yourself so much that you forget to go home', but recently my parents haven't been too well so I want to go back and take stock before deciding anything. Ah – a year has passed really quickly, how time flies.

Li   You're a real old China hand, as Chinese as the Chinese. No wonder your students like you so much, hard-working (conscientious), capable plus a great sense of humour. Aili, you don't want to leave either do you?

S   No, I've really got a lot out of this year. What a pity I can't stay any longer.

Li   You really are returning with a sack full of goodies!

S   I suppose you could put it like that.

Mrs Li   Come and eat. I've made the dumplings and they're cooking. Let's have some wine first. Here's a plate of hors d'oeuvres. Wenhua, how about opening the wine?

Li   This is a pretty good bottle. It's white wine from (made by) a joint venture. Most Chinese wine is sweet but we know that you're not too keen on sweet wines. Right, bottoms up! Bon voyage (safe journey) and come back soon!

S   Here's to your good health and your heart's desire!

Li   Let's take a few photos. Hang on (wait though,) let's take them after the dumplings have come, there'll be more of a Chinese atmosphere (flavour!) then. Ah, here they are.

K   Have you got a flash?

Li   Yes. Is everybody ready? Smile please! Oh, I've forgotten to take the lens cap off.

Mrs Li   You're so muddleheaded (you're such a twit!), wasting (other) people's expressions, now hurry up!

K   I'll take a few snaps too. When I've had them developed, I'll post (mail) them to you. Have you got our address in England?

Li   No.

K   I'll write it down for you. Aili, have you got a pen? My ballpoint doesn't work. (is broken).

S   Yes, here you are. Zhou Dejin, your dumplings are really delicious, next time you'll definitely have to teach me how to make them.

Mrs Li No problem (fine), I hope you'll come back as soon as possible...the soya sauce and vinegar are both here.

S   Thanks. I'll have a little soya sauce. There's no way that a person like me can take vinegar (be jealous), ha ha!

Mrs Li You see, Yongshou, if you were to stay for another year there'd be absolutely no problem!

K   I'm quieter and more stable than Aili. She has friends all over the world. If anybody's going to be jealous it would certainly be me!

S   What rubbish my dear! How many female students of yours have told me how handsome (attractive) you are!

Li   Come on, let's have another drink. May our friendship last for ever! Bottoms up!

K   Next Friday is your birthday, (Mr/teacher) Li, what a shame that we'll have already left China by then so we're going to propose a toast to you now and wish you 'a life as long as the Southern Mountain and as blessed as the Eastern Sea' in advance. We've also got you a little something.

Li   You can't do that! You've already given (us) some things when you came, how come you're giving some more?

S   They were for you both, this is a birthday present. We hope you can add a little tiger energy to the Year of the Tiger!

Li   You really shouldn't have.

Mrs Li What's the matter Aili? Don't cry, we'll meet again some day(!) Come back (again) after you've graduated.

S   Don't take any notice of me. It's OK (it's nothing), I'm just being sentimental! Whenever I part from friends, I always think of the phrase 'meeting and parting are both difficult'.

Mrs Li　That is true. Your coming from so many thousands of miles away was really quite something but you'll still have plenty of opportunities to come to China in the future.

Li　How about our having a get-together when you come back? Come on, another toast, to our meeting again next year or the year after.

Mrs Li　You have to (can't not) go back, this time Aili, you've still got one year of studying to do but later on there'll be masses of opportunities.

Li　When's the plane leaving?

K　4.40 pm. We should get there by 3.

Li　We'll come and see you off eh?

S　There's no need. The airport's miles away, it's much too inconvenient. Let's count this evening as our goodbye otherwise I won't be able to stand it if we have to say yet another one.

Li　We'll see. If I can get off class a bit earlier we'll definitely go. All right, that's enough of that (the subject's closed). Let's drink a last toast.

Mrs Li　No more for me (I've had it!), I'll be drunk if I drink any more. Look, my face is all red.

Li　Never mind, you're not driving! Come on, joy and happiness to us all! Bottoms up!

Mrs Li,　⎫
　　　　⎬ Bottoms up!
K and S　⎭

Exercise 22.3

1 *Zhǔnbèi hǎo le ma? Wǒ liǎng diǎn zhōng* **jiù** *yào zǒu le.*
2 *Yúnnán zài Zhōngguó de* **xīnán** *bù.*　3 **Bù kěyǐ** *bǎ zhàoxiàngjī jiè gěi tā.*　4 *Wǒ yǒu* **bǎifēn zhī sìshí** *de bǎwò.*　5 *Yīngguó de shēnghuófèi bǐ Zhōngguó* **guì duō** *le (de duō).*　6 *Gǔdiǎn yīnyuè gēn xiàndài yīnyuè* **yíyàng hǎo tīng.**　7 *Fánshì lǎoshī* **dōu** *xǐhuan jiāo shū.*　8 *Chúfēi nǐ yuánliàng wǒ, wǒ* **cái** *bù kū.*　9 *Zài guówài shíjiān hěn cháng, kǒngpà* **fēi** *huàn qián* **bùkě.**　10 *Shàngjí*

hǎoxiàng *bù xǐhuan tā, bù zhīdao shénme yuányīn.* **11** *Nǐ* **dài** *shang tàiyángjìng qù cānjiā liánhuānhuì tài bù héshì ne!* **12** *Tā* **bèi** *dǎ le yì tā hútu.* **13** *Shèhuìzhǔyìzhě yīnggāi tóngqíng qióng rén.* **14** *Wǒ* **bù tóngyì nǐ** *– tā bìng bú shi ge huài rén.* **15** *Qǐng nǐ bǎ èrshí'èr kè de kèwén fānyì* **chéng** *Yīngwén.*

Chinese–English Vocabulary

Pinyin (alpha-betical order)	Characters	Chap. No.	English
à	啊	4	ah, oh (expressing sudden realisation)
àiren	爱人	2	husband, wife
āiyā	哎呀	20	oh dear (expressing surprise)
àn (zhào)	按（照）	8	according to, on the basis of
ānjìng	安静	5	quiet
ba	吧	2	particle indicating suggestion
bā	八	14	eight
bǎ	把	18	preposition showing disposal; also MW for things with handles
bàba	爸爸	7	daddy, dad
bái	白	22	white; blank
bǎi	百	19	hundred
bǎifēn zhī–	百分之_	19	per cent
bān	搬	8	remove, move
bàn	半	7	half
bàn	办		handle, attend to, do
bàn dào	办到	10	get something done, accomplish
bàn shì	办事	21	arrange for something to be done

Pinyin (alpha-betical order)	Characters	Chap. No.	English
bànfǎ	办法		method
bàng	棒	11	excellent (coll.)
bāngmáng	帮忙	19	help, do a favour
bāngzhù	帮助		help
bànlǐ	办理	20	conduct, handle, transact
bāo	包	14	packet (of), package
bāo	包	22	make (*jiǎozi*); to wrap; include
bào (zhǐ)	报（纸）	11	newspaper
MW *zhāng* or *fèn(r)*	张、份儿		
bǎocún	保存	20	keep, preserve
bāoguǒ	包裹	18	parcel, package
bāoguǒdān	包裹单	18	parcel form
bāokuò	包括	9	include
bāo shang	包上		wrap up
bàoxiāo	报销		reimbursement of expenses
bǎwò	把握		certainty
bēi	杯	2	cup(ful)
běi	北	17	north
Bèiduōfēn	贝多芬	22	Beethoven
Běihǎi Gōngyuán	北海公园	10	Beihai Park
Běijīng Dàxué	北京大学	4	Beijing University
Běijīng Fàndiàn	北京饭店	7	Beijing Hotel
Běijīng Yǔyán Xuéyuàn	北京语言学院	7	Beijing Languages Institute
bēizi	杯子	6	cup
bèizi	被子	6	duvet, quilt
MW *chuáng*	床		
běn	本	14	MW for books, magazines
bèn	笨		stupid
běndì	本地	21	this locality
béng	甭	20	needn't
běnlái	本来		originally
běnrén	本人	20	in person; oneself

Pinyin (alphabetical order)	Characters	Chap. No.	English
bǐ	比	7	compared with
biàn	变	10	change
biǎoqíng	表情	22	expression; to express one's feelings
biāozhǔn	标准	8	criterion; standard
bié	别	4	don't
bǐfang shuō	比方说	11	for example
bǐjiào	比较	7	relatively
bīng	兵	7	soldier
bìng	并	10	negative emphasiser
bīngguì	冰柜	6	freezer
bīngxiāng	冰箱	5	refrigerator
bìngrén	病人		patient, sick person
bǐrú	比如	10	for example, such as
bìxiūkè(chéng)	必修课（程）	22	obligatory or required course
bìyè	毕业	22	graduate
bō	拨	16	dial
bōlibēi	玻璃杯	6	glass (tumbler)
bǔ	捕		arrest
bù	布		cloth
bù	不	1	not
bù	部	15	MW for films
bù shǎo	不少	19	quite a bit, quite a few
bú shi…ér shi	不是…而是	11	not…but
bú shi…jiù shi	不是…就是	11	if it's not…then it's…
bù tóng	不同	20	different
bù yuǎn wàn lǐ ér lái	不远万里而来	22	not considering 10 000 *li* too far to come
bù zěnmeyàng	不怎么样	4	not up to much
bù…le	不…了	5	not…any more
búbì	不必		not have to
búcuò	不错	4	pretty good
búdàn…érqiě	不但…而且		not only…but also
bùdé bù	不得不	9	cannot but, have to
bùduì	部队	7	army

Pinyin (alpha-betical order)	Characters	Chap. No.	English
bùfen	部分	9	part, section
bùguǎn	不管		no matter
búguò	不过	22	but, however, only
búyòng	不用	22	need not
bùzhì	布置	5	decorate
cāi	猜	11	guess
cái	才	11	not…until…; only
cài	菜	4	dish, vegetable
càidān	菜单	9	menu
cǎisè	彩色	5	colour; multicoloured
cānjiā	参加	8	join; attend
cāo xīn	操心	20	worry about
cèsuǒ	厕所	6	toilet
chá	茶	1	tea
chá	查	11	check; investigate
chà	差		lack, short of
chá zìdiǎn	查字典	11	consult a dictionary
chábēi	茶杯	9	teacup
chàbuduō	差不多	22	almost, nearly
cháguǎn	茶馆	10	teahouse
chájī	茶几	6	coffee-table
cháng	长	11	long
chángshòu	长寿	16	long life
cháng (cháng)	常（常）	7	often
Chángchéng	长城		Great Wall
chángtú diànhuà	长途电话	18	long-distance telephone call
chǎnpǐn	产品	22	product
chǎojīdàn	炒鸡蛋	9	scrambled eggs
chāozhòng	超重	22	overweight
chātóu	插头	6	plug (electric)
cháyè	茶叶	9	tea (leaves)
chāzi	叉子	6	fork
chāzuò	插座	6	socket

Pinyin (alpha-betical order)	Characters	Chap. No.	English
chēkù	车库	6	garage
chéng	成		become
chéng qiān shàng wàn	成千上万	9	thousands and thousands
chēnghū	称呼	21	form of address; to address
chéngniánrén	成年人	11	adult
chéngrèn	承认	9	admit (e.g. mistake)
chéngshì	城市	20	city, town
chènshān	衬衫	14	shirt, blouse
MW *jiàn*	件		
chī bǎo	吃饱	5	eat one's fill
chī cù	吃醋	22	feel jealous
chī fàn	吃饭	3	eat (meal)
chízi	池子	6	sink
(chōng)xǐ	(冲)洗	22	develop (as of film); to wash
chōu yān	抽烟		smoke (v-o)
chū	出	10	come or go out
chū chāi	出差	21	be on a business trip
chuān	穿		wear (clothes)
chuán	船		boat (n)
chuáng	床	8	bed
chuángdān	床单	6	sheet
chuángdiàn	床垫	6	mattress
chuānghu	窗户	6	window
chuānglián	窗帘	6	curtain
chúfáng	厨房	5	kitchen
chúfēi	除非	20	unless
chūjìng	出境	20	leave the country
chúle... (yǐwài)	除了…(以外)	8	except, apart from
chūntiān	春天	10	spring (season)
chūshì	出示	20	show, produce
cì	次	11	time, occasion
		19	MW with number of train
cídài	磁带	22	tape
cóng	从	4	from (movement involved)

Pinyin (alphabetical order)	Characters	Chap. No.	English
cóngqián	从前	9	previously, in the past
cù	醋	6	vinegar; jealousy (as in love affair)
cún qián	存钱	20	deposit money
cuòwù	错误	21	mistake, error
dà	大	7	grown up; big
dǎ diànbào	打电报		send a telegram
dǎ diànhuà	打电话	16	telephone (v-o)
dǎ gē(r)	打嗝（儿）		belch, burp, hiccup (v-o)
dǎ gǔ	打鼓		beat a drum
dǎ hān	打鼾		snore (v-o)
dǎ hāqian	打哈欠		yawn (v-o)
dǎ hū(lu)	打呼噜		snore (colloq.) (v-o)
dà máojīn	大毛巾	6	bath towel
dǎ pái	打牌	10	play cards or mahjong
dǎ pìgu	打屁股		spank (v-o)
dǎ qì	打气		pump, inflate (v-o)
dǎ qiú	打球		play ball
dǎ tàijíquán	打太极拳	10	do taijiquan
dǎ zhēn	打针		give/have an injection
dǎ zì	打字		type (v-o)
dǎchéng yípiàn	打成一片	22	become one with, identify with
dàgài	大概		probably
dàhòutiān	大后天	16	day after the day after tomorrow
dāi	待	10	stay (v)
dài	带	20	bring; take
dài	戴	21	wear (hats, gloves, glasses etc.)
dàibiǎo	代表	9	representative
dàifu	大夫		doctor
dàjiā	大家	15	everybody
dǎkāi	打开	22	open (up); switch on
dāndiào	单调	7	monotonous, dull
dāng	当	5	serve as; be

Pinyin (alphabetical order)	Characters	Chap. No.	English
dāngrán	当然	9	of course, naturally
dānrénchuáng	单人床	6	single bed
MW *zhāng*	张		
dānrénfángjiān	单人房间	9	single room
dànshi	但是	4	but
dānwèi	单位	8	unit
-dào	到	7	manage to do action of verb up to; to
dào	到	17	arrive, go to
dào…qù/lái	到…去/（来）	10	go/come to…; to arrive at…
dàochù	到处	10	everywhere
dàoqī	到期	20	become due, expire
dàoshì	倒是	11	indeed, as it happens
dāozi	刀子	6	knife
dǎrǎo	打扰	11	disturb
dàren	大人		adult
dàshēng (de)	大声（地）	21	loudly
dǎsuàn	打算	22	intend, to plan
dǎtīng	打听	20	enquire
dàtóng-xiǎoyì	大同小异	20	similar in major area but different on minor points
dàyī	大衣		overcoat
MW *jiàn*	件		
de	的	3	marker
de shíhou	的时候	8	when
Déguó	德国		Germany
děi	得	5	must, need
děng	等	8	etc.
děng	等	19	wait
děngyú	等于	19	be equal to; be equivalent to
dì	地	10	locality, land; the earth
dì	第	11	ordinal prefix
diǎn	点	11	point, aspect
diǎn	点	20	count, check (e.g. money to see if correct)

Pinyin (alpha-betical order)	Characters	Chap. No.	English
diǎn zhōng	点钟	3	o'clock
diànbào	电报	18	telegram
MW fèn	份		
diàndēng	电灯	6	electric light
diànhuà (jī)	电话(机)	6	telephone
diànhuà hàomǎ	电话号码		telephone number
diǎnr (coll.)	点儿	20	spot, small branch
diànshàn	电扇	6	electric fan
diànshì (jī)	电视(机)	5	television
MW tái	台		
diànxiàn	电线	6	electric cable
diànyǐng	电影	15	film
MW bù	部		
dìdào	地道	22	genuine
dìdi	弟弟	7	younger brother
dìfang	地方	5	place
dìlǐ	地理		geography
dǐng	顶	19	top, peak; MW for hats
dǐng	顶	22	go against
dìng	订	9	order (in advance)
dìng	订	19	book, reserve; subscribe to
dìnghūn	订婚	19	be or get engaged
dìngqī cúnkuǎn	定期存款	20	deposit account
dírén	敌人		enemy
dìtǎn	地毯	6	carpet
dìtú	地图	14	map
MW zhāng	张		
diū	丢	20	lose
dìxiōng	弟兄		brothers
dìzhǐ	地址	18	address
dōng (bianr)	东(边儿)	17	east(side)
dǒng	懂	11	understand
Dōngjīng	东京		Tokyo
dōngtiān	冬天	8	winter
dōngxi	东西	14	thing(s)

Pinyin (alphabetical order)	Characters	Chap. No.	English
dōu	都	4	both, all
dòu	逗	19	funny
dú shū	读书	5	study
duǎn	短	10	short (in length)
duì	对	3	correct
duì…lái shuō	对…来说	11	as far as…/is concerned
duìbuqǐ	对不起	19	sorry; excuse me
duìhuàn	兑换	20	exchange (money)
duìmiàn	对面	17	opposite
duìxiàng	对象	3	steady boy- or girlfriend
duìzhào	对照	20	compare
duō	多	4	many; more
duō	多	11	more than, odd
duō(me)	多(么)	22	how
duō dehěn	多得很	22	very many
duōshao	多少	14	how many, how much
duōshù	多数	9	majority
è	饿	4	hungry
èi	欸		yes (verbal response to enquiry)
ér	而	19	but; and
èr	二	14	two (number)
èrlóu	二楼	6	first floor
érqiě	而且	9	moreover
érzi	儿子	5	son
fādá	发达	8	developed, advanced
Fǎguó	法国		France
Fǎguórén	法国人		French (person)
fǎn'ér	反而	10	on the contrary
fàng (zài)	放(在)	5	put (in or on)
fàng jià	放假	21	have a holiday or vacation
fàng xīn	放心	16	set one's mind at rest
fāngbiàn	方便	20	convenient

Pinyin (alpha- betical order)	Characters	Chap. No.	English
fángfèi	房费	9	room charge
fǎnguòlái	反过来		conversely
fángjiān	房间	5	room
fāngmiàn	方面	9	aspect, respect
fángzi	房子	5	house
MW *suǒ/ge*	所/个		
fángzū	房租	8	rent (for house)
fānqiézhī	蕃茄汁	9	tomato juice
fánshì	凡是	20	every, any, all
fàntīng	饭厅	6	dining room
fānyì	翻译		translate, interpret
fǎnzhèng	反正	10	anyway, in any case
fāxiàn	发现		discover
fāyīn	发音	11	pronunciation
fāzhǎn	发展	21	develop
fēicháng	非常	4	extremely
fēijī	飞机	22	aeroplane
MW *jià*	架		
(fēi) jīchǎng	（飞）机场	22	airport
fèijìn(r)	费劲（儿）	22	strenuous, energy consuming
féizào	肥皂	9	soap
MW *kuài*	块		
Fēizhōu	非洲		Africa
fēn	分	14	portion; MW for money
fēn	分	22	divide; distribute; distinguish
fèn(r)	份（儿）		copy
fēng	封	17	MW for letter
fēng	风	22	wind
féng shang	缝上		sew up
féngrènjī	缝纫机	8	sewing-machine
MW *tái*	台		
fēnháng	分行	20	branch (bank)
fǒuzé	否则	20	otherwise, or else
fù	付	9	pay
fùjìn	附近	10	nearby

Pinyin (alphabetical order)	Characters	Chap. No.	English
fùmǔ	父母	8	parents
fùnǚ	妇女		woman
fùqīn	父亲		father
fūrén	夫人	22	Mrs; Madame (formal)
fúwù	服务	9	service; to serve
fúwùyuán	服务员	7	attendant
fùyú	富于	22	rich in, full of
fùzá	复杂		complex, complicated
gǎi	改	21	alter, change, correct
gān bēi	干杯	22	drink a toast
gǎn xìngqù	感兴趣		be interested in something
gànbù	干部	10	cadre
gāng	刚	19	just
gāngcái	刚才	11	just now
gānjìng	干净		clean
gǎnjué	感觉	21	feeling, sense
gǎnkuài	赶快		hastily
gǎnqíng	感情	7	feeling, emotion
gǎnxiǎng	感想	22	reflections, thoughts
gāo	高	4	tall, high
gāo bízi	高鼻子	21	big nose
gàobié	告别	22	take leave of
gàosu	告诉		tell, let know
gāoxìng	高兴	2	happy
gébì	隔壁	18	next door
gēge	哥哥	7	elder brother
gègè	各个	21	each, every
gěi	给	2	to, for; give
gēn	跟	10	with; and
gēn...yíyàng	跟…一样	19	the same as...
gèng	更	11	even more, still more
gēnshang	跟上	9	keep pace with
gèrén	个人		individual (person)
gōngchǎng	工厂	10	factory
gōnggòng	公共	9	public

Pinyin (alphabetical order)	Characters	Chap. No.	English
gōnggòngqìchē MW liàng	公共汽车 辆		bus
gōngjīn	公斤	18	kilogram
gōnglǐ	公里		kilometre
gōngrén	工人	7	worker
gōngsī	公司	9	company
gōngyuán	公园	10	park
gōngzī	工资	8	wages
gōngzuò	工作	7	work; to work
gōngzuòzhèng	工作证	9	ID card (employee's)
gòu	够	19	rather, quite; enough
gòuwùzhī- fùzhèng	购物支付证		preferential card (new type)
guàhào	挂号	18	register
guàhàofèi	挂号费	18	registration charge
guài	怪		strange, odd
guǎn	管	22	bother about; be in charge of
guàng dà jiē	逛大街	10	go window-shopping
Guǎngdōng	广东	10	Canton
guāngyīn sì jiàn, rìyuè rú suō	光阳似箭, 日月如梭	22	time flies
guàntóu	罐头	6	tin, can
guānxi	关系	7	relation(ship)
gǔdiǎn	古典	22	classical
Gùgōng	故宫	17	Forbidden City (Imperial Palace)
guì	贵	9	expensive
guīdìng	规定	20	rule, regulation
guìtái	柜台	18	counter
guìxìng	贵姓	16	may I ask your name?
gǔlǎo	古老		ancient
guò	过	5	pass, cross
-guo	过	9	verbal suffix
guóchǎn	国产	8	made in one's country

Pinyin (alphabetical order)	Characters	Chap. No.	English
Guójì Fàndiàn	国际饭店	19	International Hotel
guójiā	国家	8	country
guǒjiàng	果酱	9	jam
guòjiǎng	过奖	11	you flatter me
guòqù	过去		(the) past
guówài	国外	20	overseas, abroad
hāhā	哈哈	22	ha ha
hái	还	7	still, in addition
háishi	还是	5	or (used in questions)
háishi	还是	11	after all; still (emphatic)
hǎishuǐ	海水		sea-water
háizi	孩子	5	child
hǎn	喊	21	shout, cry out
hángkōng	航空	18	airmail
Hángzhōu	杭州	21	Hangzhou
Hànyǔ	汉语	4	Chinese language
Hànzì	汉字	11	Chinese character(s)
hǎo	好	1	good
-hǎo	好	11	do the action of the verb satisfactorily
hào	号	15	number, date
hǎo chī	好吃	5	tasty, delicious
hǎo jǐ	好几	19	a good many
hàomǎ	号码	20	number (e.g. telephone)
hǎowán(r)	好玩（儿）	19	entertaining, enjoyable
hǎoxiàng	好象	21	seem
hǎoxiào	好笑		funny
hē	喝	1	drink
hé	和	5	and
héhuǒ	合伙	21	form a company or partnership
hēi-bái	黑白	5	black and white
hěn	很	1	very
héng	横	16	horizontal
héshì	合适		suitable

Pinyin (alphabetical order)	Characters	Chap. No.	English
hézī qǐyè	合资企业	22	joint venture
hóng	红	22	red
hóngchá	红茶	6	black tea (Indian)
hòu	厚		thick
hòubianr	后边儿	17	back, behind
hòuhuì yǒu qī	后会有期	22	we'll meet again some day
hòunián	后年	22	year after next
hòutiān	后天	16	day after tomorrow
hòuzhě	后者	22	the latter
huā	花	6	flowers; to spend
huà	话	21	remark, words(s)
MW *jù*	句		
huá bīng	滑冰	10	skate (*Lit.* slide ice)
huà huàr	画画儿		draw, paint (v-o)
huá xuě	滑雪		ski (v-o) (*Lit.* slide snow)
huāchá	花茶	6	jasmine tea
huài	坏	21	bad; broken
huáiyí	怀疑	20	suspect
huán	还		give or pay back, return
huàn qián	换钱	20	change money
huángyóu	黄油	9	butter
huānyíng	欢迎	5	welcome
huāpíng	花瓶	6	vase
huàr	画儿	6	painting
MW *zhāng*	张		
huāyuán	花园	6	garden
huí	回	5	return
huì	会	2	know how to, can; will
huì	会	9	will (showing possibility)
huí guó	回国	19	return to your own country
hújiāo	胡椒	6	pepper
hǔnián	虎年	22	year of the Tiger
huò (zhě)	或 (者)	9	or, perhaps
huò	货	8	goods
huǒchē	火车	19	train

Pinyin (alpha-betical order)	Characters	Chap. No.	English
huǒchēzhàn	火车站	19	railway station
huópo	活泼		lively
huóqī cúnkuǎn	活期存款	20	current account
huǒtuǐ	火腿	9	ham
hǔqì	虎气	22	vigour
húshuō	胡说	22	nonsense; talk nonsense
hútu	糊涂	22	muddle-headed
hùzhào	护照	20	passport
jí	即	9	that is, *viz*
jǐ	几	3	how many (less than 10)?; several
jǐ	挤	8	crowded; squeeze
jì	寄	18	post, mail (v)
jì (xiàlai)	记下来	16	note down, record
jiā	家	3	home; family
jiā (shang)	加（上）	8	add (on)
jiǎ	甲	17	A (as in A says…)
jiājù	家具	8	furniture
jiān	间	5	MW for room
jiǎn	剪		cut (as of hair)
jiàn	见	9	see; meet
jiàn	件	14	MW for piece, article, item e.g. clothing
jiǎndān	简单	8	simple
Jiānéng	佳能	21	Canon
jiǎng	讲	19	speak; to explain
jiàngyóu	酱油	6	soya sauce
jiānjīdàn	煎鸡蛋	9	fried egg(s)
jiànkāng	健康	22	healthy, sound
jiànwén	见闻	21	what one sees and hears
jiànxíng	饯行	22	give a farewell dinner
jiāo	教	7	teach
jiào	叫	7	call, be called
jiàotáng	教堂		church

Pinyin (alphabetical order)	Characters	Chap. No.	English
jiàoyù	教育	21	education; to educate
jiàoyuán	教员	7	teacher
jiǎozi	饺子	22	kind of ravioli, dumpling
jiàozuò	叫做	22	be called, be known as
jiàqī	假期		holidays, vacation
jiàqián	价钱	9	price
jīběn (shang)	基本（上）	20	basic(ally)
jīdàn	鸡蛋	9	egg
jìde	记得	20	remember
jiē	接	16	take hold of, receive; to meet
jiē	街		street
jiè	借		borrow; lend
jié bīng	结冰	10	freeze, ice over
jié hūn	结婚	3	marry, get married
jiēchù	接触	9	come into contact with
jiēdài	接待	20	receive; admit
jiějie	姐姐	7	elder sister
jiěmèi	姐妹		sisters
jièmo	芥末	6	mustard
jièshào	介绍	2	introduce
jiēzhe	接着	19	carry on; to follow
jīguān	机关	10	offices, organisation
jīhuì	机会	22	opportunity, chance
jìjiànrén	寄件人	18	sender
jìjié	季节	10	season (of year)
-jíle	极了	4	extremely
jīn	斤	14	catty (½ kilogram)
jìn	进	9	enter
jìn	近	17	near
jìng	敬	22	propose (a toast), toast
jǐngchá	警察		police, policeman
jīngcháng	经常	10	regularly, frequently
jīngguò	经过	19	go through, pass
jǐnguǎn	尽管	20	feel free to; even though, despite
jìngtóugài	镜头盖	22	lens cap

Pinyin (alpha-betical order)	Characters	Chap. No.	English
jìngzi	镜子	6	mirror
-jìnlai	进夹	8	verb + in
jīnnián	今年	7	this year
jīntiān	今天	4	today
jǐnzǎo	尽早	22	as soon as possible, at the earliest possible date
jíshǐ	即使	9	even if, even though
jìshù	技术	4	technique
jìsuàn	计算	20	count, to calculate
jìsuànjī	计算机	9	calculating machine, computer
jiǔ	酒	2	alcohol
jiǔ	九	14	nine
jiù	就	3	then; just, only, merely
jiù	旧		old
jiǔpíng	酒瓶	6	wine bottle
jiùshì	就是	11	precisely
juéde	觉得	21	feel
juéduì	绝对	22	absolute(ly)
jùlèbù	俱乐部		social club
júzizhī	桔子汁	2	orange juice
kāfēi	咖啡	1	coffee
kāi	开	19	start; to open; to drive
kāi chē de	开车的	22	person who drives, driver
kāiguān	开关	6	switch (n)
kāilǎng	开朗		open (personality)
kāishǐ	开始	11	begin
kāishuǐ	开水	9	boiled water
kàn	看	5	look, see, watch, read
kàn xì	看戏		see; watch a play
kǎomiànbāo	烤面包	9	toast
MW piàn	片		
kě	可	21	emphasises tone of speaker
kè	刻		quarter; carve
kě' ài	可爱		lovable
kěbúshì	可不是	21	exactly; that's just the way it is

Pinyin (alphabetical order)	Characters	Chap. No.	English
kěkào	可靠		reliable
kěkě	可可	9	cocoa
kělián	可怜		pitiable; pitiful
kèmǎn	客满	16	sold out, full house
kěndìng	肯定	21	definite(ly); affirm
kěpà	可怕		terrifying, frightening
kèqi	客气	4	polite
kěshì	可是	8	but
kètīng	客厅	5	living room, lounge
kèwén	课文	9	text
MW kè	课		
kěxī	可惜	10	it's a pity that
kěxiào	可笑		laughable, ridiculous
kěyǐ	可以	5	can, may
kǒngpà	恐怕		be afraid that...
kǒu	口	7	MW for family members
kū	哭	22	weep, cry
kuài	快	5	quick, fast
kuài	块	14	MW for money
kuàilè	快乐	22	happy, joyful
kuàizi	筷子	4	chopsticks
MW shuāng	双		
kùnnan	困难	11	difficult; difficulty
lā	拉	21	pull; to play (of stringed instrument)
là(de)	辣 (的)		hot or spicy food
lái	来	4	come
lǎn	懒		lazy
làngfèi	浪费	22	waste, squander
làngmàn	浪漫	19	romantic
lǎngsòng	朗诵	19	recite, read aloud with expression
lǎo	老	5	old
lǎo	老	22	always

Pinyin (alpha-betical order)	Characters	Chap. No.	English
lǎobǎn	老板		boss
láojià	劳驾	17	excuse me
lǎorén	老人	10	old people
lǎoshī	老师		teacher
lǎoshì	老式	21	old-fashioned
lǎowài	老外	21	'old foreigner'
le	了	3/4	particle *le*
lěng	冷	8	cold
lěngpán	冷盘	22	cold dish; hors d'oeuvres
lí	离	17	from (static)
lǐ	里		$^1/_3$ mile or $^1/_2$ kilometre
-lǐ	里	4	inside
liǎ	俩	3	two
lián	连		even (conj.)
liǎn	脸	22	face
liáng	凉	4	cool
liǎng	两	3	two (of a kind)
liánhuānhuì	联欢会	22	get together, party
liànxí	练习		exercise, practise (n and v)
liáo tiān(r)	聊天（儿）	10	chat
liǎojiě	了解	21	find out, understand, know
líkāi	离开	22	leave (place or person)
lǐmào	礼貌	21	courteous; manners
líng	零	14	zero
lǐngdài	领带		tie
lǐngdǎo	领导		leader(ship)
lìng (wài)	另（外）	20	another; separately
(línyù) pēntóu	（淋浴）喷头	6	shower
liú	留	16	keep, remain; let grow; leave (behind or for somebody)
liù	六	14	six
liúlì	流利		fluent
liúlián wàng fǎn	流连忘返	22	enjoy oneself so much as to forget to go home
liúxuéshēng	留学生	7	student studying abroad

Pinyin (alpha-betical order)	Characters	Chap. No.	English
lìwài	例外		exception
lǐwù	礼物	22	present, gift
MW *jiàn/ge*	件/个		
lìxī	利息	20	interest (e.g. bank)
lì(xī)lù	利(息)率	20	rate of interest
lóngtou	龙头	6	tap
lóushàng	楼上		upstairs
lóutī	楼梯	6	stairs, staircase
lóuxià	楼下	15	downstairs
lù	路		road
lù yīn	录音		record (v-o); recording (tape)
lǜchá	绿茶	6	green tea (Chinese)
lǚguǎn	旅馆	9	hotel
Lúndūn	伦敦		London
lúnliú	轮流	10	take turns; in turn
lùrén	路人	17	passerby, stranger
lǚtú	旅途	21	journey, trip
lùxiàngjī	录像机	6	video recorder
lǚxíng	旅行	10	travel
lǚxíng zhīpiào	旅行支票	20	traveller's cheque
lùyīnjī	录音机	6	tape recorder
lǚyóu	旅游	21	tourism; to tour
ma	吗	2	question particle
mǎ	马		horse
mà	骂		swear at, curse
máfan	麻烦	5	trouble; troublesome
mǎi	买	14	buy
mài	卖	16	sell
mǎi dōngxi	买东西	14	go shopping
māma	妈妈	7	mummy, mum
mǎn	满	22	full; to reach the limit, expire
màn	慢	5	slow
mǎn zài ér guī	满载而归	22	return with fruitful results
máo	毛	14	MW for money

Pinyin (alpha-betical order)	Characters	Chap. No.	English
Máo Zhǔxí Jìniàntáng	毛主席纪念堂	17	Mao Zedong (Chairman Mao) Mausoleum
máobìng	毛病		defect
máojīn	毛巾	9	towel
máojīnjià	毛巾架	6	towel rail
máoyī MW *jiàn*	毛衣 件	14	sweater, woolly
màozi	帽子		hat
mǎshàng	马上		immediately
méi	没	3	not (used with *yǒu*)
měi	每	8	each, every
méi shénme	没什么	5	it's nothing
méi (yǒu) guānxi	没(有)关系	4	it doesn't matter
Měiguó	美国	18	USA, American
Měiguórén	美国人	11	American
mèimei	妹妹	7	younger sister
měirén	美人	21	beautiful woman
méishìr	没事儿	22	it's OK, it's nothing; have nothing planned
Měiyuán	美元	20	US dollar
mén	门	6	door, gate
mǐ	米	14	metre, rice
miànfěn	面粉	6	flour
miànjīn MW *tiáo*	面巾 条	6	face flannel
miáoxiě	描写	19	describe
mìmì	秘密		secret
míngbai	明白	20	understand; clear
míngtiān	明天	3	tomorrow
míngzi	名字	16	name (given)
Mòsīkē	莫斯科	19	Moscow
mótuōchē MW *liàng*	摩托车 辆		motorbike
mǒu	某	9	(a) certain

Pinyin (alpha-betical order)	Characters	Chap. No.	English
Mòzhātè	莫扎特	22	Mozart
mùbiāo	目标		objective
mǔyǔ	母语	11	mother tongue
na	哪	22	particle showing mood
nǎ (or něi)	哪	4	which?
nà (or nèi)	那	3	that
ná chū	拿出	19	take out
nǎipíng	奶瓶		milk bottle
nàme	那么	1	so, in that case
nán	男	3	male
nán	难	10	difficult
nán	南	17	south
nánnǔ lǎoshào	男女老少	10	men and women, old and young
nánguài	难怪	19	no wonder
nàozhōng	闹钟	6	alarm clock
nǎr	哪儿	3	where?
nàr (nàlǐ)	那儿（那里）	8	there
ne	呢	2	question particle
néng	能	16	be able to, can
nénggàn	能干	22	capable, competent
ǹg	嗯	4	hm, uh-huh
nǐ	你	1	you
nián	年		year
niàn	念	17	read aloud
niánjì	年纪	7	age
niánqīng	年轻	19	young
Níkòng	尼空	21	Nikon
nǐmen	你们	2	you (plural)
nín	您	2	you (polite form)
Niújīn	牛津		Oxford
niúnǎi	牛奶		milk
nǔ	女	3	female
nǔ' ér	女儿	5	daughter
nuǎnhuo	暖和	22	warm

Pinyin (alpha-betical order)	Characters	Chap. No.	English
nuǎnqì	暖气	6	central heating
nuǎnqìpiàn	暖气片		radiator
nǚshēng	女生	22	female student(s)
ò	哦	22	oh
Ōuzhōu	欧洲	10	Europe
pá	爬	19	climb
pà	怕	21	fear, be afraid of
pái	排	15	row, line
pái	牌	20	plate; brand; card
páijià	牌价	20	market quotation (exchange rate)
pàng	胖		fat
pángbianr	旁边儿	21	side
pǎo	跑	10	run
péi	陪	5	accompany
pèifú	偏服		admire
pèng(dào)	碰到	20	bump (into)
péngyou	朋友	3	friend
piānjiàn	偏见	21	prejudice, bias
piányi	便宜	8	cheap
piào	票	15	ticket
MW *zhāng*	张		
piàojià	票价	19	ticket price
piàoliang	漂亮	5	beautiful, pretty
píjiǔ	啤酒	11	beer
píng	凭	9	rely on, depend on
píng	瓶	22	MW for bottles
píngcháng	平常	9	usually, ordinary, commonplace
píngguǒ	苹果	14	apple
píngzi	瓶子	6	bottle
píqi	脾气		temperament
pòfèi	破费	22	go to some expense

Pinyin (alphabetical order)	Characters	Chap. No.	English
pútáo	葡萄		grape
pútáojiǔ	葡萄酒	22	wine
pǔtōnghuà	普通话	11	common spoken languange (modern standard Chinese)
qī	七	14	seven
qí	骑	22	ride (as of horse, bicycle)
qiān	千		thousand
qián	钱	14	money
qiān zì	签字	20	sign; signature
qiánbianr	前边儿	17	front, in front of
Qiánmén	前门	17	Qianmen
qiānwàn	千万	20	whatever you do
qiánzhě	前者	22	the former
qiǎokèlì	巧克力		chocolate
MW *kuài*	块		
qìchē	汽车	19	car
MW *liàng*	辆		
qǐfēi	起飞	22	take off (of aircraft)
qíguài	奇怪	10	strange
qìhòu	气候	10	climate
qíng	晴	10	fine, clear, bright (of weather)
qǐng	请	1	invite
qǐng kè	请客		invite somebody for a meal
qīngchu	清楚	11	clear; clearly
Qīngdǎo	青岛	11	Qingdao
qíngkuàng	情况	7	situation
qīnmì	亲密	21	close, intimate
qióng (rén)	穷（人）		poor (person)
qíshí	其实	9	actually, as a matter of fact
qiūtiān	秋天	10	autumn
qǔ	取	16	get, fetch
qù	去	3	go
qǔ qián	取钱	20	withdraw money
quánlì	权利		right(s)

Pinyin (alphabetical order)	Characters	Chap. No.	English
què	却	9	however
quèshí	确实	22	really, indeed; true, certain
qún	群	10	MW for group, flock
qǔqiánbiǎo	取钱表	20	cash withdrawal form
ràng	让	22	let, to allow
rè niúnǎi	热牛奶	9	hot milk
rén	人	16	person
rènào	热闹	10	bustling, exciting
rénjiān lèyuán	人间乐园	21	paradise on earth
Rénmín Dàhuìtáng	人民大会堂	17	Great Hall of the People
Rénmín Yīngxióng Jìniànbēi	人民英雄纪念碑	17	Monument to the People's Heroes
rénmínbì	人民币	19	RMB (Chinese currency)
rènshi	认识	2	know, recognise
rènwéi	认为	21	think, consider
rènzhēn	认真	22	conscientious
rèqíng	热情	5	warm-hearted, enthusiastic
rèshuǐpíng	热水瓶	6	Thermos flask
Rìběn	日本	8	Japan
rìchū	日出	15	sunrise
rìluò	日落	19	sunset
Rìyuán	日元		yen
rìzi	日子	7	day; date
róngyì	容易	11	easy
ruǎnwò	软卧	19	soft sleeper
ruǎnzuò	软座	19	soft seat (train)
rúguǒ	如果	19	if
rúguǒ...(de huà), jiù...	如果…(的话），就…	9	if...then
Ruìshì	瑞士		Switzerland
sāizi	塞子	6	plug (for sink, etc.)
sān	三	14	three

Pinyin (alpha-betical order)	Characters	Chap. No.	English
sàn bù	散步	10	to take a stroll, walk
sānmíngzhì	三明治	21	sandwich
MW *kuài*	块		
shāfā	沙发	6	sofa
MW *tào*	套		suite (settee and two easy chairs)
shài tàiyáng	晒太阳	10	sunbathe
shàng	上		last; up
shàng cèsuǒ	上厕所	9	go to the toilet
Shàngdì de Chǒng'ér	《上帝的宠儿》	16	'Amadeus'
shāngdiàn	商店	10	shop
shānggǎnzhǔyìzhě	伤感主义者	22	sentimentalist
shàngjí	上级		superiors
shàngpù	上铺	19	upper berth
shāngrén	商人	9	businessman
shǎnguāngdēng	闪光灯	22	flash (light)
shàngwǔ	上午	19	morning
shāo	烧	8	burn
shǎo	少	4	less, few
sháozi	勺子	6	spoon
shèbèi	设备	9	equipment, facilities
shěbude	舍不得	22	be unwilling to part with, grudge
shéi (or *shuí*)	谁	9	who?
shèng (*xiàlai*)	剩(下来)	19	be left (over); remain
shēngchǎn	生产	10	produce, manufacture
Shèngdànjié	圣诞节		Christmas
shēngdiào	声调	11	tone
shēnghuó	生活	4	life; to live
shénme shíhou	什么时候		when?
shēngrì	生日	22	birthday
shēngyì	生意	9	business
shénme	什么	3	what?
shénmede	什么的	9	and so on

Pinyin (alphabetical order)	Characters	Chap. No.	English
shēntǐ	身体	7	health, body
shī	诗	19	poem
MW *shǒu*	首		
shì	是	2	be
shì (qing)	事情	11	matter, thing
MW *jiàn*	件		
shífēn	十分	21	extremely, very
shīgē	诗歌		poetry
shíjiān	时间	5	time
shìjiè	世界	10	world
shíkèbiǎo	时刻表	19	timetable, schedule
shíwǔ	十五	14	fifteen
shìyè	事业	21	undertaking, cause
shízài	实在	22	really, honestly; true, real
shōu (hǎo)	收(好)	18	put away; receive
shǒu	手	21	hand
shòu	受	21	receive, be subjected to
shòu bǐ Nánshān fú rú Dōnghǎi	寿比南山福如东海	22	may you live as long as the Southern Mountain and be as blessed as the Eastern Sea.
shòu bù liǎo	受不了	22	be unable to bear or endure
shǒudū	首都		capital
Shǒudū Jùchǎng	首都剧场	16	Capital Theatre
shōuhuò	收获	22	gains, results; harvest
shòuhuòyuán	售货员	14	shop-assistant
shōujiànrén	收件人	18	addressee, recipient
shǒujīn	手巾	6	hand towel
shōujù	收据	18	receipt
shòupiàoyuán	售票员	15	box office clerk; ticket seller
shōushi	收拾	22	pack; tidy up, put in order
shǒutào	手套		glove(s)
shǒutíbāo	手提包	22	bag, handbag
shōuyīnjī	收音机	6	radio
MW *tái/ge*	台/个		
shū	书	6	book

Pinyin (alphabetical order)	Characters	Chap. No.	English
shǔ	属		belong to
shù	树	6	tree
shù	竖	16	vertical
shuā yá	刷牙		brush teeth
shuài	帅	22	handsome; beautifully (coll.)
shuāngrénchuáng MW *zhāng*	双人床 张	6	double bed
shuāngrénfángjiān	双人房间	9	double room
shūcài	蔬菜	6	vegetables
shūfáng	书房	8	study room (n)
shūfu	舒服	8	comfortable
shuǐ	水		water
shuì (jiào)	睡觉	8	sleep, go to bed
shuǐdiànfèi	水电费	8	water and electricity charges
shuǐguǒ	水果	22	fruit
shuǐguǒzhī	水果汁	9	fruit juice
shuǐpíng	水平	11	level, standard
shuǐtǒng	水桶	6	bucket, pail
shūjià	书架	6	bookcase, bookshelf
shuō	说	15	speak, say
shuō huà	说话	4	speak, talk
shuōfǎ	说法		way of saying things
shuōmíng	说明		show, explain, illustrate
shūzhuō	书桌	8	desk
shūzi MW *bǎ*	梳子 把	6	comb, brush
sǐ	死		die
sì	四	14	four
sīchóu	丝绸	14	silk
Sìchuān	四川	10	Sichuan
sìshēng	四声	11	the four tones
sòng	送	22	give as a present; see somebody off; send
Sū 、 Háng	苏、杭	21	Suzhou and Hangzhou
suàn	算	22	regard as, count as

Pinyin (alpha-betical order)	Characters	Chap. No.	English
suàn le	算了	20	forget it, let it pass
suàn zhàng	算帐	9	work out bill, make bill
suān(niú)nǎi	酸(牛)奶	9	yoghurt
suànpan	算盘	9	abacus
Sūgélán	苏格兰		Scotland
súhuà	俗话	21	common saying, proverb
MW *jù*	句		
suì	岁	3	year (of age)
suíbiàn	随便	4	do as one pleases
suīrán...dànshi	虽然…但是	8	although
suíshí	随时	9	at any time
Sūlián	苏联		USSR
suǒyǐ	所以	5	therefore
suǒyǒu (de)	所有（的）	20	all
tā	他	2	he, him
tā	她	2	she, her
tā	它	21	it
tài	太	3	too, extremely
táidēng	台灯	6	table lamp
tàitai	太太	2	Mrs, wife
tàiyángjìng	太阳镜	21	sunglasses
MW *fù*	副		
tāmen	他们	2	they
tán huà	谈话	5	chat, conversation
Táng	唐	19	Tang Dynasty (618–907 AD)
táng	糖	6	sugar, sweets, candy
tàngyījià	烫衣架	6	ironing board
tǎnshuài (de)	坦率（地）	21	frank(ly)
tǎnzi	毯子	6	blanket
tào	套	14	set
tèbié	特别	9	especially; special
tèquán	特权	9	privilege
tiān	添	5	add, increase
tiān	天	8	day; sky, heaven

Pinyin (alpha- betical order)	Characters	Chap. No.	English
tián	甜	22	sweet
tián (xiě)	填（写）	18	fill in (e.g. form)
Tiān'ānmén *Guǎngchǎng*	大安门广场	17	Tiananmen Square
tiānpíng	天平	18	scales (for weighing)
tiānqì	天气	8	weather
Tiāntán	天坛	17	Temple of Heaven
tiāntáng	天堂	21	heaven, paradise
tiānxià	天下	22	land under heaven – the world
tiē(shang)	贴（上）	18	stick (on)
tīng	厅	5	hall
tīng	听		listen
tǐng	挺	15	very, rather
tīng qǐlai	听起来	21	sound (verb)
tīngshuō	听说	8	be told, hear of
tíqián	提前	22	bring forward a date
tōngguò	通过	20	go through
tóngqíng	同情	9	sympathise with
tóngshí	同时	8	at the same time; moreover
tóngshì	同事	7	colleague, fellow worker
tóngxiāng	同乡	21	person who was born in the same place as oneself
tóngxué	同学	21	fellow student
tóngyì	同意	21	agree with
tóngzhì	同志	18	comrade
tóufa	头发		hair (on head)
tuìxiū	退休	7	retire
wàibì	外币	20	foreign currency
wàibīn	外宾	9	foreign guest, visitor
wàiguó	外国	7	foreign (country)
wàihuì (quàn)	外汇（券）	20	foreign exchange (certificate)
wàimiàn	外面	5	outside
-wán	完	5	finish (doing)
wán(r)	玩（儿）	3	have fun
wǎn	晚		late

Pinyin (alphabetical order)	Characters	Chap. No.	English
wàn	万		ten thousand
wǎncān	晚餐	22	supper, dinner
wǎnfàn	晚饭		evening meal, dinner
wàng (jì)	忘 (记)	20	forget
wàng	往	17	towards, to
wǎngqiú	网球		tennis
wàngǔ chángcún	万古长存	22	last forever, be everlasting
wǎngwǎng	往往	9	more often than not, frequently
wánquán	完全	21	complete(ly)
wǎnshang	晚上	3	evening
wànshì rúyì	万事如意	22	your heart's desire
wèi	位	4	MW for persons (polite)
wèi	喂	16	hello (on telephone)
wèi	为	22	for, for the sake of
wèi shénme	为什么	19	why?
wēibōlú	微波炉	6	microwave oven
wèidao	味道	22	flavour, taste
wèihūnfū	未婚夫	19	fiancé
wèihūnqī	未婚妻		fiancée
wèile	为了	22	for the sake of, in order to
Wēinísī	威尼斯	21	Venice
wèishēngzhǐ MW juǎn	卫生纸 卷	6	toilet paper
wèn	问	15	ask
wèn lù	问路	17	ask the way
wěndìng	稳定	22	stable, steady; to stabilise
wénhuà	文化		culture
wénmíng	闻名	21	well-known, famous
wèntí	问题	20	question, problem
wénzì	文字		script (writing system)
wǒ	我	1	I, me
wòjīdàn	卧鸡蛋	9	poached egg(s)
wǒmen	我们	2	we, us

Pinyin (alpha-betical order)	Characters	Chap. No.	English
wòshì	卧室	5	bedroom
wūdǐng	屋顶		roof
wǔdǒuchú/ wǔdǒuguì	五斗橱/五斗柜	6	chest of drawers
wūlǐ	屋里	22	in the room
xì	戏		play
xī yān	吸烟		smoke (v-o)
-xià	下	8	have the capacity to (follows verb)
xià	下	15	next
xià bān	下班	10	finish work
xià qí	下棋	10	play chess
xià xuě	下雪	10	snow (v-o)
xià yǔ	下雨	10	rain (v-o)
xiàbianr	下边儿	9	under(neath), below
xiān	先	18	first (adv)
xiàndài	现代		modern
xiǎng	想	3	feel like doing something; think
xiàng	象	10	resemble
xiàng	向	22	towards; to face
xiǎng qǐlai	想起来	22	remember, call to mind
xiāngdāng	相当	9	quite (a bit)
xiāngfǎn	相反		opposite, contrary
Xiānggǎng	香港		Hong Kong
xiānghuì	相会	22	meet one another
xiāngjiàn shí nán bié yì nán	相见时难别亦难	22	meeting and parting are both difficult (quotation from poem by Li Shangyin)
xiǎngshòu	享受	9	enjoy rights etc; treat
(xiāng) yān MW zhī, bāo	香烟 支、包	14	cigarette
xiāngzào	香皂	6	toilet soap
xiānsheng	先生	1	Mr, gentleman

Pinyin (alpha-betical order)	Characters	Chap. No.	English
xiànyú	限于	9	be confined to
xiànzài	现在	7	now, at present
xiǎo	小	5	small
xiào	笑	22	smile, laugh
xiǎoháir	小孩儿	3	child (small)
xiǎohuǒzi	小伙子	21	young fellow
xiǎojie	小姐	4	Miss, young lady
xiǎoshí	小时		hour
xiǎoshuò	小说	6	novel
MW *běn*	本		
xiǎoyìsi	小意思	22	small token, mere trifle
xiàpù	下铺	19	bottom berth
xiàtiān	夏天	10	summer
xiàwǔ	下午	16	afternoon
xiàyìshí	下意识	21	subconsciousness
Xībānyáwén	西班牙文		Spanish (language)
xībianr	西边儿	17	west (side)
Xīcān	西餐	9	Western food
xié	鞋		shoe(s)
xiě (zì)	写（字）	11	write (characters)
xièxie	谢谢	1	thank; thank you
Xīfāng	西方	8	the West
Xīfāngrén	西方人	11	Westerner
Xīhú	西湖	21	West Lake
xǐhuan	喜欢	1	like (v)
xǐliǎnpén	洗脸盆	6	wash basin
xīn	新		new
xìn MW *fēng*	信 封	18	letter
xìnfēng	信封		envelope
xíng	行	1	be all right
xìngfú	幸福	22	enjoy good fortune, happy
xínglǐ	行李	22	luggage, baggage
xìngmíng	姓名	18	(full) name
xīngqī	星期	10	week
xīngqīwǔ	星期五	16	Friday

Pinyin (alpha-betical order)	Characters	Chap. No.	English
xīnlǐ	心里	21	in the heart or mind
xīnshì	新式	21	latest type, new-style
xīnxiān	新鲜	21	fresh
xīnyì	心意	22	kindly feelings, regard
xiōngdì	兄弟	8	brothers
xīshēng	牺牲		sacrifice (v)
xiūxi	休息	8	rest (v and n)
xǐwǎnchí	洗碗池	6	sink (n)
xīwàng	希望	19	hope (v and n)
xǐyījī	洗衣机	5	washing machine
xǐzǎojiān	洗澡间	6	bathroom
xǐzǎopén	洗澡盆	6	bath (tub)
xuǎn	选	19	choose
xué(xí)	学(习)	4	study (v)
xuésheng	学生	7	student
xuéshēngzhèng	学生证	9	student card
xuéxiào	学校	4	school
xūyào	需要	22	need, require; needs (n)
ya	呀	21	particle indicating surprise
yágāo	牙膏	6	toothpaste
MW tǒng	筒		
yān	烟		tobacco (cigarette)
yán	盐	6	salt
yǎn	演	16	perform, act
yàng	样	11	type, kind
yángguǐzi	洋鬼子	21	foreign devil
yàngshì	样式	20	form, pattern
yángwèi(r)	洋味(儿)	11	foreign flavour
yàngzi	样子		appearance, the way somebody looks
yānhuīgāng	烟灰缸	6	ashtray
yāo	幺	19	one (used in speech instead of *yī* in telephone and train numbers)

Pinyin (alpha-betical order)	Characters	Chap. No.	English
yào	要	5	want to; must, to want
yào (shi)…(de huà), jiù	要(是)…(的话),就	10	if…then
yàoshi	要是	9	if
yàobù(rán)	要不(然)	4	otherwisc
yáshuā	牙刷	6	toothbrush
MW bǎ	把		
Yàzhōu	亚洲		Asia
yě	也	3	also, too
yī	一	2	one
yǐ	乙	17	B (as in B says)
yī…jiù	一…就	10	no sooner…than…, as soon as
yì	亿		hundred million
yìbān	一般	8	generally; general
yìbān lái shuō	一般来说	21	generally speaking
yīcǐ lèituī	依此类推	20	others can be deduced similarly
Yìdàlì	意大利		Italy
Yìdàlìrén	意大利人		Italian (person)
yìdiǎn(r)	一点 (儿)	4	a little
yídìng	一定	4	certainly, definitely
yīfu	衣服	14	clothes
MW jiàn	件		
yígòng	一共	14	altogether
yīguì	衣柜	6	wardrobe
yíhàn	遗憾	22	regret; to regret, be a pity
Yíhéyuán	颐和园	10	Summer Palace
yǐhòu	以后	8	after, afterwards
yíhuìr	一会儿	10	a short while, after a moment
yìjiàn	意见		opinion
yǐjīng	已经	7	already
yìlóu	一楼	6	ground floor
yílù píng'ān	一路平安	22	*bon voyage*
yìmó yíyàng	一模一样	20	exactly like
yīn	阴	10	cloudy, overcast

Pinyin (alpha-betical order)	Characters	Chap. No.	English
Yīngbàng	英镑	20	pound sterling
(yīng)gāi	（应）该	5	ought, should
Yīngguó	英国	4	Britain, England
Yīngguórén	英国人	4	British
yǐngjùyuàn	影剧院	15	cinema and theatre (buildings)
yìngwò	硬卧	19	hard sleeper
yíngyèyuán	营业员	18	clerk, shop employee
Yīngyǔ	英语	11	English language
yìngzuò	硬座	19	hard seat (train)
yīnlì	阴历		lunar calendar
yīnwèi (yīnwei)	因为	11	because
yīnyuè	音乐	22	music
yīnyuèhuì	音乐会	15	concert
yìqǐ	一起	10	together
yǐqián	以前	7	previously, before
yíqiè	一切		all, every, everything
yīshēng	医生	7	doctor
yìsi	意思	3	meaning
(yì)xiē	（一）些	8	some
yíyàng	一样	20	alike, the same
yīyuàn	医院	7	hospital
yízhènzi	一阵子	19	period of time, spell
yǐzi	椅子	6	chair
MW *bǎ*	把		
yòng	用	4	use
yǒngyuǎn	永远	16	forever
yǒu	有	3	have, there is/are
yǒu (de) shí-hou	有（的）时候	9	sometimes
yǒu kòng	有空	3	have free time
yǒu míng	有名		be famous
yǒu yìsi	有意思	11	be interesting
yǒu yòng	有用		useful
yòu…yòu	又…又	5	both…and
yōudài	优待	9	preferential treatment

Pinyin (alphabetical order)	Characters	Chap. No.	English
yōudàizhèng	优待证	19	preferential card
yǒude	有的	8	some
yǒudeshì	有的是	10	have plenty of, there's no lack
yóudiànjú	邮电局	18	post and telecommunications office
yóufèi	邮费	22	postage
yóujì	邮寄	18	send by post or mail
yóukè	游客	9	tourist, sightseer
yóulǎn	游览		visit (v), sightsee
yōumògǎn	幽默感	22	sense of humour
yóupiào	邮票	14	postage stamp
MW zhāng	张		
yǒuyì	友谊	22	friendship
Yǒuyì Shāngdiàn	友谊商店	20	Friendship Store
yóuyǒng	游泳		swim (v-o)
yuán	圆	8	round
yuǎn	远	17	far
Yuándàn	元旦		New Year's Day
yuánliàng	原谅	4	forgive
Yuánmíngyuán	圆明园	10	Old Summer Palace
yuànyì	愿意	5	be willing, want
yuányīn	原因		reason, cause
yuánzhūbǐ	圆珠笔	22	ballpoint pen
MW zhī	枝/支		
yuè	月	10	month
yuè lái yuè	越来越	9	more and more
yuèbǐng	月饼	19	mooncake
yuèguāng	月光	19	moonlight
yuèliàng	月亮		moon
yǔfǎ	语法	11	grammar
yùjīn	浴巾	6	bath towel
MW tiáo	条		
yúkuài	愉快	19	happy, pleased

Pinyin (alpha-betical order)	Characters	Chap. No.	English
yùndǒu	熨斗	6	iron
yùpén	浴盆	6	bath (tub)
yùshì	浴室	6	bathroom
zài	在	3	be at; at
zài	再	5	again
zài	在	16	in the middle of -ing
zài shuō	再说	22	not tackle a problem until some other time
zàijiàn	再见	5	goodbye
zāng	脏		dirty
zánmen	咱们	21	we (including listener)
zǎo	早	5	early
zǎo…jiù	早…就		long since
zǎocān	早餐	9	breakfast
zǎorì	早日	22	at an early date; soon
zǎoshang	早上	9	morning (early)
zázhì	杂志	14	magazine
MW běn	本		
zěnme	怎么	11	how
zěnme bàn	怎么办	20	what's to be done?
zěnme le	怎么了	22	what's the matter?
zěnmeyàng	怎么样	3	what about (it)?; how?
zhàn	站	22	stand; station, stop (bus etc)
zhāng	张	14	MW for flat, rectangular objects
zhànghù	帐户	20	account (bank)
zháo	着		potential resultative verb ending
zhǎo	找	7	look for
zhǎo (qián)	找（钱）	14	give back (as of change)
zhào xiàng	照相	10	take a photo, have one's picture taken
zhàocháng	照常	10	as usual

Pinyin (alpha-betical order)	Characters	Chap. No.	English
zhāodài	招待	5	hospitality; entertain
zhàopiàn	照片		photograph
MW *zhāng*	张		
zhàoxiàngjī	照相机	21	camera
MW *tái*	台		
-zhe	着	10	verbal suffix
zhè (or *zhèi*)	这	2	this
zhè yàng	这样	11	this kind of
zhème	这么	22	so, this way, like this
zhēn	真	2	really; true, real
zhèngfǔ	政府		government
zhěnggè	整个	10	whole, entire
zhèngcháng	正常	10	normal, regular
zhènghǎo	正好	20	just right; to happen to
zhèngmíng	证明	20	certificate; to prove
zhèngzài...ne	正在···呢	10	in the middle of -ing
zhèngzhì	政治		political
zhěntào	枕套	6	pillow case
zhěntou	枕头	6	pillow
zhèr (*zhèlǐ*)	这儿（这里）	4	here
zhèyàng	这样	19	like this, in this way, so
zhī	织		knit, weave
zhǐ	只	5	only
zhǐ	指	11	refer to, point at/to; finger
...*zhī jiān*	之间	22	between, amongst...
...*zhī zhōng*	之中		between, amongst...
zhīdao	知道	11	know (a fact)
zhíde	值得	17	be worth, deserve
zhǐhǎo	只好	5	have to
zhíjiē	直接	20	direct
zhíyè	职业	21	occupation, profession
zhǒng	种	7	sort, kind
zhòng	重	18	heavy
Zhōngguó	中国	1	China

Pinyin (alphabetical order)	Characters	Chap. No.	English
Zhōngguó Gémìng Bówùguǎn	中国革命博物馆	17	Museum of (the Chinese) Revolution
Zhōngguó Guójì Xìntuō Tóuzī Gōngsī	中国国际信托投资公司	20	CITIC
Zhōngguó Lìshǐ Bówùguǎn	中国历史博物馆	17	Museum of National History (of China)
Zhōngguó Lǚxíngshè	中国旅行社	19	China Travel Service
Zhōngguó Yínháng	中国银行	20	Bank of China
Zhōngguóhuà	中国话	19	Chinese language (older term)
Zhōngguótōng	中国通	22	expert on China
zhōngjiān	中间	17	middle, between
zhōngtóu	钟头		hour
Zhōngwén	中文	9	Chinese language (usually written form)
zhòngyào	重要		important
zhǒngzú	种族	21	race (as in racism)
zhōumò	周末		week-end
zhǔ	煮	22	boil, cook
zhù	住	8	live in, at
zhù	祝	19	offer good wishes
zhuǎn	转	22	turn; transfer
zhuānjiā	专家	9	expert, specialist
zhuānjiāzhèng	专家证	19	expert card
zhùfáng	住房	8	housing, accommodation
zhǔjīdàn	煮鸡蛋	9	boiled egg(s)
zhǔnbèi	准备	19	prepare
zhuōzi MW *zhāng*	桌子 张	6	table
zhǔyào	主要	21	principal(ly)
zhùyì	注意	21	pay attention to, take note of

Pinyin (alpha-betical order)	Characters	Chap. No.	English
zì qī qī rén	自欺欺人	21	deceive yourself as well as others
zìdiǎn	字典	6	dictionary
MW *běn*	本		
zìjǐ	自己	4	oneself
zǐmèi	姊妹	8	sisters
zīwèi	滋味	22	good taste, flavour
zìxíngchē	自行车	19	bicycle
MW *liàng*	辆		
zìyóu	自由		free; freedom
zìzài	自在	21	at ease, comfortable
zǒng (shi)	总（是）	8	always
zǒnglǐ	总理		premier
zǒngtǒng	总统		president
zǒu	走	5	leave, walk, go
zū	租	21	rent, hire
zǔhéyīnxiǎng	组合音响	8	hi-fi
MW *tào*	套		
zuì	最	4	most
zuì	醉	22	drunk
zuìhǎo	最好	4	had better; best
zuìjìn	最近	22	recently; nearest, latest
zuìhòu	最后	22	the last; finally
zuò	坐	1	sit
zuò chē	坐车	17	go by transport
zuò	做／作	4	do, to make
zuòfǎ	作法	9	way of doing something
zuótiān	昨天		yesterday

English–Chinese Vocabulary

English words	Chinese words
English words	**Chinese words**

a good many   *hǎo jǐ*
a little   *yìdiǎn(r)*
a short while, after a moment
   yíhuìr
abacus   *suànpan*
able to, can   *néng*
absolute(ly)   *juéduì*
accompany   *péi*
accomplish, get something done
   bàn dào
according to, on the basis of
   àn(zhào)
account (bank)   *zhànghù*
actually, as a matter of fact
   qíshí
add, increase   *tiān*
add (on)   *jiā(shang)*
address   *dìzhǐ*
addressee, recipient
   shōujiànrén
admire   *pèifú*
admit (e.g. mistake)   *chéngrèn*

admit, receive   *jiēdài*
adult   *chéngniánrén* or *dàren*
aeroplane   *fēijī*
afraid that   *kǒngpà*
after all, still   *háishi*
after (conj.), afterwards   *yǐhòu*
afternoon   *xiàwǔ*
again   *zài*
age   *niánjì*
agree with   *tóngyì*
airmail   *hángkōng*
ah, oh   *à*
airport   *fēijīchǎng*
alarm clock   *nàozhōng*
alcohol   *jiǔ*
alike, the same   *yíyàng*
all + noun   *suǒyǒu (de)* + *noun*
all right   *xíng*
all, both   *dōu*
almost, nearly   *chàbuduō*
already   *yǐjīng*
also, too   *yě*

English words   Chinese words   **English words   Chinese words**

alter, change, correct   *gǎi*

although   *suīrán...dànshi*

altogether   *yígòng*

always   *zǒng (shi)*

always (doing something)   *lǎo*

'Amadeus'   《*Shàngdì de Chǒng'ér*》

America, USA   *Měiguó*

American (person)   *Měiguórén*

ancient   *gǔlǎo*

and   *hé*

and so on   *shénmede*

another, separately   *lìng(wài)*

anyway, in any case   *fǎnzhèng*

appearance   *yàngzi*

apple   *píngguǒ*

army   *bùduì*

arrange for something to be done   *bàn shì*

arrest   *bǔ*

arrive, go to   *dào*

as far as...is concerned   *duì... lái shuō*

as soon as possible, at the earliest possible date   *jǐnzǎo*

as usual   *zhàocháng*

ash tray   *yānhuīgāng*

Asia   *Yàzhōu*

ask   *wèn*

ask the way   *wèn lù*

aspect, respect   *fāngmiàn*

at, in   *zài*

at an early date, soon   *zǎorì*

at any time   *suíshí*

at ease, comfortable   *zìzài*

at the same time; moreover   *tóngshí*

attend, take part in, join   *cānjiā*

attend to, handle, do   *bàn*

attendant   *fúwùyuán*

autumn   *qiūtiān*

await, treat   *dài*

back, behind   *hòubianr*

bad, broken   *huài*

bag, handbag   *shǒutíbāo*

ballpoint pen   *yuánzhūbǐ (MW zhī)*

Bank of China   *Zhōngguó Yínháng*

basic(ally)   *jīběn (shang)*

bath (tub)   *yùpén* or *xǐzǎopén*

bath towel   *dà máojīn* or *yùjīn (MW tiáo)*

bathroom   *xǐzǎojiān* or *yùshì*

be   *shì*

beat a drum   *dǎ gǔ*

become   *chéng*

belong to   *shǔ*

berth (lower)   *xiàpù*

berth (upper)   *shàngpù*

beautiful, pretty   *piàoliang*

beautiful woman   *měirén*

because   *yīnwèi (yīnwei)*

bed   *chuáng (MW zhāng)*

bedroom   *wòshì*

beer   *píjiǔ*

Beethoven   *Bèiduōfēn*

begin   *kāishǐ*

English words   Chinese words

Beihai Park *Běihǎi Gōngyuán*
Beijing Hotel *Běijīng Fàndiàn*
Beijing Languages Institute
  Běijīng Yǔyán Xuéyuàn
Beijing University *Běijīng Dàxué*
belch, burp, hiccup *dǎ gē(r)*
best; had better *zuìhǎo*
between, amongst ...*zhī jiān*
  or...*zhī zhōng*
bicycle *zìxíngchē (MW liàng)*
big *dà*
birthday *shēngrì*
black *hēi*
black and white *hēi-bái*
black tea (Indian) *hóngchá*
blanket *tǎnzi*
boat (n) *chuán*
boil, cook *zhǔ*
boiled water *kāishuǐ*
bon voyage, have a pleasant
  journey *yílù píng’ān*
book *shū*
book, reserve, subscribe to
  dìng
bookcase, bookshelf *shūjià*
borrow; lend *jiè*
boss *lǎobǎn*
both, all *dōu*
both...and *yòu...yòu*
bother about, be in charge of
  guǎn
bottle *píngzi*
box office clerk *shòupiàoyuán*
branch (bank) *fēnháng*

English words   Chinese words

breakfast *zǎocān*
bring forward a date *tíqián*
bring, take *dài*
Britain, England *Yīngguó*
British (person) *Yīngguórén*
brothers *xiōngdì/dìxiōng*
brush teeth *shuā yá*
bucket, pail *shuǐtǒng*
bump (into) *pèng (dào)*
burn *shāo*
bus *gōnggòngqìchē (MW liàng)*
business *shēngyì*
businessman *shāngrén*
bustling, exciting *rènào*
but *dànshi* or *kěshì*
but, and *ér*
but, however, only *búguò*
butter *huángyóu*
buy *mǎi*

cadre *gànbù*
calculating machine, computer
  jìsuànjī (MW jià)
call, be called *jiào*
calculate, count *jìsuàn*
camera *zhàoxiàngjī*
can, know how to *huì*
can, may *kěyǐ*
can (physically able) *néng*
cannot but, have to *bùde bù*
Canon *Jiānéng*
Canton *Guǎngdōng*
capable, competent *nénggàn*
capital *shǒudū*

English words Chinese words	**English words Chinese words**

Capital Theatre   *Shǒudū Jùchǎng*

car   *qìchē (MW liàng)*

carpet   *dìtǎn*

carry on, follow   *jiēzhe*

cash withdrawal form   *qǔqiánbiǎo*

catty (½ kilogram)   *jīn*

central heating   *nuǎnqì*

certain (as in 'a certain person')   *mǒu*

certainly, definitely   *yídìng*

certainty   *bǎwò*

certificate, to prove   *zhèngmíng*

chair   *yǐzi (MW bǎ)*

change   *biàn*

change money   *huàn qián*

chat   *liáo tiān(r)*

chat, conversation   *tán huà*

cheap   *piányi*

check; investigate   *chá*

check (e.g. money to see if correct)   *diǎn*

chest of drawers   *wǔdǒuchú, wǔdǒuguì*

child   *háizi*

child (small)   *xiǎoháir*

China   *Zhōngguó*

China Travel Service   *Zhōngguó Lǚxíngshè*

Chinese language   *Hànyǔ*

Chinese language (older term)   *Zhōngguóhuà*

Chinese character(s)   *Hànzì*

Chinese language (usually written form)   *Zhōngwén*

chocolate   *qiǎokèlì (MW kuài)*

choose   *xuǎn*

chopsticks   *kuàizi (MW shuāng)*

Christmas   *Shèngdànjié*

church   *jiàotáng*

cigarette   *(xiāng)yān (MW zhī/bāo)*

cinema and theatre   *yǐngjùyuàn*

city, town   *chéngshì*

classical   *gǔdiǎn*

clean   *gānjìng*

clear, clearly   *qīngchu*

clerk, shop employee   *yíngyèyuán*

climate   *qìhòu*

climb   *pá*

close, intimate   *qīnmì*

cloth   *bù*

clothes   *yīfu (MW jiàn)*

cloudy, overcast   *yīn*

club (social)   *jùlèbù*

cocoa   *kěkě*

coffee   *kāfēi*

coffee table   *chájī*

cold   *lěng*

colleague, fellow worker   *tóngshì*

colour, multicoloured   *cǎisè*

comb, brush   *shūzi*

come   *lái*

come into contact with   *jiēchù*

come or go out   *chū*

comfortable   *shūfu*

common saying, proverb   *súhuà*

English words   Chinese words

common spoken language
(Modern Standard Chinese)
pǔtōnghuà
company *gōngsī*
compare *duìzhào*
compared with *bǐ*
complete(ly) *wánquán*
complicated, complex *fùzá*
comrade *tóngzhì*
concert *yīnyuèhuì*
conduct, handle, transact
bànlǐ
confine to *xiànyú*
conscientious *rènzhēn*
consult a dictionary *chá zìdiǎn*
convenient *fāngbiàn*
conversely *fǎnguòlái*
cool *liáng*
portion; MW for money;
minutes *fēn*
copy *fèn*
correct *duì*
count, check (e.g. money to see
if correct) *diǎn*
counter *guìtái*
country *guójiā*
courteous, manners *lǐmào*
criterion, standard *biāozhǔn*
crowded, squeeze *jǐ*
culture *wénhuà*
cup *bēizi*
cup(ful) *bēi*
current account *huóqī*
cúnkuǎn
curtain *chuānglián*
cut (as of hair) *jiǎn*

English words   Chinese words

daddy, dad *bàba*
daughter *nǚ'ér*
day after the day after
tomorrow *dàhòutiān*
day after tomorrow *hòutiān*
day, date *rìzi*
day, sky, heaven *tiān*
deceive yourself as well as
others *zì qī qī rén*
decorate *bùzhì*
defect *máobìng*
definite(ly), affirm *kěndìng*
deposit account *dìngqī*
cúnkuǎn
deposit money *cún qián*
describe *miáoxiě*
desk *shūzhuō (MW zhāng)*
despite; feel free to *jǐnguǎn*
develop *fāzhǎn*
develop (as of film), to wash
(chōng)xǐ
developed, advanced *fādá*
dial *bō*
dictionary *zìdiǎn (MW běn)*
die *sǐ*
different *bù tóng*
difficult *nán*
difficulty; difficult *kùnnan*
dining room *fàntīng*
direct *zhíjiē*
dirty *zāng*
discover *fāxiàn*
dish, vegetable *cài*
disturb *dǎrǎo*
divide, distinguish *fēn*
do as one pleases *suíbiàn*

English words Chinese words   **English words Chinese words**

do taijiquan *dǎ tàijíquán*

do the action of the verb
  satisfactorily –*hǎo*

do, to make *zuò*

doctor *yīshēng*

doctor *dàifu*

don't *bié*

door, gate *mén*

double bed *shuāngrénchuáng*
  (*MW zhāng*)

double room
  shuāngrénfángjiān

downstairs *lóuxià*

draw, paint *huà huàr*

draw up, subscribe to, order
  dìng

drink *hē*

drink a toast *gān bēi*

drive (v-o) *kāi chē*

driver *kāi chē de*

drunk *zuì*

dumpling, kind of ravioli *jiǎozi*

duvet, quilt *bèizi*

each, every *měi*

each and every *gègè*

east (side) *dōng(bianr)*

easy *róngyì*

eat one's fill *chī bǎo*

eat (meal) *chī fàn*

education, to educate *jiàoyù*

egg(s) *jīdàn*

egg(s) (boiled) *zhǔjīdàn*

egg(s) (fried) *jiānjīdàn*

egg(s) (poached) *wòjīdàn*

eggs (scrambled) *chǎojīdàn*

eight *bā*

elder brother *gēge*

elder sister *jiějie*

electric cable *diànxiàn*

electric fan *diànshàn*

electric light *diàndēng*

enemy *dírén*

engaged (of people) *dìnghūn*

English language *Yīngyǔ*

enjoy rights, etc., treat
  xiǎngshòu

enjoy good fortune, happy,
  well-being *xìngfú*

enjoy oneself so much as to
  forget to go home *liúlián
  wàng fǎn*

enquire *dǎtīng*

enter *jìn*

entertaining, enjoyable
  hǎowán(r)

envelope *xìnfēng*

equal to, be equivalent to
  děngyú

equipment, facilities *shèbèi*

especially, special *tèbié*

etc. *děng*

Europe *Ōuzhōu*

even (conj.) *lián*

even if, even though *jíshǐ*

even more, still more *gèng*

evening *wǎnshang*

evening meal *wǎnfàn*

everlasting, last forever *wàngǔ
  chángcún*

English words   Chinese words

every, any, all   *fánshì*
everybody   *dàjiā*
everything   *yíqiè*
everywhere   *dàochù*
exactly like   *yìmó yíyàng*
exactly, that's just the way it is
   kěbúshì
excellent (coll.)   *bàng*
except, apart from   *chúle...*
   (yǐwài)
exception   *lìwài*
exchange (money)   *duìhuàn*
exchange rate (market
   quotation)   *páijià*
excuse me   *láojià*
exercise (n and v)   *liànxí*
expensive   *guì*
expert, specialist   *zhuānjiā*
expert card   *zhuānjiāzhèng*
expire, become due   *dàoqī*
explain, speak at length   *jiǎng*
expression, to express one's
   feelings   *biǎoqíng*
extremely   *fēicháng or shífēn*
extremely (follows adjective)
   – *jíle*

face   *liǎn*
face flannel   *miànjīn*
facing, towards   *xiàng*
factory   *gōngchǎng*
family, home   *jiā*
famous   *yǒu míng*
far   *yuǎn*
fat   *pàng*

English words   Chinese words

father   *fùqīn*
fear, be afraid of   *pà*
feel   *juéde*
feeling, sense   *gǎnjué*
feelings   *gǎnqíng*
fellow student   *tóngxué*
female   *nǚ*
female student(s)   *nǚshēng*
few   *shǎo*
fiancé   *wèihūnfū*
fiancée   *wèihūnqī*
fifteen   *shíwǔ*
fill in (e.g. form)   *tián(xiě)*
film   *diànyǐng*
find out, understand, know
   liǎojiě
finally, the last   *zuìhòu*
fine, clear, bright (of weather)
   qíng
finger   *zhǐ*
finish work   *xià bān*
first (adv)   *xiān*
flash (light)   *shǎnguāngdōng*
flavour, taste   *wèidao*
floor (first)   *èrlóu*
floor (ground)   *yìlóu*
flour   *miànfěn*
flower(s)   *huā*
fluent   *liúlì*
for, for the sake of   *wèi*
for; give   *gěi*
for example   *bǐfang shuō or*
   bǐrú
for the sake of, in order to
   wèile

English words **Chinese words**

Forbidden City (Imperial Palace) *Gùgōng*
foreign country *wàiguó*
foreign currency *wàibì*
foreign devil *yángguǐzi*
foreign exchange (certificate) *wàihuì(quàn)*
foreign flavour *yángwèi(r)*
foreign guest, visitor *wàibīn*
forever *yǒngyuǎn*
forget *wàng(jì)*
forget it, let it pass *suàn le*
forgive *yuánliàng*
form a company or partnership *héhuǒ*
form of address, to address *chēnghū*
form, pattern *yàngshì*
former *qiánzhě*
four *sì*
France *Fǎguó*
frank(ly) *tǎnshuài (de)*
free, freedom *zìyóu*
freeze, ice over *jié bīng*
freezer *bīngguì*
French (person) *Fǎguórén*
frequently, more often than not *wǎngwǎng*
fresh *xīnxiān*
Friday *xīngqīwǔ*
friend *péngyou*
friendship *yǒuyì*
Friendship Store *Yǒuyì Shāngdiàn*
from (movement involved) *cóng*

English words **Chinese words**

from (static) *lí*
front, in front of *qiánbian(r)*
fruit *shuǐguǒ*
fruit juice *shuǐguǒzhī*
full, to reach the limit; expire *mǎn*
funny, laughable *hǎoxiào*
funny (colloq.) *dòu*
furniture *jiājù*
gains, results, harvest *shōuhuò*
garage *chēkù*
garden *huāyuán*
generally speaking *yìbān lái shuō*
generally, general *yìbān*
genuine *dìdào*
geography *dìlǐ*
Germany *Déguó*
get, fetch *qǔ*
get-together, party *liánhuānhuì*
give; far *gěi*
give a farewell dinner *jiànxíng*
give/have an injection *dǎ zhēn*
give as a present; see somebody off *sòng*
give back as of change; to look for *zhǎo*
glad, happy *gāoxìng*
glass (tumbler) *bōlibēi*
glove(s) *shǒutào*
go *qù*
go against (e.g. wind) *dǐng*
go by transport *zuò chē*
go shopping *mǎi dōngxi*
go to some expense *pòfèi*

English words   Chinese words

go to the toilet   *shàng cèsuǒ*
go through (e.g. solicitor)
  tōngguò
go window shopping   *guàng dà
  jiē*
go/come to, to arrive   *dào...
  qù/lái*
good   *hǎo*
good taste, flavour   *zīwèi*
goodbye   *zàijiàn*
goods   *huò*
government   *zhèngfǔ*
graduate   *bìyè*
grammar   *yǔfǎ*
grape   *pútáo*
Great Hall of the People
  Rénmín Dàhuìtáng
Great Wall   *Chángchéng*
green tea (Chinese)   *lùchá*
group, crowd, flock   *qún*
grown up, big   *dà*
grudge doing something
  shěbude
guess   *cāi*
ha ha   *hāhā*
had better; best   *zuìhǎo*
hair   *tóufa*
half   *bàn*
hall   *tīng*
ham   *huǒtuǐ*
hand   *shǒu*
hand towel   *shǒujīn (MW tiáo)*
handsome; beautifully (coll.)
  shuài
handle, attend to, do   *bàn*
hat   *màozi*

English words   Chinese words

happy, joyful, cheerful   *kuàilè*
  or *yúkuài*
hastily   *gǎnkuài*
have   *yǒu*
have a holiday or vacation
  fàng jià
have an injection   *dǎ zhēn*
have free time   *yǒu kòng*
have fun   *wán(r)*
have plenty of   *yǒudeshì*
have the capacity to   *-xià*
have to, had better   *zhǐhǎo*
he   *tā*
health, body   *shēntǐ*
healthy, sound   *jiànkāng*
hear of, be told   *tīngshuō*
heart's desire   *wànshì rúyì*
heaven, paradise   *tiāntáng*
heavy   *zhòng*
hello (on telephone)   *wèi*
help, do a favour (colloq.)
  bāngmáng
help   *bāngzhù*
her   *tā*
here   *zhèr (zhèlǐ)*
hi-fi   *zǔhéyīnxiǎng*
him   *tā*
hm   *ǹg*
holidays, vacation   *jiàqī*
home, family   *jiā*
honestly, really; true, real
  shízài
Hong Kong   *Xiānggǎng*
hope   *xīwàng*
horizontal   *héng*
hors d'oeuvres   *lěngpán*

English words   Chinese words

horse *mǎ*
hospital *yīyuàn*
hospitality, entertain *zhāodài*
hot *rè*
hot milk *rè niúnǎi*
hotel *lǚguǎn*
hour *xiǎoshí/zhōngtóu*
housing, accommodation
  zhùfáng
how (as in 'how do you know?')
  zěnme
how (as in 'how long?' or 'how
  lovely') *duō*
how many *duōshao*
how many (less than 10)?;
  several *jǐ*
however *què*
hundred *(yì)bǎi*
hundred million *yì*
hungry *è*
husband, wife *àiren*
I, me *wǒ*
ID card (employees)
  gōngzuòzhèng
identify with, become one with
  dǎchéng yípiàn
if *rúguǒ or yàoshi*
if it's not…, then it's… *bú
  shi…jiù shi*
if…then *yào(shi)…(de huà),
  jiù*
if…then *rúguǒ…(de huà), jiù*
immediately *mǎshàng*
important *zhòngyào*
in, at *zài*

English words   Chinese words

in person, oneself *běnrén*
in the heart or mind *xīnlǐ*
in the middle of -ing
  zhèngzài…ne
in the room *wūlǐ*
include *bāokuò*
indeed, really, true, certain
  quèshí
individual (person) *gèrén*
inflate, pump *dǎ qì*
inside *lǐ*
intend, to plan *dǎsuàn*
interest (e.g. bank) *lìxī*
interested in something *gǎn
  xìngqù*
interesting *yǒu yìsi*
International Hotel *Guójì
  Fàndiàn*
interpret *fānyì*
introduce *jièshào*
invite *qǐng*
invite somebody for a meal
  qǐng kè
iron *yùndǒu*
ironing board *tàngyījià*
it *tā*
Italy *Yìdàlì*
Italian (person) *Yìdàlìrén*
it doesn't matter *méi (yǒu)
  guānxi*
it's a pity that *kěxī*
it's nothing *méi shénme*

jam *guǒjiàng*
Japan *Rìběn*

English words   Chinese words

jasmine tea   *huāchá*
be jealous   *chī cù*
join, attend   *cānjiā*
joint venture   *hézī qǐyè*
journey, trip   *lǚtú*
just   *gāng*
just now   *gāngcái*
just right, to happen to
   zhènghǎo

keep pace with   *gēnshang*
keep, preserve   *bǎocún*
kilogram   *gōngjīn*
kilometre   *gōnglǐ*
kitchen   *chúfáng*
knife   *dāozi*
knit, weave   *zhī*
know (a fact)   *zhīdao*
know how to, can   *huì*
know, recognise   *rènshi*
known as   *jiàozuò*

last, up   *shàng*
latest type, new-style   *xīnshì*
latter   *hòuzhě*
laugh, smile   *xiào*
laughable, ridiculous   *kěxiào*
lazy   *lǎn*
leader, leadership   *lǐngdǎo*
learn, study   *xué(xí)*
leave (place or person)   *líkāi*
leave the country   *chūjìng*
leave, walk, go   *zǒu*
leave (behind or for somebody)
   liú
left over, remain   *shèng(xiàlai)*

English words   Chinese words

lend; borrow   *jiè*
lens cap   *jìngtóugài*
less, few   *shǎo*
let, to allow   *ràng*
letter   *xìn*
level, standard   *shuǐpíng*
life, to live   *shēnghuó*
like (v)   *xǐhuan*
like this, in this way   *zhèyàng*
listen   *tīng*
live in, at   *zhù*
lively   *huópo*
living room, lounge   *kètīng*
locality, land; the earth   *dì*
London   *Lúndūn*
long   *cháng*
long distance telephone call
   chángtú diànhuà
long life   *chángshòu*
look for   *zhǎo*
look, see, watch, read   *kàn*
lose   *diū*
loudly   *dàshēng(de)*
lovable   *kě'ài*
luggage, baggage   *xínglǐ*
lunar calendar   *yīnlì*

made locally (here, in China)
   guóchǎn
magazine   *zázhì*
majority   *duōshù*
make   *zuò*
make (*jiaozi*); to wrap; to
   include   *bāo*
male   *nán*

English words   Chinese words

manage to do action of verb,
  -up to; *-dào*
many, more *duō*
Mao Zedong Mausoleum
  Máo Zhǔxí Jìniàntáng
map *dìtú*
market quotation (exchange
  rate) *páijià*
marry, get married *jié hūn*
matter, thing *shì (qing) (MW
  jiàn)*
mattress *chuángdiàn*
meaning *yìsi*
meet (by appointment) *jiē*
meet one another *xiānghuì*
men and women, old and young
  nánnǚ lǎoshào
menu *càidān*
merely *jiù*
method *bànfǎ*
metre *mǐ*
microwave oven *wēibōlú*
middle, between *zhōngjiān*
milk *niúnǎi*
milk bottle *nǎipíng*
mirror *jìngzi*
Miss, young lady *xiǎojie*
mistake, error *cuòwù*
modern *xiàndài*
money *qián*
monotonous, dull *dāndiào*
month *yuè*
Monument to the People's
  Heroes *Rénmín Yīngxióng
  Jìniànbēi*

English words   Chinese words

moon *yuèliàng*
mooncake *yuèbǐng*
moonlight *yuèguāng*
more, many *duō*
more and more *yuè lái yuè*
more often than not, frequently
  wǎngwǎng
moreover *érqiě*
morning (early) *zǎoshang*
morning *shàngwǔ*
Moscow *Mòsīkē*
most *zuì*
mother tongue *mǔyǔ*
motorbike *mótuōchē (MW
  liàng)*
Mozart *Mòzhātè*
Mr, gentleman *xiānsheng*
Mrs, Madam (formal) *fūrén*
Mrs, wife *tàitai*
muddle-headed *hútu*
mummy, mum *māma*
Museum of National History
  Zhōngguó Lìshǐ Bówùguǎn
Museum of Revolution
  Zhōngguó Gémìng Bówùguǎn
music *yīnyuè*
must, need *děi*
mustard *jièmo*

name (full) *xìngmíng*
name (given) *míngzi*
naturally *dāngrán*
near *jìn*
nearby *fùjìn*
need not *búyòng or béng*

English words   Chinese words

need, require, needs (n)   *xūyào*
new   *xīn*
New Year's Day   *Yuándàn*
newspaper   *bào(zhǐ) (MW zhāng)*
next   *xià*
next door   *gébì*
Nikon   *Níkòng*
nine   *jiǔ*
no matter   *bùguǎn*
no sooner...than..., as soon as   *yī...jiù*
no wonder   *nánguài*
nonsense, talk nonsense   *húshuō*
normal, regular   *zhèngcháng*
north   *běi*
not   *bù*
not (used with *yǒu*)   *méi*
not have to   *búbì*
not only...but also   *búdàn... érqiě*
not up to much   *bù zěnmeyàng*
not...any more   *bù...le*
not...but   *bú shi...ér shi*
not...until...; only   *cái*
novel   *xiǎoshuō (MW běn)*
now, at present   *xiànzài*
number   *hào*
number (telephone)   *hàomǎ*
o'clock   *diǎn zhōng*
objective, aim   *mùbiāo*
obligatory or required course   *bìxiūkè(chéng)*
occupation, profession   *zhíyè*

English words   Chinese words

odd, strange   *guài*
of course, naturally   *dāngrán*
offer good wishes   *zhù*
offices, organization   *jīguān*
often   *cháng(cháng)*
oh!   *ò*
oh dear   *āiyā*
old   *lǎo* (of people)
old   *jiù* (of things)
old China hand; expert on China   *Zhōngguótōng*
'old foreigner'   *lǎowài*
old person or people   *lǎorén*
Old Summer Palace   *Yuánmíngyuán*
old-fashioned   *lǎoshì*
on business   *chū chāi*
on the contrary   *fǎn'ér*
one   *yī*
one (used in speech instead of *yi* in telephone and train numbers)   *yāo*
oneself; own   *zìjǐ*
only   *zhǐ*
open; switch on   *kāi*
open (personality)   *kāilǎng*
open (up); switch on   *dǎkāi*
opinion   *yìjiàn*
opposite, i.e. facing   *duìmiàn*
opposite, contrary   *xiāngfǎn*
opportunity, chance   *jīhuì*
or (used in questions)   *háishi*
or, perhaps   *huò(zhě)*
orange juice   *júzizhī*
order (in advance)   *dìng*

English words	**Chinese words**	**English words**	**Chinese words**

originally *běnlái*

otherwise *yàobù(rán)*

otherwise, or else *fǒuzé*

ought, should *(yīng)gāi*

outside *wàimiàn*

overcoat *dàyī (MW jiàn)*

overseas, abroad *guówài*

overweight *chāozhòng*

Oxford *Niújīn*

pack, tidy up, put in order *shōushi*

pail, bucket *shuǐtǒng*

painting *huàr*

parcel form *bāoguǒdān*

parcel, package *bāo(guǒ)*

parents *fùmǔ*

park *gōngyuán*

part, section *bùfen*

pass, go via *jīngguò*

pass, cross *guò*

passerby, stranger *lùrén*

passport *hùzhào*

past (the) *guòqù*

patient, sick person *bìngrén*

pay *fù*

pay attention to, take note of *zhùyì*

pepper *hújiāo*

per cent *bǎifēn zhī...*

perform, act *yǎn*

period of time, spell *yízhènzi*

person *rén*

photograph (n) *zhàopiàn*

pillow *zhěntou*

pillowcase *zhěntào*

pitiable, pitiful *kělián*

place *dìfang*

plate, brand; card *pái*

play (n) *xì*

play ball *dǎ qiú*

play cards or mahjong *dǎ pái*

play (stringed instrument) *lā*

play chess *xià qí*

plenty of *yǒudeshì*

plug *sāizi*

plug (electric) *chātóu*

poem *shī (MW shǒu)*

poetry *shīgē*

point at *zhǐ*

point, aspect *diǎn*

police, policeman *jǐngchá*

polite *kèqi*

political *zhèngzhì*

poor (person) *qióng(rén)*

post and telecommunications office *yóudiànjú*

post, mail (verb) *jì*

postage *yóufèi*

pound sterling *Yīngbàng*

practise *liànxí*

precisely *jiùshì*

preferential card *yōudàizhèng* or *gòuwùzhīfùzhèng* (new type)

preferential treatment *yōudài*

prejudice, bias *piānjiàn*

prepare *zhǔnbèi*

premier *zǒnglǐ*

present, gift *lǐwù*

pretty, beautiful *piàoliang*

English words   Chinese words

president *zǒngtǒng*
pretty good *búcuò*
previously; before (conj.)
  yǐqián
previously, in the past
  cóngqián
price *jiàqián*
principal(ly) *zhǔyào*
privilege *tèquán*
probably *dàgài*
produce, manufacture
  shēngchǎn
product *chǎnpǐn*
pronunciation *fāyīn*
propose (a toast), toast *jìng*
prove *zhèngmíng*
public *gōnggòng*
pull, to play (of stringed
  instrument) *lā*
pump (v-o), inflate *dǎ qì*
put (in or in) *fàng(zài)*
put away, receive *shōu(hǎo)*

question, problem *wèntí*
quick, fast *kuài*
quiet *ānjìng*
quite (+adj.) *xiāngdāng*
quite a bit, quite a few *bù shǎo*

RMB (Chinese currency)
  rénmínbì
race (as in racism) *zhǒngzú*
radiator *nuǎnqìpiàn*
radio *shōuyīnjī*
railway station *huǒchēzhàn*

English words   Chinese words

rain (v-o) *xià yǔ*
rate of interest *lì(xī)lù*
rather, quite, enough *gòu*
read *kàn*
read aloud *niàn*
really, true *zhēn*
reason, cause *yuányīn*
recall, call to mind *xiǎng qǐlai*
receipt *shōujù*
receive, accept *shōu*
recently, nearest, latest *zuìjìn*
recite, read aloud with
  expression *lǎngsòng*
record (v); recording (tape) *lù
  yīn*
red *hóng*
refer to *zhǐ*
reflections, thoughts *gǎnxiǎng*
refrigerator *bīngxiāng*
regard, kindly feelings *xīnyì*
regard as, count as *suàn*
register *guàhào*
registration charge *guàhàofèi*
regret; to regret, be a pity
  yíhàn
regularly, frequently *jīngcháng*
reimbursement of expenses
  bàoxiāo
relation(ship) *guānxi*
relatively *bǐjiào*
reliable *kěkào*
rely on, depend on *píng*
remark, word *huà*
remember *jìde*
remove, move *bān*

English words   Chinese words

rent (n) for house   *fángzū*
rent, hire (v)   *zū*
representative   *dàibiǎo*
resemble   *xiàng*
reserve for someone; remain;
    let grow; leave   *liú*
rest   *xiūxi*
retire   *tuìxiū*
return (as of money)   *huán*
return   *huí*
return to your own country
    huí guó
rich in, full of   *fùyú*
ride (as of horse, bicycle)   *qí*
right(s)   *quánlì*
road   *lù*
romantic   *làngmàn*
roof   *wūdǐng*
room   *fángjiān*
room charge   *fángfèi*
round   *yuán*
row, line   *pái*
rule, regulation   *guīdìng*
run   *pǎo*

sacrifice (v)   *xīshēng*
salt   *yán*
sandwich   *sānmíngzhì*
scales (for weighing)   *tiānpíng*
school   *xuéxiào*
Scotland   *Sūgélán*
script (writing system)   *wénzì*
season (of year)   *jìjié*
seat (in train) hard   *yìngzuò*
seat (in train) soft   *ruǎnzuò*

English words   Chinese words

sea-water   *hǎishuǐ*
secret (adj.; n)   *mìmì*
see, meet   *jiàn*
see, watch   *kàn*
seem   *hǎoxiàng*
sell   *mài*
send   *sòng*
send a telegram   *dǎ diànbào*
send by post or mail   *yóujì*
sender   *jìjiànrén*
sense of humour   *yōumògǎn*
sentimentalist
    shānggǎnzhǔyìzhě
serve as; be   *dāng*
service, to serve   *fúwù*
set (n)   *tào*
set one's mind at rest   *fàng xīn*
seven   *qī*
several   *jǐ*
sew up   *féng shang*
sewing-machine   *féngrènjī*
she   *tā*
sheet   *chuángdān*
shirt, blouse   *chènshān*
shoe(s)   *xié*
shop   *shāngdiàn*
shop-assistant   *shòuhuòyuán*
short (in length)   *duǎn*
shout, cry out   *hǎn*
show, produce   *chūshì*
show, explain, illustrate
    shuōmíng
shower   *(línyù)pēntóu*
sick person   *bìngrén*
side   *pángbiānr*

English words	Chinese words	English words	Chinese words

sign, signature *qiān zì*

silk *sīchóu*

simple *jiǎndān*

single bed *dānrénchuáng*

single room *dānrénfángjiān*

sink *chízi or xǐwǎnchí*

sisters *jiěmèi/zǐmèi*

sit *zuò*

situation *qíngkuàng*

six *liù*

skate (v) *huà bīng*

ski (v) *huá xuě*

sleep, go to bed *shuì (jiào)*

sleeper (in train) hard *yìngwò*

sleeper (in train) soft *ruǎnwò*

slow *màn*

small *xiǎo*

small token, mere trifle
 xiǎoyìsi

smile, laugh *xiào*

smoke (v-o) *chōu yān* or
 xī yān

snore (v-o) *dǎ hān*

snore (colloq.) (v-o) *dǎ hū(lu)*

snow (v-o) *xià xuě*

so, in that case *nàme* or *zhème*

soap *féizào (MW kuài)*

soap (toilet) *xiāngzào*

socket *chāzuò*

sofa, settee *shāfā*

sold out, full house *kèmǎn*

soldier *bīng*

some *(yì)xiē*

some (subject or topic position
 only) *yǒude*

sometimes *yǒu(de) shíhou*

son *érzi*

soon *zǎorì*

sorry, excuse me *duìbuqǐ*

sort, kind *zhǒng*

sound (v) *tīng qǐlai*

south *nán*

soya sauce *jiàngyóu*

Spanish language *Xībānyáwén*

spank (v-o) *dǎ pìgu*

speak *shuō*

speak, talk (v-o) *shuō huà*

spend *huā*

spicy or hot (food) *là(de)*

spoon *sháozi*

spot *diǎnr (coll.)*

spring (season) *chūntiān*

stable, steady, to stabilise
 wěndìng

stairs, staircase *lóutī*

stamp (postage) *yóupiào*

stand *zhàn*

start, to open; to drive *kāi*

stay *dāi*

steady boy- or girlfriend
 duìxiàng

stick (on) *tiē(shang)*

still, in addition *hái*

stop (bus etc) *zhàn*

street *jiē*

strange *qíguài*

strenuous, energy consuming
 fèijìn(r)

student *xuésheng*

student card *xuéshēngzhèng*

English words   Chinese words   **English words   Chinese words**

student studying abroad
  liúxuéshēng

study (v), learn   *dú shū* or *xuéxí*

study (n)   *shūfáng*

stupid   *bèn*

subconsciousness   *xiàyìshí*

subject to; receive   *shòu*

sugar, sweets, candy   *táng*

suitable   *héshì*

suite, (settee and two easy
  chairs)   *shāfā (MW tào)*

summer   *xiàtiān*

Summer Palace   *Yíhéyuán*

sunbathe   *shài tàiyáng*

sunglasses   *tàiyángjìng*

sunrise   *rìchū*

sunset   *rìluò*

superiors   *shàngjí*

supper, dinner   *wǎncān*

suspect   *huáiyí*

swear at, curse   *mà*

sweater, woolly   *máoyī*

sweet   *tián*

sweets, sugar   *táng*

swim (v-o)   *yóuyǒng*

switch (n)   *kāiguān*

Switzerland   *Ruìshì*

sympathise with   *tóngqíng*

table   *zhuōzi (MW zhāng)*

table lamp   *táidēng*

take a photo   *zhào xiàng*

take a stroll, walk   *sàn bù*

take hold of, receive, to meet *jiē*

take leave of   *gàobié*

take off (of aircraft)   *qǐfēi*

take out   *ná chū*

take turns, in turn   *lúnliú*

tall, high   *gāo*

tap   *lóngtou*

tape   *cídài*

tape recorder   *lùyīnjī*

tasty, delicious   *hǎo chī*

tea   *chá*

tea (Chinese)   *lǜchá*

tea (Indian)   *hóngchá*

tea (jasmine)   *huāchá*

tea (leaves)   *cháyè*

teach   *jiāo*

teacher   *jiàoyuán* or *lǎoshī*

teacup   *chábēi*

teahouse   *cháguǎn*

technique   *jìshù*

telegram (n)   *diànbào*

telephone (n)   *diànhuà(jī)*

telephone (v-o)   *dǎ diànhuà*

telephone number   *diànhuà
  hàomǎ*

television   *diànshì(jī) (MW tái)*

tell, let know   *gàosu*

temperament   *píqi*

Temple of Heaven   *Tiāntán*

ten thousand   *(yí) wàn*

tennis   *wǎngqiú*

terrifying, frightening   *kěpà*

text   *kèwén (MW kè)*

thank, thank you   *xièxie*

that   *nà (or nèi)*

that is, viz.   *jí*

the same as…   *gēn…yíyàng*

English words   Chinese words

theatre and cinema   *yǐngjùyuàn*
then   *jiù*
there   *nàr* or *nàlǐ*
there is/there are   *yǒu*
therefore   *suǒyǐ*
Thermos flask   *rèshuǐpíng*
they   *tāmen*
thick   *hòu*
thing(s)   *dōngxi*
think; feel like doing something
   xiǎng
think, consider   *rènwéi*
this   *zhè (or zhèi)*
this kind of   *zhè yàng*
this locality   *běndì*
this year   *jīnnián*
thousand   *(yì) qiān*
three   *sān*
Tiananmen Square
   Tiān'ānmén Guǎngchǎng
ticket   *piào*
ticket price   *piàojià*
ticket seller   *shòupiàoyuán*
tie   *lǐngdài*
time (length of)   *shíjiān*
time, occasion   *cì*
timetable, schedule   *shíkèbiǎo*
tin, can   *guàntóu*
to   *dào*
toast   *kǎomiànbāo*
tobacco, cigarette   *yān*
today   *jīntiān*
together   *yìqǐ*
toilet   *cèsuǒ*
toilet paper   *wèishēngzhǐ*

English words   Chinese words

toilet soap   *xiāngzào*
tomato juice   *fānqiézhī*
tomorrow   *míngtiān*
tone   *shēngdiào*
too, extremely   *tài*
toothbrush   *yáshuā (MW bǎ)*
toothpaste   *yágāo (MW tǒng)*
top, peak; MW for hat   *dǐng*
tourism; to tour   *lǚyóu*
tourist, sightseer   *yóukè*
towards, to, in the direction of
   wàng
towel   *máojīn (MW tiáo)*
towel rail   *máojīnjià*
town, city   *chéngshì*
train   *huǒchē*
translate   *fānyì*
travel   *lǚxíng*
traveller's cheque   *lǚxíng*
   zhīpiào
tree   *shù (MW kē)*
trouble, troublesome   *máfan*
turn, transfer   *zhuǎn*
two   *liǎ*
two (number)   *èr*
two (of a kind)   *liǎng*
type (v-o)   *dǎ zì*
type, kind   *yàng*

US dollar   *Měiyuán*
uh-huh   *m̀*
unbearable   *shòu bù liǎo*
uncover, open   *jiēkāi*
under(neath), below   *xiàbianr*
understand   *dǒng*

English words	Chinese words	English words	Chinese words

understand, clear *míngbai*

undertaking, cause *shìyè*

unit *dānwèi*

unless *chúfēi*

up, last *shàng*

upper berth *shàngpù*

upstairs *lóushàng*

us *wǒmen*

use *yòng*

useful *yǒu yòng*

USSR *Sūlián*

usually, ordinary *píngcháng*

vase *huāpíng*

vegetables *shūcài*

Venice *Wēinísī*

vertical *shù*

very *hěn*

very many *duō dehěn*

very, rather *tǐng*

video recorder *lùxiàngjī*

vigour *hǔqì*

vinegar; jealousy (as in love affairs) *cù*

visit, sightsee *yóulǎn*

wages *gōngzī*

wait *děng*

walk *zǒu*

want to, must *yào*

wardrobe *yīguì*

warm *nuǎnhuo*

warm-hearted, enthusiastic *rèqíng*

washbasin *xǐliǎnpén*

washing machine *xǐyījī*

waste, squander *làngfèi*

watch, see *kàn*

water *shuǐ*

water and electricity charges *shuǐdiànfèi*

way of saying something *shuōfǎ*

way of doing something *zuòfǎ*

we *wǒmen*

we (including listener) *zánmen*

we'll meet again some day *hòuhuì yǒu qī*

wear (clothes) *chuān*

wear (hat, gloves, glasses, etc) *dài*

weather *tiānqì*

week *xīngqī*

weekend *zhōumò*

weep, cry *kū*

welcome *huānyíng*

well-being, happy *xìngfú*

well-known, famous *wénmíng*

West, the West *Xīfāng*

West Lake *Xīhú*

west (side) *xī(bianr)*

Western food *Xīcān*

Westerner *Xīfāngrén*

what *shénme*

what about (it)?; how? *zěnmeyàng*

whatever you do *qiānwàn*

what one sees and hears *jiànwén*

what's the matter? *zěnme le*

English words   Chinese words

what's to be done? *zěnme bàn*
what? *shénme*
when *de shíhou*
when? *shénme shíhou*
where? *nǎr*
which? *nǎ (or něi)*
white *bái*
who? *shéi (or shuí)*
whole, entire *zhěnggè*
why? *wèi shénme*
will (showing possibility) *huì*
willing *yuànyì*
wind *fēng*
window *chuānghu*
wine *pútáojiǔ*
wine bottle *jiǔpíng*
winter *dōngtiān*
with, and *gēn*
withdraw money *qǔ qián*
woman *fùnǚ*
work out bill, make bill *suàn zhàng*
work, to work *gōngzuò*
worker *gōngrén*

English words   Chinese words

world *shìjiè*
worry about *cāo xīn*
worth, deserve *zhíde*
wrap up *bāo shang*
write (characters) *xiě (zì)*

yawn (v-o) *dǎ hāqian*
year *nián*
year (of age) *suì*
year after next *hòunián*
yen *Rìyuán*
yesterday *zuótiān*
yoghurt *suān (niú)nǎi*
you *nǐ*
you (plural) *nǐmen*
you (polite form) *nín*
you flatter me *guòjiǎng*
young *niánqīng*
young fellow *xiǎohuǒzi*
younger brother *dìdi*
younger sister *mèimei*

zero *líng*

Character Texts

1

Making Friends (i)

第一课　交朋友(1)

李	王先生，你好！
王	李先生，你好！
李	请坐。
王	谢谢。
李	请喝咖啡。
王	谢谢，我不喝咖啡。
李	那么，中国茶行不行？
王	行，谢谢你！我很喜欢喝中国茶。

2

Making Friends (ii)

第二课　交朋友 (2)

李	王先生，我给你介绍一下，这是我爱人，周德津。
王	李太太，您好！
李太太	王先生，您好！认识您，我真高兴。
王	请坐，请坐。喝一杯酒吧。
李	谢谢，我喝一杯。
王	李太太呢？
李太太	谢谢，我不会喝酒。
王	那么，桔子汁好吗？
李太太	好，谢谢您。

3

Making Friends (iii)

第三课　交朋友 (3)

王　　李先生，你们有小孩儿吗？

李　　有，我们有两个，一个男孩儿，一个女孩儿。

王　　男孩儿几岁？女孩儿几岁？

李　　男孩儿十四岁，女孩儿九岁。

李太太　王先生结婚了吗？

王　　没有。

李太太　有对象吗？

王　　'对象' 是什么意思？

李　　'对象' 是女朋友的意思。你有女朋友吗？

王　　有。

李太太　她在哪儿？她也在中国吗？

王　　对，她也在中国。

李　　我想请你们去我们家玩儿，好吗？

王　　那太好了。

李太太　你们明天晚上有空吗？

王　　有空。

李　　那么，请你们俩明天晚上去我们家吃饭吧。

王　　那太谢谢你们了！几点钟去呢？

李太太　六点怎么样？

王　　行，就六点吧。

4

At the Lis' (i)

第四课　在李先生家(1)

王　　我给你们介绍一下，这位是我的女朋友，史爱理。这位是
　　　李先生，这位是李太太。

李
李太太　史小姐，您好！

史　　李先生、李太太，你们好！

李　　请随便坐吧。

李太太　史小姐，您也是从英国来的吗？

史　　是，我也是从英国来的。

李　　啊，你们俩都是英国人。

李太太　史小姐，您在这儿作什么？

史　　我在这儿学习汉语。

李　　您在哪个学校学习汉语？

史　　我在北京大学学习汉语。

李　　学校里生活怎么样？

史　　很不错。

李太太　你们一定很饿了。我们吃饭吧。今天晚上吃中国菜行吗？

王　　好极了！

李　　别客气，自己来吧。你们会用筷子吗？

王　　会用，但是用得不好。

李　　没关系……嗯，你们都用得不错啊！

李太太　我做菜做得不好，请原谅。

史　　您做菜做得很好。

李太太　史小姐会做菜吗？

史　　会一点儿，但是技术不高。

王　　她英国菜做得非常好。

李　　中国菜做得怎么样？

史　　我中国菜做得不怎么样。

李太太　你们最好少说话，多吃饭吧，要不然菜都凉了！

5

At the Lis' (ii)

第五课　在李先生家(2)

李　　别客气，再多吃一点儿。

王　　吃饱了，菜都很好吃。

李太太　你们愿意喝咖啡还是喝茶？

王　　我随便。

史　　喝茶吧。

（喝完了茶）

李太太　史小姐，看一看我们的小房子吧？

史　　好，谢谢您。永寿，你陪李先生谈话吧。

李太太　这是厨房，地方很小，所以冰箱、洗衣机都放在外面厅里。
　　　　我们只有三个房间，儿子一间，女儿　间。

史　　孩子们有自己的房间可以安安静静地读书。

李太太　我和老李的房间只好又当卧室又当客厅。

史　　你们的客厅布置得很漂亮。电视是彩色的还是黑白的？

李太太　是彩色的。要不要看一下？

史　　不用了。时间不早了，我们（应）该回去了。

王　　时间过得真快。李先生、李太太，我们得走了，谢谢你们的
　　　　热情招待。我们玩儿得非常高兴，给你们添了不少麻烦。

李　　没什么，欢迎你们再来玩儿。

王/史　一定来，谢谢你们。再见。

李　　慢走，慢走。

7

My Family

第七课　我的家庭

　　我叫张占一。我家在北京。我家有五口人—爸爸、妈妈、哥哥、姐姐和我。我没有弟弟，也没有妹妹。

　　我姐姐三十岁，还没有找到对象呢（还没有结婚呢！），这种情况在中国很少。哥哥比姐姐小两岁，比我大一岁半。

　　爸爸、妈妈年纪比较大了。爸爸今年六十一岁，是（一）个老教员，在北京语言学院教外国留学生汉语。

　　妈妈比爸爸小三岁，以前是个工人，现在已经退休了。他们俩身体非常好。

　　姐姐在医院当医生，哥哥在部队当兵，所以他们不常在家。

　　我在北京饭店当服务员，工作有一点儿单调，但是我和同事们的关系很好，所以还过得去。

　　我们一家人感情也都很好，日子过得还不错。

8

My Home

第八课　我的家

我们住得很简单，只有三间房加上厨房和厕所。父母的卧室同时也当客厅。

我和哥哥睡（在）一个房间，我们每（个）人（都）有一张书桌，在那儿读书总（是）比在客厅里安静得多。

姐姐的房间比我们兄弟俩的那间还小，只放得下一张床、一张小小的桌子和一把椅子。

我们兄弟、姊妹参加工作以后，除了休息那天以外，很少在家，所以住得没有以前那么挤，父母也比以前住得舒服一些。

我想在西方一般住房比我们大些。你们除了卧室以外还有客厅，有的有书房，有的还有饭厅，听说有花园的也很多。

我们家家具不多，客厅里有一张双人床、一个沙发、一个衣柜、一台电视（机）。还有一套组合音响，是日本货。缝纫机是国产货。

吃饭的时候，大圆桌和椅子都搬进来。冬天天气冷的时候，单位给我们烧暖气。虽然你们发达国家工资比我们高得多，但是我们房租、水电费等都比你们便宜多了。

我们家地方不大，可是按中国现在的标准，我们过得还不错。

9

Hotels

第九课　旅馆

北京的旅馆单人房间特别少。多数是双人房间。

要是你愿意一个人住双人房间，当然也可以，但是往往要付双人房间的房费。

外国专家和留学生凭工作证或（者）学生证，平常可以享受优待。

住外宾的大部分房间都包括浴室和厕所。浴室里有浴盆和淋浴喷头，也都有毛巾、浴巾、肥皂、卫生纸、玻璃杯等。

每个房间里都有电话、电视、热水瓶、茶叶、茶杯、凉开水什么的。（大）多数住我们饭店的外宾早上吃西餐。

有的人想用汉语订菜。您以前见过中文菜单没有？如果没见过的话，就看看课文下边的菜单吧。服务员从前用算盘算帐，但是现在用计算机的越来越多了。

北京的饭店很多。除了成千上万的游客以外，一部分外国公司的代表（即商人）也住饭店，所以饭店的生意总是很不错的。价钱却越来越贵了，而且服务、设备还不一定跟得上。

我在北京饭店工作，接触过的外国人很多。我们中国人不得不承认他们在某些方面享受一定的特权，即使这些特权有（的）时候只限于随时都可以进饭店上厕所！其实谁用过中国公共厕所，谁都会同情他们这种作法的！

10

Weather, Dates and Seasons

第十课　气候、日期和四季

今年北京的天气很不正常。冬天不冷，夏天也不热。应该下雪的时候并没有下，应该下雨的时候也没有下，真奇怪！

是不是整个世界的气候正在变呢？欧洲平常没有北京那么冷，但是今年反而有的时候比北京还冷。

春天、秋天是北京最好的季节但是可惜太短了。要是在中国旅行的话，五月和九月天气最好，晴天多，阴天少。　天气一好，公园里的人就很多。老人下棋的下棋，打牌的打牌，聊天儿的聊天儿，早上打太极拳的有的是。中国有些地方比如四川、广东等地在茶馆里坐着喝茶的也很多。

中国人一般一个星期工作六天，不象大部分欧洲国家星期六也休息。虽然机关干部星期天休息，有的工厂星期天也照常生产，工人轮流休息。

今天是星期天，天气特别好，男女老少一群一群都出去玩儿。公园里散步的散步，照相的照相，有的喜欢逛大街，商店里总是很挤，整个北京热闹极了。

在中国要（是）想找一个安静的地方，一个人呆一会儿，是很难办到的。你要想晒太阳，就得跟成千上万的人一起晒！反正星期天到处都是人！

今年冬天结冰以后，我经常去滑冰，一下班就跑到北海公园去滑。如果在家就到附近的圆明园或颐和园去滑。

11

In the Restaurant

第十一课　在饭馆里

张	你们菜订好了没有？
史	订好了，谢谢你。啤酒来了。啊！不是北京啤酒而是青岛啤酒。
张	没关系，青岛啤酒更好喝。您普通话说得真好。
史	过奖，过奖，说得不好。
张	说得很好。您是哪国人？
史	你猜猜吧。
张	不是美国人就是英国人。
史	我是英国人。你怎么知道呢？
张	因为刚才您是跟您朋友说英语！您朋友也会说汉语吗？
史	也会说。
王	说得没他好。
张	啊！你们俩的汉语真棒，学了几年了？
史	学了两年了。
张	您呢？（指的是王永寿）
王	学了四年了。
张	你们在中国待了很长时间了吧？
王	不长，来了三个多月了。
张	这是你们第一次来中国吗？
王	不，她是第一次，我是第二次。
张	你们真行，发音很清楚，没什么洋味儿，很标准的普通话。学中文不是很难学吗？
王	难是难，可是也有它容易的地方，比方说中文发音、语法都并不难，难的是声调。对我们西方人来说，中文的四声还是相当困难的。
张	写汉字呢？

史　　写汉字很不容易，因为我们外国人一般是成年人才开始学
　　　中文，不象你们六、七岁就开始了。当然还有一点，中文就
　　　是你们的母语。

张　　那倒是。象你们这样的水平，报纸看得懂吗？

史　　看得懂。

张　　小说呢？

史　　也行，但是不认识的字还要查字典。啊！菜来了，真漂亮
　　　啊！看起来一定很好吃。

张　　那么，你们慢慢儿吃吧，不再打扰你们了。有什么事，随时
　　　可以叫我。

王　　好了，谢谢你，有什么事一定找你。跟你聊天儿很有意思。

Index to Grammar Notes
and Cultural References

The first number in each entry refers to the Chapter, the second to the section within the Grammar of the Chapter.